International Development in a Changing World

International Development

This book forms part of the series *International Development* published by
Bloomsbury Academic in association with The Open University. The two books
in the series are:

International Development in a Changing World
(edited by Theo Papaioannou and Melissa Butcher)
ISBN 978-1-78093-234-7 (hardback)
ISBN 978-1-78093-237-8 (paperback)
ISBN 978-1-78093-235-4 (Epub eBook)
ISBN 978-1-78093-236-1 (PDF eBook)

New Perspectives in International Development
(edited by Melissa Butcher and Theo Papaioannou)
ISBN 978-1-78093-243-9 (hardback)
ISBN 978-1-78093-251-4 (paperback)
ISBN 978-1-78093-248-4 (Epub eBook)
ISBN 978-1-78093-249-1 (PDF eBook)

This publication forms part of the Open University module
TD223 *International development: making sense of a changing world*. Details
of this and other Open University modules can be obtained from the Student
Registration and Enquiry Service, The Open University, PO Box 197, Milton
Keynes MK7 6BJ, United Kingdom (tel. +44 (0)845 300 60 90,
email general-enquiries@open.ac.uk).

www.open.ac.uk

International Development in a Changing World

Edited by Theo Papaioannou
and Melissa Butcher

The Open University

BLOOMSBURY ACADEMIC

Published by

Bloomsbury Academic
an imprint of Bloomsbury Publishing Plc
50 Bedford Square
London WC1B 3DP
United Kingdom

and

175 Fifth Avenue
New York
NY10010
USA
www.bloomsburyacademic.com

In association with

The Open University
Walton Hall, Milton Keynes
MK7 6AA
United Kingdom

First published 2013

Edited and designed by The Open University.

Typeset by The Open University.

Printed and bound in the United Kingdom by Latimer Trend and Company Ltd, Plymouth.

CIP records for this book are available from the British Library and the Library of Congress.
ISBN 978-1-78093-234-7 (hardback)
ISBN 978-1-78093-237-8 (paperback)
ISBN 978-1-78093-235-4 (Epub eBook)
ISBN 978-1-78093-236-1 (PDF eBook)

1.1

Contents

Introduction

Theo Papaioannou and Mellissa Butcher

Welcome to *International Development in a Changing World*, the first volume of a companion text book to the Open University module TD223 *International development: making sense of a changing world*. This book will introduce you to some of the key issues, debates and ideas about development and international politics in the 21st century. The following chapters focus on the contested concepts of development, poverty, inequality and livelihood, and examine the emergence of 'new powers' that pose challenges to the existing system of international relations. A key thread throughout the book is the development of an understanding of the historical and contemporary make-up of the international system and its relationship to development as a process of economic and social transformation. In examining development as a process of change, we locate it within broader themes, including the examination of power relations, ideas around human agency, and the interaction between different scales of development, local, national, international and transnational. You will see that these different themes of history, power, agency and scale run throughout the book. Without them, development cannot be adequately understood as a complex process of interaction.

With this focus on interaction, the book is premised on an understanding of development as relational, that is, it is both process and practice that depends on not only an interaction between people but also between people and institutions such as governments and non-governmental organizations. You will also see interaction between different academic disciplines, incorporating theories and tools from social sciences and development studies, to provide a more holistic understanding of the social, economic and political transformations involved. Every subject has its own 'language' with a 'vocabulary' of terms (which we call concepts) that are used to engage with, describe, analyse and interpret the subject. Development is no different and the book is designed to introduce you to its vocabulary. Learning any language becomes easier with practice, although if you have a social science background you will already be familiar with some of the language of development introduced here. If you come from a natural science or technological background, you may need to be a bit more patient, although there's no need to feel daunted. In order to help you with the 'vocabulary and language' of development, we have produced a glossary that is located at the end of this book, key terms are highlighted in the text in bold.

The theoretical concepts of development discussed in the following chapters provide general and normative explanations about how social transformations and deliberative human actions do and should occur, informing policy and practice. It is important to bear in mind that all theories are context dependent and therefore cannot be understood in abstraction from the concrete relations of history, power, agency and scale. Therefore, chapters move from the theoretical to also, in a series of case studies, look closely at the deliberate actions of people to improve their livelihoods, communities and societies.

Similarly, as you read through *International Development in a Changing World* you will come across many activities that give you an opportunity to apply the theories you read about to real world examples. These activities are of three kinds:

- Activities that allow you to check particular skills. For example, checking that you can interpret numerical data about poverty and inequality that is presented in graphic form; or identifying the main points made in a quotation.

- Activities that ask you to check your understanding of a topic or concept, or to relate that understanding to your own experience and prior knowledge. Often such activities will ask you to make notes which can become the basis of personal and critical reflection. International development is, after all, inherently personal as well.

- Activities that ask you to critically engage in a hypothetical discussion about a development idea, debate or issue for which there is no clear 'right' answer, only arguments one way or the other. In such activities you are an active part of the story or argument, and can take ownership of it.

These different kinds of activity start from the basic assumption that you only really learn something when you have to teach it, even if that is teaching yourself. However, we follow these activities with a 'Discussion' text of our own which can give you ideas to build on or compare your own thoughts with.

In terms of content, *International Development in a Changing World* begins with introducing international development, and contesting its theory and practice. Chapter 1 provides a foundation through exploring some of the different meanings of the word 'development', and addressing the question of why and how we should think about it as an inherently international issue. Chapter 2 offers insights into the key debates, theories and current research in the disciplines of international development and international studies, identifying new centres of power, state and non-state actors and new forms of organization and public action in the context of development, such as aid and humanitarian intervention.

Incorporating our concern with scale, the book focuses on the international system and world economy, using the key debates and theories of earlier chapters to examine contemporary shifts in the world system with the rise in power of countries such as China, India and Brazil. Where do these countries get their power from? What does this mean for the international system and for development? We explore these questions by looking in more detail at the history of the international system, factors such as colonization and the trajectories of China, India and Brazil. These three countries are not the only rising powers in evidence today. Some would, for example, add Russia or Indonesia, Turkey and Nigeria. However, we have chosen to focus on these three as they are the most clear-cut examples of emerging powers today from the global South and therefore overturning the 'old' geography of the international order. More importantly, the aim is to appreciate the general point that powers rise and fall and that with these changes come different outcomes for the theory and practice of development. Chapter 3, in particular, focuses on China, beginning with the idea of this country as a new threat from the USA's point of view. Linking with the use of historical analysis, we examine how these rising powers fit into a longer history of the world economy. Chapter 4 continues to address the international scale of development but from a more political perspective. That is, how do rising powers reshape patterns of development internationally and reorient political relations between states? Chapter 5 shifts our viewpoint (partially at least) from the international to the state. Given that the power of emerging countries is founded on their tremendous economic growth in recent years we address the question of what has driven this. Chapter 6 shifts our spatial lens again and looks at how the rising powers work through, and also transform, certain geographical patterns including the organization of production, migration and environmental impacts. Two increasingly important transnational centres of power are highlighted in this and Chapter 7: namely, global cities and transnational corporations. Both sites have been key agents of interaction and change with differential linkages to states and uneven impacts on the well-being of people.

Perhaps the most common view of development is as a process that addresses poverty and inequality. As with Chapter 1's challenge to our understanding of what is development, Chapter 8 contests the meaning of poverty, how it is measured, and the explanations given for its existence and persistence. This chapter also explores perceptions (and misperceptions) of how it might be experienced. Complicating the link between development and poverty, Chapter 9 proposes that it is inequality that we need to take more account of, examining how it is reproduced and measured globally. The question of whether inequality between and within countries matters is important for us in relation to the rapid changes resulting from the rising powers (and decline of others) and what inequalities are being created, reinforced or possibly reduced by them. In recent years, aid and development have come to focus more intently on livelihoods as a means to alleviate poverty, yet here again the picture is complicated. Chapter 10 concentrates on livelihoods, exploring the experience of making a living in different contexts that often involve searching for multiple sources of income. This section introduces the connection between culture and development that has been implicated in the failure of many 'western' development projects in other contexts. The livelihoods of poor and low income populations are also placed in the wider context of international development by examining the impact of global value chains on the ability of people to make a living. Global value chains demonstrate the importance of linking local and international structures and processes of economic and social change, understanding the various interactions and associated power relations at different points in the chain, from local to global. Chapter 11 takes up these themes by examining different types of interventions that can be adopted to promote livelihoods – from technological change to education. The interventions they discuss here are based on specific case studies and give you an opportunity to apply theories and concepts from earlier chapters to the real world. What do you think is the best way to reduce poverty? Bi- and multilateral aid is one of the best-known methods of intervening in development, but, as Chapter 12 examines, it is also a contentious area with many arguments for and against its effectiveness.

Again, we can see how power relations between donors and clients can impact on development, and what different bargaining positions are possible, bringing together ideas from international relations and development studies.

In conclusion, we summarize the key messages of this volume and remind you that making sense of important development events in today's changing world is a matter of critical analysis of historical processes, power relations and agency at different scales.

This is a lot of material to cover in 12 chapters but we hope that by the end you will have gained a good grounding in understanding development in a changing world, with reference to key thinkers in the field as well as applied responses from development organizations. Some of these illustrations will be current or only a few years old, but it's also important to recognize continuity with the past, to see the patterns in the rise and fall of powerful countries, or the use of aid as both a beneficial tool and a bargaining chip, for example. Development is a fast-changing subject area, as indeed is the real world to which it relates, but the conceptual and practical analysis offered in these chapters will provide you with tools that can be applied in different contexts and times. We hope you will use these tools not only to reflect on development in your own context and time but also to contribute to positive developmental change in the globalizing world.

In writing this introduction we would like to acknowledge the input of Giles Mohan, Hazel Johnson and Gordon Wilson.

Introducing international development

1

William Brown and Rebecca Hanlin

Introduction

There are many reasons to study international development. You may have become interested in the subject because you want a better understanding of the changing world in which we live and the reasons behind the multiple problems or issues that we face. You may have come into this field through a career-related sideways step, from banking or working in agriculture or the healthcare sector, for instance. Or your motivations for studying international development could be a combination of these and other reasons. For many of us who study or work in the field of international development, the interest is also because we want to see change for the better in the world. For many people all over the world, if not all of us, 'development' is also part of everyday life.

From a long-term perspective, studying 'development' might mean studying what the historian Eric Hobsbawm called the 'central historical question' (Rosenberg, 2006). Given that humans have remained biologically much the same since the Stone Age:

> [...] how did humanity get from caveman to space-traveller, from a time when we were scared by sabre-toothed tigers to a time when we are scared of nuclear explosions?
>
> *(Hobsbawm, 1997, p. 40)*

Studying development in this sense means asking how we understand, explain and evaluate the huge economic and political transformations that societies have undergone, and the technological and cultural changes that form such an important part of those transformations.

Alternatively, with a somewhat more focused view, studying development might imply finding out about the efforts of people at national, international or local community level to make improvements in their own and others' lives. This kind of 'intentional' change concerns the wish that many of us no doubt have about being part of something good, working with other members of our communities both locally and globally to promote change. Development here implies actions aimed at achieving something that is desirable or progressive.

This chapter, and this book, will address both views – the broad social transformations that development involves, and the more focused, deliberate actions to improve livelihoods, communities and societies. Indeed, as you will see in this chapter, the word 'development' has different and contested meanings. Certainly, 'development' relates to social change in some way, whether to an event ('there's been a new development') or to cumulative change over time ('this developed out of that'). In fact, it can be seen as both an 'unplanned' process of change as well as something that is intended, i.e. the outcome of deliberate collective decisions. In both forms, 'development' is acknowledged in day-to-day practice – in its own field of study, its own budget line in national accounts, in dedicated charities, state agencies and private companies and in areas of social action such as 'international aid' or 'community development'.

A central aim of this chapter, then, is to explore some of the different meanings of the word 'development' and Section 1.1 will be returning to these ideas of 'unplanned' and 'intentional' change, where we will also be asking about the different, and equally contested, goals of development. However, we also want to explore the idea of *international* development, that is, asking why, and how, we should think about development as an inherently international issue and this is discussed in Section 1.2.

In summary, the aims of the chapter are to:

- explore some of the different meanings of the term 'development'
- investigate the ways in which development is an international process.

While a fair amount of ground is covered in this chapter, we aim to introduce you to some ways of thinking about these issues rather than definitive accounts of them, while the following chapters in this book provide deeper explorations. Here we aim to offer a way of beginning to think about the subject of international development in a changing world and the debates and puzzles it presents us with today.

1.1   What is development?

In many accounts, the idea of development relates to the notion of human progress – of a betterment or improvement in society – and that development is inherently 'good change' (Chambers, 1997). However, as Thomas (2000) has pointed out, even this somewhat bland definition leads to a series of other questions. These relate to the goals of development: for example, what is the end point or direction of travel that is seen to be good? They also relate to the routes to get there: for example, what kinds of development practice will help us achieve those goals? This section sets out one way to think about the diverse meanings that development has. To do this we will make a broad working distinction between the 'goals' of development and the 'routes' to development. The term 'development goals' attempts to identify some of the very different ideas about what it means to become developed. The term 'routes to development' tries to differentiate some of the different ways in which societies, communities and people develop, i.e. what the 'practice' of development amounts to. First, though, look at Activity 1.1, which identifies different claims about what development 'is'.

Activity 1.1

Read the statements below and identify which of them, for you, encapsulate what development means. (You can choose more than one.) You will return to this activity at the end of the chapter, so keep a note of your answers so you can compare what you think now and what you think at the end.

- Development means progress and good change.

- Development is about industrialization, adopting new technology and becoming a modern country.
- Development means reducing poverty and improving education, health and social welfare.
- Development is something that only concerns the poorer countries of the world.
- Development is about achieving higher economic growth.
- Development involves conflict, including violent conflict.
- Development is something that happens in each country individually.

Do not spend more than 15 minutes on this activity.

Discussion

There isn't a right or wrong answer to this activity. Someone has argued the case for each of these ideas at one time or another. Nor are all the options mutually exclusive. In what follows, we will suggest some of our ideas about these and other aspects of development.

In fact, people disagree as to whether most processes of change in society are good or bad, not least because change will almost inevitably involve winners and losers, so development is an inherently contested process. One of the most important questions to ask of any process of change – especially where some people are claiming such change is 'progress' – is who benefits and who loses from this process.

Road building in Africa might be a case in point. In 2010 the Chinese government provided millions of pounds worth of investment into infrastructure projects in Africa, including the building of a new ring road around Nairobi in Kenya (see Figure 1.1).

This new road was designed to ease congestion in Nairobi, enhancing the productivity of Nairobi-based businesses. However, there was concern that this investment was part of a business deal that allowed China access to Kenya's consumers through import of its own goods, and which therefore would have a detrimental impact on local manufacturers. Similar questions about winners, losers and progress arise in respect of other development projects. Large-scale dams in India and China, seen by their governments as essential to those countries' development, have been opposed by others because of the displacement, environmental damage and loss of livelihoods that their construction has also involved. So when we say that development is 'contested' we do not mean (just) as an abstract set of debates – contested development means very serious, sometimes life and death, struggles for lives, livelihoods and prosperity.

Figure 1.1   'Good change'? China's involvement in Africa creates winners and losers

Judging what kind of social change should be seen as 'good' and identifying the routes by which those goals might be reached, shape the different ways in which the term development is used. The rest of Section 1.1 outlines a way of thinking about those different uses. Table 1.1 summarizes our way of organising the discussion. Across the top there are 'goals of development', which are split into 'broader' and 'narrower' goals. Down the side there are 'routes to development' – the ways in which development comes about – which in turn are split into 'unplanned' and 'intentional' change. The content of each of the four cells are some of the examples of each category. You may well wish to think of more now and add more as you study this book. Read through Table 1.1 now. Subsections 1.1.1 and 1.1.2 will refer back to Table 1.1. and unpack each of the different goals and routes in more detail.

1.1.1   The goals of development

If development is seen as a goal, what is the destination, or direction of travel, that is desired or seen to be 'good'? Activity 1.1 and Table 1.1 hinted at some of the wide range of possible answers that might be given to this question. However, goals of development may range from very broad aims to much more specific ones. We'll take each in turn.

Broader goals: the structural transformation of society

At its broadest, development refers to a set of transformations of societies as a whole, and a cumulative process of change in the human condition, represented by the first column in Table 1.1. Hobsbawm's quote at the start of the chapter, referring to the transformed conditions of human life, speaks to this notion of development over the long run. However, both in terms of the pace of change unleashed, and in terms of its importance for contemporary development, the key structural transformations of society that we are concerned with are the rise of capitalism and industrialization. These twin transformations became established originally in Britain by the late 18th century, spreading to Western Europe, the United States of America and Japan in the 19th and early 20th centuries, and to parts of the **South**, most notably China, more recently.

Table 1.1 Development goals and routes

		Goals of development	
		Broader goals: the structural transformation of society	Narrower goals: achieving specific social targets and improvements
Routes to development	Unplanned processes of social change	Transition from agricultural to industrial society Dynamic growth and change inherent to capitalism Urbanization Modernization Unintended impacts of warfare and conflict 'Shocks' – economic crisis, political upheaval or environmental disaster	Impact of economic growth on incomes Positive impacts of technological change on livelihoods
	Intentional collective action in international, state and non-state forms	Macroeconomic and governance reforms State promotion of industrialization Promotion of technological change Promotion/regulation of urbanization	International and national efforts at poverty reduction National social policies to promote literacy, health, education, etc. State and non-governmental aid Rural and urban community improvement and fair trade schemes

You will study more about industrialization and different models of capitalism in Chapter 5, but for now it is useful to have a broad definition of each. **Capitalism** is a system of social relations in which owners of capital hire labour in return for wages; production is for sale in the **market** rather than direct consumption by producers; and profits are realized by owners of capital after payment of costs of production. **Industrialization** involves the mechanization of social productive activity with the use of inanimate sources of power (fossil fuels and electricity rather than horses and oxen); the invention and diffusion of new technical knowledge; and changes to how work is organized, especially the use of wage labour and large-scale factory production. In many cases, including Britain, these two transformations have been closely linked; Britain's industrial revolution followed close on the heels of, and accelerated, the rise of capitalist social relations. However, historically there have been many different patterns of transformation. Indeed, there have been some non-capitalist routes to industrialization (such as the Soviet Union and the earlier stages of China's industrialization, both of which were followed by transitions from communism to capitalism) as well as great variance in the kinds of capitalism that have emerged across the world.

So why do we talk about this as being 'structural change'? Taken together, industrialization and capitalism imply large-scale changes in the patterns of social relationships in societies. Not least among these is what is produced in a society and how the economy grows. Capitalist industrialization, for example, typically involves the movement of large numbers of people from work on the land (characteristic of agricultural and non-capitalist societies) to urban areas and industrial employment as well as the rise of markets as a key mechanism through which economic activity is organized. Industrialization has therefore often been associated with processes of large-scale urbanization as seen in cities like Detroit in the 20th century and Shanghai in the 20th and 21st centuries. A host of other institutional changes can also occur, for example, to legal systems, forms of politics and government, levels of education and health provision, and so on. So overall, this kind of broad developmental change involves a transformation in the make-up of a country, what its economy is based on and how its people make a living.

As you will explore more in Chapter 4, part of the reason structural transformation in the form of industrialization and capitalism is seen as a desirable goal is because of the dynamic effect they have on economic growth and technological change. Transformation creates the ability to move society onto 'a permanent different economic trajectory' (Mokyr, 1999, p. 3). Industrial capitalism is perhaps one of the dominant goals of many development actors precisely because it is seen as being the 'engine of 'development'' (Thomas, 2000). Industrialization enables sustained increases in productivity through the deployment of new technologies in production and new ways of organising production. Capitalist economies, driven on by competition between capitalist firms in the market, make such productive innovation a central dynamic of the economy. Although prone to periodic crises and characterized by large inequalities and environmental damage, capitalist industrialization has proved capable also of generating large increases in economic growth and wealth over the long term. In addition, the **technological innovation** central to capitalism also makes possible major improvements in standards of living, health and life span, even if it doesn't always realize these for many people.

However, as well as introducing a new dynamism into processes of social change in the form of constant technological innovation and increasing productivity and output, such 'gains' come at a cost, including an environmental cost (Robbins, 2013). The era of industrial capitalism has also been one of enormous unevenness in the extent of development. This is true within individual countries in terms of inequalities between different classes and regions. But it is perhaps even more marked in terms of unevenness between countries. The development of some countries ahead of others, broadly Western Europe and its 'offshoots' (North America and Australia (Maddison, 2001)) before much of the **global South**, created a marked and long-lasting divergence in growth rates and income. This divergence established patterns of inequality in wealth and power internationally that have shaped much of the subsequent history of, and debates about, development. Indeed, the specific problems faced by those 'coming later' to industrial capitalism arguably defines a key part of what studying development is about (Brett, 2009).

Activity 1.2

Do you think industrialization is essential to development? As this section has suggested, the goal of industrialization – and emulation of the countries of the **North** – has influenced much development thinking and practice. But it is not seen in unqualified positive terms. Consider these two quotes, both from a BBC documentary, Requiem for Detroit, broadcast in the UK in 2010. Make a few notes on what they tell you about different views of the role of industrialization?

> One hundred years ago the birth of the automobile in Detroit heralded the second American revolution, unleashing forces of mass production and consumerism which shaped the 20th century and powered the wheels of American success.

> The auto industry has come to the end of the line. To think that they are the answer to the evolution of civilization and humanity is childish. To get so excited about a few decades of mass production and think that's heaven … that's crazy.

> *(Requiem for Detroit, 2010)*

Do not spend more than 15 minutes on this activity.

Discussion

The documentary shows industrial development, especially automobile production (Figure 1.2), in Detroit underpinned not just the growth and expansion of the city, but lay at the heart of 'Americanism' as a dominant force in the 20th century world, driving technological change and new forms of production, as well as a whole culture based on mass production and consumption. Add to that the international political influence that the USA wields, based in no small part on its industrial strength, and you can see why industrialization and mass consumption and production is a form of development that was, and for many still is, very attractive.

The second quote draws our attention to some of the down sides and Requiem for Detroit outlines many others. Here, the crisis in Detroit's car industry, which came to a head in 2010, is seen as the beginning of the end not just for the firms involved but for an entire city and culture on which it was based. Industrial mass production is portrayed instead as a passing phase, 'a few decades' from human history. Some environmentalists would agree with this sentiment. Where do you stand in relation to these views?

Figure 1.2   The Model T Factory, Detroit: the automobile created opportunities for Detroit but also created the route of its own downfall

Narrower goals: specific social improvements

If this discussion suggests the broader goals that development is often identified with, it also hints at the more limited, narrower goals that development entails, represented in Table 1.1 by the second column. While achieving capitalist industrialization has been a broad goal in and of itself, it is also desired because it is seen to deliver other more specific benefits – rising incomes, better health, education, and so on. For many people it is these aims, rather than some abstract notion of 'becoming a modern society', that are the real goals associated with development.

In societies where the transition to industrialization has not happened, or is still in its early stages, much development effort is aimed at achieving these benefits directly, through funding for education, say, or community development projects aimed at raising incomes. However, the impact of capitalism and industrialization has always been very uneven, as already noted. In fact, there are a host of negative social changes associated with structural transformation, such as displacement of people, loss of livelihood, unemployment and low wages. For all its positive impact historically, industrial capitalism creates many losers and is an inherently conflicted process for that very reason. As a result, where social improvements fail to arise, where capitalism and industrialization are seen to have a negative affect on people's health or wellbeing or to increase inequalities, then these more specific goals come into even sharper focus. The goals of development here are defined by the need to 'ameliorate the disordered faults of progress' (Cowen and Shenton, 1997).

Therefore, this second, narrower way of thinking about the goals of development is defined by more specific objectives, the achievement of ends that are seen to be good in themselves. Some of the debates about development therefore revolve around the priorities that are given to different specific goals. For some, the goal of economic growth is a dominant concern because it is seen to enable the achievement of many other goals – growth will raise incomes and provide the wealth necessary to improve education, health, and so on. For others, the uneven distribution of the benefits of economic growth (even where it occurs) means that specific attention to other targets is necessary. Policies that favour economic growth at all costs may adversely affect livelihoods of many people. The Millennium Development Goals (MDGs) adopted by the United Nations (UN) in 2000 are a good example of an attempt to specify a list of more definite, measurable development objectives by 2015 (see Box 1.1).

Box 1.1   The United Nations and the Millennium Development Goals

The United Nations (UN) is an international organization set up in 1945 to maintain global peace and security and to help nations around the world improve the lives of the poorest people. More than 190 **nation states** are members of the UN.

It has five main bodies, including the General Assembly, the Security Council and the International Court of Justice. It also has a variety of programmes, agencies and committees that report to one of the five main bodies. These include regional Economic Commissions, UN organizations such as UNICEF, the International Labour Organisation (ILO) and the World Health Organisation (WHO).

The Millennium Development Goals (MDGs), adopted by the UN in 2000, are an example of a global response to the most pressing economic and social development issues of the late 20th century. They defined the responses of states, development agencies and charities in a range of issues in the early part of the 21st century. You will read more about this type of development and the role of different development actors in Chapters 8–12 of this book, but here is a list of the targets.

Goal 1   Eradicate extreme poverty and hunger

Halve, between 1990 and 2015, the proportion of people whose income is less than $1 a day

Achieve full and productive employment and decent work for all, including women and young people

Halve, between 1990 and 2015, the proportion of people who suffer from hunger

Goal 2   Achieve universal primary education

Ensure that, by 2015, children everywhere, boys and girls alike, will be able to complete a full course of primary schooling

Goal 3   Promote gender equality and empower women

Eliminate gender disparity in primary and secondary education, preferably by 2005, and in all levels of education no later than 2015

Goal 4   Reduce child mortality

Reduce by two thirds, between 1990 and 2015, the under-five mortality rate

Goal 5   Improve maternal health

Reduce by three quarters the maternal mortality ratio

Achieve universal access to reproductive health

Goal 6   Combat HIV/AIDS, malaria and other diseases

Have halted and begun to reverse, by 2015, the spread of HIV/AIDS

Achieve, by 2010, universal access to treatment for HIV/AIDS for all those who need it

Have halted and begun to reverse, by 2015, the incidence of malaria and other major diseases

Goal 7   Ensure environmental sustainability

Integrate the principles of sustainable development into country policies and programmes and reverse the loss of environmental resources

Reduce biodiversity loss, achieving, by 2010, a significant reduction in the rate of loss

Halve, by 2015, the proportion of the population without sustainable access to safe drinking water and basic sanitation

Achieve, by 2020, a significant improvement in the lives of at least 100 million slum dwellers

Goal 8   Develop a global partnership for development

Develop further an open, rule-based, predictable, non-discriminatory trading and financial system

Address the special needs of least developed countries

Address the special needs of landlocked developing countries and small island developing states

Deal comprehensively with the debt problems of developing countries

In cooperation with pharmaceutical companies, provide access to affordable essential drugs in developing countries

In cooperation with the private sector, make available benefits of new technologies, especially information and communications

(United Nations, 2010)

1.1.2   Routes to development: unplanned change and intentional action

As well as considering the goals implied by the idea of 'development' we also need to focus on the routes that reaching those goals entails. Here we make a distinction between what we term 'unplanned' processes of change and deliberate 'intentional' development actions. This distinction turns on the difference between what Brett (2009, p. 9) identifies as the 'incremental but compulsory and spontaneous process' of development and the 'conscious and collective enterprise' of development.

Unplanned change

The idea of development as entailing unplanned processes of social change, shown as the first row in Table 1.1, is an attempt to get at the extent to which developmental goals might be achieved by historical change that isn't a deliberate outcome of policy or action but rather the result of an accumulation of events, trends and shifts in society as a whole. It is a view of development that sees it as an inherent self-generating process or as Thomas (2000, p. 25) writes, it is a 'spontaneous and unconscious ("natural"?) process of development from within'.

There are various forms in which unplanned change has become a key route to development. In some cases the shift from feudal agriculture to industrial capitalism was itself the product of numerous underlying social changes – changes in the productivity of agriculture, the economic impact of Britain's empire abroad, and changes in class structure among them. In this way, unplanned change involved 'the destruction of the old in order to achieve the new' (Thomas, 2000, p. 25). And as mentioned in Table 1.1, in some cases the impact of wars or natural disasters can have large but unplanned developmental impacts. Warfare can be seen – perhaps paradoxically – as having a developmental impact on society by uprooting the previous forms of government and economy and stimulating widespread social change (Brown, 2013).

However, it is the inner dynamic of capitalist industrialization, discussed in Section 1.1.1, that gives us the most prominent example of the idea of development as unplanned change.

Some of the early attempts to understand capitalism – by Adam Smith in the late 18th century and Karl Marx in the 19th century, for example (Figure 1.3) – focused on this idea.

Both saw in capitalism an 'internal' motor of change that develops society in terms of economic output, incomes, technology and welfare. Although a strident critic of capitalism, Marx was nevertheless in awe of the transforming impact capitalism had. For his part, Adam Smith emphasized the way the market mechanism drove forward the creation of the 'wealth of nations'.

Indeed, it is this latter view – of the importance of the unplanned outcomes of market interactions – which has most purchase on contemporary debates about development. As you will see in Chapter 2, for many people, neoliberal theorists chief among them, 'allowing markets to work' is the key problem for development, as it is through markets that social development will be achieved. For such theorists, both the goal of social transformation and more specific development targets are met through the unplanned outcomes of capitalist markets.

(a) (b)

Figure 1.3 (a) Adam Smith, philosopher and political economist (1723–1790) and (b) Karl Marx, writer and revolutionary (1818–1883)

Intentional development

In contrast to the idea of unplanned social change, development also clearly – perhaps more obviously – involves very deliberate actions and practice. In this guise, development has been at the centre of much more conscious, collective actions. As Brett noted:

> Development exists as a normative aspiration, is institutionalized in systems designed to facilitate progressive change, is embodied in conscious policy projects … and operates as a set of teleological expectations about the future.

(Brett, 2009, p. 9)

Development here is an idea that animates collective, social action. Indeed, some define development more exclusively in just these terms. Nederveen Pieterse (2010, p. 21) refers to development as '… the organised intervention in collective affairs according to a standard of improvement'. For Hettne (2009, p. 6), on the other hand, development 'in the modern sense implies intentional social change in accordance with societal objectives'.

You will be able to think of many development activities that have been associated with development in this guise; some are mentioned in Table 1.1. As you will see there, these include development activities that are designed specifically to bring about or manage the broader structural transformations mentioned above, such as the deliberate promotion of industry. Such activities can be termed 'intentional development' as they imply deliberate efforts by governments to achieve a predetermined set of objectives. We also cite the changes to macroeconomic policy promoted by international organizations like the International Monetary Fund (IMF) and the World Bank (see Box 1.2) as well as many governments, and government policies aimed at promoting and regulating urbanization, as other examples.

Box 1.2 The International Monetary Fund and World Bank

The IMF is tasked with encouraging economic cooperation to maintain global financial stability.

The World Bank is in charge of financing economic development and reconstruction, initially in the countries affected by World War II and latterly the developing countries of the world. One of its activities is to provide financing to countries in the form of loans, often with 'conditionalities' or rules attached. Many developing countries have received these through what are known as Structural Adjustment Programs (SAPs). The IMF also makes loans and is responsible for SAPs.

The IMF and the World Bank are sometimes known as the Bretton Woods Institutions after the conference at Bretton Woods in New Hampshire, USA in 1944 which led to their creation.

Deliberate action is also directed at achieving some of the narrower targets as well. Many such intentional activities are specifically designed to improve the situation of those who are the poorest in society, who need specific assistance (in the case of wars, famine, floods, etc.) or who are deemed to have a less 'developed' state of being and therefore need to be provided with the opportunity to become wealthier or similar to other countries in terms of their economic growth status, educational standards, etc. The MDGs cited in Box 1.1 are a key example of intentional development action at the level of the UN, and the issue of poverty and poverty reduction has been a central concern of intentional development efforts for many decades. You will study poverty in depth in Chapters 8 and 9.

We lay stress on collective and intentional action in this category in order to differentiate these sorts of social activity from more individualistic responses, such as those of business people or workers responding to market incentives. These latter responses are of course 'intentional' but they lack the public nature of collective actions and are not explicitly directed towards achieving development per se in the same way as the actions of organizations like governments, development agencies, charities and non-governmental organizations (NGOs – sometimes referred to as the 'third sector').

1.1.3 Consolidating our study so far

The preceding subsections set out to explain a fourfold framework (Table 1.1) for understanding the different meanings of development. Two kinds of goals of development have been outlined (broader structural transformation of society and narrower specific goals of social improvement) and two routes by which development happens (unplanned processes of social change and intentional collective actions).

Activity 1.3

To test your understanding of this section, note down three or four development issues that particularly concern you. Then look back at Table 1.1 and spend a few minutes deciding where you would place those issues in the four cells of the table (any one issue might go into more than one cell).

Do not spend more than 15 minutes on this activity.

We hope that the framework is useful in prompting you to think about the different meanings of development and the way that many different types of social change and collective action form the subject of 'development'. The rest of the book focuses on a number of key areas that we think are central to development today. Chapters 3–7 address one of the most dramatic contemporary areas of change – the rise of new emerging powers such as China, India and Brazil. This issue certainly fits into the idea of development as structural transformation with all three of these countries undergoing massive social upheaval associated with industrialization. But you will also see how broad social change in these countries has come about both through unplanned processes, notably the effects of the international economy, as well as more deliberate actions, not least the policies adopted by governments to promote industrialization. Furthermore, the experience of development in these countries contains within it the realization, or attempt to realize, specific developmental objectives. Perhaps chief among these, aside from the promotion of economic growth, is the reduction of poverty. It is the issue of poverty that is the focus of Chapters 8–12. The continuing existence of poverty also signals the uneven way in which the developmental benefits of transformation are distributed within society. Unplanned processes of change mean that specific development goals – in this case levels of poverty – remain to be tackled. But attempts to reduce poverty are also the object of much deliberate collective action both within countries and internationally.

It is important to bear in mind the different meanings of development when you encounter statements about development. However, as you may notice, using the different categories that have been introduced should always be done with caution because 'real life' doesn't necessarily divide easily and neatly into these boxes. Many issues you will encounter straddle different goals and routes to development.

1.2   Development as an international process

If we think about development as processes of both unplanned social change, in the modern era dominated by capitalist industrialization, and intentional collective action aimed at broad societal transformation as well as more specific improvements in various aspects of the human condition, then what does it mean to talk of international development?

There are several ways to approach this issue and, in choosing to study 'international development', you will no doubt have some ideas about what you think the term means. This section is going to think through this question by first addressing the issue of what we take the word 'international' to mean (and by extension what we understand by the subject of 'International Studies' – the study of 'the international'). We then address the different ways in which development, in the senses we have discussed already, can be thought of as 'international'.

At its broadest, the term international refers to what Justin Rosenberg, a leading thinker in International Studies, identified as the obvious but 'surprisingly consequential' fact that the world exists and has always existed as more than one society and that – with possibly some very rare exceptions – they always interact with others 'outside' of their own (Rosenberg, 2006, p. 316). If you pause for a moment to think about this, you can see Rosenberg's point. In earlier historical eras, the ways different societies were organized politically varied a great deal – we've had ancient empires, city states, tribes, and so on. In addition, the extensiveness and intensiveness of their interaction also varied. But the world has always consisted of multiple political entities that interact with others. Today's world is organized into nation states and for the most part we will refer in what follows to '**states**' or 'countries' rather than 'societies'. Indeed, the fact that our world is divided into multiple different countries, reflected in more than 190 members of the UN, is so obvious that it seems almost ridiculous to point this out. Yet this fact, and the extent and range of interactions that exist between those states, is strikingly important to almost all development issues. Before reading on, look at Activity 1.4.

Activity 1.4

Reflect on what you know about a key rising power today. China, India or Brazil are obvious examples, but you can choose any country. How far can you give an account of contemporary development issues facing your chosen country without bringing in the role of countries, organizations, businesses or NGOs that are outside that country?

Do not spend more than 15 minutes on this activity.

Discussion

This activity is quite a challenging exercise. Let's take China as an example. Contemporary development issues might include the country's rapid industrialization; environmental problems that are linked to that; or issues to do with urbanization. In some sense all these issues have aspects to them that are national, distinctively Chinese and stemming from the unique developmental path that China has followed. However, in each case you quickly find that, both historically and today, the 'international' intrudes. China's rapid industrialization is closely linked to its ability to export manufactured goods to other countries and this in turn is governed by a series of trade agreements with those countries and China's membership of the World Trade Organization (WTO), the governing body for world trade. Its environmental problems have been highlighted both by organizations within China and by international NGOs, and China is also one of the key countries involved in negotiations around an international agreement on climate change.

China's urbanization includes the growth of cities such as Shanghai (Figure 1.4), whose history is peppered with the interventions of outside powers (the USA, Britain and France, and later Japan) and whose development today is based on the city as an intersection for international flows of finance and goods.

Figure 1.4   Shanghai is a city that has been influenced by external intervention throughout its history

If you think of other examples involving 'development' you will no doubt also note the importance of international trade and investment, travel and migration, diplomacy, warfare, cultural interaction via the internet, and so on. As we hope you will see in the rest of this chapter and in the rest of the book, this feature of our world has an enormous bearing on how we understand and engage with the subject of development.

1.2.1 What do we mean by 'international system'?

Following this line of thinking, the word 'international' and the discipline of International Studies can be taken to refer to 'that area of social life that arises specifically from the co-existence of multiple societies' (Rosenberg 2006, p. 316). As a subject International Studies often goes under other titles such as International Relations and covers a wide range of issues from international politics and diplomacy to war and security, international economics and other international social, environmental and cultural issues.

However, as an academic discipline, International Studies often collates these different issues within a broader and overarching idea of an **international system**. Indeed the study of the character, emergence and change in the international system as a whole is an important part of the subject of International Studies. The debate as to how one characterizes the international system is beyond the scope of this chapter, so we will offer some broad outlines only.

The idea of a 'system' generally implies regularized and substantial interaction between the units that comprise the system. In International Studies it is the existence of multiple societies – in the present day, 'nation states' or 'countries' – that gives the term 'international' its meaning. In fact, the word 'international' was first used by the English philosopher and writer Jeremy Bentham in the late 18th century to differentiate international law from domestic law (Buzan and Little, 2001, p. 32).

In trying to characterize any particular international system, it is necessary therefore to identify both the 'units' that are interacting and the types and extent of interaction (Buzan and Little, 2001). Looking across the span of human history, it is possible to identify different international systems with different constituent units. Fortunately for our purposes in this book, we will focus for the most part on the modern international system in which the primary building blocks, or units, are nation states. Although there are debates as to when one can identify the modern international system coming into being – some argue it originates with the emergence of separate European states in the mid-17th century while others argue that it only really becomes established with the spread of capitalism and modern states from the 18th to 19th centuries – we don't need to get into those debates here. Suffice to say that today's international system is global in scope, that is, the system of states covers the whole planet.

If the primary units of the modern international system are the 190-plus states that make up the system, the range of interactions between them covers a lot of ground. Buzan and Little (2001) argue that we can identify a number of different kinds or areas of interaction:

- Warfare and military interaction: the use of force across state boundaries.
- Political and diplomatic activities: such as the recognition of independence of other countries, negotiations, international campaigns by non-governmental and civil society groups, and the creation of international organizations.

- Economic interactions across borders: such as international trade, investment and financial flows and the operations of transnational businesses.

- Sociocultural interactions: such as the exchange or transmission of ideas, migration, the spread of international norms, such as human rights norms, the spread of religious beliefs, and language.

Different ideas about international systems prioritize different kinds of interaction, or may argue for others to be added to the picture. Buzan and Little argue, for instance, that there is an increasingly important field of environmental interaction. For our purposes we want to leave this open and you will read more about different approaches to understanding the international system in Chapter 4. While we take the system of states as the foundation of the international system – it is what makes the international system 'international' – we suggest that in studying different aspects of international development, all of these areas of interaction play an important role.

1.2.2 Anarchy and power in the international system

One further point should be made before addressing international development itself. In terms of how politics is organized – broadly how collective decisions are arrived at and upheld – the subject of International Studies suggests that there is a crucial distinction between what goes on within states and what goes on between them. Within countries, politics is based around systems of government, law and enforcement. This means that collective decisions of that society – laws and policies of the country – can be arrived at and upheld, ultimately by the use of force (by the police force or army). However, the fact that our world is divided into many, separate independent states creates an arena of politics between countries – international politics – where there is no such single authority, no world government or global means of enforcing laws.

International Studies typically characterizes this situation and the international system as, in formal terms, an '**anarchy**'. Here the term anarchy is not used in the everyday sense meaning chaos and disorder. Instead it is used to indicate the absence of a single, recognized 'world' government with the ability to make and uphold laws. Indeed, international anarchy is the flip side of the existence of multiple independent states. Because each of those states claims the exclusive right to make and uphold laws within its own territory – the basis of state **sovereignty** – it necessarily means that there is no external, higher authority. This means that the range of interactions between countries that were discussed earlier – trade, migration, human rights norms, and so on – are not governed in the same way when they occur within a single country. Instead, states (or rather the governments of states representing independent countries) engage in processes of bargaining, competition, conflict, cooperation and coercion to manage these interactions. Sometimes conflicts arising from these processes descend into warfare between states, indeed many theorists argue that international politics is inherently war-prone. But this is far from always the case. Indeed, states have found ways to create quite elaborate processes of cooperation to manage issues of shared concern. The UN system is perhaps the most developed of these and it seeks to regulate the political, diplomatic and military relations between states as well as a host of other issues like the environment, economic issues and, importantly, development. International organizations like the IMF and World Bank are also products of states collectively cooperating with each other to create bodies that can help to tackle economic and development issues.

However, even these extensive organizations, with their associated bureaucracies and the various rules by which they operate, are not the same as having a 'world government' and states will typically look out for their own interests, however those interests are defined. Indeed, one important consequence of the anarchic nature of the international system is that how much **power** different states have can have a large bearing on the outcome of processes of cooperation and conflict internationally. The organizations just mentioned are a case in point. Within the UN system, in the UN General Assembly, every state is represented and each carries equal weight. However, the critical decisions, especially those concerning the use of force, are taken by the UN Security Council. Here the permanent members (the USA, Britain, France, China and Russia) carry veto powers reflecting their status as victorious powers at the end of World War II. Within the IMF and World Bank, influence is decided by the financial contributions each country makes through weighted voting on their governing bodies – a system which has traditionally ensured that the most developed countries get the biggest say.

In summary, then, the anarchic nature of the international system also means that questions of power are never far from the surface in international politics. Different theoretical traditions in International Studies, which you will study in Chapter 4, give different interpretations of the role of anarchy and power in international politics, but most agree they are important to some extent. Indeed, the fact that the most developed states have for most of recent history been the most powerful has been a major influence on the international politics of development. Additionally, as you will examine in more detail in the following chapters, countries that experience surges forward in development (like China) can also be seen as rising powers in the international system.

1.2.3   The international system and development

Let's sum up where we have got to so far. We know that development refers both to the broad structural changes in society, particularly associated with capitalism, and to the deliberate collective efforts to achieve specific development goals. We also know that these take place in an international system characterized by great unevenness in terms of levels of development of the countries that make it up. We now need to think about what difference it makes to thinking about development if we build in this idea of interaction between countries across all the areas identified above.

Approaching social development as if it occurs within single countries has been a feature of some of the academic study of development, as well as the wider social sciences. It is also evident in the actual practice of development, particularly in governments' 'national development plans' and some of the everyday accounts of countries' histories. However, in the subject of

Development Studies itself, the international dimension of development has often featured as a central part of the overall problem of development. Indeed, to the extent that Development Studies as an academic subject is 'about' the problems facing societies trying to 'catch up' with the more developed, there is a recognition of the international, multi-society context in which development unfolds. Moreover, many of the key theoretical approaches to development discussed in Chapter 2, as well as many of the substantive debates addressed by Development Studies, are concerned with the processes of interaction between different countries. This is true whether we are looking at, for example, the economic areas of interaction in the world economy around trade or debt; cultural questions about rights and indigenous communities; or more political or military issues around independence, power or intervention.

This book tries to build on this awareness of the interconnections between the international system and development and make it explicit. From our discussion above, we know that interaction between societies is a more or less permanent feature of the world and that each individual society exists in an international system. This means that when we think about development we need to acknowledge that development:

- occurs in more than one country at the same time, but in very different ways
- in any individual society is connected in fundamental ways with development in other societies with which it interacts and that may be much more or less, or just differently, developed
- unfolds across the international system as a whole.

This means that any particular country's development is 'international' in the sense that it is shaped to a greater or lesser extent – but always to some extent – by that fact that it occurs in a world consisting of other countries with which it interacts and which are also developing (Rosenberg, 2006). In this sense, development in one society is always related to development in others. This relationship may be very negative – one society develops at the expense of, or by exploiting, another, as was the case with many colonial relationships. Or it may be a more mutually beneficial relationship – one society is able to develop by utilizing the technological or other advances of another.

Whether viewed across the world as a whole, or seen from the perspective of a single country, development is therefore an internationally interactive process. This means that any single, national instance of development (China's development, say, or Brazil's) embodies within it aspects – technologies, ideas, institutions – drawn from outside. Taken across the world as a whole, the development of, say, industrial capitalism, from its origins in Britain in the 18th and 19th centuries to the vast expansion of industrialization in Asia today, is shaped by the different patterns of interaction between different societies.

However, viewed over a long time span, the national and historical circumstances in which development occurs is always changing. For any individual society, the 'external' factors that shape that society's development combine with the particular history and culture of each individual society in unique ways. Furthermore, the international context within which any particular society develops changes from one time to the next. Britain became an industrial society in a world in which there were no other industrialized countries. The circumstances for those that followed – France, Germany and the USA in the 19th century – were therefore different, giving them a different developmental experience. The circumstances for much of the South in the post World War II era has been one of a world dominated by western states that had gone far down the path of industrialization. And today, for countries in Africa, development occurs in a context where not only the **West** but much of Asia is industrialized.

This means that as well as being an interactive process, development is also made up of multiple different paths – the mosaic of different development experiences at different places and different historical times. There is no single line to be followed, or no single path to development. In this sense we can say that development is multilinear.

Both of these ideas – of development as an internationally interactive process and as multilinear when looking at the international system as a whole – change the way we view the unplanned and intentional processes of development.

Understood as an unplanned process, in particular around the structural transformations associated with the rise of industrial capitalism, we can now see more clearly that this process is one that occurs in interaction with the international system. Rather than a view of each country successively going through an essentially similar process of development, following the same paths to those that have gone before (as proposed by some leading theorists like Rostow (1961)), we now see a succession of very different experiences of capitalist industrialization. Here the 'international context' acts differently in each case, producing varied results. The kind of industrialization taking place in Asia is producing a very different outcome to that experienced in Latin America or Europe.

Secondly, however, the unfolding story of development itself then helps to reshape the international system, generating new kinds of interaction. For example, trade between China and Europe, say, in the early 21st century where China is a highly competitive exporter of manufactured goods is now very different from the trade between China and Europe in the 19th century when China was subjected to 'unequal treaties' by European powers and forced to participate in the opium trade (see Figure 1.5). But development also has the power to reshape the relations between states, making some stronger and more powerful and others weaker, as the changing political relationship between China and Europe also shows. You will consider more of this aspect of international development in Chapters 3 and 4.

Figure 1.5 The signing of the Nanjing Treaty ended the Opium War between Britain and China

The idea of development as intentional, collective actions also changes when we consider it as an international process. Indeed, here we can introduce a distinction between actions that are mostly national or local in their nature and those that are inherently international.

Activity 1.5

In Subsection 1.1.2 (and in Table 1.1), we mentioned a number of examples of intentional development actions. Looking at some of those examples, which would you class as 'international'?

Do not spend more than 10 minutes on this activity.

Discussion

There isn't a hard and fast distinction between 'national' and 'international' development. Even local community efforts, for example to improve marketing of produce, may connect with the international arena in the form, say, of **fair trade** exports, and national efforts to raise literacy levels may rely on external actors for funding.

However, other actions – for example, development aid given by donor countries – is inherently international because it occurs between one country (or group of countries) and another. In this it is very different from a national government providing finance for a local area. The latter is set up and operated by a single national government. In international aid, there is a political process between states, while in the domestic actions of national government there are political processes that remain largely within states.

The importance of this is that, when it comes to international intentional development efforts, as represented by the MDGs, for instance, or international efforts at debt reduction, the political processes that arise involve efforts to achieve cooperation between states. As you have seen in Subsection 1.2.2, such international political processes around development inevitably raise questions as to how far international cooperation, as opposed to international competition or conflict, characterize development and about the exercise of power in such development efforts.

Summary and looking forward

This chapter has introduced you to a way of thinking about what studying international development involves. It began by suggesting a framework with which to organize some of the different and contested meanings of development. You have seen that studying development involves attention to a wide array of actions and historical processes. This chapter then outlined some ideas about what the term 'international' can be taken to mean and how this impacts on our understanding of the goals and routes to development.

Activity 1.6

Pause now and look back at the notes you made in response to Activity 1.1. Now, think about development in a country you know well and decide which of the following are ways to achieve development:

- Developing industry that is very efficient.
- Redistribution of wealth so that the poor have more resources.
- Improving education and skills, health and/or the position of women.
- General economic growth.
- Providing the conditions for people to become self-reliant.
- Resolving violence and other social conflicts.
- Ensuring that government is accountable and well managed.
- Other (please state).

Have you changed your views on what development entails? If so, why?

Consider why you have chosen the statements you have. What reasoning did you use? How does it relate to what you have just read?

Do not spend more than 15 minutes on this activity.

In many of the subsequent chapters in this book you will be able to put some much richer empirical detail on the skeleton outlined here and may find it useful to refer back to these discussions about international development as you proceed. Chapter 2 will outline, again in skeleton form, some of the key theoretical debates that have been developed within Development Studies, and indeed through the practice of development itself. As you will see in Chapter 2, the different ways in which development is 'international' has been a key issue within different debates within Development Studies over the years.

References

Brett, E.A. (2009) *Reconstructing Development Theory: International Inequality, Institutional Reform and Social Emancipation*, Basingstoke: Palgrave Macmillan.

Brown, W. (2013) 'War, states and development' in Butcher, M. and Papaioannou, T. (eds) *New Perspectives in International Development*, London, Bloomsbury Academic/Milton Keynes, The Open University.

Buzan, B. and Little, R. (2001) *International Systems in World History: Remaking the Study of International Relations*, Oxford, Oxford University Press.

Chambers, R. (1997) Whose Reality Counts? Putting the First Last, ITDG Publishing.

Cowen, M.P. and Shenton, R.W. (1997) *Doctrines of Development*, Routledge.

Hettne, B. (2009) *Thinking about Development*, London, Zed Books.

Hobsbawm, E.J. (1997) *On History*, London, Weidenfeld and Nicolson.

Maddison, A. (2001) *The World Economy: A Millennial Perspective*, Paris, OECD.

Mokyr, J. (1999) 'Editor's Introduction: the new economic history and the industrial revolution' in Mokyr, J. (ed.) *The British Industrial Revolution: an economic perspective* (2nd edition), Oxford, Westview Press.

Nederveen Pieterse, J. (2010) *Development Theory: deconstructions/reconstructions* (2nd revised edition). London, Sage and TCS books.

The Open University (2008) U213 *International Development: challenges for a world in transition*, 'Introducing Development', Milton Keynes, The Open University.

Requiem for Detroit, BBC television programme, 13 March 2010.

Robbins, P. (2013) 'History of technological innovation and critiques' in Butcher, M. and Papaioannou, T. (eds) *New Perspectives in International Development*, London, Bloomsbury Academic/Milton Keynes, The Open University.

Rosenberg, J. (2006) 'Why is there no international historical sociology?', *European Journal of International Relations*, vol. 12, no. 3, pp. 307–340.

Rostow, W.W. (1961) *The Stages of Economic Growth: A Non-communist Manifesto*, Cambridge, Cambridge University Press.

Thomas, A. (2000), Meanings and views of development' in Allen, T. and Thomas, A. (eds), *Poverty and Development in the 21st Century*, Oxford, Oxford University Press.

Thomas, A. and Allen, T. (2000) *Poverty and Development in the 21st Century*, Oxford, Oxford University Press.

United Nations (2010) *Millennium Development Goals at a Glance* [online], http://www.un.org/millenniumgoals/pdf/MDGs%20at%20a%20Glance%20SEPT%202010.pdf (Accessed 8 April 2011).

Further reading

If you are interested in reading more about international development theory, a good additional source is:

Brett, E.A. (2009) *Reconstructing Development Theory: International Inequality, Institutional Reform and Social Emancipation*, Basingstoke, Palgrave Macmillan.

Potter, R., Binns, T., Elliot, J. and Smith, D.W. (2008) *Geographies of Development*, 3rd edition, Pearson.

Contesting development in theory and practice

Rebecca Hanlin and William Brown

Introduction

In Chapter 1 we asserted that development, like any process of social change, is contested. Not only does it create winners and losers, but it opens up conflicts over different visions of the future, of what ought to happen. The different meanings of development, as well as the different aspects of development as an international process, have not surprisingly led to a number of debates in development thinking that have also had important impacts on development practice. It is important to make clear, however, that these have been debates and, while at some times there have been definite shifts from one side of the argument to the other, this is never total and at all times there are those who do not agree with the current 'mainstream' view. Often this is because, as you have seen, development is a multilinear process. It is complex. There are always winners and losers and issues that arise that create chaos, 'contradicting all that the concept of 'development' represented' (Hettne, 2009).

In fact, different views about development and how it happens are based on our values on how development should occur (a **normative** judgement), and our understanding of how it does occur in practice (an **analytical** judgement). As you will see, there isn't a hard and fast distinction between normative and analytical arguments as one will often lead into the other. Nevertheless, it is a useful distinction to keep in mind. Such conflicting normative and analytical views form the everyday content of development practice, the cut and thrust of political debates in the North and South, the arguments of development campaigners, and the proposals and actions of official development agencies and development non-governmental organizations (NGOs).

However, it is possible to stand back somewhat from the intricate detail of such everyday practice in order to identify a number of more general theories that both arise from, and influence, debates about development. Indeed, the formulation of theories about development – that is, generalized explanations of how development does and should occur – informs policies and practice on how to push it in certain directions through active intervention. As you read this book you will become aware of how difficult it is to actually divide development theory from development practice, especially when the same words are used, although often with different meanings (Lund, 2010). As Section 2.4 will suggest, all theories need to be understood in relation to the practical social contexts in which they arise and which they seek to influence. Nevertheless, in grouping together a number of viewpoints that share general propositions about development, we can help to clarify some of the key aspects of debate about development over time, the central shifts in thinking that have occurred and their impact on development practice.

Sections 2.1–2.3 look at development debates through three themes: history, agency and power, and scale. Of these, most attention is given to the history of development ideas and practice in order to provide grounding in some of the key historical turning points in this field. History here provides the framework for looking at development debates. The other themes – agency and power, and scale – are used as ways of differentiating between different positions in development debates. Thinking about issues of agency and power, and scale provides a backdrop to major issues debated within different ways of thinking about development theory and practice. As such, they come to frame development debates but also, as with the theme of history, can provide a lens through which to analyze critically these debates and the wider arena of development practice as a whole.

As we go through each theme, four main approaches to development will be introduced that have had a key role in shaping the debates about development: neoliberalism; structuralism; interventionism; and people-centred approaches. Each of these is summarized in its own box to provide an idea of the main claims. The importance of other ways of thinking about development, sometimes termed 'southern views of development', will be discussed briefly. Finally, Table 2.2 provides an overview of the four main approaches.

In summary, the aims of this chapter are to:

- introduce the history of theoretical thinking about development and the main approaches to development that have emerged since World War II

- look at some of the issues of agency and power that emerge in these theoretical debates and particularly the role of power in shaping theoretical debates themselves

- consider some of the issues about scale and the different perspectives on development that considerations of scale give rise to.

As with Chapter 1, we provide introductions to these issues, many of which are referred to in subsequent chapters in this book.

2.1 The history of development thinking

Quite where you would date thinking about the history of development from is itself a debatable point. In part this is down to different interpretations of development as an intentional or unplanned process. As you will see in other chapters, some writers date the structural transformations talked about in Chapter 1 back 500 years, to the beginning of the European expansion into non-European areas of the world. Others trace the idea of a goal of continual progress in society to the **European Enlightenment** dating back to the 17th century (see Figure 2.1) and the scientific and philosophical advances that accompanied Europe's rise.

Figure 2.1 A picture of 'An Experiment on the Bird in the Air Pump' captures the spirit of the European Enlightenment

Certainly both of these notions have an impact on contemporary debates in the shape of the legacies of historic inequalities between Europe and much of the South, as well as in debates about the European focus of development thinking (also see Section 2.2). One can even make a case that the idea of development has an even longer history in that most literate societies appear to have had some notion of social change over time.

If the focus is on the structural transformations wrought by industrial capitalism, however, as you have seen, this dates back to the late 18th to 19th centuries. And it is within the context of Britain's industrialization that we also begin to see some contours of debates about development that are familiar today. Karl Polanyi (1944, 1957) has written about these in terms of a tension, or what he calls a 'double movement', between market and society that has continued through the 'Great Transformation' of industrialization. Much of the debate about development turns on the relative roles of markets or government and state, and their actions as key drivers of development. You will come back to these discussions throughout this book.

For example, seen as intentional development actions, efforts to relieve severe poverty, such as the Poor Laws and public health initiatives in Britain in the 18th and 19th centuries (Figure 2.2), prefaced much more substantial and effective efforts adopted in the 20th century when state governments in industrialized countries saw poverty as a major cause for concern, and sought to tackle inequality in order to promote stable societies. In many of these countries there were also moves towards socially inclusive policies in education, housing and welfare, all requiring state action.

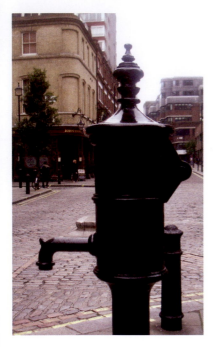

Figure 2.2 One of the first public health initiatives in Britain was the water pump pioneered by John Snow in London to reduce the incidence of cholera and other water borne diseases

However, the struggle to enact such social improvement was waged against a prevailing 'laissez-faire' doctrine in the early part of the 19th century, a liberal tradition which forms the historical grounding of what today goes under the title of neoliberalism (see Box 2.1). This view laid greater stress on markets as the key mechanism through which development would happen.

Box 2.1 Neoliberalism

Neoliberal views dominated much development thinking and practice in the 1980s and 1990s, and in those decades were reflected in the policies favoured by many governments (North and South) and organizations like the World Bank and the International Monetary Fund. In fact, in many respects, this is a modern variation of the original liberal ideas about capitalism that can be traced back to Adam Smith over 200 years ago. Neoliberalism emphasizes the action of free markets, the unfettered activity of buying and selling, as the best means of providing development. Neoliberals do not trust the state to act in the interests of its people, but believe rather that, because it is an institution, it will act in its own interest and in the interest of people who have power over the state. As a result, they emphasize the need for the state to be restricted in the scope of its actions and they concentrate on upholding the conditions necessary for markets to work, in particular by enforcing the law, upholding contracts and providing a stable currency. Competition within markets, carried out mainly by private individuals and companies, will bring about the most efficient and effective production and distribution of goods and services. As a total economy grows as a result of this efficiency, the new wealth generated will benefit everyone and will eventually trickle down even to the poorest. Thus, neoliberals stress development initiatives that help markets function well. They would emphasize the following actions:

- General economic growth.

- Developing industry that is very efficient.

- Providing the conditions so individuals can become innovative, entrepreneurial, and able to make choices and to become self-reliant.

This follows from the importance they place on individual responsibility and the value of competition.

It will be clear from this that neoliberalism emphasizes ideas of unplanned development in the sense that the workings of the market and competition are seen as the main driver of economic growth. As a form of intentional development it is more limited to actions that remove state barriers to markets. In terms of the relationship between national processes of development and the international system, neoliberalism emphasizes the benefits of open economies that are well integrated with the international economy, that allow a free flow of imports and exports, open the national economy to international competition, and are open to investment. It thus posits a particular kind of liberalized international economic interaction at the centre of development. Because these are seen to generate benefits to all countries, it creates, according to its adherents, the opportunity for international cooperation to achieve these ends.

Deliberate efforts to tackle poverty and use state action to stimulate economic prosperity grew through the late 19th century, both in terms of social policies aimed at ameliorating the ill-effects of industrialization and in a broader sense of using the state to encourage the growth of industry in those countries (like Germany and Japan) that industrialized later than Britain. Indeed, for some development writers (Gershenkron, 1962) 'late industrialization' has typically been characterized by an increased role for the state in managing the process of industrialization.

In the South, some development efforts had been enacted by colonial powers such as Britain and France, as you will see in Chapter 3. However, it was in the post-World War II period, with many Southern countries becoming independent sovereign states, that structuralism (see Box 2.2) came to the fore. Countries that had recently gained independence after periods of colonialism were concerned to develop their economies and improve the material conditions of their populations, often through state-directed development plans. It was also during this period that we see the acceleration of intentional development in the form of aid, loans and technical assistance from industrialized countries as you will see further in Chapter 12. Certainly in some countries of the South, such as India, the existence of a non-capitalist, state-planned process of industrialization in the form of the Soviet Union played a crucial role in supporting the idea that state intervention in markets was necessary for development to take place. Even in many industrialized countries, mixed economies involving elements of state planning and ownership were prevalent for a time. Levels of state intervention varied from country to country.

Box 2.2 Structuralism

Structuralist views hold that markets only bring economic growth to some, and in order to ensure development you have to look at economic and social structures – who has power and who owns what. These structures greatly affect one's ability to enter and survive in markets. Structuralism therefore takes a critical view of unfettered markets and argues the need for state governments and international agencies to control markets, to make sure that competition is fair, and to distribute the benefits of wealth. Many of the strategies followed in the post-World War II period by governments in the South and North had structuralist elements. Although often associated with the Marxist and socialist left, in fact there are both left- and right-wing versions of structuralism (Brett, 2009).

In terms of intentional development actions, therefore, structuralism sees state actions – such as restrictions on imports, controls over financial flows, subsidies to particular industries, say – as necessary to combat what are seen as entrenched obstacles to development. In terms of domestic policies, some structuralists would certainly agree with redistributing wealth so that the poor have more resources and, while aiming for higher economic growth, would want equal attention paid to improving social wellbeing, such as access to education and healthcare, and enhanced physical environments. However, structuralism also implies a very different kind of relationship between national economies and the international system, with deliberate and highly politicized interventions in international economic flows of trade and investment. In part, such actions are seen as necessary in order to offset the negative effects of the 'unplanned' developmental tendencies within capitalism which, left unhindered, will exacerbate inequalities within and between countries and create obstacles to the development of the poorer countries.

However, a broader set of structuralist arguments about the place of the South in the international economy strengthened the view that states needed to manage international economic flows (trade, investment and technology transfer) if development was to happen. By the 1970s, many Southern countries argued for the need for reform of the international economy itself, in a campaign for a **New International Economic Order** which would seek to control international markets in commodities and raw materials in order to deliver greater benefits for developing countries.

In the event, the campaign came to little, and by the end of the 1970s, crisis in the industrialized economies and significant political shifts saw a resurgence of neoliberal ideas and practice. Those on the right of the political spectrum saw state interference as hindering the dynamic of private enterprise, and argued that politicians and civil servants were not competent to direct economic growth. These shifts were reflected in policies of major international organizations like the World Bank and, combined with crises in structuralist approaches to development, saw many Southern countries adopt neoliberal ideas. In 1989 the Soviet bloc of communist-inspired, state-led development collapsed, giving greater ascendancy to neoliberal ideas. Since then, most countries, including much of the South, have to some extent embraced the liberal capitalist view of development.

Due to the severe impact on poor people of many neoliberal policies, the 1990s and 2000s saw considerable shifts towards taking greater account of poverty and a renewed emphasis was placed on **accountable governance** in order to further improve the actions of the market. In what some term interventionism (see Box 2.3), governments in both the North and the South combine efforts to limit state public expenditure, encourage private enterprise, and increase exports with more interventionist policies aimed at improving the conditions of the poorest in society. Thus the emphasis on markets from neoliberalism is combined with a set of intentional actions aimed at specific developmental goals. There have also been moves to increase the accountability of the state by devolving services to local government, and encouraging the participation of citizens in planning and evaluating services. Governments differ in their response to the provision of services (healthcare, education, planning) by providing services directly, working through partnerships with the private sector, or facilitating the private sector to provide services. Accompanying this, the increasing integration of world markets where all countries trade and compete with each other, known by some as **globalization**, provides a critical political and economic context for development activity.

Box 2.3   Interventionism

Many observers claim that a combination of policies, both structuralist (state-led) and neoliberal (market-led) strategies are often necessary. Much development debate now focuses on the extent and form of intervention. This approach, referred to as interventionism, argues that both markets and states are important to development and that both need to operate well in order to create the right conditions for development. Drawing on some of the 'Third Way' ideas of the Labour government in Britain (1997–2010) and Bill Clinton's presidency of the USA (1993–2001) as well as from the criticisms of neoliberal policies of the 1980s and early 1990s, interventionism represents something of a synthesis of the other two approaches (Brett, 2009). The World Bank's view in 1997 gives a flavour of it:

> Development – economic, social and sustainable – without an effective state is impossible [...] an effective state – not a minimal one – is central to economic and social development, but more as a partner and facilitator than as director. States work to complement markets, not replace them.

> *(World Bank, 1997, p. 18)*

2.2   Agency and power in development

In Chapter 1, you have already come across many different agents of development – states, individuals and businesses operating in markets, international organizations, NGOs and groups of local people. For example, we discussed the power of individual nation states in the UN system. However, Activity 1.2, which looked at attitudes towards the car industry in Detroit, highlighted the power of business entities and particularly the power of what have become large multinational firms and transnational corporations (TNCs).

These actors (states and TNCs) are part of a set of macro level agents of development. There are, however, many other agents of development both as collectives, that is groups of individuals, and individuals themselves. Examples include:

- the influence of individuals in social movements such as the American Civil Rights Movement
- the UK's Make Poverty History campaign
- international activity around the World Social Forum

- smaller community level activity such as in China with respect to the Three Gorges Dam, a controversial building project to create the world's largest hydropower plant on the Yangtze River.

We as individuals, as discussed in Chapter 1, also act as development agents in our day-to-day activities, both consciously and unconsciously, through the decisions and actions we take.

All agent's of development, whether they are working at the macro level (state and market) or the micro level (individual and community), are qualitatively different in the way they operate, maintain themselves and evolve. Linked to this, the agency, or degree to which these agents are free to make their own decisions and follow their own chosen path of action, is also an important issue that needs consideration. This agency is determined by both individual and collective action but is also influenced by a wider context and the interaction of an agent with wider society.

You will read more about the various agents of development in a number of the following chapters. For now the short examples in Box 2.4 should help you contextualize this discussion a bit more.

Box 2.4   Agents of development at work

Computers and their programmes

In 2007 a European Union court found Microsoft guilty of breaching anti-trust rules. The case against Microsoft related to the dominance of its operating system, which was being used by over 95% of the world's computers at the time. *The* Economist (2007) magazine wrote: 'Microsoft's pride may have been hurt by the court, but its dominance is hardly under immediate threat.'

Latin America's development

In the 1950s and 1960s many Latin American countries started to move their economic activity towards more inward-looking markets through a policy known as **Import Substitution Industrialization (ISI)**. Instead of importing industrial products from abroad, tariffs were used to protect industry so that goods needed by national consumers (both individuals and firms) were produced domestically. One argument (from Dependency theory, discussed later) to explain this decision was that Latin American countries were on the periphery, that is they were not key players in the global system both politically and economically, and were therefore prone to 'underdevelopment'.

Baby milk advertising

An international boycott of Nestlé products from the 1970s by concerned consumers due to their aggressive marketing of powdered baby milk, particularly in developing countries, led to the setting up of a range of consumer groups and social movements, including Baby Milk Action and the International Baby Food Action Network, as well as the development of the International Code of Marketing on Breastmilk Substitutes by the World Health Organization (in the 1980s). In 2009, the boycott had resulted in a ban on all Nestlé products in 73 student unions and 102 businesses in the UK (see Figure 2.3).

Figure 2.3 Nestlé's promotion of its baby milk products was a source of civil society action

Activity 2.1

Once you have read through the examples in Box 2.4, answer the following questions:

1 Who were the main agents of development involved in each of these case studies?

2 What do you think was a major factor in determining the outcome of the agents' activities?

Do not spend more than 15 minutes on this activity.

Discussion

In answering the first question it is important to realize that there are the obvious agents of development – the main actors of the story – such as a TNC, a state government and individuals often acting within social collectives. However, they have not operated in isolation. In each of these examples there are multiple agents of development involved.

The degree to which the TNC, the state, the individual and the social collective were successful in their activities is determined in part by the degree of power that they hold in relation to other agents or actors, which in turn determines their ability to act. Power is therefore an issue that is intricately bound to the notion of agency. People often define power in terms of control and influence over others but it is also important to consider power in terms of the degree of freedom an individual has, or in other words the degree to which power is enabling or constraining. As such, power is relational because it is determined by your interaction with others. Related to this, it is also ever present because we exist within a society where we are constantly in contact with other people, organizations or institutions, resulting in a constant juggling of power relations.

The extent to which agents can (or can be enabled to) act together while recognizing their own interests is a major issue for development. As you may have noted, much of the historical evolution of debates about development turns in part on arguments about who or what are the primary agents for development. In particular a tension exists between those approaches that emphasize state-based actions, and those that emphasize market operators as the best drivers of development. Many neoliberal interventions in development are based on a critique of the negative impact of states as agents in guiding policy. Conversely, much structuralist analysis is based on a critique of the structure of markets as a limiting factor in the development prospects of the poorest. Both critiques shaped the interventionist compromise that came to dominate official development discourses in the early 21st century.

In understanding these different takes on agency, it is important to realize that, at different times, different theories have been heralded as correct for understanding the present, explaining the past and providing a framework for the future. However, we would do well to remember Brett's words of caution:

> Development studies, unlike mathematics or chemistry, has to deal with a conflict-ridden reality and produce future-oriented predictions and prescriptions that will constantly be undermined by unforeseen events. The fashionable orthodoxies of the day will always be threatened by dissolution, but they incorporate all the knowledge we have about how to proceed, and are constantly being criticized, corrected and improved as the development community responds to its successes and failures.
>
> *(Brett, 2009, p. xviii)*

In recognizing this, it should become clear that visions of development are dependent on whose understanding of development becomes the most dominant. It is difficult not to recognize that the dominance and prominence of different views of development relate to the knowledge, power and politics of those involved.

This, to some extent, is an argument as to why many Southern theories of development, which developed outside of the North (this is discussed further in Section 2.3), have not taken hold, although more often than not it relates to the specificity of their development and scope. Such a view builds on arguments of neocolonialism whereby, in a similar way to during the colonial history, agents of development often seen as being located in the North exerted their influence over the countries and populations of the South.

Recognizing the power and inequality inherent even in theory accepts that 'each development theory can be read as a **hegemony** or a challenge to hegemony' due to its role in building support or opposition for theories in order to influence policy discussions and ultimately policy implementation (Nederveen Pieterse, 2010, p. 27). As analysts we bring our values, ideals and perspectives to issues and with that also our politics and existing dominant power relations (Clifford and Marcus, 1986; Crewe and Harrison, 1998).

It is perhaps unsurprising therefore that there is a set of theorists who reject all other theories of development because they are critical of the political processes by which those theories were produced. These theorists and practitioners argue for a more critical reflection on what 'development' actually means. For some this requirement is premised on the argument that what is seen as the dominant view of 'development' has come about because of the 'universalizing power' of the relationship between the market and the state determining how all economic, political and social activity takes place (Sachs, 1992). Thus, these theorists argue for the theory and practice of international development to become more self-critical (Rahnema and Bawtree, 1997) or 'reflexive' (Nederveen Pieterse, 2010). By this they mean that we (that is, those studying or working in international development) must recognize our place within the world and our impact on it. At the same time this approach calls for more inclusive development research and practice, requiring ownership by those for whom development is taking place. There is thus an emphasis placed on investigating alternative representations and practice within local settings (Escobar, 1995) so that the 'multiple narratives' of all those involved in development activities are heard reflecting the importance of participatory approaches to development (Peters, 2000), but also the politics inherent within such an approach (Mosse and Lewis, 2005). This approach acknowledges difference and therefore power relations from the outset (Hettne, 2009).

2.3   Questions of scale

Our final theme focuses on how different approaches to development conceptualize the scale of these processes and actions. Questions of scale can be divided into a number of registers – local community or household level, sub-national regional level, national level, international and global. We have made a case already in Chapter 1 that in studying 'international development' we think that the international scale has a unique role in conceptualizations of development, so there is no need to repeat those points here. But it is apparent from the history of development ideas discussed in Sections 2.1 and 2.2 that scale matters in defining goals of development and in understanding the unplanned and intentional routes towards those goals.

Activity 2.2

Review Table 2.1. This was first introduced to you in Chapter 1. Note down whether these examples are focused at local, regional, national or international scales. We have numbered each goal to help with this task, and provided a couple of examples to start you off.

Do not spend more than 15 minutes on this activity.

Table 2.1 Development goals and routes

		Goals of development		Scale levels
		Broader goals: the structural transformation of society	Narrower goals: achieving specific social targets/improvements	
Routes to development	Unplanned processes of social change	1.1 Transition from agricultural to industrial society 1.2 Dynamic growth and change inherent to capitalism 1.3 Urbanization 1.4 Modernization 1.5 Unintended impacts of warfare and conflict 1.6 'Shocks' – economic crisis, political upheaval or environmental disaster	2.1 Impact of economic growth on incomes 2.2 Positive impacts of technological change on livelihoods	1.1 National 2.2 Local
	Intentional collective action in international, state and non-state forms	3.1 Macroeconomic and governance reforms 3.2 State promotion of industrialization 3.3 Promotion of technological change 3.4 Promotion/regulation of urbanization	4.1 International and national efforts at poverty reduction 4.2 National social policies to promote literacy, health, education, etc. 4.3 State and non-governmental aid 4.4 Rural and urban community improvement and fair trade schemes	3.4 National 4.1 International

Discussion

You may have found it quite difficult to put an issue into a single level of scale. This is because often issues cross traditional boundaries or the issue may depend on the contextual environment on which you are focusing. So, for example, there are interactions between national-level development processes and the international implied in relations between international organizations and national governments. At the same time, there is an argument that suggests all issues impact at the local level even if they start out as international issues.

Therefore, it is important to spend a few moments reviewing a key debate in development that we have not yet touched upon, which focuses our attention very firmly on issues of scale. People-centred development (see Box 2.5) arose in the early 1970s in part as reaction to the large-scale state-directed development efforts inspired by structuralism. As you can see from Box 2.5, it has two key differences when compared with other approaches. The first is a disagreement about the goals of development, making a strong case that they focus too heavily on economic growth rather than the narrower specific goals of improving the lives of poor people. However, the second difference is about scale, with the focus of development efforts being the need to bring people more directly into control over change, supporting localized action, participatory processes and local ownership of development projects. As such, they are critical of the role of donors, large NGOs and even the state in acting for people. But it is also a critique of these actors as being too remote because of the scale at which they operate.

Box 2.5 People-centred development

People-centred development is highly critical of all economic approaches instead emphasizing:

- redistribution of wealth so that the poor have more resources
- improving education and skills
- improving the health of the people
- providing the conditions for people to become self-reliant
- ensuring that government is accountable and well managed.

It emphasizes **participation** and **empowerment** rather than economic growth and the satisfaction of human needs as the purpose of development. Dudley Seers (1969, 1979) pioneered this approach to development. His original six 'conditions for development' build on the five key issues raised above and have been extended by the experience of the decades since the 1970s (points 7 and 8 below). These eight key 'conditions of development' form a human-needs-centred development approach (an extension of the people-centred approach):

1 low levels of material poverty
2 low level of unemployment
3 relative equality
4 democratization of political life
5 'true' national independence
6 good literacy and educational levels
7 relative equal status for women and participation of women
8 sustainability, the ability to meet future needs.

The people-centred approach has also been presented as a juxtaposed stance against other 'mainstream' Western approaches. The people-centred approach and others similar to it were influential in the 1980s as a counterpoint to the rise of neoliberalism. Since then they have remained a constant force. In fact, by the beginning of the 21st century there was something of a return to this approach within mainstream international development policy arenas of social as well as economic concerns of development. The development of the MDGs discussed in Chapter 1 is an example of this. As the WHO's Commission on Social Determinants of Health put it:

> Take the central policy importance given to economic growth: Economic growth is without question important, particularly for poor countries, as it gives the opportunity to provide resources to invest in improvement of the lives of their population. But growth by itself, without appropriate social policies to ensure reasonable fairness in the way its benefits are distributed, brings little benefit to health equity.
>
> *(Commission for Social Determinants of Health, 2008, p. 1)*

The dominance of Western approaches to development thinking and practice has led some to argue that much development tradition is based on 'Western ways of creating the world' (Strathern, 1988; Escobar, 1995). However, there are a variety of 'Southern' theories of development that have been influential at various times and places. Examples of these are listed in Box 2.6. The discussion above has concentrated on Western theories of development because of their international prominence. However, this is not because we elevate these in importance over other theories of development. These alternative theories of development that originated in the South have at times been extremely important in shaping the international development debates. For example, dependency theory was key to shaping much structuralist theory and has also contributed to **world systems theory**, which has been applied to a wide range of fields not just that of international development. As the global forces of power change axis (see Chapters 3 and 4 in this book), it is possible that future Southern theories of development will have the potential to eclipse these current dominant Western theories. The experience of some Asian countries has already made many development economists reconsider their understandings of how development happens.

Box 2.6   Examples of Southern theories of development

Dependency theory: argues that the reason some economies have not developed as others have (resulting in 'underdevelopment') is because they stand on the periphery of technological innovation which is seen as crucial for promoting economic growth. Some proponents of the theory believe that countries can 'catch up' with the central countries but for other theorists this would result simply in a new set of dependencies being created. This approach was developed in Latin America and has been influential since the late 1950s.

Gandhian economics: building on the writings of Gandhi from the early 1900s, this approach views small-scale, community-based self-sufficiency as the key to economic and social sustainability. The emphasis is on wellbeing as the driver of economic activity, and limits to the amount of wealth required. In addition there is a strong emphasis on trusteeship and the notion that those with wealth would act in the service of wider society. Gandhi's ideas on a village-based economy are said to have had some influence in shaping alternative approaches to development such as

Tanzanian socialism of the 1960s–1980s. Gandhianism has occasionally resurfaced in Indian politics (as with the protests over corruption in India in 2011), though has had little influence over India's overall approach to development.

2.4   The key approaches to development

This chapter has outlined a series of key approaches to development that have been influential within development studies theory and international development practice. These key approaches have been introduced through a framework of thinking about the context within which development occurs and three key themes that need to be considered: history, power and agency, and scale. Table 2.2 provides an overview of these approaches to development, outlining their main concerns, the time period they were most influential, key thinkers associated with each approach, examples of this approach in practice and, finally, the specific international implications of each approach. The aim of this table is to provide a good overview of the key 'take-home' points from each approach, building on what you have already read. Take some time to go through this table and understand it. It will become a useful tool, along with Table 1.1 in Chapter 1, to help you understand many of the arguments and issues raised in the rest of this book.

Table 2.2   Summary of key approaches to development

	Neoliberalism	Structuralism	Interventionism	People-centred
Main claims/ concerns	Emphasis on free market solutions and limitations on state/government action. For a strong but limited state, allowing markets to emerge and work.	Emphasis on the structural bias in world economy against growth and industrialization in developing countries. Need for strong public action in the form of national controls on economic flows (investment, trade) and international regulation to change international commodity markets, technology transfer, etc. More radical versions emphasized 'de-linking' from world economy and national or autarchic development.	Something of a mid-point between neoliberal and structuralism. Has neoliberalism emphasis on market solutions and on capitalism as the motor for development but recognizes market limitations and failures and need for state intervention to address social problems (poverty, education).	Emphasis on meeting human needs (poverty, unemployment, education, housing, etc.) and for policies directed to these ends rather than macro-level aims (economic growth, industrialization, etc.). Emphasizes the negative effects of industrialization strategies.
When influential	Intellectual background in classic political economy of Adam Smith and Ricardo in the late18th to19th centuries, whose ideas influenced 'laissez-faire' British policy in the early 19th century, as well as the inter-war Austrian school of economics. More recently came back into favour (hence 'neo-') from mid-1970s. Dominant in UK and USA from 1980 and over the international finance institutions. Continuing, albeit more qualified, influence from mid-1990s on.	Early versions in work of German economist Friedrich List in 19th century but key ideas were post-World War II analyses of the problems of 'catch-up' facing developing countries. Major influence in 1950s and 1960s on development policies of the South. More radical versions in the dependency theory of Gunder-Frank and Wallerstein had less practical influence.	In some versions, influence of Keynesian ideas of economic regulation which were influential in 1950s and 1960s in the industrialized world, but mainly to the fore from mid-1990s with much less Keynesian influence. Evident in policies of New Labour in the UK and Clinton administration in the USA; and increasingly in World Bank policies towards the South, especially from 1997 onwards.	Originally developed in the 1970s as a response to what was seen as the top-down nature of development strategies (e.g. structuralist). Influence on some policies (e.g. World Bank rural development) in 1970s but growing influence within development NGOs in 1980s and 1990s. Some ideas are reflected in poverty reduction strategies of late 1990s and beyond.

Table 2.2   Summary of key approaches to development (continued)

	Neoliberalism	Structuralism	Interventionism	People-centred
Key thinkers	Ludwig Von Mises, Fredrich Von Hayek, Milton Friedman, Peter Bauer	Raúl Prebisch, Fernando Henrique Cardoso, Andre Gunder Frank	Joseph Stiglitz, Jeffery Sachs	David Korten, Dudley Seers, Amartya Sen
Examples of development practice	Structural adjustment policies of the IMF and World Bank, trade liberalization, e.g. through World Trade Organisation (WTO)	Import Substitution Industrialization (ISI) policies of 1960s and 1970s, campaigns for New International Economic Order of 1970s	Poverty Reduction Strategy Papers (PRSPs) from the late 1990s on social sector spending combined with market liberalization and governance reforms in the 2000s	Community-level aid (and empowerment) projects funded by governments and NGOs
International implications	Implies that development occurs through liberalized integration between national and world economy, with free flow of trade, investment and finance. Politically for stringent conditions on granting public money through international aid efforts and the like.	Implies a highly regulated and managed relationship between national and international economies; nationalist in political orientation and an anti-colonial/-imperialist political rhetoric.	Entails liberalization of international economic flows, but also for international public action to achieve social goals. Political rhetoric of international consensus around markets, governance reform and social improvements.	Can contain anti-corporate discourses against TNCs as well as radical critiques of impact of World Bank aid projects. Presents a picture of communities struggling against outside (national and international) impositions and exploitation.

Summary and looking forward

In this chapter you have seen how many of the contested ideas about development, introduced in Chapter 1, turn exactly on different ways that development actors and theorists define development in relation to the different goals and routes of development. Indeed, you might find it useful to look at the boxes outlining different development approaches to confirm this claim. In between, we have explored how both the meanings of development and the contests around development theory and practice have to be interpreted through a framework of the international system which both sets a context for, and shapes the nature of, development in its different guises. We emphasized in particular how development is both interactive between different countries and multilinear in the sense that no one country is fated to follow exactly the same historical trajectory as another. It is partly because of this complex and fluid terrain that studying international development is such a stimulating and challenging prospect. It is also a necessary one if we are to contribute to achieving change for the better in the world.

References

Brett, E.A. (2009) *Reconstructing Development Theory: International Inequality, Institutional Reform and Social Emancipation*, Basingstoke, Palgrave Macmillan.

Clifford, J. and Marcus, G. (eds) (1986) *Writing Culture: The Politics and Poetics of Ethnography*, Berkeley, USA, University of California Press.

Commission for Social Determinants of Health (2008) *Closing the Gap in a Generation: Health Equity Through Action on the Social Determinants of Health*, Geneva, World Health Organization.

Crewe, E. and Harrison, E. (1998) *Whose Development? An Ethnography of Aid*, London, Zed Books.

The Economist (2007) 'EU v. Microsoft', 7 September 2007.

Escobar, A. (1995) *Encountering Development: The Making and Unmaking of the Third World*, Princeton, Princeton University Press.

Gardner, K. and Lewis, D. (2000) 'Dominant Paradigms Overturned or "Business as Usual"? Development Discourse and the White Paper on International Development', *Critique of Anthropology*, vol. 20, no. 1, pp. 15–29.

Gerschenkron, A. (1962) *Economic Backwardness in Historical Perspective: A Book of Essays*, Cambridge, Belknap Press of Harvard University Press.

Hettne, B. (2009) *Thinking about Development*, London, Zed Books.

Lund, C. (2010) 'Approaching development: an opinionated review', *Progress in Development Studies*, vol. 10, no. 1, pp. 19–34.

Mosse, D. and Lewis, D. (2005) *The Aid Effect: Giving and Governing in International Development*, London, Pluto Press.

Nederveen Pieterse, J. (2010) *Development Theory: Deconstructions/Reconstructions* (2nd revised edition) London, Sage and TCS books.

Peters, P.E. (2000) *Development Encounters: Sites of Participation and Knowledge*, Harvard Institute for International Development.

Polanyi, K. (1944, 1957) *The Great Transformation: The Political and Economic Origins of Our Time*, Boston, Beacon Press.

Rahnema, M. and Bawtree, V. (1997) *The Post-Development Reader*, London, Zed Books.

Sachs, W. (1992) *The Development Dictionary: A Guide to Knowledge as Power*, London, Zed Books.

Seers, D. (1969 [1979]) 'The meaning of development' in Lehmann, D. (ed.) *Development Theory: Four Critical Studies*, London, Frank Cass.

Strathern, M. (1988) *The Gender of the Gift: Problems with Women and Problems with Society in Melanesia*, Berkeley, University of California Press.

World Bank (1997) *World Development Report: The State in a Changing World*, Washington, World Bank.

Further reading

Nederveen Pieterse, J. (2010) *Development Theory: Deconstructions/Reconstructions*, (2nd revised edition) London, Sage and TCS books.

Thomas, A. (2000) 'Development as practice in a liberal capitalist world', *Journal of International Development*, vol. 12, issue 6, pp. 773–787.

Rising powers

Giles Mohan

Introduction

Consider this commentary on India.

> The notable thing about India's rise is not that it is new, but that its path has been unique. Rather than adopting the classic Asian strategy – exporting labor-intensive, low-priced manufactured goods to the West – India has relied on its domestic market more than exports, consumption more than investment, services more than industry, and high-tech more than low-skilled manufacturing. ... But what is most remarkable is that rather than rising with the help of the state, India is in many ways rising despite the state. ... And since 1991 especially, the Indian state has been gradually moving out of the way.
>
> *(Das, 2006, p. 2)*

Here is a country growing rapidly and moving up the rank of world economies. The extract talks of India's 'rise' and this chapter will be looking at what we are calling *the rising powers*. Chapter 1 discussed the idea that development could be spontaneous or planned and that each country pursues its own pathway. In the extract above we see all of this – India has a unique approach that is largely driven by individuals although the state does have some planning role, albeit a diminishing one. It also mentions the 'classic Asian strategy' and how India is different. The chapters that follow will look at the 'classic' strategy through engaging with the other great rising power in Asia – China.

But where do the rising powers get their power from? What does this mean for countries in the international system, and how does this affect the way we think about the process of development itself? To address these questions this chapter aims to:

- establish the broad characteristics of rising powers
- outline the key concepts of power and change within the international system
- give some detail of the actual changes in the balance of power within the international system over the past few centuries
- outline the development trajectories of India, Brazil and China.

One of these rising powers stands out as playing an unprecedented role in reshaping the international system and as such has generated considerable anxiety among the major world powers, which tells us much about what drives and constitutes a rising power. That country is China and Section 3.1 begins by looking at what makes it a powerful development actor and how its rise is perceived to affect the power of the USA.

3.1 China's rise as a threat

The international system is made up of multiple states and these states interact to a greater or lesser extent as they develop. Understanding this dynamism is at the heart of International Studies. What, then, might the rise of one power mean for other powers and the international system as a whole?

Activity 3.1

The following extract from 'How we would fight China' (Kaplan, 2005) is taken from a US publication and concerns the rise of China, with the author suggesting how the USA might respond. As you read it, think about the following questions:

1   How does the author present the 'threat' from China?

2   What characterizes the development process in China?

3   What does China's power tell us more generally about power within the international system?

Spend about 15 minutes on this activity.

For some time now no navy or air force has posed a threat to the United States. … This will soon change. The Chinese navy is poised to push out into the Pacific … In the coming decades China will play an asymmetric back-and-forth game with us [the USA] in the Pacific …

… It [China] has growing increments of 'soft' power that demonstrate a particular gift for adaptation. While stateless terrorists fill security vacuums, the Chinese fill economic ones. All over the globe, in such disparate places as the troubled Pacific Island states of Oceania, the Panama Canal zone, and out-of-the-way African nations, the Chinese are becoming masters of indirect influence – by establishing business communities and diplomatic outposts, by negotiating construction and trade agreements. Pulsing with consumer and martial energy, and boasting a peasantry that, unlike others in history, is overwhelmingly literate, China constitutes the principal conventional threat to America's liberal imperium. …

… China's rulers may not be democrats in the literal sense, but they are seeking a liberated First World lifestyle for many of their 1.3 billion people – and doing so requires that they safeguard sea-lanes for the transport of energy resources from the Middle East and elsewhere. Naturally, they do not trust the United States and India to do this for them. Given the stakes, and given what history teaches us about the conflicts that emerge when great powers all pursue legitimate interests, the result is likely to be the defining military conflict of the twenty-first century: if not a big war with China, then a series of Cold War-style standoffs that stretch out over years and decades.

(Kaplan, 2005)

Discussion

1   The Chinese threat

The author certainly seems worried about the Chinese! Kaplan is a provocative commentator who tends to focus on what he sees as the major tensions in world politics. He also views these tensions from the perspective of his home country – the USA – and how he believes they will negatively affect that country's power. Like any viewpoint it is not a simple 'fact' but a claim that is open to contestation, so you need to bear this in mind as you analyze his position.

Kaplan sees the Chinese as a threat militarily; so much so that he foresees a new '**Cold War**' being fought in the Pacific.

2   What characterizes development

But underlying that military might is rapid economic development allied to new technologies. Chapter 1 discussed the 'goals' and 'routes' of development and here Kaplan is arguing that the Chinese share a desire for the same 'lifestyles' as those in the 'First World', but China's route is unique and is currently not 'liberated' given its relative lack of democracy. This suggests that development is made up of multiple aspects – not just economic growth, but forms of governance, technology, military power, and the size and skills of the population. This means, as Chapter 1 discussed, that to understand *international* development it is also important to look at the ways in which 'internal' development proceeds, since development is an interactive process between internal and external factors.

3   Power and the international system

As noted, Kaplan writes from a perspective of how this all affects the USA but this is not the only view circulating in the USA (e.g. see Ikenberry, 2008). How does the author see the balance between China's rise and the USA's status? He seems to say that a gain for China will be a loss for the USA. The whole tone of the piece is about China as a threat. It's about 'fighting' the Chinese. Interestingly the author also talks about the **soft power** that China uses so effectively, which is all about influencing others without resorting to military threats. He mentions the global spread of China and its use of trade, diplomacy and infrastructure deals. This is about development as multiple interactions with others. Here then are two alternative ways of viewing China's rise. One is a win–lose scenario. China gains while the USA (or some other power) loses. The other is a win–win scenario. China's growth and influence has positive impacts on some other countries.

We will be using these two broad scenarios of win–lose and win–win in looking at what happens when any power rises.

Before proceeding it is worth outlining the defining features of rising powers, either historically or today, which frame these chapters (see Box 3.1).

Box 3.1 What makes a rising power?

Politically a rising power, by its very nature, is powerful although there is no necessary link between economic and political power. In looking at differential power within the international system we will use the idea of hegemony: the complex power of a dominant actor over others. Hegemony is not just a political phenomenon but includes the economic and cultural dimensions which will also be examined in this book.

Economically a rising power becomes a centre of both world consumption and production. These countries industrialize at rapid rates for a period of time although there are different routes to industrialization. The other important upshot is that, as centres of production/consumption, rising powers have to enter relations with others as suppliers of raw materials or components and/or as markets for manufactured goods. These industrial transitions also mean the conversion of the natural environment into productive elements, first 'at home' and then externally through trade, investment and cross-border flows, giving rise to, for example, pollution.

Culturally a rising power has a strong sense of national purpose. First, we often see major powers taking a view of the world as centred upon themselves, and other countries with whom they interact 'lacking' certain features that would make them equal. In extreme cases this becomes the focus for interventions as a power sees its role as bringing order to the less civilized or development to the underdeveloped. Second, culture is something which helps shape – but does not determine – the nature of regional capitalisms. In Chapter 1, capitalism was defined as possessing certain features, but some important differences relate to culture in terms of how business is organized. Third, powers have tended to project their own culture as the 'norm' through things like language, though this is contested and appropriated in interesting ways.

Spatially a rising power possesses both a 'core' city-region and extensive international networks through the out-migration of its 'people', extension of its state institutions and operation of its firms. Industrialization is an urban phenomenon that creates centres of production (e.g. Detroit), but also of finance and politics, to which people migrate. These become the key hubs in the coordination of the international system and connect to other nodes. While much of the international system can be orchestrated at arms length it generally requires the physical presence of people from one country in other countries. And even when formal political control ends there are multiple other mechanisms for maintaining relationships of influence over others, for example aid, transnational corporations (TNCs). Chapters 5 and 7 will explore these.

These are factors that characterize *all* rising power to some degree. However, there are two important factors that make the contemporary rising powers *different* from previous ones. The first is population size, which Kaplan mentions with regard to China in the earlier extract, but India and Brazil also have very large populations. Only the USA has a sizeable population as a world power whereas the UK, Spain, Portugal, France and the Netherlands, which were the rising powers of the 18th and 19th centuries, were tiny by comparison. The population issue is key to discussions of growth, consumption, urbanization, migration and the environment. The second difference is histories of colonization and stages of development. China, India and Brazil were colonized by European (and some regional) powers, albeit at different times and in different ways. This experience of colonization not only altered their development paths for anything up to 200 years and tied them into particular spheres of influence, but has shaped their attitudes to self-determination in development matters.

3.2 Power in the international system

In Chapter 1 you were introduced to the idea of the 'modern' international system which is made up of states and the interactions between them. The important point of Chapter 1 was that each state has unique features of its own development, which in turn shape the ways in which it interacts with other states. So, while we can for the sake of analysis look at 'internal' factors, they are always and inevitably also shaped by 'external' relations, and these are characterized by differences in power. The very idea of (rising) powers implies that some actors in the international system possess more power than others, and this section examines this in more detail. Who holds power in the international system and where does their power come from?

But first, let us examine what power means at a more general level. We can think about power concerning how an entity is able to influence its environment. In some texts, power is seen as a thing in itself, something which an actor must possess and deploy. This is very much about unequal power relations and a win–lose mentality in which a more powerful actor uses their power to make a less powerful actor act in a way it would not normally do. In terms of international relations this conceptualization of power is routinely used by **realist** theorists, which is discussed further in Chapter 4. It is also ultimately tied to military or 'hard' power since the threat (or use) of force can move another actor to behave in a certain way.

However, power can be used in more enabling ways. We can see power as an actor's ability to exercise influence over others through a relationship with them. This influence can be through a form of persuasion or attraction. The mechanisms of influence are multiple but could include economic interaction or pressure, diplomacy and cultural exchanges. For example, in the Kaplan piece the idea of soft power is a means of influence since it is about using aid to secure access to resources and garner political support.

3.2.1 Order and disruption in the international system

The idea of a system implies a degree of coherence and order. Yet the notion of rising powers implies a disruption to a settled order. So how does the international system achieve both stability *and* an openness to change? This question will be explored through a series of linked concepts relating to power. These are anarchy, hegemony and **imperialism**.

Anarchy

Given that the building blocks of the international system are states, you might think that it is chaotic as every state acts individually. In this sense a leading thinker on the international system, Bull (1977), put forward the idea of anarchy, which you were first introduced to in Chapter 1. You might think anarchy means precisely a lack of order, but Bull argued that it simply means the absence of some overarching institutional framework for enforcing actions, a kind of world government. Rather, he believed, we have a 'society of states', which implies something more than the sum of individual states. He wrote:

> A society of states (or international society) exists when a group of states, conscious of certain common interests and common values, form a society in the sense that they conceive themselves to be bound by a common set of rules in their relations with one another, and share in the working of common institutions.

> *(Bull, 1977, p. 13)*

Bull implies that something beyond the individual state exists. He uses the words 'group', 'society', 'common interests' and 'relations'. Some states within the society of states do operate collectively via common interests, values and rules that are agreed consensually rather than being imposed from outside.

Activity 3.2

Can you think of any ways in which states act 'in common' to achieve certain goals?

Spend no more than 5 minutes on this activity.

One of the ways in which Bull's model of international society could be achieved is through **diplomacy** between states, namely the ordered negotiations intended to smooth the functioning of inter-state relations. Another method of organizing these relations is through **international law**, which has grown up alongside the modern international system and seeks to enshrine the principles of sovereignty into a variety of international interactions, such as trade or war. A final building block of international society is **international organizations**, most notably the United Nations. We also see regional state groupings such as the European Union. While all these arrangements seek to promote and ease the relations between states they are explicitly based on the sanctity of states as the ultimate building blocks of the system.

But Bull's idea of order does not imply that all states are equally powerful, since:

The contribution of the great powers to international order derives from the sheer facts of inequality of power as between the states that make up the international system.

(Bull, 1977, p. 199)

For him the great powers have a pivotal role to play in ensuring order, although he goes on to say that 'the great powers cannot formalize and make explicit the full extent of their special position'. Here he picks up a key strategic tension, since powerful states clearly have power but to deploy it too crudely would undermine the idea that the state system is made up of equal states. In the Kaplan extract China and the USA are seen as the key players, so Bull is right to see some states as having more power and more influence and holding out the possibility for shaping the 'common interests'. How might we account for some states having more power and how do they achieve it?

Hegemony

Here some analysts in international studies have used the idea of hegemony based on the ideas of Antonio Gramsci. Gramsci was an Italian **Marxist** living in the first half of the 20th century. One of his main contributions to political theory was a focus on the interplay of culture and capitalism. Cox (1987) applied Gramsci's concepts to international relations. Cox wanted to know how world orders have come into being and, in turn, how certain norms and institutions emerged. Hegemony is more than just outright domination of one power over others. If we only ever threatened people with violence to get things done then the world would simply escalate into all-out war. To achieve influence it is more productive to use less confrontational means. It is in understanding this more complex and arguably subtle exercise of power that the idea of hegemony is useful.

Hegemony in a Gramscian sense is where certain social classes within a particular state achieve leadership through their control over the production process, the political apparatus and, crucially, the intellectual sphere. Here is how Cox defines hegemony:

> Hegemony is a *structure of values and understandings about the nature of order* that permeates a whole system of states and non-state entities. In a hegemonic order these values and understandings are *relatively stable and unquestioned*. They appear to most actors as the natural order. Such a structure of meanings is *underpinned by a structure of power*, in which *most probably one state is dominant* but that state's dominance is not sufficient to create hegemony. Hegemony derives from *the dominant social strata* of the dominant states in so far as these ways of doing and thinking have acquired the acquiescence of the dominant social strata of *other states*.

> *(Cox, cited in Gill, 1993, p. 42, italics added)*

This is a complex paragraph and we have italicized some of the key elements. Cox is saying that hegemony is about how we understand order, but what makes it so powerful is that it 'permeates a whole system of states and non-state entities'. It is not about the naked use of power but a more subtle and, for that reason, all-encompassing form of power. Ultimately it rests on shared 'values' or a set of beliefs about how things should be organized, which once in place are 'stable' and 'unquestioned'. For example, Chapter 2 discussed neoliberalism as a dominant approach to development that emerged in the 1980s and 1990s and was, more or less, accepted by powerful actors as the best way to achieve development. Hence, some talk about *neoliberal hegemony.*

While these values become pervasive, for Cox it is usually one state that drives this systemic order, although he concedes in the phrase 'most probably' that more than one state could be involved. However, it is not enough for that one state to dominate; what is crucial is that the 'dominant social strata' in that state not only dominates the domestic lower strata but also dominates the dominant strata of other states. This analysis of social power is rooted in Gramsci's Marxism since it is about a dominant 'class' in one country entering into unequal alliances with the dominant classes of other countries (discussed further in Chapter 4). For example, during the period of British hegemony, the dominant British classes co-opted powerful leaders in the colonized countries in order to govern rather than simply resort to warfare (though there was plenty of that too).

What is absolutely crucial for our analysis of the rising powers from the idea of hegemony is that we focus on the importance of 'production' as a basis for power. This means that while there is no simple linkage between economic and political power, a rising power does need to oversee significant economic activity within its borders. We saw in the extracts on India and China how they were being taken seriously by established powers because of their economic growth.

Imperialism

As seen in the analysis of Bull and Cox, some states do not have much power and are the subject of hegemonic ordering. Here we can add the idea of imperialism to our conceptual toolkit. The word imperialism derives from 'empire' and refers to 'the creation and maintenance of an unequal economic, cultural and territorial relationship, usually between states and often in the form of an empire, based on domination and subordination' (Clayton, 2000, p. 375). Empires have existed in history and are not simply something of the recent past, or as some Marxists would have it, only a feature of capitalism.

We can think of formal imperialism as involving colonization of one country by another and with it the subordination of its people. This is about projecting power through control and domination in pursuit of resources and territory. But colonization is only one aspect of imperialism. Imperialism can also be informal and organized more 'at arms length'. This is about power through influence and is where the goals of resource control, for example, are achieved through forms of persuasion such as aid, bribery or the structuring of international organizations. Here no formal sovereignty is violated but influence is achieved by other means. Like Bull, Cox also analyzes international organizations as a key element of the international system. For a study of global hegemony, the rising powers and international development organizations like the World Bank and the International Monetary Fund (IMF) are very important due to their ability to dictate policy in developing countries (see Subsections 3.3.3 and 3.3.4).

3.2.2 Sources of power

So far we have looked at the idea of a system of states without an overarching rule setter. Yet this was tempered by stating that historically there has tended to be one or two key powers that can determine the 'order' of the world, which implicates other countries and actors into this. But still power has been talked of in quite abstract terms so we will look in more detail at what the sources of this power are.

Strange (1994, p. 23) provides a useful framework for examining the ways in which power operates. Crucially she argues that 'it is not enough … to ask where authority lies – who has power. It is important to ask why they have it – what is the source of power?' Her framework introduces two forms of power: relational and structural. The former corresponds to the commonsense idea of differential state power such that Country A can make Country B do something they would not ordinarily do. This form of power is increasingly being replaced by structural power which is 'the power to shape and determine the structures of the global political economy within which other states, their political institutions, their enterprises and (not least) their scientists and other professional people have to operate' (Strange, 1994, p. 25). This is closer to the idea of hegemony put forward by Cox, although Strange wanted to downplay production as the motivating force behind change.

Strange further disaggregates structural power into four intersecting facets from which authority is derived (see Figure 3.1). These are the control over production, the control over finance and credit, the control over knowledge and ideas, and the control over people's security. Crucially we cannot separate out one of the four factors as the sole determinant of dynamism in the international system so Strange represents them in a 'pyramid of power' with each one having a different influence in any given situation. This is helpful in avoiding thinking about processes and outcomes of the international system as simply either 'good' or 'bad'. In Chapter 1 and after the extract by Kaplan we discussed the idea of win–lose and win–win scenarios. In the language of social science we term these two outcomes zero-sum and positive-sum respectively.

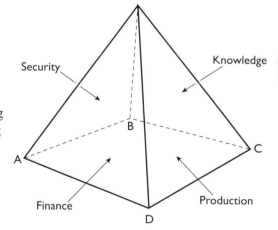

Figure 3.1   Strange's pyramid of power

The zero-sum effects are where the gains for one actor are matched by the losses of another actor. This plays out across the economic, political and cultural realms and has a spatial manifestation. For example, certain colonial export crops came at the expense of domestic food production, which sees regional agricultural patterns change and with it the local ecology and social relations of production. In terms of theories of development we see such approaches in dependency (as discussed in Chapter 2) and realist frameworks (which will be discussed in more detail in Chapter 4).

The positive-sum effects are where the sum of the benefits minus the overall losses is positive. This does not mean that both actors have to gain, though this is one type of positive-sum outcome. There can be occasions where one gains and another loses or where one gains but another gains much more, so long as the sum is positive at the end. These positive-sum interpretations are shared by many liberals, some Marxists and many politicians. Economically, as will be seen in Chapter 5, trade of commodities can benefit the production processes and growth of the importing country while also boosting prices and demand in producer countries. In what follows we will be assessing the outcomes of the rising powers for international development.

3.3 The world economy from pax-Britannica to pax-Americana to ...?

Now we have a sense of what a rising power looks like and how power operates in order to provide stability in the international system but also disruption. Following Cox we can see periods of hegemony when one power tended to dominate the international system. Broadly speaking we have seen a period of Western European hegemony in the 18th and 19th centuries with Britain as the dominant world power (pax-Britannica). From the late 19th century the USA began to rise and by the mid-20th century had attained great power status, which it arguably holds to this day at the time of writing (pax-Americana). Why the first few decades of the 21st century are so interesting is that we are witnessing the rise of China, India and Brazil, which are already playing major roles in the world. The remainder of this chapter gives an overview of these key countries.

3.3.1 The Asian millennia?

India and China were major powers for much of the past two millennia, with well-developed economic and political systems as well as established linkages with other parts of the world. In India the Mughal Empire was established from the early 16th century and encompassed much of what is modern Northern India. The Mughals ruled their empire through tributary relations – a formal recognition of the rulers of other kingdoms but subjugated through the paying of tribute to the more powerful centre. India produced spices that were traded across the Indian Ocean or over land along the Silk Route (see Figure 3.2) and sold in the Middle East and Europe. The Mughal Empire was gradually weakened from the early 18th century by the rise of smaller tributary states and the arrival of European traders.

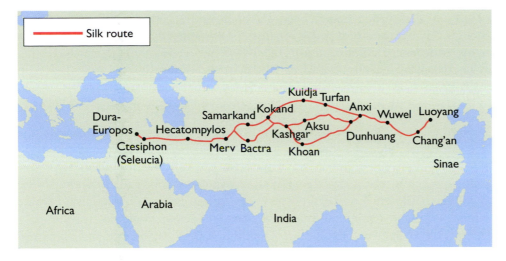

Figure 3.2   The Silk Route (active from at least the 2nd century BC to 1400)

China also had a series of 'internal' dynastic empires, but always, like India, facing threats from along its borders. There were complex bureaucracies for administering these large lands and, as with India, there were well-developed tributary relations with other kingdoms and states. China was quite urbanized by the 14th century and cities enabled the growth of private industry and manufacturing of goods such as paper and porcelain that were traded by sea or across land. Trade was a major part of the economy and early trade missions were launched, most famously by the Muslim Admiral Zheng He, who reached East Africa in the early 15th century (see Figure 3.3), thus initiating what the Chinese government talks about in the early 21st century as China's 'peaceful' relations with Africa.

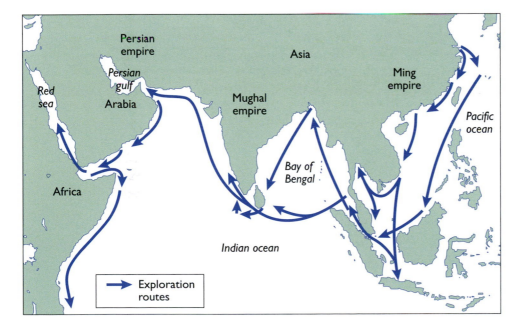

Figure 3.3   The voyages of Zheng He (early 15th century)

In both cases European traders were active from the 16th century onwards although this became most intensive in the 18th and 19th centuries, ultimately leading to forms of colonization in the 1840s and 1850s through various treaties that were heavily loaded in favour of the Europeans.

3.3.2 British hegemony and the age of imperialism

Although there had been trading networks dating back to at least classical times the era of intensive trading activity took off between 1500 and 1800. This saw European sea powers trading exotic goods with pre-industrial societies, when it was relatively easy to access these goods for ridiculously low values. Different European powers – Belgium, Denmark, England, France, Holland, Portugal, Spain and Sweden – utilized various strategies for the organization of their mercantile interests though they established their empires at slightly different times. Much of the activity was along coastal routes with fortifications built to protect the European soldiers and traders and to store goods for shipment back to markets in Europe (Figure 3.4).

Figure 3.4 Christiansbourg Castle built by the Danish in the 1660s in what is modern-day Accra, Ghana

This early incorporation into the international system effectively transferred economic **surplus** out of what was to become the developing world. The sophistication of these ventures increased with such things as the British and Dutch Charter Company formula (the British and Dutch East India Companies), which saw state-backed commercial enterprises taking over the management and governance of the trading settlements.

Nowhere was such trade as infamous as the slave trade that emerged from the mid-1600s and lasted for the next two centuries. The west coast of Africa became the source of slaves for plantations in the Americas and the Caribbean. The crops produced in the Americas – cotton and tobacco most notably – were then shipped to Western Europe for processing. Finished goods from the growing industries of Europe were then taken out to West Africa where they were sold for cash or exchanged for more slaves. And so the circulation of people and goods as commodities continued in this triangular fashion leading to the system being termed the 'triangular trade'. The slave trade displaced an estimated 10 million Africans and fuelled the industrial development of Western Europe while simultaneously siphoning off labour and skills from Africa.

As Hirst and Thompson (1996, p. 14) noted, the international economy at this time was 'the product of the complex interaction of economic relations and politics, shaped and reshaped by the struggles of the Great Powers'. Not only was rivalry more intense but the states themselves were much more sophisticated in their governance and technology than they had been during early colonization of Latin America. The pinnacle of this was the Raj in India. Ideologically, the colonial mission was justified through a twin movement of protecting the competitiveness of the metropole vis-à-vis other imperial powers, but also as a process of 'enlightening' colonial subjects. The colonies thus became national property to be nurtured and milked of their surplus. In this way a project of economic exploitation was tied to a discourse of modernity.

Given the competition between rival European powers the imperative was the establishment of hegemony over the colonial territory (see Figure 3.5). The Berlin Conference of 1884–5 to partition Africa enshrined this principle stating that 'effective occupation' required a colonizer to validate their claim by establishing the rudimentary infrastructure of hegemonic institutions. This meant military outposts and a basic network of administrative centres within a demarcated territory. The result was the imposition of state forms by the core countries and the creation of colonial territories.

Figure 3.5   Cartoon of European powers dividing up China (1890s)

The heightened demand for tropical products in Europe saw more formal colonization from the 1870s as systems were established for intensive production, which in turn led to the emergence of an international division of labour based around states and nationally centred 'transnational corporations' (TNCs). The firms internationalized through imperial ties but were nationally oriented, such as Lever Brothers and Cadbury. The nascent TNCs, which will be discussed in more detail in Chapter 7, although relatively small in size, were geographically extensive and impacted heavily upon local production systems.

The period of European colonialism and British hegemony (see Figure 3.6) was highly successful but the system began to break-down for various reasons in the late 19th and early 20th centuries. These included the low productivity of many colonies, the draining effects of two world wars on national coffers, the activities of well-educated nationalists and anti-colonial guerrilla movements, and the assumption that virtuous relations would exist post-colonially. Independence came to Latin America around a century before Asia and Africa, but countries remained tied into imperialist relations. As such, it was no coincidence that many of the radical underdevelopment theories discussed in Chapter 2 emerged from this region and quickly found resonance among the newly independent countries of Africa and Asia.

Figure 3.6   Map of the British Empire

3.3.3 US hegemony the Cold War, and global regulation

During the early part of the 20th century economic power began to shift from Western Europe towards the USA, ushering in the 'American Century'. Whereas capitalist competition in Europe had manifested itself in colonial expansion and overseas investment, the US economy had been growing through new production systems and innovation. For most of the 19th century the USA was an agricultural country and inward migration was largely from North-West Europe. The North began to industrialize in the mid-19th century, which set in train tensions with the slaveholding plantations of the South. In 1861 the South tried to break away to protect the institution of slavery, leading to the Civil War.

Industrial capacity was boosted during the Civil War, largely to meet military needs. The federal government paid for this by issuing 'greenbacks', paper money that could be used as real money because the government promised that anyone who wished could trade the greenbacks in for gold or silver money. This amounted to a national debt, and the government began to pay it off by restricting new gold and silver money and by retiring the paper currency. This policy had the effect of reducing the amount of money in circulation and increased the value of the gold and silver money owned by the banks. This saw the concentration of capital in the hands of a few very wealthy men, such as J. Pierpont Morgan and Cornelius Vanderbilt, who then invested it in projects of industrial development.

By the end of the 19th century US industries were able to compete with European firms. In 1889, the USA began building an overseas empire of its own. The Spanish–American War of 1898 was supposedly fought to assist the people of Cuba in gaining independence from Spain, but in the process the USA took other Spanish possessions, including Puerto Rico, some Pacific islands and the Philippines. In the same year, the USA annexed the kingdom of Hawaii. This ushered in US hegemony as the country transformed from an agrarian nation based on democratic ideals into an industrial and imperialist power.

Rapid economic growth, fuelled by entrepreneurs who created major new industries in railroads, steel, coal, oil, textiles and machinery, required new labour sources and so millions of immigrants from Europe and Asia arrived. During World War I US money, arms and soldiers helped turn the tide and allowed the USA to determine the terms of peace. The crash of 1929 started the worldwide Great Depression, which was long and severe for the entire country, but the New Deal Coalition of the inter-war years began an era of federal regulation of business, support for labour unions and provision of relief for the unemployed and social security for the elderly.

The ability of the USA to intervene decisively in World War II and lead the post-war reconstruction effort marked the transfer of hegemony away from Britain. The period between the end of World War II and the early 1970s was regarded as boom years for US, Western European and East Asian capital, even though the relative fortunes of these regions differed. The war severely damaged the Western European and Japanese economies and the US government intervened through large aid programmes to reconstruct and revitalize these capitalist centres. They succeeded although it diminished the USA's economic power in relative terms while putting in place a liberal capitalist world in the face of communism (Ikenberry, 2008).

With the ending of formal colonization in the period from 1947 to the mid-1960s, control of the international system was achieved via new forms of intervention in the developing world, which operated, in many respects, at arms length. New forms of US-backed economic governance were established through the Bretton Woods Institutions (primarily the IMF and the World Bank, see Chapter 1), ideological legitimization was actively stoked through the Cold War, and development policy in the developing world was based around a seemingly benign theory of modernization and 'catch up'.

The Bretton Woods System was set up at an international summit in 1944, which drew together statesmen and academics from the leading economic powers and sought to put in place a system for managing the global economy following the rivalries which had, in part, precipitated World War II. The Bretton Woods System began to break down in the 1970s, largely because the international regulation of exchange rates was abandoned for flexible, market-based rates that coincided with the deregulation of international banking and the oil price boom of the 1970s (Hirst and Thompson, 1996). This meant that creditworthy countries could borrow money privately to finance their deficits and fund development projects. During this period the IMF lost much of its *raison d'être* and was restructured and re-oriented towards being a 'development' institution.

The Cold War represented the logical extension of geopolitical rivalries that had been emerging since the end of World War I. The effects of the Cold War were significant in generating military blocs and in the proliferation of imperial wars in the developing world. These wars involved either direct involvement, such as in Vietnam and Korea, or were proxy wars where the superpowers armed various factions that were seen to be loyal to their cause. Paradoxically, this gave many developing states a degree of bargaining power as they could play Washington off against Moscow or Beijing. In this way those developing countries that were seemingly quite powerless could exploit the bipolar 'East–West' international system to their own advantage, although it was a dangerous game to play given that the major powers could destabilize individual countries through military and economic interventions.

In the immediate post-independence period many newly liberated states were keen to avoid being dragged into the ideological battles that had split the world into East and West. Hence, under a banner of 'non-alignment' and 'Third Worldism' these countries acknowledged their shared experience of colonization but proclaimed their desire to develop under their own steam. This early 'South–South' cooperation – cemented at the Bandung Conference (see Box 3.2 and Figure 3.7) – foreshadowed the rise of the new group of rising powers.

Box 3.2 Bandung Conference

The Bandung Conference was an international conference of world leaders held in Indonesia in 1955. It aimed to foster cooperation between developing nations and to oppose imperialism in all its forms.

Figure 3.7 The Bandung Conference of 1955

The period of independence was one of optimism. Newly liberated countries often had Keynesian aspirations, which were discussed in Chapter 2. Here the role of policy was to ensure full employment, which meant using state spending to stimulate demand. Such ideas were influential in advanced liberal democracies, but were also at the heart of development economics which informed policy in newly independent countries, such that 'development necessitated plans, written by economists, and strong, active governments to implement them. Development was an art of large-scale social engineering' (Hettne, 1995, p. 38).

However, these steps to stimulate development in the former colonies were stifled by a variety of factors. The former colonies generally lacked the levels of economic development required to generate enough surplus for investment in industry. Technologically, many developing countries lacked the means of production and were reliant on imported capital goods which worked against economic independence. Their political structures were fashioned under colonialism and were still tied strongly to the former colonizers. This created the so-called 'dependency' syndrome, which meant that developing countries were unable to develop and is an example of a zero-sum relationship.

3.3.4 The oil crises, debt and neoliberalism

While the Cold War lasted until the late-1980s, changes were already afoot that signalled its demise. In the early 1970s labour unrest in the core capitalist countries was rife and the power of the unions was seen by some politicians as excessive. At the same time, the oil-producing states of the Middle East raised oil prices and so precipitated a period of recession that fuelled labour unrest. The price rises and recession also hit the developing world hard as the markets for their raw materials declined and their oil bill increased.

What was an oil crisis for many developed industrial economies was a windfall for the oil producers whose revenue flooded the banks of the industrialized economies. These so-called 'petrodollars' needed to be put to use, so at a time when the Bretton Woods System began to break down there was a great deal of cheap credit available to developing countries. They needed to shore themselves up against their own economic recessions and seek finance to stave off legitimacy crises, that is, internal protests. Debate exists about the efficacy of this lending but it turned even sourer when interest rates rose sharply in the late-1970s and ushered in the debt crisis for most developing countries.

The response of manufacturers in Europe and the USA in some sectors was to move production offshore, mainly to South-East Asian countries that were beginning to industrialize – the so-called Newly Industrializing Countries (NICs), such as Singapore, Taiwan and Hong Kong, which had an export-oriented policy backed up by a strong and centralized state. This saw a 'new' international division of labour, which in contrast to the colonial 'old' division of labour was not oriented around formal colonies and was increasingly managed through web-like TNCs. In terms of the management of production there was also a shift towards 'flexibility' that weakened the power of labour.

However, while the state in the NICs was critical to their success there was a number of crucial geopolitical factors. First, the NICs' 'special relationship' with the USA saw them exporting labour-intensive, standardized products to the vigorously expanding US market. The place of the NICs as bulwarks against communist threats resulted in huge inflows of aid and investment, and also meant that while the Bretton Woods Institutions were promoting the removal of protectionist barriers, the USA turned a blind eye to the heavy restrictions and subsidies issued by the NIC governments. The second factor was the NICs' close relations with Japan, which had been the regional imperial power in the middle part of the 20th century and left behind reasonable infrastructure and, more importantly, the legacy of post-colonial ties. When the Japanese economy faced rising labour costs, firms relocated to their former colonies where labour was cheaper while Japanese trading houses integrated regional trading relations. Additionally, a measure of technology transfer occurred from Japan to the NICs so that a virtuous circuit existed between the manufacturing NICs, the technologically advanced Japanese and US markets.

Hence, from the late 1970s, a period of restructuring began. With the collapse of the Soviet bloc a decade later, the way was open for a new form of hegemony that was based less around a single power and more around the logic of capitalism, a discourse of neoliberalism and a politics of thin multilateralism among a handful of powerful liberal states (Agnew and Corbridge, 1995). For many developing countries in the 1980s and 1990s, it was the Bretton Woods Institutions that were key to their destiny through **Structural Adjustment Programmes** (SAPs). These adjustment programmes arose out of the problems of debt and the logic of liberalization, and could be enforced even more virulently once the ideological counterweight of the Soviet 'threat' had ended. This was known as the 'Washington Consensus', which has of late given way to a 'post-Washington' position that is firmly embedded in liberal capitalist ideology.

3.4 The stories of China, Brazil and India

So far we have looked at changing hegemony and the move from a world dominated by Britain in the 19th century to the USA in the 20th century. This section looks at three countries and how they emerged from colonial rule to begin their somewhat stuttering pathways to rising power status. These are China, Brazil and India. All three countries were colonized by European powers but in quite different ways and at different times. During the colonial period Brazil and India largely supplied raw materials whereas China's role was much more about manufactured goods that were bought using the proceeds of sales from India. A crucial similarity for all these countries, though again realized in very different ways, was how to balance the needs of development with those of state-building. Colonialism tended to create economies that functioned to serve European markets and put in place administrations designed for control rather than well-being. At independence, which came at different times to these three countries, the central states tended to assume a directing role in development, at the same time using development as a key source of legitimacy – to greater or lesser degrees of success. In their shared belief in the force of industrialization all three have at times ignored agriculture. Finally, all three countries liberalized at different times in the past 30 years, which created growth but also growing inequality.

3.4.1 China

In the early 20th century China was largely an agricultural country with a small industrial sector and a significant presence of foreign powers on its soil. Although the republic of 1911 brought an end to the feudal empire, the nationalists, first under Sun Yat-sen, then from 1925 under Chiang Kai-shek, were unable ever to gain full control of the country. The world outlook of these leaders was inspired by the West, which they saw as modern, scientific and technologically advanced. In the 1930s the Japanese attacked China, and the communists, defeated in the urban centres, embarked on 'The Long March' to the province of Yan'an in 1933–4. This move to develop a rural rather than urban base for communist forces saw the rise to prominence of Mao Zedong. After the defeat of Japan in 1945, it was under Mao's leadership that the communists fought the civil war against Chiang Kai-shek's nationalists and led the revolution of 1949.

According to Mao, the bourgeois revolution of Sun Yat-sen failed because the foreign colonial powers in China sided with the feudal forces. Before China could embark on the socialist revolution it first had to complete this failed revolution. A programme of land reform confiscated the land of the landlords and distributed it to peasants. In the early 1950s, the policy towards Chinese capitalists was liberal insofar as they were allowed to continue their business provided it was not monopolistic.

After World War II, as discussed in Section 3.3.3, the USA took the lead in creating an international system based on international organizations, many colonies gradually gained independence, and the world was divided by the Cold War. The victory of the communists over the nationalists in the Civil War (1945–9), the ensuing Korean War (1950–3) where China fought directly against US forces, and tensions between the Western allies (the USA, Britain and France) and the Soviet Union regarding the future of Europe effectively placed China in an internationally isolated position.

During the first years of the People's Republic of China, rural non-agricultural production collapsed. The movement to mobilize people to build new rural industries was known as the Great Leap Forward, and aimed at rapid industrialization of rural China through local initiatives to build an industrial infrastructure. Inexperience and the disruption of normal village functions led to serious misjudgements and the relatively good situation in agriculture during the mid-1950s turned bad.

Urban China developed separately. Industry and trades were, from the mid-1950s, to become publicly owned. Companies owned by Chinese capitalists were gradually transformed into state-owned enterprises. In addition to these state-owned enterprises there were also urban collective enterprises owned by the small artisans, traders and petty producers who were induced to form cooperatives in the early 1950s. The state established an elaborate system for planning and managing the production of state-owned enterprises that divided the population into two large categories – urban and rural – that enjoyed different rights vis-à-vis the state. People working for state-owned enterprises also received substantial social welfare benefits such as education, health, childcare and other social provision – a package of rights known as the 'iron rice bowl'.

In China, the turbulent years between the late 1960s and late 1970s were known as the 'Cultural Revolution', and were an attempt to remove capitalist thought from the country. In order to restore some order, the People's Liberation Army was put in charge of administration, which brought a certain level of normality. Externally things began to change with the United Nations General Assembly naming the People's Republic of China as the rightful government of China while the USA began a process of rapprochement. As a result, from the early 1970s China became increasingly integrated in the world system. Together these developments weakened the position of the hard-line communists, allowing the return to influence of more moderate politicians.

In December 1978 the Central Committee of the Chinese Communist Party confirmed the rise of the moderates by initiating a series of reforms to the economy and state intended to tackle the political and economic crises afflicting the country. Their project was to make China a strong socialist state by building up the economic and technological base. Deng Xiaoping's famous saying 'It does not matter whether a cat is black or white so long as it catches mice' indicates the break with the doctrinaire attitudes of the more othodox members of the communist party.

The reforms, as they gradually unfolded, have affected almost every part of China's economic and political system. They allowed more freedom to private enterprises in the areas of production and employment and sought to transfer ownership of some state-owned industries to a more private footing. There were reforms to political structures and systems involving some decentralization and a more output-based system of rewards for party officials. Peasants and workers were freed from production and residential controls, but equally many lost social protection from the state. Inward investment was encouraged and Special Economic Zones were set up in Southern China, initially to give additional incentives to these firms. The reform measures helped to stimulate high growth rates in the Chinese economy, averaging around eight per cent over almost three decades, much of it built on export-oriented manufacturing as shown in Figure 3.8.

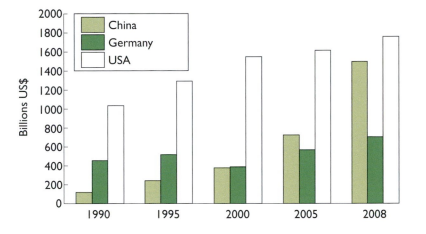

Figure 3.8   Value added in manufacturing (current US$ 1990–2008)

While **Gross Domestic Product** (GDP) growth has been very high throughout the 1990s and 2000s, this has been unevenly distributed in geographical terms with a concentration of high incomes in the coastal regions where **Foreign Direct Investment** (FDI) was greatest. (GDP will be looked at in more detail in Chapter 5.)

3.4.2 Brazil

Like China, Brazil was also tied into European spheres of influence and later colonized. The Portuguese came in the early 16th century but it was not until the 17th century that a more intensive production system for sugarcane was established in the coastal northeast. These essentially economic interactions became more political in the early 19th century when the Portuguese court fled Europe following Napoleon's invasion of Portugal during the Peninsular War.

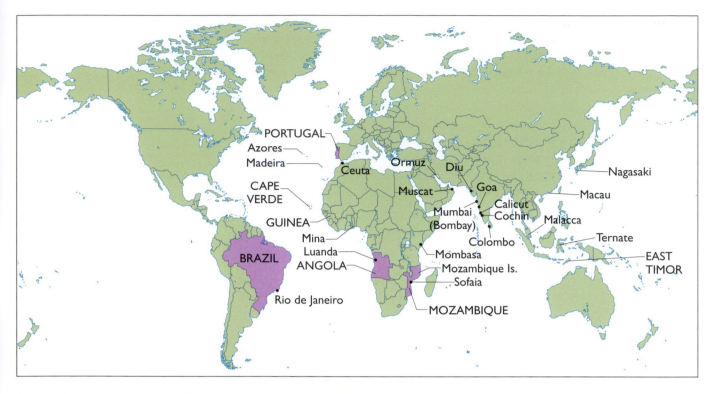

Figure 3.9 The Portuguese Empire from the 17th to 20th centuries

By this time Portugal had a sizeable empire including parts of Africa, India, and South and East Asia, which it ruled from Brazil (see Figure 3.9). On return to Portugal in 1821 the king's son, Pedro, stayed on to govern and advocated the country's secession from Portugal. This move was opposed by the landed elites who were, and remained for much of the 19th and 20th centuries, a conservative force in Brazilian politics.

From 1930 Brazil came under the rule of Getulio Vargas. Although from the landed **oligarchy** he was also a pragmatic politician who realized the need to develop the economy away from agriculture and to bring new voices to the political process. While he centralized political power Vargas began to break down the monopoly of power held by the landed aristocracy by making space for urban workers and the new middle class. However, Vargas' period in office coincided with a global financial crisis and recession in the late 1920s that saw demand for Brazil's exports decline.

The post World War II period was one of optimism and saw a continuation of attempts to diversify the economy away from agricultural commodities. A landmark policy framework was 'import-substitution industrialization' (ISI), which was based on the realization that newly independent countries in the developing world needed to move away from primary products but lacked the necessary capital and entrepreneurial skills to do so. The logic was essentially Keynesian and saw the state taking the role of lead industrialist by securing funding and infrastructure for industries and erecting tariff barriers to allow these fledgling industries to develop without excessive foreign competition. This remained a feature of Brazil's development policy for much of the 1940s through to the 1970s.

The period from the mid-1960s to the mid-1980s was one of what O'Donnell (1970) terms bureaucratic–authoritarian government. Here the state centralized further and its priorities focused on economic growth, partly as a means of maintaining legitimacy, and the preservation of order. Brazil was still heavily dependent on agricultural exports even though ISI had meant that the agricultural sector had been relatively ignored. Much of the industrialization and infrastructure was financed through international loans so that the country was heavily indebted, although the temporarily high growth rates suggested this would not be a problem. However, the oil crises of the 1970s saw oil prices rise for importing countries and a general stagnation of the global economy, which hurt most developing countries. When interest rates rose Brazil was faced with high debt repayments that further hampered the country's ability to re-invest in the economy since it was servicing debts.

Despite this precarious economic position, the political climate was gradually shifting towards a more open system of governance. The government of the mid-1980s attempted various economic plans and continued to resist the IMF's call for orthodox adjustment. While the 1980s was a lost decade for Brazil it was in the early 1990s that Fernando Henrique Cardoso became finance minister and introduced what was called the 'Real Plan'. This centred on fiscal discipline, cutting government expenditure yet also protecting the poorest, which saw an immediate upturn in the economy. Based on his success, Cardoso won the 1994 presidential elections and was empowered to push even further with the economic strategy he had pioneered. Much of what Cardoso implemented was familiar from other countries and can be seen as part of the wider 'Washington Consensus' – downsizing government, privatizing state-owned enterprises, introducing foreign competition and reforming tax systems. The Real Plan brought down inflation and boosted GDP growth as well as improving international creditworthiness.

In the 1994 elections Luiz Lula de Silva of the Partido dos Trabalhadores (PT, Workers Party) was a strong candidate but he appealed mainly to workers and peasants with his quite vociferous left-wing ideals. He won the 2002 elections on an anti-neoliberal platform but once in office maintained many core elements of Cardoso's strategy. Where Lula differed and arguably made strides was in social protection for the poorest. He managed to push through quite hard reforms around curbing the benefits of civil servants and streamlining the tax system, but also introduced the 'Bolsa Familia' ('The Family Basket') programme, which provided cash transfers to poorer families on condition of school attendance of the families' children.

The 2000s have seen very strong export growth in Brazil. Brazil's economy is not, as so often assumed, based solely on agricultural commodities, but an increasingly diversified and sophisticated manufacturing sector. And with a growing domestic middle class much of the output of this industry is consumed within Brazil rather than being exported. In particular, trade with China has been very strong as China procures the natural resources that Brazil produces. With this growing economic stability has come political influence. Crucially Brazil engages with the other rising powers, especially the IBSA Dialogue Forum (IBSA being India, Brazil and South Africa), which seeks to be a collective voice for these emerging economies.

3.4.3 India

Earlier we saw that India and China were well integrated into trade routes in the 16th and 17th centuries. In 1600 The British East India Company was incorporated and competed with its main rival the Dutch East India Company. Operations in the 18th century were largely mercantile but inter-imperial rivalry with the French and Portuguese and the need to expand the sources of raw materials saw them move further inland. Following the Indian Rebellion of 1857 the British turned India into a Crown Colony, ushering in the period called 'The Raj', with India being the 'jewel in the crown' of the British Empire.

While colonization was about accessing resources it was also about changing values. One of the paradoxes is that, as a result, many colonized people developed a well-reasoned and organized opposition to external rule, often using the concepts of nationalism, liberty and equality that were the underpinnings of western political discourse. In India the late 19th century and first half of the 20th century saw growing opposition from mass movements led by Mahatma Gandhi and Jawaharlal Nehru. One upshot was that the colonies became more expensive to control so that the cost-effectiveness of empire was gradually eroded.

A dominant theory of Indian development was based on a sense that India's lack of development was a zero-sum outcome of its relationship with the UK. As a result, post-colonial thinking was driven by a strong economic nationalism that India should be self-reliant. At the time of Indian independence in 1947 Keynesian theory was ascendant. India had a large, legitimate and well-organized state that intervened in the economy to promote certain industrial sectors, under a policy of ISI. Where India was different from Brazil was that it focused on capital goods substitutions (e.g. machinery) as opposed to consumer goods substitutions (e.g. fridges). India was also wary of allowing massive inward investment and so developed its key industrial sectors through joint ventures, often with British TNCs as part of a legacy of the colonial era. Since India lacked a large industrial sector or domestic middle class its savings base was narrow so, in addition to state support for industry, foreign aid was targeted at these sectors. With growing Cold War tensions in the region India was adept at brokering between major powers to secure aid.

The focus on the manufacturing sector for much of the 1950s and early 1960s meant that agriculture was relatively neglected. The government had assumed agricultural modernization would take place through administrative dictate rather than meaningful investment and technological innovation. Moreover, in support of India's ISI the USA gave a great deal of aid in the 1950s that brought food but disguised the problems in agriculture. By the mid-1960s food production was lagging and famines occurred in Bihar in 1966 and Maharashtra in 1972. When India sought the USA's support, the USA used this to exert greater control over India's politics, largely to bolster US anti-communist activities in Asia. But in the 1970s India rebuilt its food production systems through the 'Green Revolution', that is, the application of new seeds, chemical and irrigation technologies, which saw the scale of farming increase as well as the concentration of land in the hands of larger famers (see Robbins, 2013). Food security had been achieved but many poorer farmers were forced to become labourers, either in the rural areas or increasingly by moving to the rapidly growing cities. Rural–urban migration is looked at in more detail in Chapter 6.

The stumbling industrial economy of the 1970s called into question the authority and legitimacy of the government. Nehru, India's first post-independence leader, staked his authority on being 'The Father of the Nation' and in him was embodied the twin ambitions of a coherent state and national development. Nehru's daughter, Indira Gandhi, governed from 1966 to 1977, then 1980–4, and while her father had overseen 'command politics' (a top-down approach based on planning) she gave over to 'demand politics' (based on responding to requests from interest groups) where different political factions saw the state as a source of finance. Reciprocally it is argued she used state largesse to buy off opposition, although she is clearly not the first or the last Indian politician to do this. Hence the 1970s was a period of disorder and economic mismanagement and one in which more personalized and identity-based politics began to emerge in contrast to the secularism of Nehru. This was also a period when the government strongly advocated home-grown production, with a 'Be Indian, Buy Indian' campaign and restrictions on TNCs.

Throughout the 1980s there was growing disenchantment from some powerful sections of Indian society about the state-led development model. This saw the shift to liberalization, but contrary to Africa in the 1980s where reform was pushed through on the back of SAPs, liberalization was more of an internal affair in India. Following an economic crisis in 1991, the Congress Party, now led by P.V. Narasimha Rao, sped up a process of economic transformation that had begun in the late-1980s under the premiership of Indira Gandhi's son, Rajiv. Hence the main thrust of liberalization began in 1991 and was overseen by the Congress Party from 1991 to 1996. However, the rapid transformation of the economy and social structures during this period led to an 'anti-Westernization' backlash and the rise of the Bharatiya Janata Party, a right-wing Hindu party that governed as a coalition between 1998 and 2004.

Liberalization saw reductions in import restrictions, removal of administrative controls on food pricing and distribution, privatization of public assets and invitations to overseas TNCs to invest in key sectors of the economy. It was an uneven process, however, with some interests opposing it, others welcoming it, and initial problems such as imports exceeding exports and a resulting imbalance of payments. But it also allowed quite sophisticated electronics and telecommunications industries to be developed by well-educated Indian entrepreneurs, a story picked up in Chapter 6. While India's growth between 1950 and 1980 had been around the world norm it increased sharply from the early 1980s and has stayed high ever since.

Summary and looking forward

This chapter has focused on the rising powers, notably a group of countries that have risen up the economic and political order from the 1980s and 1990s. However, this phenomenon is not unique in history and is part and parcel of the functioning of the international system. The rest of the chapter deepened your understanding of what constitutes a rising power. Specifically we:

- looked at what the 'new' rising powers might mean for the 'established' powers in the international system, in terms of threats or opportunities

- outlined the main features of a rising power using the concept of hegemony, which is rooted in economic explanations but also incorporates the political and cultural

- explored in more detail the meanings and sources of power and their operation in the international system. Specifically we looked at anarchy and hegemony and the different sources of power when analyzing the international system

- set out a brief history of the international order from the 18th to 20th centuries, focusing on the periods of UK and US hegemony

- outlined briefly the trajectories of the three most important rising powers in order to look at where these trajectories shared similar features and where they differed.

So far a number of related themes have been touched on – power, international system, change and interaction, but these have not been dealt with systematically. The discipline of international relations focuses on the relationships between states, which are also a major building block in understanding development. How might a combined focus on international relations and development illuminate both strands of study in enriching ways and how, then, can that help us understand the more recent rising powers? It is to this that we now turn in the next chapter.

References

Agnew, J. and Corbridge, S. (1995) *Mastering Space: Hegemony, Territory and International Political Economy*, London, Routledge.

Bull, H. (1977) *The Anarchical Society: A Study of Order in World Politics*, New York, Columbia University Press.

Clayton, D. (2000) 'Imperialism' in Johnston, R., Gregory, D., Pratt, G. and Watts, M. (eds) *The Dictionary of Human Geography*, Oxford, Blackwell.

Cox, R. (1987) *Production, Power and World Order: Social Forces in the Making of History*, New York, Columba University Press.

Das, G. (2006) 'The India Model', *Foreign Affairs*, vol. 85, no. 4, pp. 2–16.

Gill, S. (1993) 'Epistemology, ontology and the "Italian School"' in Gill, S. (ed.) *Gramsci, Historical Materialism and International Relations*, Cambridge, Cambridge University Press.

Hettne, B. (1995) *Development Theory and the Three Worlds*, Harlow, Longman.

Hirst, P. and Thompson, G. (1996) *Globalisation in Question*, Cambridge, Polity Press.

Ikenberry, J. (2008) 'The rise of China and the future of the West', *Foreign Affairs*, vol. 87, no. 1, pp. 23–37.

Kaplan, R.D. (2005) 'How we would fight China', *The Atlantic Magazine*, June 2005.

O'Donnell, G. (1970) *Modernization and Bureaucratic-Authoritarianism,* Berkeley, University of California.

Robbins, P. (2013) 'History of technological innovation and critiques' in Butcher, M. and Papaioannou, T. (eds) *New Perspectives in International Development*, London, Bloomsbury Academic/Milton Keynes, The Open University.

Strange, S. (1994) *States and Markets*, London, Pinter.

Further reading

Alden, C. (2007) *China in Africa*, London, Zed Books.

Brautigam, D. (2009) *The Dragon's Gift: The Real Story of China in Africa*, Oxford, Oxford University Press.

Harvey, D. (2005) *A Brief History of Neoliberalism*, Oxford, Oxford University Press.

Nye, J. (2004) *Soft Power: The Means to Success in World Politics*, New York, Public Affairs.

Roett, R. (2010) *The New Brazil*, Washington DC, Brookings Institution Press.

Sen, A. (2006*) The Argumentative Indian: Writings on Indian History, Culture and Identity*, London, Penguin Books.

Acknowledgements

Much of the thinking for this chapter benefited from not only an excellent module team but also the work of the Asian Drivers research group at the Open University (see http://asiandrivers.open.ac.uk/), especially our colleague Professor Raphie Kaplinsky.

Change, politics and the international system

Ray Kiely

Introduction

Chapter 3 introduced the idea that there are a number of rising powers in the international system. The emergence of these powers gives rise to a number of questions, such as: 'what factors explain their development?' and 'what implications does their rise have for other developing countries?' These questions will be addressed in later chapters, though they are touched on in this one. What this chapter focuses on is how one of these rising powers, China, alters the character of the international system.

This is an important question as international orders, and 'great powers' within those orders, have changed over time. Does the rise of China constitute the beginnings of a new international order, and if so, what kind of order? What does this mean for the dominant power in the current international order, the USA? And what does this mean for development which, as seen in Chapter 1, must in part be examined in an international context, and which is always influenced by the wishes of the dominant power. Does China's rise mean not only the beginning of the end of US primacy, but also of neoliberal policies that have been promoted by the dominant power?

To answer these questions we need to draw on empirical material. But also an explanation as well as description is needed, and that means that we need to draw on theory, and specifically theories of international order, and how these explain the rise and fall of great powers. This chapter then combines the theories of international relations with those of Development Studies. Combining these theories is important for three reasons:

1 Development is not simply a national process, but also an international one, in that it is influenced by international processes such as inter-state relations, foreign investment, aid, and so on.

2 International relations can be viewed as relations of power, not least between developed and developing states.

3 Related to these points, the policy preferences of the dominant state in the international order are bound to influence 'national' development policies throughout the globe.

The chapter therefore starts by introducing you to a number of theories: in particular, it looks in some depth at realist, liberal and Marxist theories of international order. These theories will be introduced both generally and specifically in relation to what they have to say about so-called great powers. These three theories are not the only theories of international order; however, examining them will hopefully give you not only an idea of what these theories claim, but also how different comments and perspectives you might read in the media regarding China's rise are implicitly informed by theory. The chapter then moves on to examine what these theoretical approaches have to say about the rise of China. China has been deliberately chosen as it is the rising power that has the greatest claim to be a potential, if not actual, great power. Finally, the chapter provides a more narrative-based account of how China's rise is related to US power, which attempts to show how such factual accounts are still necessarily informed by theory.

In summary, the aims of this chapter are to:

- introduce some important theories of international order
- examine what these theories have to say about the rise of China
- provide a narrative account – informed by theory – of China's rise and its limitations.

The overarching point that permeates all this is that theories are necessary – and unavoidable – in explaining the nature of the international system, and that any convincing understanding of development must take into account this international system and the role of great powers in it.

4.1 Perspectives on international order

This section examines a number of perspectives that seek to explain the core features of the international system. The approaches examined are realism, liberalism and Marxism. To facilitate clarity and understanding, a brief exposition of realism and liberalism is presented first, followed by a comparison and contrast between these approaches, and then finally a look at Marxism. The section introduces the broad contentions of all these approaches, and particularly focuses on what they have to say about great powers. In doing this, the aim is to show that these historical debates retain their relevance for understanding something as contemporary as China's rise.

4.1.1 Realism

Realist theories of international relations are in many respects the most influential ones. The first point that realism makes is that the international system is composed of nation states, and these states exist in a relationship of anarchy, something you read about in Chapter 3. You may recall that anarchy in this sense means the absence of a world government at the international level. At the domestic level, relations between individuals are ultimately regulated by a coordinator, the nation state.

This domestic–international analogy is central to the structural realist work of Kenneth Waltz. Waltz argued that it is the structure of the international system that ultimately determines the behaviour of states in that system. For him, all states, regardless of their domestic character, are similar, and all are ultimately concerned with self-preservation. In the absence of international government, states must look after themselves – the international system is therefore a self-help system. States are above all concerned with their own security, and this is bound to lead them into conflict with other states.

The international system is thus one where states exercise their own interests and so it is one principally concerned with power. What is crucial for understanding the structure of international order is the distribution of power, and in particular the balance of power between states. For Waltz (1979, p. 73), the study of great powers is central to any theory of international politics. States try to increase their power against other states, which can lead to a balance of power between competing states. This is a dynamic, uncertain and conflict-ridden process, but it is one that simply reflects the anarchical structure of international politics. What this means is that the rise of a potential new power (such as China) is likely to lead to resistance from the existing great power (such as the USA) and this could give rise to different forms of conflict. We saw this view coming out strongly in the extract from Kaplan in Chapter 3.

4.1.2 Liberalism

From this we can see that realism's concern is with interests and power, and that these ultimately determine international politics. Liberalism instead argues that the defining feature of international order is not anarchy but *interdependence*. The international order is not one based on an endless pattern of conflict between states, though such conflict can and does occur. Rather, it will depend on how states interact with each other, and this in turn is strongly influenced by the domestic character of such states. In contrast to the strong claims made by realism, liberals argue that states can, and indeed do, cooperate with each other, and this is because there are mutual gains to be made from such cooperation. In other words, interdependence can promote shared, mutual interests so that, for example, commercial relations of trade and investment replace war-like relations.

In terms of great powers, of crucial importance is how these behave in the international order. They must be prepared to exercise leadership in a way that interacts positively with other powerful states, thus giving the latter an incentive not to balance against the primary power. For some liberal internationalists, this is precisely what the USA has done as a hegemonic power since 1945, and since the end of the Cold War (Ikenberry, 2008). Indeed, with the extension of liberal democracies, the end of the power politics of the Cold War, and the increase in free trade since the 1980s and 1990s onwards, liberals argue that their time has come – and as will be seen, even non-liberal states like China can be integrated into a liberal international system.

4.1.3 Liberalism and realism: further exposition and comparison

This revival of liberalism has happened before. In the period between 1919 and 1939, when the academic discipline of international relations was first developed there was the first flourishing of liberal theories of international politics. Following the carnage of World War I, the US President Woodrow Wilson (see Figure 4.1) set out 14 points for international peace that essentially was a liberal account of international politics. This argued that war came about because of the militarism of undemocratic **autocracies**, and there was the need for an extension of liberal democracy across the world, alongside national self-determination and a need for international structures, such as a League of Nations. For Wilson, this was possible because states had mutual interests, because of the

Figure 4.1 Woodrow Wilson was the 28th US President. He served two terms from 1913 to 1921

interdependent nature of international politics, which would promote positive-sum interactions between states. This was in contrast to zero-sum interactions, whereby the gains by one state would be at the expense, or loss, of another – the realist position outlined above.

This liberal optimism was quickly shattered by the events that followed. As well as the Bolshevik revolution in Russia in 1917, there was the rise of fascism in Italy, the Nazis in Germany, the Great Depression, military expansion by the new dictatorships, and ultimately World War II. However, the response to such conflict from liberal theorists is that states did not conform to the liberal ideal – the USA did not join the League of Nations, the most aggressive states were not liberal democracies, and the Great Depression was associated with excessively protectionist policies rather than free trade policies. A number of critics suggested that the fact that liberal policies were not embraced suggested that there was something intrinsically wrong with the liberal account of international politics.

The international relations theorist and historian Edward Hallett Carr claimed that the liberal position on international relations was utopian, and not realistic. He argued (Carr, 2001 [1939]) that in a world of scarcity, there was a basic division between the 'haves' and 'have-nots' and that international law reflected the wishes of the powerful, and not those of the relatively powerless. The notion that any international rule of law would be a neutral instrument was naïve and international institutions would ultimately be dominated by the interests of the powerful. Two very brief examples illustrate this. First, Wilson's argument for the extension of liberal democracy in 1918 is hard to swallow given the lack of democracy in the segregated USA at the time. Second, the peace process that followed World War I was very much a victors' peace. Reparations were imposed on Germany that had catastrophic consequences for the domestic politics of that country, and so essentially helped the Nazis in their rise to power (in part through liberal democratic means).

Carr's realist critique of liberalism was a powerful one. However, some caution is necessary. Unlike Waltz, Carr was not suggesting that his account of a conflict-ridden international political order was relevant for all periods of history. Indeed, though critical of the utopianism of liberalism, he retained the view that the international order could, under historically specific conditions, be changed for the better. What should be taken from Carr then, and perhaps developed further, is the idea that the liberal view of mutual gains through interdependence needs to be treated with some scepticism, and indeed, may itself be linked to the exercise of power.

A brief example illustrates the point. The 19th century liberal Richard Cobden believed that free trade represented an example of mutual gains in an interdependent international order. Cobden was involved in the promotion of free trade agreements between Britain and other countries in the 1860s (Bell, 2006). A number of countries signed these agreements but by the 1880s had effectively broken from them and embarked on a series of **protectionist** policies at home, often combined with colonial policies abroad. In other words, they broke from Cobden's hopes of an expanded zone of liberal states. Why did they do this? One answer is that the free trade policies promoted by

Britain and their respective partners led to (absolute) gains for both sides, but these gains were relatively much greater for Britain. In this scenario, free trade is promoted by states that have more to gain from it, precisely because their economies are more productive and thus more competitive than other economies (Chang, 2002). France, Germany and the USA thus began to carry out protectionist policies in order to develop domestic industries that, under free trade conditions, would not have been able to compete with cheaper imports from the established industrial producer of the time, Great Britain. In other words, in terms of development theories examined in Chapter 1, these countries began interventionist policies of governing the market in order to catch up with – and overtake – Britain. Britain was effectively the neoliberal power of the time, but other countries responded by adopting policies that ran counter to neoliberalism. Seen in this way, both neoliberal economic policies and liberal theories of international relations are complicit in the exercise of power.

What this also suggests, though, is that the issue of gains in a situation of interdependence is a complex one, and sometimes relative gains – that is, gains measured relative to those of other states – may be more important than absolute ones. But be careful here – the realist claim is that relative gains are *always* more important than absolute ones, which makes cooperation very difficult. While the example just mentioned is one where relative gains outweighed absolute ones, this is not the same thing as saying that all concrete examples will confirm the realist position. Think of issues of cooperation in recent times, for example the rise of the European Union or the formation of the World Trade Organization (WTO). How can we account for these if we argue, like realism, that cooperation is difficult in an anarchical system of self-interested nation states? The realist response is that international institutions ultimately reflect the balance of power in the international system, but this still leaves aside the issue of how such cooperation emerges in the first place. Realists might be correct that power relations pervade these institutions, but it is less clear how the cooperation that gives rise to these organizations could even begin to occur.

Activity 4.1

What are the key points of realist and liberal perspectives on international order? Compare and contrast these, and particularly focus on how the two positions understand international cooperation and the nature of gains in the international system.

Spend about 15 minutes on this activity.

Discussion

To summarize these issues:

1   Realism sees the order as one based on conflict, in which self-interested states strive to increase their power and security in an anarchical international order. In this context, cooperation is difficult as any potential gains for one state may be 'trumped' by greater gains for the other state – the relative gains for the latter state may prevent the former from cooperating in the first place.

2   Liberalism argues that the international order can and does change, and that cooperation is possible in a situation of interdependence. This is most likely in the case of interaction between liberal states, which share similar values and are committed to free trade, and so on. In these cases, the prospect of absolute gains for both states makes cooperation not only feasible, but likely.

The discussion above suggests that liberalism has a more contingent account of the international order. What we mean by contingent is that the international system can change and indeed it can change for the better. For liberals, this would involve an extension of liberal states across the world. Realism on the other hand, is often said to avoid normative and prescriptive questions, but in fact has been centrally involved in them. Though often characterized as a theory narrowly concerned with the question of power, realists have also examined how such power should be used in promoting the national interest. Interestingly, this has led to realist thinkers being used to criticize the actions of great powers. One prominent realist, Hans Morgenthau, criticized US involvement in Vietnam in the 1960s as it was not in the national interest, and another, John Mearsheimer, did the same over the US-led war in Iraq in 2003 (Mearsheimer, 2005).

This suggests some contingency in realist accounts of international relations – states exercise their national interests in the international order, but what this national interest might be varies across time and place. The problem though for realism is that it does not provide us with the theoretical tools to explain how the national interest might vary across time and place, and indeed how it is constructed in the first place. This discussion suggests that liberalism's strength is that it is more open to change and variation in the international order than realism, even though the latter has some strong criticisms to make of the former's complicity with power relations.

4.1.4 Marxism

Marxism is a variety of structuralist theory, as discussed in Chapter 2. It is of course associated with the failed socialist alternative represented by the former Soviet Union, but we are interested less in Marxism as a political ideology, and more as a theoretical analysis of international politics.

For Marxists, the international order is above all a capitalist order. Capitalism is based on an unequal social relationship between the owners of the means of production, wealth and so on – the capitalist class or bourgeoisie – and those who do not own any significant source of wealth beyond their capacity to work. In feudal times, the exploited class would have direct access to sources of wealth such as land, and would grow food and would have to pay landlords a rent. In capitalist society, however, the exploited class has no such access and so has to find work – that is, be employed by the owners of wealth – in order to gain a wage that allows them to buy food, clothing and shelter. This account is, of course, a crude simplification, but the key point is this – in capitalist society the working class, or proletariat, have to work for the capitalist for a wage in order to access the key things in life. However, the capitalist pays a wage lower than the value of the goods produced by the workers, and this is the immediate source of capitalist profit. Workers are therefore exploited in capitalist society, just as peasants are – albeit in different ways – in feudal society. Reforms may be won by working class pressure, but the basic fact of capitalism remains the social relationship of class exploitation by capitalist over worker. Ultimately the state represents the interests of the capitalist class according to Marxists.

There is rather a lot missing from this all too brief account! In particular, it says little about the nature of the international system. However, what we should bear in mind so far is that Marxists distinctively focus on the capitalist nature of the current international order. Of great importance in this respect is the fact that capitalism is dynamic – the competition between capitalist firms and so on gives rise to technological innovation to stay ahead of rivals. This leads to an increase in the size and scope of capitalist firms – or what Marx called the concentration and centralization of capital. In this sense, the capitalist economy is internationalized from the outset.

It was only after Marx's death in 1883 that Marxists developed a fuller theory of the international. Above all, this was done through the development of Marxist theories of imperialism, which was mentioned in Chapter 3. Imperialism usually refers to the domination of some territories by others. This typically, but not always, means formal colonization to form empires, which have existed throughout history. Writing in the early 20th century, Marxists began to develop new theories of imperialism in the context of a new wave of colonial expansion by, among others, Belgium, Britain, France, Germany, Japan and the USA. Like other approaches to imperialism, some of this writing was concerned with the effects of colonial expansion on the colonies themselves, and how some empires or strong states dominate weaker states. However, what was distinctive about Marxist approaches is that they attempted to explain the changing relationship between the more developed capitalist powers, the so-called great powers.

A number of Marxists developed theories of imperialism at this time, but the most famous was associated with the Russian revolutionary leader Lenin (see Figure 4.2). His basic argument was that the international expansion of capital was a process full of conflict, as each great power sought to maximize its share in an increasingly competitive and restricted world market. For Lenin (1977 [1914], pp. 177–231), this new and 'highest stage of capitalism' gave rise to a close linkage between economic, political and military competition between great powers, which had intensified at an international level and led to major conflict in the shape of World War I. This formed the basis of classical Marxist interpretations of imperialism as being based on inevitable conflict between imperialist powers.

Figure 4.2 Vladimir Ilyich Lenin (1870–1924)

For Leninists, the key claims made regarding imperialism were that:

- the late 19th century saw a growing centralization and concentration of capital, and with that an increasing internationalization of capital beyond the borders of nation states

- this altered the nature of competition and Lenin argued that so-called monopolistic capitalism increased competition within states. Moreover, competition between capitalist companies, and between their 'national representatives', their home nation states, had intensified

- this gave rise to conflict – inter-imperialist rivalries – and ultimately to war, both in 1914 and in 1939.

By emphasizing the centrality of tensions between great powers, there is obviously some overlap with realist theories of international relations.

This was not, however, the only way in which imperialism was theorized by Marxists in the period before 1914. The German Marxist Karl Kautsky fully recognized that the 1914–18 war was about great power rivalry, but in contrast to Lenin, he questioned whether this was an *inevitable* consequence of relations between imperialist powers. Like those who focused on inter-imperialist rivalries, Kautsky recognized that tensions had intensified as a result of the rise of challengers to British hegemony in the late 19th century.

Specifically, both Western Europe and the eastern USA responded to British industrial dominance and support for free trade by promoting industrialization through protectionist policies at home, and colonial expansionist policies abroad (Kautsky, 1970 [1914], p. 43).

Kautsky went on to question whether these tensions inevitably gave rise to war, or that they would necessarily do so again in the future:

> (t)here is no *economic* necessity for continuing the arms race after the World War, even from the standpoint of the capitalist class itself, with the exception of at most certain armaments interests. On the contrary, the capitalist economy is seriously threatened precisely by the contradictions between its states.
>
> *(Kautsky, 1970 [1914], pp. 44–5)*

Thus, at some point in the future, capital and capitalist states would have to unite to avoid the destructiveness of war, and this would be based on growing cooperation rather than conflict between capitalist states, 'a holy alliance of the imperialists' (Kautsky, 1970 [1914], p. 46), who would agree on how the world should be divided.

What we have then is two very different approaches to understanding (capitalist) imperialism, and the relationship between advanced capitalist states within this imperialist international order. Lenin stressed that the tensions within this order made cooperation, in the long run at least, unfeasible. Kautsky, on the other hand, argued that cooperation – and by implication, peaceful relations between the great powers – was possible. These two positions clearly overlap with realist and liberal perspectives, with Lenin in the former camp and Kautsky in the latter. As we will see, these differences re-occur in the context of the rise of China and US hegemony.

One other factor that has been important to Marxist debates is the idea that imperialism entails the domination of some states over others. This was clear in the context of the build-up to the two world wars, when competing great powers dominated colonies and weaker independent states. Since Lenin's time, Marxists have tended to argue that imperialism in this sense of domination continues to the present, even in an era when most territories have won their independence from colonial rule. In this way, the USA might be regarded as an imperialist power, even if it is not formally colonizing territories.

So far a number of perspectives have been introduced that seek to make sense of international order, and of the place of great powers in that order (see Figure 4.3).

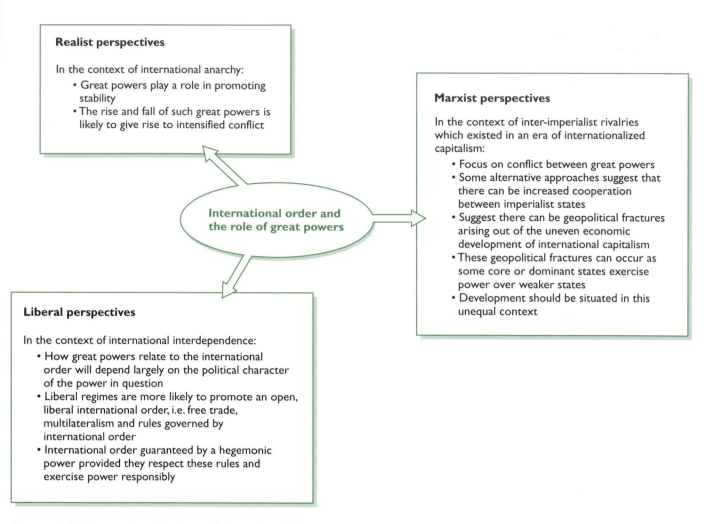

Realist perspectives

In the context of international anarchy:
- Great powers play a role in promoting stability
- The rise and fall of such great powers is likely to give rise to intensified conflict

Marxist perspectives

In the context of inter-imperialist rivalries which existed in an era of internationalized capitalism:
- Focus on conflict between great powers
- Some alternative approaches suggest that there can be increased cooperation between imperialist states
- Suggest there can be geopolitical fractures arising out of the uneven economic development of international capitalism
- These geopolitical fractures can occur as some core or dominant states exercise power over weaker states
- Development should be situated in this unequal context

International order and the role of great powers

Liberal perspectives

In the context of international interdependence:
- How great powers relate to the international order will depend largely on the political character of the power in question
- Liberal regimes are more likely to promote an open, liberal international order, i.e. free trade, multilateralism and rules governed by international order
- International order guaranteed by a hegemonic power provided they respect these rules and exercise power responsibly

Figure 4.3   International order and the role of great powers

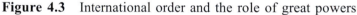

Activity 4.2

By now you should have grasped the main characteristics of the three approaches – realism, liberalism and Marxism – addressed in this chapter. But why does any of this matter? Why has this chapter looked in depth at realist and liberal debates between 1919 and 1939, for example? Step back and think why this may be the case and how it might relate to understanding China's rise, before moving on to consider that subject in more depth.

Spend about 15 minutes on this activity.

Discussion

It can be argued that these debates matter not only for understanding history, but also for understanding contemporary international politics. Realists (and Leninists) might argue that there is much to learn from this period, or indeed the period before 1914, and that there may be grounds for thinking that there are striking similarities between then and now. Liberals (and Kautskyites) might argue that there is indeed much to learn from history, but in this case this would be to draw out the differences, more than the similarities, between now and then. Before reading the next paragraph, jot down some possible similarities and differences between the two periods.

For similarities, one could point to possible decline by the dominant power (Britain then, the USA now), and potential challengers to that power (Germany then, China now). For differences, one might point to greater levels of integration between states (reflected in international institutions, foreign investment across states), and unchallenged military power now compared to the 1930s.

These are issues taken up in depth in the sections that follow, but for now, it should be clear that in examining China's rise, we should be looking for evidence of competition and conflict to back up both the realist and Leninist case, and cooperation to support the liberal and Kautskyite views.

4.2 Perspectives on China's rise

So far then, this chapter has looked at a number of perspectives on the international system, and tried to show how these explain the role of great powers in that system. Now we want to move on to show concretely what each perspective would have to say about the rise of China. This can briefly be done by taking each theory's specific claims related to China, and how they might use evidence to support their case. The treatment of this issue here will be quite brief, as we then want to turn to a more narrative-based account of US hegemony in the international order, and where China's rise might be situated in that order so as to deepen understanding of how each of the theories might be used to illustrate China's emergence as an international power.

4.2.1 Realism

Realists are not united on the rise of China, but the basic realist position is, unsurprisingly, that China's growing power will lead it to try to reshape the international order, and this will lead to resistance from the existing hegemonic power, the USA. The result is likely to be tension and conflict, though we will see that some realists believe things will be more complex than this. Mearsheimer (2001, p. 41) argues that:

> If China continues its impressive economic growth over the next few decades, the United States and China are likely to engage in an intense security competition with considerable potential for war.

Mearsheimer (2001, p. 42) also argues that the USA should 'do what it can to slow the rise of China. In fact, the structural imperatives of the international system, which are powerful, will probably force the USA to abandon its policy of constructive engagement in the near future.'

Mearsheimer therefore not only attempts to explain the significance of the rise of China for the USA-led international order, he also argues that the USA should 'do what it can' to slow down China's rise. As seen earlier, this is where a theory based on analysis can quickly become one based on prescription – Mearsheimer did not see the US decision to launch a war against Iraq as being in the national interest, but he does think that a more forceful policy towards China is justified, as its rise is considered to be a threat to the national interest. This in turn was linked to a rejection of the Clinton administration's policy of treating China as a strategic partner, rather than as a strategic competitor, which was the initial wish of the Bush administration.

What evidence could be cited to support the view that China's rise represents a threat to US hegemony in the international order? Some of these issues are addressed in depth in later chapters, but the following factors come to mind:

- ongoing disputes over human rights, including in terms of the policy of dispensing aid
- ideological differences between the liberal USA and 'communist', or perhaps 'authoritarian capitalist', China
- the issue of Taiwan, a state with which China is, as of 2011, still officially in conflict
- differences over the environmental crisis
- competing interests over access to primary commodities, particularly oil
- differences over regional alliances made by the two powers
- economic differences over the respective value of both the dollar and the Chinese currency, the *renminbi* (see below).

In each of these cases there are important areas of contention, even conflict, between China and the USA. However, there are two issues at stake here: first, to what extent can a realist mode of analysis explain these differences; and second, and related to the first point, how significant are these differences? Remember that, for realists, the main issue of conflict in the international order is over the attempt by states to secure self-preservation, or security, in the international order. Ideological differences do not actually come into it – a realist account of the Cold War for instance argued that the communist or capitalist character of inter-state conflict was irrelevant; the issue was the anarchical nature of the international order. So, a realist would essentially argue that conflicts over the nature of human rights, for example, actually hide a deeper source of tension, which is that of the shifting balance of power in the international order. And this could certainly be backed up with some kind of evidence-based argument – for example, the USA may talk the language of human rights, but it has a strong track record of breaching human rights in its support for authoritarian regimes, and support for torture and detention policies.

But it does seem problematic to simply reduce all the tensions outlined above to the struggle for security in an international order, and a shift in the balance of power that has resulted from such a struggle. Perhaps the most basic measure of security is military power, and Mearsheimer (2001, p. 5) himself argues: 'Great powers are determined on the basis of their relative military capability.' However, if this is the case, then a question to ask, that is difficult for a realist to answer, is why has there been no serious attempt to challenge US military superiority in recent years? Based on constant (2005) values, US military spending stood at approximately US$550 000 million in 2008, compared to US$70 000 million for China. This represented an increase of US$40 000 million for China since 2000, but US spending increased by US $350 000 million over the same period (Young, 2010, p. 8). The USA spends about 45.3 per cent of the total global military budget, more than the next 45 largest military spenders combined. In contrast, China spends just 4.3 per cent of the global military budget (Breslin, 2010, p. 59; Dumbrell, 2010, p. 19).

An alternative realist account suggests that there has not been any overt challenge to the USA, because it is essentially a uni-polar power (Brooks and Wohlforth, 2008). What this means is that the USA is so powerful it makes no sense for any rising power to challenge it, and instead states such as China are more likely to adopt a policy of cooperating with it, albeit selectively. What this suggests is that they consciously choose to embrace the USA-led international order, so as to share in the gains of that order, and thus avoid a confrontation with a stronger power. This 'defensive realist' approach implies that China's rise might be exaggerated, or at least it is not so significant that it can present a real threat to US hegemony in the foreseeable future (Chan, 2008). This remains a realist account because its focus is still on the balance of power – it simply suggests that China's rise is not significant enough to alter this balance of power. Liberals, however, suggest something quite different, and focus on the question of particular kinds of power.

4.2.2 Liberalism

Liberals suggest that China's rise will not inevitably provoke conflict in a changing international order. Like the defensive realists, the argument is made that US hegemonic decline – and by implication, China's rise – has been exaggerated (Ikenberry, 2008). But more important, and in contrast to all realist positions, the liberal argument is that this is in part because of the nature of US power and of the international order that it leads.

In the words of Ikenberry:

> The rise of China does not have to trigger a wrenching hegemonic transition. The US–Chinese power transition can be very different from those of the past because China faces an international order that is fundamentally different from those that past rising states confronted. China does not just face the United States; it faces a Western-centred system that is open, integrated and rule-based, with wide and deep political foundations.
>
> *(Ikenberry, 2008, p. 24)*

What is crucial for Ikenberry is the nature of the liberal international order. This open, transparent order allows rising powers to work within it, rather than against it and this is precisely what China is doing. There is evidence of this interdependence, which in turn has facilitated cooperation between the USA and China. For example, China is a permanent member of the United Nations Security Council, and in 2001 it joined the WTO. China has liberalized in terms of its trade and investment policies, and as a result increasingly trades with the USA, and indeed is a major recipient of US foreign direct investment. Furthermore, while there may be tensions over currency values and the US trade deficit with China, it is the latter which plays a significant role in financing both the US trade and budget deficits through, for instance, buying up US debt in the form of US Treasury bonds (see Section 4.3). This is not to deny that there remain significant sources of tension, as discussed above, but the liberal position tends towards the view that the increasingly interdependent relationship between China and the USA can facilitate peaceful relations between them.

There are, however, two qualifications that might be highlighted here. First, one that Ikenberry (2008, pp. 33–4) points to, is that continued cooperation will in part depend on how the hegemonic power, the USA, responds to China's rise. Some liberals at least were concerned with the way that the Bush administration ignored its allies, at least in its first term of office from 2001 to 2004. But second – and here we revisit the question of liberalism and power – the domestic nature of China's political system does complicate a liberal position. You may recall that liberals argue that cooperation is more likely between liberal democratic regimes. China is most certainly not a liberal democratic regime, and one could argue – from a position of 'offensive liberalism' – that actually the USA should take a more hostile position towards an authoritarian regime like China. Interestingly then, while a liberal position does envisage a more cooperative international regime than a realist one, liberal prescriptions may in certain cases actually provoke conflict – an issue explored later in the book. On the whole though, most liberal positions suggest that the USA-led international order is both transparent and flexible enough to accommodate rising powers, and indeed such powers may not actually undermine US hegemony.

4.2.3 Marxism

Marxist positions in many respects echo these debates, with some arguing, like realists, that China's rise will exacerbate geopolitical competition and conflict in the international order. This is essentially the theory of inter-imperialist rivalries updated for current times. For those Marxists who emphasize the primacy of geopolitical competition, uneven development plays a similar role to that of anarchy in realist accounts. Uneven development is linked to the competition within the international capitalist order, and how this leads to some regions, and their respective states, gaining at the expense of rivals. This does not mean, however, that the winners in this competitive process are always the same powers, and in this regard 'China's rise is already destabilising the existing pattern of global relationships' (Callinicos, 2009, p. 219). The net result is a redistribution of global economic power, and while this might occur in the context of increased interdependence, there is a great deal of instability within this international order. Indeed, writing in 2009, Callinicos (2009, p. 218) suggests that the economic crisis of 2007 onwards was likely to intensify instability as it led to slower growth alongside shifts in the balance of power between the USA and China. This might not lead to war, as in 1914 or 1939, but it would give rise to intensified competition and conflict.

A sense of what this approach concretely means can be gleaned from briefly focusing on the question of oil. You may recall the protests against the war in

Iraq. There were a number of points made by critics of the war, one of which essentially suggested that it was really about getting access to Iraq's considerable oil reserves (see Figure 4.4). Some Marxists similarly suggested that the USA was 'looking to control oil supplies as a means to counter the power shifts threatened within the global economy' (Harvey, 2003, pp. 80–1). In other words, gaining access to Iraqi oil might give the USA some kind of strategic power against potential competitors, such as China.

Figure 4.4 An anti-war march in London in February 2003

Certainly there is greater global demand for oil with the rise of new powers, and it is likely that Middle East oil will be the main source for this increased demand in the foreseeable future, and this might provoke competition between great powers (Klare, 2004). But, we also need to be more specific about the *form* of international order promoted by the USA. This is not the same as that promoted by imperialist powers in the late 19th century who, except for Britain, upheld territorially exclusive policies with their respective colonies. In other words, French colonies traded only with France, Belgian colonies with Belgium, and so on. Even if the USA gained exclusive access to Iraqi oil, it is unclear how this alone could provide meaningful strategic influence over potential rivals like China. This is because the international oil industry is not based on territorially exclusive trading policies – for example, Saudi Arabia trades with a number of countries. In other words, even if the USA gained exclusive access to and control over Iraqi oil, this is not sufficient for them to exercise significant leverage over China, either economically or geopolitically. Furthermore, the USA is actually far less dependent on oil supplies from the Middle East than Japan, the EU and China, and the USA has made considerable efforts to diversify its energy sources in recent years. Even if its dependence on Middle East oil is likely to grow, the fact remains that 'by underwriting transnationally-orientated political economies in the Middle East the US has (by default) guaranteed security of oil supply to *world* markets' (Stokes, 2007, p. 251). In other words, the USA is effectively acting on behalf of all capitalist states, rather than simply in its own interest. The USA might benefit the most, but other great powers are also beneficiaries.

This point leads to the second approach, which suggests that the nature of the international order has changed so much that it renders Leninist-type theories irrelevant in the current order. This account can point to the evidence also drawn on by liberal accounts of the international order. The Marxist twist to the argument is that this interdependence reflects a growing internationalization of capital, reflected in the rise of TNCs and financial flows of capital across national borders. These issues are examined in depth in Chapter 7, but the basic point here is that the internationalization of capital through increased financial flows and the increase in the prominence of global production networks has been led by the USA, in alliance with other developed capitalist states (Panitch and Gindin, 2003). While there were significant flows of capital across national borders before 1914, the nature of these flows is now quantitatively and qualitatively different. As seen in the case of oil, trade is far more open than it was in the days of colonialism. Similarly, foreign investment by transnational companies (TNCs) makes it very difficult to link nation states to a particular nationality of capital. This does not mean that nation states are irrelevant, but it does mean that such states are increasingly internationalized alongside capital. It also does not mean that all states benefit from this system, and it might be the case that the developed capitalist states cooperate and effectively subordinate less developed capitalist states, where gains are highly uneven and unequal between developed and developing countries.

Another question that needs to be addressed further – and the evidence cited in relation to the liberal case is relevant here – is whether China is part of, or outside of, this USA-led liberal international order. This discussion also has implications not only for understanding contemporary interdependence, but also for questioning the alleged decline of the USA, as will be discussed in Section 4.3.

But perhaps first we need to take stock, and think again about why the theories discussed in this chapter are important. One common charge made against theory is that it is always guilty of being selective with the facts, and even of fitting facts into preconceived theoretical boxes. Look again at the comments about realism in relation to China above, and specifically whether all of the areas of contention and conflict can really be reduced to security issues. This might frustrate you, however – for if all the perspectives try to fit the evidence into their preconceived theory, what is the point of theory? Well, as suggested earlier, that theory is needed in order to explain – facts alone will not suffice. This is because some facts might be more important than others, and facts alone can only describe. Section 4.3 provides a more 'factual' account of China's rise, and does so in relation to the question of a USA-led international order since 1945. This, we hope, will be useful in itself, but we also want you to think critically about the narrative that is provided. Writing as a social scientist, the attempt here is to provide as 'objective' a picture as possible. However, this narrative will be informed by a personal perspective, which we want you to try to tease out. The point of this is to try to show not only that theory is necessary, but also that it is unavoidable, and that it always informs 'the facts'.

4.3 China's rise in a USA-led liberal international order

Chapter 3 described some of the features of the post-war liberal international order. We can, therefore, be quite brief here. The post-war international order was one led by the USA, and was quite different from that which preceded it. Before that there was an era of great power rivalries, colonialism and conflict. There was an attempt to implement a liberal order after 1918, but as seen, that was a failure. After 1945, the liberal order was (selectively) implemented, the United Nations was formed, and other multilateral agencies such as the International Monetary Fund (IMF) and the World Bank were created. The commitment was to an open international order based on rules that were binding for all, free trade, open door policies towards investment, and so on.

Realists argue that this order could only be created as a result of the unprecedented power of the USA. The great power – in the case the USA – was so powerful that it could impose a liberal international order on the capitalist world (Webb and Krasner, 1989). At the same time, the USA was not all-powerful and there emerged a balance of power between the USA and the Soviet Union. This led the capitalist states to ally with the USA, but it also led the USA to make compromises in terms of its promotion of a liberal international order. Indeed, **Marshall Aid** was crucial to the post-war reconstruction of Europe, and the USA allowed countries to protect themselves from competition from US companies, a policy that was also allowed to occur in the Third World, where import substitution industrialization (ISI) was carried out. The USA also compromised on multilateralism through making the dollar the main international currency, and through the veto powers granted to certain countries at the United Nations Security Council.

Activity 4.3

The above paragraph briefly outlines how realists explain the rise of a liberal international order after 1945. Focusing on the Cold War explanation – that capitalist states cooperated in the context of a common enemy, the Soviet Union – how convincing is this as an explanation?

Discussion

In some respects – the specifics of the Cold War and cooperation between capitalist states – the argument is quite convincing. But – and this is the key point – for such an explanation to be fully compatible with a realist position, we need to generalize from these specifics a bit more. Concretely, if cooperation between capitalist states occurred because of the Cold War, then we should expect competition and conflict to re-occur between capitalist states once the Cold War had ended (and similarly from a Leninist perspective, we should expect the return of inter-imperialist rivalries). However, cooperation continued and we did not see the revival of conflict between capitalist states.

This, then, presents a problem for a realist account (but see the discussion of defensive realism in Section 4.2.1 for a realist response).

However, this post-war reconstruction was accompanied by a longer-term commitment to a liberal order, and tariff rates were gradually reduced through periodic General Agreement on Tariffs and Trade (GATT) talks and through foreign direct investment by TNCs. In a sense this reconstruction came to an end with the effective breakdown of some parts of the Bretton Woods System in the early 1970s, and the shift to neoliberal policies in the 1980s. In the 1980s these policies, in part at least, were not successful and there was low growth and significant setbacks in social development indicators in developing countries. But the 1990s saw a boom in foreign investment and a revival of US strength in the international order, reinforced by the collapse of the communist alternative.

China, meanwhile, began to shift its policies following the death of Mao in 1976. Under Deng Xiaopeng, liberalization policies were implemented from 1978 onwards, and these were enhanced in the early 1990s just at the start of the foreign investment boom in emerging markets. As Chapter 5 shows, this led to a massive increase in both foreign investment and growth in China. But it also led to concerns that China was a threat to US hegemony, not least as the domestic character of Chinese policies puts it outside the liberal core.

And there are indeed ongoing tensions over trade, market access and what the USA regards as an undervalued Chinese currency, which exacerbates the US trade deficit with China. In terms of geopolitics, there is concern that China allies itself with a number of rogue regimes such as Sudan and Zimbabwe. It has also been claimed that:

> China's new ideas are having a gigantic effect outside of China. China is marking a path for other nations around the world who are trying to figure out not simply how to develop their countries, but also how to fit into the international order in a way that allows them to be truly independent, to protect their way of life and political choices in a world with a single massively powerful centre of gravity.

(Ramo, 2004, p. 3)

In this way the so-called 'Beijing Consensus' could be regarded as a challenge to the USA-led (post-)Washington consensus. As Chapter 5 will detail, China's aid tends to come with no strings attached, advocacy of the principle of non-interference in domestic affairs and respect for the principle of sovereignty. For all these reasons, it could be argued that China lies outside the liberal international order.

On the other hand, there is also considerable interdependence. First, there is a great deal of foreign investment by TNCs into China. In addition to direct investment there is a great deal of subcontracting agreements between foreign and Chinese firms, in which the latter supplies the former. The USA is central to both direct foreign investment and subcontracting agreements. In 2004, US retail giant Walmart imported US$18 billion in goods from China, making it the national equivalent of the fifth largest 'national' importer of Chinese goods.

As already seen, some perspectives suggest that the US deficit is a significant cause of tension with China, particularly in relation to currency values. US national debt stood at US$3076 billion in December 2008. But what is interesting is who finances this through the purchase of debt. Overwhelmingly it is Asian countries, with China accounting for the largest amount (US$727.4 billion in December 2008) of US Treasury securities. The crisis did see periodic expressions of concern by the Chinese leadership over US debt levels. Above all, though, a massive cut in domestic consumption by US consumers would hit Chinese exporters hard, the USA being China's biggest export market (Hung, 2009, pp. 8–9).

China has indeed been selective in its acceptance of the international rules of the game, but it is hardly unique in that regard. It certainly has kept the value of its currency low, and indeed – some liberalization notwithstanding – has carried out protectionist policies, but then so too has every other power in its rise to great power status (see the discussion of the rejection of Cobden in Subsection 4.1.3). Moreover, these important policies notwithstanding, 'much of China's remarkable growth has been achieved by adjusting the domestic order to facilitate integration with the capitalist global economy' (Breslin, 2010, p. 55).

The Chinese notion of a 'peaceful rise' (Bijian, 2005) may have elements of self-justification, but it also appears to reflect acceptance that China is not a hegemonic challenger to the USA. While pursuing a strategy that attempts an increase in cooperation with the USA, such as the construction of a common counter-terrorist stance, the Communist Party elite has simultaneously hedged against the prospects of failed cooperation by developing bilateral and regional ties with the different parts of the developing world, facilitated by closer trade and investment ties (particularly in primary commodities like oil) and increased aid (Alden, 2007). These are discussed in Chapter 5. Moreover, China's relations with the rest of the developing world are based less on solidarity and more on competition with other low wage manufacturing producers, and China's need for primary commodities. This certainly undermines any notion of a Beijing Consensus that supposedly challenges the (post-)Washington consensus. On the whole then, while relations with the rest of the developing world have some significance, at present at least, they do not constitute a new coalition of forces united by a challenge to US hegemony at the level of the international state system (Foot, 2006). The analysis here thus suggests that China is simultaneously cooperating with the USA while forging possible alternative allies on a bilateral basis.

This section then has pointed in more depth to areas of cooperation and competition between China and the USA. It is hopefully clear from the argument that we question the realist and Leninist views that competition and conflict are inevitably more important than cooperation, and the related rigid separation of the domestic and the international that can be found in realist analyses. In this regard we are questioning the view that anarchy (in realism) or uneven development (in Leninism) can provide a full explanation for the character of the international system. Instead, we have suggested that cooperation is possible, and insofar as there is competition, the severity of this will depend on the reaction by both states to China's rise. This puts our position closer to the liberal and Kautskyite views addressed in Subsections 4.1.3 and 4.1.4, respectively.

One final point, though, is the issue of the capitalist nature of the international system, and how this is linked to China's rise. Certainly there has been a massive internationalization of capital in the period of neoliberalism, but this has largely been led by the already developed countries. The combined outward foreign direct investment of Brazil, Russia, India and China in 2008 was less than that of The Netherlands. China's foreign exchange reserves of US$2.3 trillion in 2009 might have been the highest in the world, but this amount is actually less than the market capitalization of the top 10 US firms in the same year (Nolan and Zhang, 2010, p. 101). Moreover, to date much of China's export growth is in low wage, low value and labour-intensive goods. This has led some observers to claim that China is simply 'playing our game', or acting as the USA's 'head servant', as it supplies cheap goods that, alongside increased debt, helped to sustain US consumption (Steinfeld, 2010; Hung, 2009). This argument, namely that China–US relations are characterized less by mutual interdependence and more by the dependence or subordination of the former by the latter, may be something of an exaggeration. But it does suggest that some scepticism about China's rise – and US decline – is necessary. In part at least, the rise of China must be seen in the context of changes in the character of international capitalism. What is being suggested then is that we need to situate China's rise in part in the context of the uneven development of international capitalism, and indeed how this might relate to the limits of China's rise.

This section has provided a more narrative-based account of the rise of China in a USA-dominated international order. The discussion above has focused on three issues:

- conflict between powers – for our purposes, China and the USA – in the context of anarchy
- cooperation between China and the USA in the context of interdependence
- the limitations of China's rise and the USA's decline.

What has been argued is that while the Kautskyite and liberal views about cooperation between great powers is more convincing than the realist/Leninist view, this does not preclude conflict between great powers and weaker states in the international order, and this reflects the uneven development of international capitalism. Rising powers in the 1860s rejected free trade policies so that they might catch up with Britain via protectionist policies, and China itself has also attempted to do this, albeit with limited success. At the same time, China has also attracted foreign investment, including from the USA – but it has tended to be in lower value areas of economic activity, which suggests that China's rise might be limited – and that many other states remain subordinated in the international system, not least because they have not rejected the free trade policies that rising powers rejected in the 1860s. This is very much a personal view, but that is less important than the fact that what this shows is we cannot think about international development without also thinking about different theoretical perspectives on the nature of the international system.

Summary and looking forward

The rising powers create the need to analyze international politics and international development together. Hence, this chapter has put international relations theory into conversation with Development Studies through a discussion of the rising powers, and China in particular. Specifically, this chapter:

- reviewed the main theoretical perspectives in international relations, and related these to general debates about the rise and fall of great powers

- took these debates and applied them in relation to the rise of China. The main debate over China's rise is essentially geopolitical, namely does its rise mean an increase in competition or cooperation between China and the USA? The realist and Leninist position argues for the former, and situates this within a wider theory of international anarchy (realism) or inter-imperialist rivalry (Leninism). Liberal and Marxist perspectives associated with Kautsky argue that relations between great powers are more contingent and a liberal core is a possibility, even as this continues to subordinate some states in the international system

- related China's rise to changes in the character of international capitalism, and suggested some reasons for being careful not to exaggerate China's emergence as a power in the international system.

Nonetheless, the fact remains that China's rise is a reality and this needs further consideration, not least in terms of the question of development. This is the subject of Chapters 5 and 6.

References

Alden, C. (2007) *China in Africa*, London, Zed Books.

Bell, D. (2006) 'Empire and international relations in Victorian political thought: historiographical sssay', *Historical Journal*, vol. 49, no. 1, pp. 281–98.

Bijian, Z. (2005) 'China's "peaceful rise" to great power status', *Foreign Affairs,* vol. 84, no. 5, pp. 18–24.

Breslin, S. (2010) 'China's emerging global role: dissatisfied responsible great power', *Politics*, vol. 30, supp. 1, pp. 52–62.

Brooks, S. and Wohlforth, W. (2008) *World Out of Balance*, Princeton, Princeton University Press.

Callinicos, A. (2009) *Imperialism and Global Political Economy*, Cambridge, Polity.

Carr, E.H. (2001 [1939]) *The Twenty Years Crisis*, Basingstoke, Palgrave.

Chan, S. (2008) *China, the US and the Power Transition Theory: A Critique*, London, Routledge.

Chang, H.-J. (2002) *Kicking Away the Ladder*, London, Anthem.

Dumbrell, J. (2010) 'American power: crisis or renewal', *Politics*, vol. 30, supp. 1, pp.15–23.

Foot, R. (2006) 'Chinese strategies in a US-hegemonic global order: accommodating and hedging', *International Affairs,* vol. 82, no. 1, pp. 77–94.

Harvey, D. (2003) *The New Imperialism*, Oxford, Oxford University Press.

Hung, H.F. (2009) 'America's head servant', *New Left Review*, no. 60, pp. 5–25.

Ikenberry, G.J. (2008) 'The rise of China and the future of the West', *Foreign Affairs*, vol. 87, no. 1, pp. 23–37.

Kautsky, K. (1970 [1914]) 'Ultra-Imperialism', *New Left Review*, no. 59, pp. 41–6.

Klare, M. (2004) *Blood and Oil*, London, Hamish Hamilton.

Lenin, V. (1977 [1916]) 'Imperialism: the highest stage of capitalism' in *Selected Works*, Moscow, Progress.

Mearsheimer, J. (2001) *The Tragedy of Great Power Politics*, New York, Norton.

Mearsheimer, J. (2005) *Hans Morgenthau and the Iraq War: Realism versus Neoconservatism*, available at www.opendemocracy.net (Accessed 11 June 2011).

Nolan, P. and Zhang, J. (2010) 'Global competition after the financial crisis', *New Left Review*, no. 64, pp. 97–108.

NSS (2002) *The National Security Strategy of the United States of America* [online], www.whitehouse.gov/nsc/nss.html (Accessed ??).

Panitch, L. and Gindin, S. (2003) 'Global capitalism and American empire' in *The Socialist Register*, 2004, London, Merlin.

Ramo, J. (2004) *The Beijing Consenus: Notes on the New Physics of Chinese Power*, London, Foreign Policy Centre.

Steinfeld, E. (2010) *Playing Our Game*, Cambridge, Cambridge University Press.

Stokes, D. (2007) 'Blood for oil? Global capital, counter-insurgency and the dual logic of American energy security', *Review of International Studies*, vol. 33, no. 2, pp. 245–64.

Waltz, K. (1979) *Theory of International Politics*, New York, Random House.

Webb, M. and Krasner, S. (1989) 'Hegemonic stability theory: an empirical assessment', *Review of International Studies*, vol. 15, no. 2, pp. 183–98.

Young, A. (2010) 'Perspectives of the changing global distribution of power: concepts and context', *Politics*, vol. 30, supp. 1, pp. 2–14.

Further reading

Breslin, S. (2007) *China in the Global Political Economy*, Basingstoke, Palgrave.

Brooks, S. and Wohlforth, W. (2008) *World Out of Balance*, Princeton, Princeton University Press.

Burchill, S., Linklater, A., Devetak, R., Donnelly, J., Nardin, T., Paterson, M., Reus-Smith, C. and True, J. (2009) *Theories of International Relations*, Basingstoke, Palgrave.

Mearsheimer, J. (2001) *The Tragedy of Great Power Politics*, New York, Norton.

Nolan, P. (2003) *China at the Crossroads*, Cambridge, Polity.

Nye, J. (2010) 'The future of American power', *Foreign Affairs*, vol. 89, no. 6, pp. 2–12.

The rising powers as drivers of development

Masuma Farooki and Giles Mohan

Introduction

The global economy is based on a wide array of networks where money, people, food, raw materials and consumer goods constantly flow from one region to another. Very few countries, whether they are rich or poor, can remain isolated from these global linkages, which are also impacted on by power relationships. As you saw in Chapter 3, international systems involve the exercise of power, which can result in positive-sum or zero-sum outcomes for the actors involved. Who controls and can affect these flows determines economic and political power in the international system. After World War II the drivers of economic and political change resided mainly in the developed economies of North America and Europe, with Soviet Russia and Japan emerging towards the latter half of the century. These actors influenced how global trade and financial markets worked, and with this came a great influence on international development.

As seen in previous chapters, from the 2000s a new group of economic powers began to emerge in the developing world: led by China, followed by India and Brazil. In 2010, the Organisation for Economic Co-operation and Development (OECD) published a report charting this shift of economic and political power from the traditional superpowers of North America and Europe to the developing regions, particularly China. The report argued:

> Developing countries have become important economic actors and demonstrate the dynamism of the new South–South economic ties. Although the process has been ongoing for 20 years, the opportunities and risks for poor countries posed by shifting wealth are only starting to be understood.
>
> *(OECD, 2010, p. 15)*

As the quote suggests, this process did not occur overnight and was the culmination of events taking place for over 20 years, as discussed at the end of Chapter 3. What is this shift in 'wealth' and why is the 'new' economic order of such concern to international development? The answer lies in the nature of the current international system, which is deeply interconnected through a multitude of channels. The rising economic and political power in Brazil, India and China has ripple effects around the world and it is for this reason that they are worth studying.

But it has also been argued that all states have unique development trajectories even as they are inevitably part of an interconnected and interdependent world. So, this chapter focuses in on the specifics of Brazil, China and India's economic growth. In order to do this the chapter develops two key themes:

- First, although the path to economic growth may be specific to a country's endowments and circumstances, there is a general model that is applicable to all countries.

- Second, when these countries become major actors in the global economy, their impact on other developing regions is of a different nature to the growth that has been driven by the advanced economies.

The path of international development when measured through the lens of economic growth looks at the nature and structure of an economy. In this chapter, then, we put on our 'economic hats', which may be new to many of you; however, economics is an essential component of understanding development. Later chapters will critique the focus on economic measures but for now, in summary, the aims of this chapter are to:

- look at the perspectives on economic growth of the neoliberal and Marxist traditions

- develop a basic understanding of patterns of economic development and the factors that drive these changes

- use these concepts to understand the recent economic growth of Brazil, India and China

- examine how these emerging economies have an impact on the development paths of other developing countries by influencing patterns of international trade and investment.

We do this by starting with a broad understanding of these influences – a 'macro' level in economic terms. Then we will move on to case studies at a more local scalel to appreciate the rising powers as drivers of international development.

5.1 Analytical perspectives on economic development

Chapter 1 talked about capitalism and industrialization and how they are an integral part of the economic development process. Within development there are two major perspectives on how industrialization can be achieved. On one hand we have the neoliberals who support the free functioning of markets and on the other hand we have the Marxists and structuralists arguing for the state to play a fundamental role in the development process. Most industrialization policies lie somewhere between these two views. Chapter 1 has already introduced these ideas so here we will examine the more economic implications of them.

The neoliberals stress development initiatives that help markets to function freely. They would emphasize the following actions: general economic growth; developing industry that is very efficient; and providing the conditions so individuals can become innovative and entrepreneurial, able to make choices and become self-reliant. These actions follow from the importance they place on individual responsibility and the value of competition. However, structuralists argue that markets only bring economic growth, and in order to ensure development you have to look at economic *and* social structures – who has power and who owns what. These structures greatly affect one's ability to enter and survive in markets. Thus, governments and international agencies need to control markets, to make sure that competition is fair and to distribute the benefits of wealth.

But whether they believe in markets or state-led economic development, the neoliberals and the structuralists agree that industrialization is necessary for development. Ever since the world's first industrial revolution in the UK more than 200 years ago, protagonists on both sides of the political spectrum have argued the case forcefully. Soviet Russia was fully in agreement about the necessity of industrialization. Communist-controlled China is following the same path. Industrialization, which is part of the process of economic development, brings with it changes in the level and use of technology, productivity and rural–urban migrations. It changes consumption and production patterns. As noted in Chapter 1 some of these changes are intentional, where the state or another institution sets up policies and plans to produce a certain kind of development path. Other changes are unintentional, or left up to the markets to generate. Whether the growth process *should be* intentional or unintentional remains contested. So how have the advanced economies of the North industrialized and are those of the South following suit?

5.2 Patterns of industrialization in economic growth

Industrialization has for many countries and people delivered higher standards of living. But this is, in turn, based on changes in the kind of economic growth that takes place, which is, in turn, based on structural changes in the economy – that is, *what is produced and how*. Primarily, we can see structural change in the decline of agriculture and the rise of industry and services. The process of transition from a commodity-based economy to an industrial one entails the rise of new kinds of production (non-agricultural, advanced technology and complex divisions of labour) organized in a particular kind of way (for sale in a market for profit) and involving patterns of social relations between classes structured around the ownership and non-ownership of property. However, the diversity amongst countries in terms of natural and human resources, country size and population, access to technology, transport and finance networks are so varied that it is difficult to model a pattern of growth that applies to *all*. There are, though, certain regularities observed in the transformation of sectoral composition and economic growth. These regularities are generation of income, improvement in technology and productivity, changes in the nature of employment and migration, and we will deal with each in turn.

Generation of national income

The national income or Gross Domestic Product (GDP) is a sum of value of the production that takes place within the boundaries of a country. The World Bank defines GDP as:

> the sum of gross value added by all resident producers in the economy plus any product taxes and minus any subsidies not included in the value of the

products. It is calculated without making deductions for depreciation of fabricated assets or for depletion and degradation of natural resources.

(World Bank, 2011a)

'Value added' is simply defined as the difference between the sale price of a product and the cost of materials to produce it. A similar concept to GDP is that of Gross National Product (GNP) – the sum of value of production of all citizens of a country, not necessarily within country boundaries. For example, a US firm produces computers in Taiwan. The value of production of this firm will be included in the GDP of Taiwan and the GNP of the USA. It will not be included in the GNP of Taiwan nor in the GDP of the USA. GDP indicators are more extensively used than GNP indicators. Box 5.1 explains how GDP can be used to compare different levels of economic development.

Box 5.1 Comparing economies using Gross Domestic Product

The GDP per capita is obtained by dividing the GDP of a country by its total population.

In 2008 the GDP per capita of the United Kingdom was US$44 000, for China US$3000 and for Cambodia US$700. The GDP per capita indicates that the first is a high-income country, the second belongs to the middle-income group while the third is a low-income country.

The World Bank defines low-income economies as those in which 2008 per capita income was US$975 or less, middle-income economies between US$976 and US$11 905, and high-income economies have per capita incomes of US$11 906 or more.

A country's GDP is composed of various sectors, usually divided into primary, secondary and tertiary (see Box 5.2)

Box 5.2 The primary, secondary and tertiary sectors

The 'primary sector' refers to income generated from growing or extracting raw materials from the earth and includes agriculture, forestry, farming, fishing and mining.

The 'secondary sector' encompasses economic activity in the industrial and infrastructure sector. Industrial activity refers to all manufacturing activities such as clothing and car production, as well as the production of intermediate goods such as metal and chemicals. Infrastructure refers to the construction industry, production of energy, and other utilities.

The 'tertiary sector' is also referred to as the services sector, and includes all businesses involved in retail and wholesale sales, tourism, financial services (such as banking and insurance), health care and transportation.

At low levels of GDP, the largest contribution to national income comes from the 'primary sector', which includes agriculture. The savings made in the agricultural sector are gradually used as investments in the 'secondary sector', particularly in industry. Governments and international loans can also be used to invest in the industrial sector. These investments allow the industrial sector to expand and, as growth accelerates, the economy begins to rely more and more on its manufacturing capabilities to generate income than on its agricultural sector. Therefore, the first shift in sectoral contribution to GDP, as a result of economic growth, occurs when the industrial sector accounts for a larger share of national income than the primary sector. This is usually seen in middle-income countries. As the industrial sector continues to expand it generates the need for services and the 'tertiary sector' expands and increased investments are made in this sector. So our second sectoral shift occurs as countries move from middle-income to high-income levels and the services sector takes over from the industrial sector as the largest contributor to national income.

Technology and productivity

One of the ways through which the primary, secondary and tertiary sectors generate savings, and therefore investable capital, is the improvement in productivity. Productivity simply refers to the inputs required to produce one unit of a product. For example, assume it takes ten workers and two machines to produce one wooden table. If the technology of the machines is improved and the workers receive more training, five workers and one machine can then produce one wooden table. The productivity of the workers and the machines in this instance has increased.

There are many ways, apart from using new technology and increasing training, to raise productivity. The essential role of productivity in industrialization is that the speed and extent of economic growth is dependent on it. More generally, an increase in productivity (see Box 5.3) across the economy as a whole is a central feature of economic growth. If we assume that a constant share of the population is employed, then an increase in output per capita is also an increase in output per worker.

> ## Box 5.3 What is productivity?
>
> Production systems use factors of production – such as labour with different skills, and capital inputs such as machines – to produce outputs from raw materials and manufactured inputs. If the amounts of labour and capital increase, then we would expect output to increase: for example, output may rise because there is an increase in the proportion of the population employed. However, if output rises faster than we would expect it to from the observed increase in capital and labour employed, then productivity is rising.
>
> The level of technology and the skill level of workers tend to be higher in richer countries than in middle- and low-income countries. This is a circular relation; to increase productivity, workers and machinery need to be better, more productive workers and higher technology machinery will lead to larger increases in productivity.

Employment

The employment structure tends to mirror the shift in sectoral composition accompanying growth. At low levels of per capita income the agricultural sector will have the largest share of employment and as incomes rise and the manufacturing sector begins to grow, employment will shift to the industrial sector. At the higher income levels, the services sector will be the dominant employer. A fundamental feature of economic growth is that it involves a sustained fall of the share of agriculture in output and employment in the economy as a whole. In the high-income capitalist countries where these changes have gone furthest, the share of the population employed on the land has fallen dramatically, to well under 5 per cent of the working population in most cases, and often as low as 2 per cent or less. On the supply side, the output produced per worker has increased in the agricultural sector so that a smaller share of the labour force is needed to feed the population. On the demand side, as incomes rise consumers have come to spend a smaller share of their total income on agricultural goods. These changes released labour from agricultural production and allowed employment in other sectors of the economy – industry and services – to grow.

Rural–urban migration

When the primary sector is the dominant income generator in an economy, a large share of the population will tend to be in the rural areas. Agriculture requires use of arable land, and therefore the labour will be organized around those areas. Manufacturing on the other hand requires clustering or the presence of a number of firms in the same area, usually around cities. As the industrial sector grows, generating more employment opportunities, people will move from rural to urban areas. Since firms providing services also tend to be located in and around cities, they will also encourage urban migration. Therefore as industrialization becomes more grounded, a larger share of a country's population will live in cities than in rural areas. This is discussed in more detail in Chapter 6. But now let us turn to the rising powers of Brazil, India and China and their patterns of economic growth.

5.3 The pattern of economic growth in Brazil, India and China

Section 5.2 sets out the typical features of industrialization and growth. It is a stylized description of structural change that all countries go through. However, while the ends – in this case industrialization, growth and urbanization – are the same, the routes to these ends vary between countries. In Chapter 3, for example, Britain's industrialization required imports from its colonies, whereas the USA's growth was more reliant on domestic raw materials. How, then, did Brazil, India and China grow? This picks up on the brief histories at the end of Chapter 3 but focusing more on the major economic changes these countries have experienced since the 1970s.

In the 1970s, Brazil, India and China were low-income developing countries, not recognized for their economic power by the developed North or the developing South. Brazil and India each accounted for only 2% of global GDP, while China had just 3% of the share. Compared to Japan's 7% and the 36% of the USA, these economies were very much behind the economic frontier. Over the next four decades their growth has seen this share more than double, while that of the North (such as Japan and the USA) has decreased. Figure 5.1 shows the share of the three rising powers as individual countries and collectively in global GDP. The USA is shown for comparative purposes. The figure shows that the share of global GDP of the rising powers collectively was still only half that of the advanced economy of the USA in 2009. However, their pace of growth is so strong that they are expected to be much closer to the position of the USA by 2040. It is their collective share of global GDP, rising from just 6% in 1995 to 12% by 2009 that has given them the status of 'rising economic powers'.

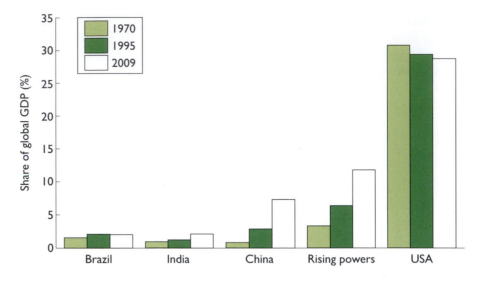

Figure 5.1 Percentage share of country in global Gross Domestic Product (Source: World Bank, 2011b)

Let's look at each of these rising powers in a little more detail.

Brazil

Since the 17th century Brazil's natural resources have been the mainstay of its economy. From sugar plantations to gold and later the discovery of oil, the region has benefited from ample resources. In the early 1970s Brazil was under military rule, which was often repressive; however, it witnessed strong economic growth in that period with GDP rising at around 8 per cent per year in the 1970s and 1980s. In the 1990s Brazil undertook many economic reforms, including moving away from centralized state-led industrialization to more market-friendly regulation. Trade was opened up (i.e. exports and imports were encouraged) and efforts made to attract foreign investment. By 2009 the country was included in the top ten largest economies of the world, and between 2000 and 2008 its GDP grew an average 4 per cent per year.

India

From the 1970s through to the end of the 1980s the Indian economy was based on social democratic ideals, with extensive central government control and regulations; the state owned most of the productive resources and market forces were allowed to operate on a limited scale. The Indian economy was essentially inward looking, that is, trade and exports did not make a major contribution to GDP. In 1991, the economy was opened up and state control was gradually replaced by market-led growth. By the start of the 21st century India had become one of the fastest growing developing economies, averaging 7 per cent annual growth rates between 2000 and 2008.

China

In the late 1970s, China was emerging from a rigid authoritarian system. Policies discussed in Chapter 3, such as the 'Great Leap Forward' (1958) and the Cultural Revolution (1966), contributed towards economic stagnation. After the death of Chairman Mao in 1976, internal political struggles ensued for a number of years. But by the early 1980s the state began to actively engage in economic and social reforms. The 1980s focused on inward-looking growth, with domestic economic development given precedence over developing international trade. The 1990s saw wide-ranging industrialization and the beginning of integration into the world trade economy. After 2000 expansive export and import regimes came into play and accelerated economic growth resulted. China had risen as a global economic powerhouse.

These three stories share two important features. First, in the 1970s each country gave more importance to domestic growth than it did to expanding trade sectors. Second, the 1970–90 period saw a stronger role for the state in economic matters (very much a structuralist approach) and only towards the 1990s and beyond did they turn towards a more market-based approach (closer to the neoliberal way of thinking). Although all three countries in the 2000s have seen their economies engaging more deeply through international trade, their economic policy remains an 'interventionist' one, that is, lying somewhere between free markets and state control.

From the discussion above it can be noted that there are similarities in the economic policies that these rising powers adapted. Now let us consider whether their path of economic growth was any different compared to the traditional patterns that were discussed earlier. We know from Section 5.2 that countries tend to move from an agricultural base to one focused on industry and then on to the services sector. By looking at the contribution to total GDP from each of the sectors, we can form an opinion as to the current state of the economy. Table 5.1 looks at the share of each sector in a country's GDP in 1980 and 2009 for the three economies individually as well as showing their GDP per capita (see Box 5.1).

Table 5.1 shows the percentage share of agriculture to GDP. In 1980, Brazil's agricultural sector contributed 11% to the value added in GDP, falling to 6% by 2009. In China and India the fall in the agricultural sector's contribution was more pronounced, from 30% to 10% for China and from 36% to 18% for India.

The table also shows the percentage share of industry's contribution to GDP. As economies grow the share of the agricultural sector decreases while that of the industrial sector increases. This is true for India where the contribution increased from 25% to 27%. In the case of China, however, the contribution of the industrial sector fell from 48% to 46% while for Brazil it dropped from 44% to 25%. Why might this be the case?

Table 5.1 Percentage share of sector in value added in Gross Domestic Product, 1980 and 2009

	Year	Brazil	China	India
Agricultural sector	1980	11%	30%	36%
	2009	6%	10%	18%
Industrial sector	1980	44%	48%	25%
	2009	25%	46%	27%
Services sector	1980	45%	22%	40%
	2009	68%	43%	55%
Trade to GDP ratio (exports + imports)	1980	20	22	16
	2009	22	49	44
GDP per capita (current US$)	1980	1932	193	267
	2009	8230	3744	1192

The answer lies in the GDP per capita for each country. Note that Brazil's GDP per capita has increased from just under US$2000 to over US$8200, while that for China increased from just under US$200 to over US$3700. We know from Section 5.2 that increases in national income are matched by a shift in GDP from the industrial to the services sector. If we look at the contribution from this sector to China and Brazil's GDP we can see a rapid increase for both economies. China's services sector contribution nearly doubled, from 22% to 49%, while that for Brazil increased from 45% to 68%.

You will also note that India's services sector contributes nearly 55% to the GDP, but the GDP per capita income levels for India suggest that it is much below the income levels of China. Why might this be the case? The answer partially lies in the large contribution that India's IT and related services make to its GDP.

The value of trade as a ratio of GDP is given for each country, and is indicative of how open the economies are towards world trade. The higher the trade to GDP ratio the more the country is open to international trade. Note that all countries have increased their trade to GDP ratio between 1980 and 2009 indicating they have become more open to international trade. This is most clearly visible in the case of India, followed by China and Brazil.

Activity 5.1

Using the data in Table 5.1, answer these questions and then read the discussion below.

1   In 1980 which countries had the highest and the lowest share of the agricultural sector in GDP?

2   Has this ranking changed in 2009?

3   In 1980 which countries had the highest and the lowest share of the industrial sector in GDP?

4   Has this ranking changed in 2009?

5   In 1980 which countries had the highest and the lowest share of the services sector in GDP?

6   Has this ranking changed in 2009?

7   For 2009 arrange the countries in a column by the share of the industrial sector in GDP. In a second column rank them by their trade to GDP ratio. Do the two columns match?

8   For 2009 arrange the countries in a column by the share of the services sector in GDP. In a second column rank them by their GDP per capita levels. Do the two columns match?

9   Based on your answers to questions 7 and 8, what can you say about the general pattern of economic development (reflect on the material discussed in Section 5.2)?

Do not spend more than 20 minutes on this activity.

Discussion

A number of observations can be made based on the statistics provided in Table 5.1. First, note that all countries individually have moved away from the agricultural sector, indicating that the economies are generating national income from other sources. In the case of China, we find that the major contribution to GDP is coming from the industrial sector, which tells us that the manufacturing and infrastructure sectors are strong in that country. For India and Brazil the services sector makes the largest contribution.

Also note that countries that have a higher trade to GDP ratio also have a higher contribution of the industrial sector to GDP. This is not necessarily a cause and effect relationship, it only indicates that countries with a large industrial sector will also tend to be more deeply engaged in international trade.

Countries with the largest share of services are not necessarily the same as countries with the highest GDP per capita. In our table, India has a higher share of services but it has lower GDP per capita than China. Although Section 5.2 suggested that richer countries will have larger contributions from services than poorer countries, we also made the point that this pattern of growth is a 'general' pattern and there will be variations in countries dependent on their resource endowments. India's IT sector and the associated business process outsourcing, including call centres, makes the services sector contribution to the economy much larger than the general pattern of economic development will predict. In general, the structural shifts in economies as income levels rise will hold true, but there will always be exceptions to the rule.

The emerging powers have followed a growth path that saw their source of economic growth start from the agricultural sector and then move on to the industrial and services sector. All three are at different stages of their growth path and in the future we expect their industrial and services sector to become larger with rising income levels.

5.4 Why do the rising powers affect other countries?

So far we have observed that patterns of economic development of the rising power economies are quite similar to the general pattern of structural change. As theorists have suggested, each of these economies has moved from being an agriculture-based economy towards an industrial- and service-based economy. Countries such as the **East Asian Tigers**, the USA and Japan have passed through similar economic phases of growth. So why are these rising powers of interest? Why do these particular rising powers matter? The East Asian Tigers also exhibited strong economic growth in the 1980s and 1990s but their influence on the global economy was not as large as that of the rising powers. There are a number of reasons for this, largely to do with the population and the size of the rising powers and their developing country status, issues raised early in Chapter 3. Let us examine these in more detail.

Size matters

In 2009 the combined population of Brazil, India and China stood at nearly 2.7 billion people (or nearly 40% of the global population). The large size of these economies, by population, means volume has a multiplier effect of any change that takes place within their borders. For example, if 1 per cent of the UK population purchased new mobile phones, it would equate to just 600 000 units sold. If 1 per cent of the Chinese or Indian population purchased mobile phones, it would mean 13 million units in China and 12 million in India! This multiplier effect of size has a large impact on global economic production and consumption systems. 80 per cent of the world's zippers are produced in factories in Qiaotou city in Zhejiang province in China. While this is positive for those seeking to buy zippers, as a single source can provide for all their needs, it does mean that other countries have to compete very hard with each other to produce the remaining 20 per cent!

The geographical size of these countries is also an important factor in how they influence the world. Mumbai and Calcutta (India), Sao Paulo (Brazil) and Shanghai (China) are ranked in the top ten largest cities of the world (by population). In 2010, 160 cities in China had populations exceeding 1 million. There are just nine in the USA and two in the UK. We will talk more about the importance of cities to development in Chapter 6. As noted in Section 5.2, with economic growth there will be a rise in urbanization and migration from the rural areas, particularly as labour moves into the manufacturing and services sectors in China, India and Brazil. This is a natural shift that occurs across many countries, as jobs and economic opportunities are more likely to be found in cities than in villages. With such a large number of cities, demand from their urban consumers for food, products, cars and residential housing also tend to be larger relative to smaller sized countries.

Developing country status matters

China, India and Brazil are developing countries, where a large portion of their population lies in the lower- rather than the middle-income groups. In 2009 per capita income for Brazil was around US$8100 and for China and India lower still at US$3700 and US$1100 respectively. In comparison, the developed North per capita incomes are much higher: US$35 000 for the UK and US$39 700 for Japan. Even with strong growth in the 2010 to 2020 period for the rising powers, their per capita incomes will remain well below other advanced economies.

The difference in per capita incomes is relevant as it helps us to identify the nature of consumption within these countries. The price elasticity of demand (see Box 5.4) for basic consumption, such as food, clothing and shelter, is low compared to that of more durable items like cars and electronic equipment. Therefore, low-income groups will focus most of their demand on basic items, but as their incomes grow a larger proportion of income will be spent on the more durable items. In 1990, a large number of households in China and India had less than US$1000 per year to spend. By 2009 less than 10% of households were left in such poverty. These households have now become consumers with needs for clothing and accessories, demands that production firms within and outside China are trying to supply. Thus, more consumers lead to more opportunities for businesses and an expansion in manufacturing activities. The manufacturing firms require raw materials as inputs, and thus increase the opportunity for raw material suppliers to expand their business as well. Subsection 5.5.4 returns to this point. Here we emphasize that, as developing countries with improving income levels, the rising powers are increasing the number of consumers and through them producers in the global economy.

Box 5.4 What is elasticity of demand?

The income earned by an individual affects his or her demand for goods and response to changes in price. In order to gauge how these demands respond to changes, we use the concept of elasticity of demand. Income elasticity of demand is defined as *the ratio of the percent change in demand to the percent change in income.* If the change in demand is less than proportionate than the change in income, a good is said to have low-income elasticity. For example, our income may increase by 10%, but our expenditure on food increases by less than 10%, therefore food has low-income elasticity of demand. Consumer items, such as electronic goods and cars, have high-income elasticity; spending on such goods rises proportionately more than increases in income.

Apart from individual consumer needs, the demands for an economy as a whole also change as its income levels increase. There is a need to connect different geographical regions: more railway tracks are laid down, more roads are constructed, urban travel systems, such as light railway services, are expanded, sea and airport facilities are built. Telephone and communication services are expanded. The country's need for energy, both oil and electricity, starts to increase. All of these infrastructure expenditures require a great deal of raw materials to construct.

The growth in income of the rising powers will increase their demand for food and raw materials, wants they cannot always fulfil from domestic resources. More consumers with purchasing power are being added to the world, and as countries move to meet those demands, more producers and workers are also required. When the rising powers find they cannot meet these consumer demands from domestic resources they increasingly turn to international markets. With their size (population), economic structure (developing country) and trading patterns (trade openness), they have a large impact on the developed world as well as on the developing world. This is a form of development interaction that was raised in Chapters 1 and 2. What are the kinds of changes they bring about in international development?

5.5 How do rising powers drive international development?

The rising powers have been called drivers of change, but what does the term 'driver' actually mean? We use the term 'driver' to define two major roles for these countries. The first is related to the importance of their size (size drivers), the second is related to their consumer behaviour or markets (market drivers). The impacts generated through these roles are felt by both the developed and developing world. Understanding and observing these impacts in an organized manner are helped if we have a conceptual framework. This is necessarily a simplified representation of the reality we seek to analyse; however, it is a useful tool for helping us organize important elements of a problem to make sure we include the most relevant aspects.

5.5.1 The rising powers framework

The rising powers conceptual framework identifies six major channels through which they interact with and impact upon the global economy: trade, investment, aid, global governance, migration and the environment. These channels allow for both direct and indirect impacts on individual sectors within countries, at a national level and within the global economy. The framework takes these positive-sum and zero-sum effects, and divides them across the six major channels (see Table 5.2).

While migration and the environment will be covered in more detail in Chapter 6, let us now use some examples to illustrate this framework from the micro level, that is, a single example of an investment project or trade between two countries. Having done that, we will expand our horizon to the macro level to examine the global patterns and implications of these flows. In practice, to get a true picture of impacts we need to combine the macro and micro.

Table 5.2 The rising powers conceptual framework

Channel	Impacts			
	Positive-sum		Zero-sum	
	Direct	Indirect	Direct	Indirect
Trade				
Investment				
Aid				
Global governance				
Migration				
Environment				

China currently accounts for nearly 40 per cent of global soybeans consumption, while Latin America is the largest exporter of soybeans. A direct impact of China's trade with Latin America is the increased revenue these countries receive for their exports to China: a positive-sum impact. Soybeans are grown on large commercial plantations (see Figure 5.2) and tend to have a smaller contribution from small-scale farmers.

Figure 5.2   Soybean crops in Sorriso, Brazil

As more land is taken over by soybean cultivation, an indirect zero-sum impact of China's demand is felt by small-scale farmers in Latin American countries. There are reports of nearly 500 smallholders being relocated in Brazil to make way for commercial farming. In Argentina, 300 000 farm workers have lost their jobs as increased soybean cultivation makes less use of labour than other agricultural crops. There are also questions over the impact of land clearance for soybean farms on the environment.

Now let us consider the case of investment in Chambishi (Zambia) where China has helped to set up one of its first export processing zones in Africa, including a US$250–350 million investment in a copper smelter plant, one of the largest facilities in the region. The export processing zone has generated 3500 local jobs in the short term and 6000–7500 direct and 15 000 indirect jobs in Zambia in the medium to long term. This has a direct positive-sum impact on Zambia. On the other hand, the large smelter facility offers direct competition to established local smelter plants and takes away investment and trained workers from them: a zero-sum indirect impact.

China's low-priced manufactured exports and investment in other countries has a direct positive-sum effect. Consumers in developing countries have access to cheaper goods, and Foreign Direct Investment (FDI) creates jobs: a positive-sum direct effect. On the other side, domestic manufacturers, unable to compete with cheap Chinese imports (see Figure 5.3), are forced out of business. Foreign investors, finding cheaper wages and a more competitive business environment in China, move their business activity away from some developing countries: a zero-sum indirect effect. For example, in Chile, between 1990 and 2000, domestic manufacturing sectors that saw the highest import penetration by Chinese imports were also the ones to see the largest fall in total employment and value added. In Mexico a fall in employment of nearly 300 000 was reported by *maquilas* (small- to medium-scale Mexican firms) in the 2000–02 period as transnational corporations (TNCs) such as Phillips, Black and Decker, and Sanyo relocated operations from Mexico to China: a zero-sum indirect effect.

Figure 5.3 Chinese goods in a Vietnamese market

India's exports of low-cost generic drugs, particularly for HIV treatment, have a direct positive-sum effect on consumers in poor countries. India's private companies such as Tata Motors and Mittal Steel, in cooperation with the Indian government, which has provided finance, are making increased investments in transport and power sectors in many African countries: a direct positive-sum effect (see Chapter 7 for more detail on Indian TNCs). These companies bring in much needed investment but unless there are efforts made to include domestic producers and local content, these large Indian firms may take away markets from the local producers: a zero-sum indirect impact.

With India and Brazil soon to follow in China's footsteps, these impacts will continue to change our understanding of the development process and economic relationships. One of the areas where China has had a major impact on development relations is that of raw materials or commodities. Soft commodities refer to agricultural goods such as grains or cereals, while hard commodities refer to mineral and metal ores. Subsection 5.5.4 briefly looks at the hard commodities story and how China has changed it.

These examples given so far illustrate the changes China and India's growth have made on individual sectors and countries and present a micro picture of events. When seen from a global perspective, these changes are amplified. Let us consider these impacts at a more macro level in three important indicators: FDI, aid and trade.

5.5.2 Shifting patterns of Foreign Direct Investment flows

The United Nations Conference on Trade and Development (UNCTAD) defines FDI as an investment made to acquire lasting interest in enterprises operating outside of the economy of the investor. Further, in cases of FDI, the investor's purpose is to gain an effective voice in the management of the enterprise. FDI is measured in stock (value of assets over a period of time) and in flows (new capital in a given year). Inward FDI flows/stocks refer to the capital a country receives, while outflow refers to investments made by the country, or company, in other regions.

Traditionally the flow of FDI has been from the North to the North. In 1992, the developed world received nearly US$111 billion in FDI flows, compared to just US$53 billion by the developing world. By 2009, the scales had considerably shifted with the North receiving US$566 billion and the South a comparable US$478 billion. Figure 5.4 contrasts the share of the rising powers with Europe and the USA in global FDI flows.

In 1999, the rising powers had less than 10 per cent of the share, much smaller than that of Europe and the USA. However, by 2009 the rising powers had overtaken the share of the USA, while that of Europe was considerably lower than a decade ago. Overall the rising economies raised their share from just 6.5 per cent of global FDI flows in 1999 to nearly 13 per cent in 2009. This greater share of FDI flows suggests more production and business being generated in developing countries, which creates opportunities for workers to benefit from greater employment opportunities and increase in income levels.

While the rising powers have been receiving FDI, they have also taken the opportunity to invest in other developing countries, with China being the sixth largest source of FDI in the world in 2009. The rising powers are becoming an important source of investment for other countries, particularly developing ones. The level and scope of technology that they export is more easily adaptable to other developing countries, relative to the technologies imported

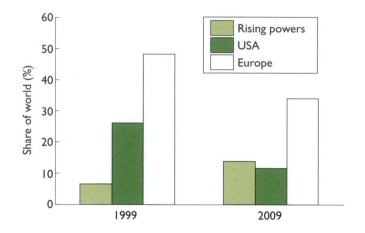

Figure 5.4 Percentage share of global Foreign Direct Investment inflows (rising powers include China, India and Brazil) in 1999 and 2009 (Source: UNCTAD, 2011)

from the North. The transfer of knowledge and skills is also easier in similar income level countries. The Indian, Brazilian and Chinese firms are used to working in often loosely regulated markets, and are more adaptable to working in other developing countries. This can have both a positive and negative impact. For example, while they can operate in countries where a constant electric supply is less than guaranteed they have also been known to pay less attention to labour and environmental standards. The case of TNCs from emerging economies is discussed in more detail in Chapter 7.

5.5.3 Shifting patterns of aid

The majority of **Official Development Assistance** (ODA) to developing countries is provided by the more advanced northern economies. However, since 2000 a number of new donors have emerged and the United Nations estimates that developing countries delivered between 7.8 per cent and 9.8 per cent of total aid flows in the decade 2000–10. These include Brazil, China, India, Malaysia, the Russian Federation, Thailand and oil-rich countries such as Saudi Arabia and Venezuela. The aid from these emerging donors still remains small: US$9077 million compared to the North's US$115 632 million in 2008. Although Saudi Arabia is the largest donor, China is the most influential donor (and the second largest by size) amongst the developing countries. Chapter 3 touched on this briefly when discussing the Kaplan extract and questions of soft power as well as in Chapter 4 on liberal interpretations of China's rise.

In recent decades, northern economies have increasingly given aid that has been untied, that is, aid that is not directly linked to a particular investment or trade agreement. The emerging economies in general, and China in particular, have a distinctive position by comparison to the northern economies. They exercise a much closer strategic integration of aid, trade and FDI. For example, China's integrated strategy in Africa is reflected in what has come to be called the 'Angolan mode' or the 'infrastructure for resources' approach. This is a scheme of financing in which China provides its large state-owned firms with export credits, securitized by access to an African country's resources through agreement with the government of the African economy. It builds into the loan considerable use of Chinese inputs, since the finance is secured in China and generally is limited to the use of Chinese (and some local) inputs.

Questions have been raised in international development about this form of aid from China. Critics argue that the strategy is self-serving in that they are trying to secure raw materials and markets for their own firms. Others argue that whatever the motivation, these countries do bring investment and know-how into developing countries.

Activity 5.2

Read the following news article published in *The Financial Times* in 2009. It reports on the case of the Democratic Republic of Congo (DRC) in Africa, as it found itself caught between the International Monetary Fund (IMF) and China. As you read the article, highlight the two different approaches that the IMF and China are taking in relation to the DRC, using them to answer the questions below.

Spend no more than 30 minutes on this activity.

1 What is the aid package that the Chinese are offering to the DRC?

2 What is the IMF insisting that the DRC do first?

3 Why do you think the two approaches differ?

> Revisions to one of China's most controversial investment deals in Africa will allow the Democratic Republic of Congo to take its first steps next week towards securing a new aid package from western donors who had objected to parts of the deal.
>
> The International Monetary Fund, which had pressed Congo to adjust its terms, 'congratulated' the government on Wednesday on making the revisions and said it would now begin the process of considering a new aid programme for the country.
>
> The deal has exemplified the tension between Chinese and western models of delivering aid to Africa as the cash-strapped Congolese government, in common with several others, has struggled to maintain access to both sources of financing.
>
> Years of war and mismanagement have left Congo one of Africa's most impoverished countries, in spite of its mineral wealth.
>
> The IMF signalled its intentions in a press release, two days after a summit in Egypt at which China pledged $10bn (€6.8bn, £6bn) of new low-cost loans to Africa and both sides lauded their relationship in the face of western critics who say China is exploiting the world's poorest continent.
>
> Under the minerals-for-infrastructure deal in Congo, initially valued at $9bn, a consortium of state-owned Chinese companies agreed to build roads, railways and hospitals in return for the right to develop a copper and cobalt mine. But against Chinese opposition, the IMF and the Paris Club of creditors urged Congo to make adjustments to

ensure the deal was consistent with Congo's management of its existing $11bn external debt.

After months of wrangling, the IMF said in August that Congo and China had agreed to two changes: eliminating a state guarantee on the $3bn mining project and reducing the overall size of the deal to $6bn by removing one of two $3bn tranches of infrastructure funding.

The IMF said it now expected to request financing assurances from Paris Club creditors … The fund requires those reassurances before it can consider a new three-year aid programme for Congo, which the government of President Joseph Kabila, who faces an election in 2011, urgently needs.

(Jopson and Wallis, 2009)

Discussion

There are two divergent approaches to aid highlighted in this article. On the one hand the Chinese government had offered an 'infrastructure for resources' deal to the DRC: they will build schools, roads and railways and in return they ask to be granted mining rights for copper and cobalt in the DRC.

The IMF on the other hand wants the DRC government to focus first on servicing its US$11 billion debt built up from the previous decades and requires assurances that the debt repayment will take precedence over any arrangements made with the Chinese. Without this commitment from the DRC, the IMF will not forward further loans to the country.

The Paris Club is an informal group of creditor governments that has met regularly in Paris since 1956 to reschedule bilateral debts. Creditors meet with individual debtor countries to negotiate debt issues, particularly when the country is pursuing an IMF-supported debt programme. It will therefore follow IMF directions.

At the time this discussion was written, the president of the DRC was facing an upcoming election! The approaches differ as the Chinese are more focused on accessing minerals (copper and cobalt) for their own economic growth and in return they will generate business for Chinese construction firms by building schools and infrastructure in the DRC. The IMF is more concerned with the idea of the DRC defaulting on its loans, which will make further loans to the country unviable as well as set a bad precedent for other developing countries who may follow suit.

Aid flows are just one avenue through which developing countries are affected by emerging powers and, as you read in Activity 5.2 in the case of the DRC, the method of delivering aid can differ between the traditional North and the emerging South. Another avenue of interaction is through international trade and again the economic nature of the trade partner can have an effect on the character of these flows. Chapter 11 will look at individual cases of how trade can impact development, but here we focus on the regional shift in trade patterns as a result of the economic growth of the emerging powers.

5.5.4 Shifting patterns of trade

In 1990, North–North trade dominated global flows, accounting for 58 per cent (US$2 trillion). But by 2008 this had fallen to 41% (US$6.6 trillion). Exports from the developing countries had increased from just 23% of global exports in 1990 to 37% in 2008. South–North trade increased from just US$0.52 trillion to US$3 trillion over the same period. As Figure 5.5 shows, a large amount of South–South trade is between the rising powers of China, India and Brazil.

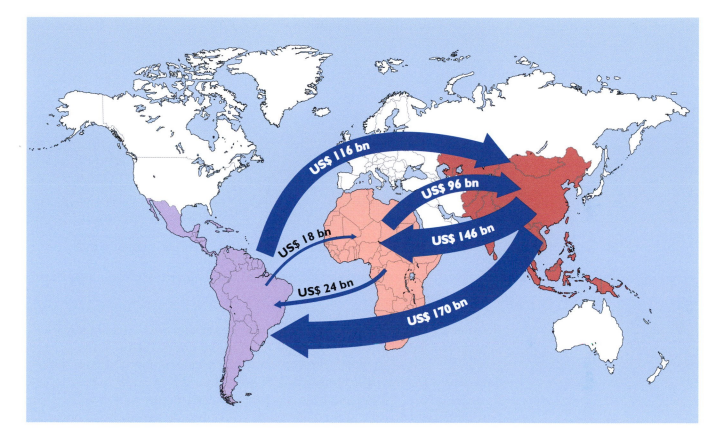

Figure 5.5 Inter-regional South–South trade flows in 2008 (US$billion) (Source: OECD, 2010, p. 72)

One of the major changes in international trade attributed to China's economic rise is the increase in commodity prices since 2003 and the impact this has had on the **terms of trade** for commodity producers. Prebisch (1950) and Singer (1950) observed the terms of trade declining over a period of time for primary commodities in relation to manufactures. This meant that commodity exporting countries were getting less manufactured imports for a single unit of their commodity exports. Looked at in a different way, commodity exporters had to pay more in commodities exported for each unit of manufactures they imported. Thus, developing countries, which were primary product exporters, became worse off over a period of time when trading with manufactures-exporting industrialized countries. From the 1950s onwards there has been pessimism in development policy about the natural resource sector and its possible contribution to development. Sachs and Warner (1995) argued that for a majority of countries that depended on their natural resources for growth, development levels had been much lower relative to other developing countries.

In late 2002 things began to change as the international prices for a number of primary commodities, particularly base metals, began to rise. Figure 5.6 shows the **price index** for major commodity groups for the period 1970–2010.

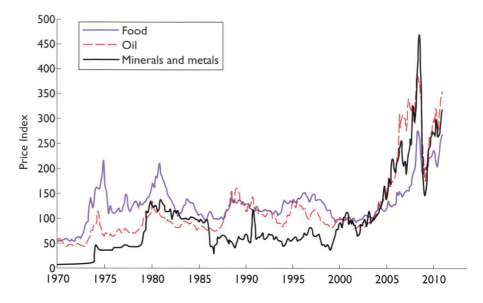

Figure 5.6   UNCTAD Monthly Commodity Price Index (200=100), 1970–2010 (Source: UNCTAD, 2010)

Between 1970 and 1980 there was a **price boom** that was linked mainly to the increase in oil prices. From 1980 to 2000 the prices for food, oil, minerals and metals tended to remain lower than in the previous period. From 2003 there was a steady rise in prices and, apart from a dip in 2008 (linked to a financial crisis), prices have been much higher than in any year before. This post-2003 period is the second commodity boom to be experienced since the 1970s.

Chinese demand, its resource-intensive economic growth linked to its expanding infrastructure and manufacturing base, has had a strong influence on the rise in commodity prices since 2003, allowing resource-rich developing countries to benefit from their natural wealth. Although a geographically large country, China is unable to meet most of its metal, energy and mineral demand from domestic resources and it relies on global commodity markets to fulfil its needs. The status of China as a developing country and not an advanced economy indicates that the country will continue its demand for commodities over the medium to long term. This means that its demand for raw materials will continue to be strong and prices of commodities will remain high in the medium term. African and Latin American countries that depend on these commodities for export revenues can therefore benefit from a medium-term rise in prices.

Commodity-led economic growth is not an easy task and accompanying stringent industrial and trade policies are important. However, commodity-exporting countries have an opportunity to benefit from this rise in prices in the medium term, particularly in Africa. In the period before the commodity price boom of 2003, sub-Saharan Africa's (SSA) economic growth rate averaged 3.5% per year (1995–2002), accelerating to 5% per year on average between 2003 and 2009. In 1995–2002, SSA received just US$66.9 billion in FDI, which more than doubled to US$162.87 billion in the 2003 to 2009 period. SSA's exports have also risen from just over US$100 billion in 2000 to over US$363 billion in 2008. A large share of the exports was commodities, of which nearly 20% was being shipped to the rising powers alone. Although there are a number of factors that have contributed to SSA's improved economic situation, the commodities sector has played an important role in its growth since 2003.

Within the rising powers, China accounts for a large share of these exports and has become one of the more important strategic partners in SSA's growth, linked to its largely under-developed reserves of oil, minerals and metals. In 2000, China accounted for 5% of SSA's exports to the world, but by 2008 this had increased to 14%, valued at US$51.6 billion. As Figure 5.7 indicates, China's imports from SSA are dominated by commodities, with oil, mineral and metal together accounting for nearly 89% of total exports to China. The share of manufactures and agricultural commodities remained below 10% between 2000 and 2009. China's interest in the commodities sector in Africa translates into increased investment, aid and trade for the continent.

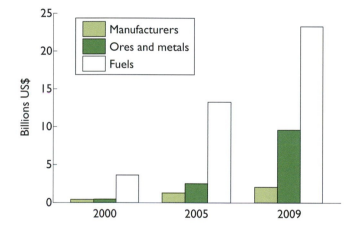

Figure 5.7 Profile of sub-Saharan Africa's exports to China (Source: COMTRADE, 2010)

China engages with a large number of African countries, often funding investment in regions that are considered politically risky by others. In terms of both trade and FDI, China's main endeavours have been in the oil and mineral sectors and in infrastructure. But the range of activities is growing rapidly, including small-scale businesses such as trading, restaurants, beauty salons and Chinese medicine centres, which Chapter 6 returns to. China's assistance to the continent has taken several forms, from health and education projects to the construction of official buildings, stadiums and roads. Trade has been dominated by oil imports and low- to medium-technology exports. There has been a significant strategic integration of aid and investment by the

Chinese and a concentration of activities in either oil- or mineral-rich economies (Angola, Nigeria and South Africa) or economies which offer potential as raw material suppliers in the future (Democratic Republic of Congo).

Summary and looking forward

The rise of Brazil, India and China is not the first shift in power that the world has seen. However, in today's highly connected markets the choices and changes made in one region impact upon others very quickly. From World War II to the late 1990s the direction of impact was mainly from the developed North to the developing South. With the rising powers in the South, this flow is now changing, with more power to affect international development coming to the developing countries. As the OECD report which opened this chapter concludes:

> Rather than see the 'rise of the rest' in terms of the 'decline of the west', policy makers should recognize that the net gains from increased prosperity of the developing world can benefit both rich and poor countries alike. Improvements in the range and quality of exports, greater technological dynamism, better prospects for doing business, a larger consumption base – all these factors can create substantial welfare benefits for the whole world.

> That is not to deny the challenges. Environmental sustainability, growing levels of inequality within countries and increased competition are three significant issues raised by shifting wealth. The birth pains of this new economic world order have also been accompanied by enormous global imbalances … Despite these challenges … the overall picture is a positive one for development.

> *(OECD, 2010, p. 20)*

Much of the discussion around the rising powers in the current international development stage comes from their economic growth and their ability to influence global production and consumption networks. In the 1970s and 1980s countries such as Japan, Singapore, Taiwan and South Korea also experienced accelerated economic growth and so we asked why the economic expansion of the rising powers was of such great interest to us. In this chapter we:

- considered the patterns of economic growth in general and those particular to Brazil, India and China

- discussed how the large size and the developing country status of these particular countries can drive changes in other developing countries. Their rising income levels generate demand for consumer goods and in turn raw materials

- developed a conceptual framework to help us map the positive- and zero-sum impacts that the rising powers can have through various channels. Apart from individual sectors we also saw how the rising powers have caused a shift in traditional patterns of international investment, aid and trade

- focused on the case of commodity prices, where China's growth has made it possible for African countries to benefit from increased investments and trade in commodities.

All of these impacts may not be positive and there will be an adjustment as the world changes the way it does business. Crucially we saw that these transformations set up flows which we only touched upon here: namely urbanization, migration and the environment. It is to these that we turn in Chapter 6.

References

COMTRADE (2010) *United Nations Commodity Trade Statistics Database* [online], available at http://comtrade.un.org/ (Accessed November 2010).

Jopson, B. and Wallis, W. (2009) 'Congo cuts back aid deal with China', *The Financial Times*, 11 November 2009.

Organization for Economic Cooperation and Development (OECD) (2010) *Perspectives on Global Development: Shifting Wealth*, 2010, Paris, OECD.

Prebisch, R. (1950) *The Economic Development of Latin America and Its Principle Problem*, Santiago, UNECLA.

Sachs, J.D. and Warner, A.M. (1995) 'Natural resource abundance and economic growth', *National Bureau of Economic Research Working Paper 6398*, Cambridge, MA, National Bureau of Economic Research.

Singer, H.W. (1950) 'The distribution of gains between investing and borrowing countries', *American Economic Review, Papers and Proceedings*, vol. 40, pp. 473–85.

United Nations Conference on Trade and Development (UNCTAD) (2010) *Commodity Price Statistics* [online] http://unctadstat.unctad.org (Accessed February 2011).

United Nations Conference on Trade and Development (UNCTAD) (2011) *UNCTADSTAT: Foreign Direct Investment* [online] http://unctadstat.unctad.org/ (Accessed February 2011).

World Bank (2011a) *ICT at a Glance: Definitions and Sources* [online] http://www.worldbank.org/ (Accessed June 2011).

World Bank (2011b) *World Development Indicators* [online] http://data.worldbank.org/data-catalog/world-development-indicator (Accessed February 2011).

Spaces of development: cities, mobilities and ecologies

Giles Mohan and Melissa Butcher

Introduction

After World War II the UK economy needed reviving, but labour was in short supply. In response, the UK government turned to its former and current colonies for workers to help rebuild the so-called 'motherland'. Many came from the Caribbean and South Asia. A former troop ship, the SS Empire Windrush (see Figure 6.1), was used to bring migrants from the Caribbean to London (see Figure 6.2). Here is a personal account, in the form of a poem, from one of these migrants. As you read it, think about the migrant's aspirations compared with the reality of the situation:

> It was 1948 on the Windrush ship. 500 men from the Caribbean was on it from warm Caribbean sand, to this cold English land. We spent twenty eight day on the ship and everyone felt real sick. … The ship docked at Tilbury, everyone began to feel merry setting foot in the mother country. Looking round it wasn't jolly, not what we imagined. The scene was drab and gloomy with plenty of chimneys that looked like factories. And so we stepped on the hallowed British soil, and looked forward to a future we dreamt would be better on this our English adventure. For many the years were rough in fact it was rough and tough. Couldn't find any place to rest our head a little. … No dogs, No Irish, No Blacks, here in the mother country Britain. Some started working all the hours God given just to make a shilling. … We the pioneers have laid a solid foundation in Britain through blood, sweat and tears, in the heat and the cold. There's NO Street Filled with Gold, that was just a story we were told. The gold is the jewel inside developed through the suffering fires of time.
>
> *(Stewart, n.d.)*

Figure 6.1   SS Empire Windrush

SOME OF THE JAMAICANS ON BOARD THE "EMPIRE WINDRUSH" : They are here to seek for work which their own island cannot provide.

Figure 6.2   Migrants from the Caribbean to London

There is clearly a lot of hope about what coming to 'the mother country' might bring. There is talk of feeling 'merry', 'future dreams' and later on a contrast with what the poet believed were 'streets of gold'. The promise was of economic prosperity and good treatment in what was a powerful nation, despite the USA taking over from Britain as the global hegemonic power, as discussed in Chapter 3. The reality was very different – dirty factories, racism and low wages. Ultimately, though, there was a sense of hope as the offspring inherited a Britain that was somewhat more tolerant and it seemed worth the 'suffering fires of time'.

Powerful stories like this have been repeated the world over as migrants set off for better times, often to be thwarted. What does it tell us about the interconnectedness of development? Remember, Chapter 3 briefly touched on the triangular slave trade. The ancestors of these Windrush pioneers were African slaves who, following the abolition of slavery, had gradually fashioned new, multicultural nations in the Caribbean. Still yoked to Britain by its Commonwealth they were now enticed back across the Atlantic to the heart of the empire – London – to once again work for the good of another society. Here are multiple connections between different places, phases of development and periods in the cycle of world powers. And in London they encountered another formerly colonized, migrant community – the Irish – who were also treated with disdain. As a powerful nation the UK forged connections around the world through trade, diplomacy and colonization, but later the 'empire struck back' as colonized peoples came to the UK creating multi-ethnic cities like London, Manchester and Birmingham. These were centres of manufacturing and commerce, but also contained pockets of deep poverty and with all of this came pollution and degradation – 'drab and gloomy' in the words of Stewart. As cities concentrate people and economic activities, they can also become sites of environmental change.

This chapter examines these complex connections in the context of the 'newer' rising powers. It develops the discussions in Chapter 2 about power and scale. There you were introduced to development at local, national and international scales. For example, Brazil developed nationally in a unique way but was also always tied into international relations with others. Here we want to complicate this story by looking at multiple and overlapping connections, of the type that Stewart demonstrated. Chapter 5 examined some of the economic interconnections between the rising powers and less developed countries but the connections we look at in this chapter, while having economic roots, are also more diverse in covering social and environmental flows. With this in mind this chapter asks the following:

- How are space and scale related in the context of the development of the rising powers?

- To what extent and in what ways are power and production concentrated in some places?

- What sorts of 'non-economic' flows does development set in motion and how do these relate to economic forces?

- How does economic activity engender environmental impacts that may affect more distant places?

In terms of the first question, the importance of the concept of scale was outlined in Chapter 2 and will be elaborated on here as we see the interconnections between space, scale and development in three case studies. The complex relationship between cities, migration and the environment will frame the narrative of the rest of the chapter.

The example above focused on migrants coming to London. The city was seen to capture the symbolic essence of British power, with a poem by Berry (2007) exclaiming:

> Now – when I get to Landan
> I jus wahn to stan-up
> unda that striking Big Ben

Big Ben is seen to embody the power and values of British civilization, which did not live up to the expectations of the new migrants. However, London was (and is) a major centre in world trade, production and finance. It grew up in tandem with British mercantilism and colonialism, discussed in Chapter 3, as a source of finance for overseas ventures and, crucially, insurance for ships and their precious cargos. It was also a centre of manufacturing and processing of imports as well as the seat of government. Hence, it became and remains a centre of coordination for connections to similar cities around the globe. In all phases of the rising powers and industrial development cities have grown up as part of that process and *concentrate economic control and production while also connecting to other cities*. This is the first of our linkages between development and space.

But all this activity tends to require people as labour. As cities grow they suck in labour from the surrounding countryside in a process of structural change that sees the relative weakening of agriculture in national development, as discussed in Chapter 5. This means migration from the countryside to the city and also from 'foreign' places to these growing cities. In the case of the Windrush generation it was a planned emigration instigated by the UK government. But migration – internally or internationally – can also be unplanned and down to the agency of individuals. It also goes in multiple directions. One of the key flows is international migration *from* a rising power to areas that serve an important economic or political function for that country. The UK saw high levels of outward migration during the colonial period as people went in search of economic opportunities or to service the empire. Today we see migrants from rising power countries also heading for areas where new opportunities are greatest, linking their countries into transnational networks. In the past, as seen in previous chapters, Brazil, India and China were poor and at times politically repressive, spurring many to leave. They still have massive levels of inequality and poverty that continues to drive outward migration. These so called **diasporas** are spread around the world in many advanced economies where economic and educational opportunities are better. Once the rising powers began to liberalize, some of these diasporic individuals returned to their 'homeland' or at least started to do business there and in turn have contributed to their economic transformation. So, international mobility is part and parcel of the development of the rising powers and puts in place *networks of exchanges* *between people and places*. This is the second of the linkages between development and space.

These two geographies of development – urban centres of control and production, and the transnational networking of people and places – produce forces that both concentrate and disperse. People, houses, factories, offices and transport hubs are concentrated in close proximity. But at the same time there are two-way connections to far-flung places where opportunities are greatest. All this economic activity has environmental impacts, be it pollution or the transfer of land or resources from one use to another. Sometimes these impacts are localized, as when a small factory dumps rubbish in the street. But other times these impacts do not stay locally contained and spread out to affect other people and places, such as through greenhouse gases from an industry affecting climate change. And don't forget that these economic activities in particular 'local' places – such as the growing of a food crop in a field – may connect to distant markets where the environmental impact goes unseen. So, economic development can *deplete the environment and spill over into other spaces*. This is the third linkage between development and space introduced in this chapter.

The next three sections expand on each of these in turn. Section 6.1 looks at the rise of global cities as centres of power in the international system and which also attract internal and international migrants. Section 6.2 develops this by looking at international migration in two directions – from a rising power to a less developed country and from a developed country back to a rising power – which link to different forms and understandings of development. Section 6.3 examines how economic development creates environmental impacts in one place, but also how international flows and interactions spread these impacts to other places.

6.1 Global cities and new centres of power

So far development at particular scales has been discussed. One has been the international scale, such as shifts in global hegemony, and another is the national scale where we have looked at bilateral trade or national development planning. Implicitly we have treated the national scale as quite uniform and not really looked at unevenness *within* a national economy in terms of our concern with power. However, in previous chapters we have discussed how industrialization sees a shift from agriculture in the country to industries in urban areas. We have mentioned cities such as London, Calcutta, Sao Paulo, Detroit, Shanghai, Moscow and Washington DC. These cities are important places in the story of power in the international system and often where industrial and service sector growth is most intense.

An important tipping point was reached in 2005 when it was estimated that more people inhabited urban centres than rural ones, with much of this growth in urbanization happening in the global South. While in developed countries many major cities are experiencing a decline, with people moving away because of urban decay (for example, Detroit), in the global South cities have become sites of economic opportunity and access to better facilities as well as concentrating inequalities and environmental problems.

In the approaches to development that you read about in Chapter 2 it was generally assumed that increasing urbanization, that is, the proportion of people living in cities, was part of the historical development of countries from rural, agrarian-based economies into so-called modern, industrial societies, following the model provided by European states. This process of urbanization has led to new forms of inequalities within cities, but cities can also highlight inequalities when they are compared against each other. For example, since the 1990s, researchers such as Saskia Sassen have argued that there is a network of powerful cities that function as hubs on which the global economy now depends. These have become known as 'global cities'.

6.1.1 The global city

Global cities, such as London and New York, act as hubs for the networks that sustain the global economy. They can be thought of as transmission points, coordinating the flow of local, regional and national resources, goods, money, people and information, around the globe and back again. According to Knox (2002), these cities are defined by their interconnectedness with each other through their concentration of:

- investment capital and financial markets (think about where major stock exchanges are based)

- clusters of specialized, high-value business services, for example legal services and property development

- major transnational and national corporate headquarters; trade and professional associations (for example, the International Association of Chartered Certified Accountants is based in London)

- headquarters for non-governmental organizations (NGOs) and media institutions.

As well as high-end and specialized work, particularly in the financial services sector, these cities attract and depend on lesser skilled service industries that fulfil a series of functions integral to that economy, for example hospitality and cleaning.

This critical mass of facilities, human resources and support services provides a high-tech infrastructure for activities that are necessary to run advanced capitalist economies, such as coordinating transnational organizations (TNCs), international banking, supranational government (for example, the EU) and the work of international agencies such as the United Nations (UN). The Globalization and World Cities (GaWC) Research Centre at Loughborough University has ranked over 100 cities by measuring their interconnectedness, and created a ranking system from Alpha++ to Gamma (GaWC, 2008). According to their measurements, London and New York are the prime examples of powerful cities coordinating the global economy.

Cities have always played an important role in international relationships and trade, with each new phase of a rising power connected to an important city. Legendary Greek city states such as Sparta and Athens gained power through military and cultural dominance. In the Middle Ages, cities such as Samarkand (in Uzbekistan) became prosperous because of their location on the Silk Route between China and Europe, which was mentioned in Chapter 3, while the Republic of Venice became a maritime power in the Mediterranean. In the 16th century, Lisbon became rich as a European hub for trade with Portuguese colonies in Africa, Asia and Brazil, and Amsterdam flourished during its 'Golden Age' in the 17th century, as a financial centre and hub for the diamond trade.

There are marked similarities between these powerful cities of the past with today's global cities, for example a good location and global connections with an expansive empire. So what makes today's global cities different? One argument is that it is the scale of their interconnectedness brought about by new communication and information technology and the ease and speed of international travel today. Knox (2002, p. 330) has also argued that it is 'the expanded management, planning and control operations of transnational corporations that have formed the nucleus of contemporary world-city formation'. The dominant economic model of neoliberalism at the core of the global economy (discussed in Chapter 2) encourages city authorities to invest in innovative research and high-tech infrastructure, but also to create incentives (for example, business parks, or a supply of skilled and unskilled labour) in order to attract foreign investment. The proliferation of international NGOs is also a relatively new phenomenon in the history of cities. Organizations such as Greenpeace, Amnesty International and the International Crisis Group require a presence in centres of international influence, such as London, New York, Brussels and Geneva.

However, there are remnants of the past that still impact on why some cities have attained global city status and others not. Note the location of Alpha global cities in 2008 in Figure 6.3.

We can see the dominance of European and North American cities. In other words, those cities at the centre of the economically powerful countries in the 20th century are the chief Alpha cities today. Wealthy economies were able to develop resources such as the technology necessary to run a sophisticated financial services industry that provided a comparative advantage for London and New York, for example. But from this map we can also see that Alpha global cities have emerged in the new rising powers as they develop the necessary infrastructure, in particular in China and the Southeast Asian hubs of Singapore, Kuala Lumpur and Bangkok. Key cities in the global network are also emerging in South America, notably Sao Paolo and Mexico City. This rise in the number of global cities in the global South can then be said to mirror the rise and fall of powers discussed in previous chapters. We might then expect that some of today's Alpha cities may lose that status in the future just as cities such as Amsterdam or Lisbon are no longer as globally important as they once were (although they are still minor Alpha cities according to the GaWC).

While the phenomenon of global cities may present a critical mass of opportunities (including creative as well as corporate industries) they have also generated problems. They have been criticized for having the potential to bypass the power of the state to the detriment of citizens, and the massive wealth they can generate is often under conditions of intense inequality (Sassen, 2001). There is competition between them and competition to become

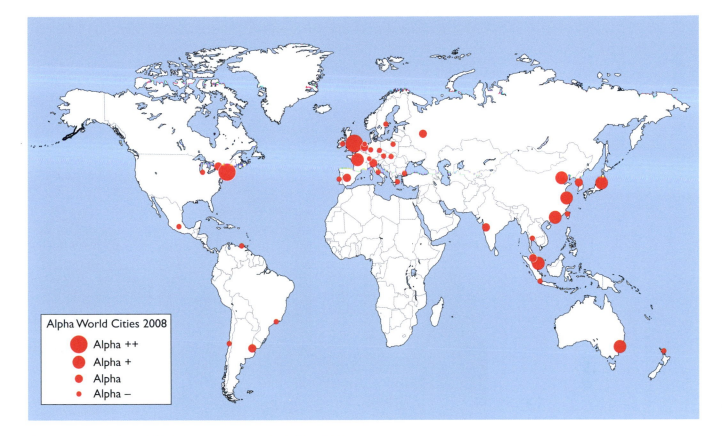

Figure 6.3 Alpha global cities (Source: GaWC, 2008)

one in order to attract more investment. Such is the perceived success of these cities that urban authorities in both the global North and South have attempted to put in place redevelopment schemes in order to try to obtain global city status, to attract more international investment. These policies have been criticized for imposing a model of urban life that favours elites and marginalizes the poor through:

- concentrating investment in high-end redevelopment projects
- intensifying state intervention such as demolitions of public housing and 'illegal' settlements
- introducing policies that explicitly fragment cities into 'deserving' and 'undeserving' areas for state support (Wilson, 2007, p. 36).

We can see the pressure on cities to conform to this model of urban development in the case of New Delhi (see Box 6.1).

Box 6.1 New Delhi

According to the GaWC index, New Delhi is a Beta+ city, so not quite an Alpha city yet, but it is striving for that status. In an effort to raise its profile Delhi began a massive programme of redevelopment to transform the city from that of a developing country to one comparable to other global cities in the world (Ministry of Urban Development, 2007). As a result, new residential and shopping enclaves have been developed within and around the edges of the city, marked by condominiums (see Figure 6.4), malls and facilities such as health, education, leisure centres and landscaped gardens.

Figure 6.4 Condominiums in Gurgaon, Delhi, 2007. Melissa Butcher

Often advertized as offering 'world class' or 'global' living, these centres are aimed at India's new middle classes who have benefited from policies of economic liberalization since 1991 (see Brosius, 2008; discussed further in Chapter 3). Hosting the Commonwealth Games in 2010 was also an opportunity to revamp the city's infrastructure, just as Beijing had done for the Olympics in 2008.

But there are other types of transformations happening as well. 'Cleaning up' the city has meant the removal of shanty towns, *jhuggis*, the closure of small traders, and whole neighbourhoods of rural migrants and poorer populations being demolished and their residents forced to move to outlying areas of the city. Those that have been displaced from inner city settlements such as Nangla Maanchi (an area demolished in 2006, displacing some 30 000 people) have been resettled in new townships on the outskirts of the city, such as Ghevra (see Figure 6.5), where infrastructure such as water supply, sanitation and schools was not yet built when the new residents began to arrive.

Figure 6.5   Ghevra, 2009. Melissa Butcher

Most of the residents were also removed from their informal employment networks near their old home (trading centres such as Old Delhi) and were now unemployed. The idea of 'geographies of margins and centres' (Sassen, 2001) is clearly seen in this spatial marginalization of those at the economic edge of the city.

Activity 6.1

Think about your city, or the nearest city to where you live. Have you noticed any changes in the city over the past few years and can you link those changes to some of the discussion above? For example, who have the changes benefited? Would you say the changes have been for the better? Who is involved in making decisions about how a city should develop?

Spend no more than 15 minutes on this activity.

In the case of New Delhi we can see the power dynamics at play. First, there is a cultural hegemony in the spread of a dominant model of urban planning associated with becoming a global city. Second, as we are seeing in other cities throughout Asia and Europe, there is the use of force or pricing to move poor and working class populations out of areas of the city that become gentrified and unaffordable. In this sense, the drive to become a global city is a powerful tool for creating urban and social change.

6.2 Networks of exchange: international migration and development

Urbanization and industrialization both capture the national processes of transformation central to the development process and indicate how connections beyond the local are forged and coordinated. The New Delhi case showed that migration to cities is inherent in this transformation. People migrate for many reasons but it is generally for a 'better life' of some sort that ties their mobility into development in a number of ways. While migration might be a general feature of society it is especially important during the growth of a rising power. Chapter 3 briefly touched upon 19th century colonialism when many people left Europe to make a living or to actively govern 'the locals' in far flung parts of their respective empires. When the USA industrialized in the late 19th and early 20th centuries it required huge amounts of cheap labour and actively encouraged migrants from Europe – such as Scandinavia, Italy and Ireland – to settle in the growing industrial cities like Detroit and Chicago. And now, with China, India and Brazil developing rapidly, we see a new wave of migration to and from these rising powers. This section is not going to explore the richness of all these migration and development stories. Rather it will focus on two that relate to India and China. The first example is the migration of Chinese entrepreneurs with skills and resources who have entered the 'frontiers' of development in parts of Africa. The second is a story of circulation in which highly skilled and relatively affluent Indian and Chinese migrants help drive development in their countries of origin.

6.2.1 Chinese entrepreneurs in Africa

The preceding discussion suggested that it is unwise to lump all migrants together. Rather we need to consider:

- who they are
- why they migrated
- what resources they have
- what they do once they resettle
- what impacts this has locally and for their wider networks.

Migration is motivated by many factors, and links to development in many ways, often in a circular fashion. For some, migration might be a response to a development intervention, such as a large dam where local communities are forced to move. It may be less direct but no less urgent as when people leave one place to seek a better life because of a dictatorial government or a very unstable economy. This latter situation was seen in the context of Zimbabwe in the early 2000s when many people migrated to South Africa to escape persecution and an economy in free fall. Others might migrate within their own country to take up jobs in a new manufacturing zone as seen taking place in China. And business executives are relocating to places where market opportunities are greatest. All these are forms of migration, but they clearly have different motivations, are driven by different social groups, and occur at different periods in history and with different impacts on development.

Migration from China to Africa arguably began way back in the 15th century with the naval mission of Zheng He to East Africa (noted in Chapter 3). However, the main impetus was after the **Opium Wars** of the 1840s and 1850s when China was forced by the colonial powers to reduce restrictions on Chinese emigration. This saw the beginning of large-scale movements of Chinese overseas in the form of the 'coolie trade' (see Figure 6.6). Most of these labour contracts were highly regulated and workers were sent back after their contracts expired, much like many of today's labour contractors in the Middle East. There were also small, but enterprising groups of independent traders that serviced Chinese labour migrants and undertook small-scale export.

Chinese Merchants and Coolie.

Figure 6.6 Chinese coolies

In 1949, when the Peoples Republic of China (PRC) was formed, there was a reversal of policy, and emigration was officially ended. During the Cold War, geopolitical strategy was played out in Africa with China challenging the major superpowers through its conspicuous targeting of aid. Between the 1960s and the beginning of the 1980s (with the exception of the Cultural Revolution), at least 150 000 Chinese technical assistants were dispatched to Africa (ECOWAS-SWAC/OECD, 2006). Although the numbers of aid workers was not huge and many stayed only temporarily, a significant number stayed on to engage in commercial activities.

More recently, given the need to access resources for industrial development and urbanization that was discussed in Chapter 5, Africa has become very important in China's (and to a lesser extent Brazil's and India's) economic and political strategies. This has seen the governments of these rising powers making 'soft power' overtures to these countries as seen in the opening extract of Chapter 3 by Kaplan. In terms of thinking about development processes, Alden (2007, p. 128) has noted: 'The behaviour of thousands of newly settled Chinese businessmen and the conduct of the African communities in which they live and work will matter as much as the diplomacy and concessions made at the government level.' Here he is saying that these high-level diplomatic interactions are important for securing Chinese resources and for the recipient governments who benefit from the aid and infrastructure deals they bring. But to understand China's impacts on African development more thoroughly we must also be attentive to the interactions at the 'everyday' level and move away from the state-to-state scale, which has dominated discussions in international relations.

Migrant flows to Africa are differentiated, with three distinct groups. First are temporary labour migrants usually associated with large infrastructure projects being built by Chinese state-owned enterprises (SOEs). They tend to be run by Chinese expatriates on fixed-term contracts who return home after a few years. Figure 6.7 shows a Chinese engineer from a large Chinese SOE working with a Ghanaian labourer on a hydroelectric dam project. The second group is petty entrepreneurs who largely operate in trade, services and light manufacturing and lack any government backing. Third are undocumented migrants that purposefully evade state surveillance (Mung, 2008).

Figure 6.7 Chinese engineer with a Ghanaian worker on a construction site in Ghana

Activity 6.2

Read the following extract by Haugen and Carling (2005), which relates to the second of the groups identified above – petty entrepreneurs. Note that 'baihuo' means 'general merchandise' in Chinese. As you read the extract consider the following questions:

- Who are the migrants?
- Why have they migrated?
- What resources (material as well as skills) do they migrate with?
- What do they do once they resettle?
- What impacts does this have locally and for their wider networks?

Spend no more than 20 minutes on this activity.

Cape Verde was apparently not a destination in Chinese migration flows within the Portuguese colonial empire … Only with the growth of the baihuo business in the late 1990s, however, was there a sharp increase in the number of Chinese residents. Today, the number probably stands at between 200 and 300 people. While this is minute in the context of the Chinese diaspora, it is sufficiently large to have had a momentous impact on the society and economy of Cape Verde. There are now baihuo shops in every urban centre in the country; on certain streets in the centres of the country's two cities, virtually every second establishment is a baihuo shop.

…

Emigration from China has grown to unprecedented levels since the onset of reforms in 1978 and the liberalization of emigration legislation in 1985. … There has been a heterogeneous migration flow to different parts of the world. A conspicuous component has been what can be called the new entrepreneurial migration. The migrants concerned do not enter established wage-labour markets in existing communities of overseas Chinese but set up their own businesses most commonly engaged in the retail or wholesale of Chinese goods, Chinese restaurants or traditional Chinese clinics. This migration flow also includes workers who are not entrepreneurs themselves but who work for relatives and often aspire to become self-employed in the same line of business.

…

Despite the shortcomings of Cape Verde, most of the Chinese entrepreneurs did not see Europe as being better in terms of opportunity. Many of the Chinese in Cape Verde have close relatives in Europe and therefore have not only first-hand information but also the necessary contacts to make onward migration a realistic option. However, they were reluctant to move to Europe because of exploitative employment conditions and a difficult business climate. The shop owners greatly appreciated the freedom and control they have in Cape Verde, and contrasted this with what they had heard about Europe. As one girl put it, 'In Europe there have been Chinese running businesses for sixty years, so it's hard to manage'. Furthermore, the Chinese in Cape Verde appreciated the respect they enjoyed due to their economic position. 'Chinese in Cape Verde are seen as having a good economy, so people will not look down upon you,' one woman said. 'But if you go to Europe you will be in the lowest social stratum. Yellow people and black people are put in the same category. They do the dirty work.'

…

Every baihuo shop sells Chinese clothes, shoes, travel accessories, knick-knacks, kitchenware and framed pictures with motives ranging from Chinese pin-ups to romantic landscapes and the Virgin Mary. About half also sell consumer electronics such as television sets and tape recorders. Toys are a seasonal product that every shop stocks in the Christmas period, but not necessarily throughout the year. The selection of goods is similar to that of the Chinese retail trade in Central and Eastern Europe. …The goods are cheap, and their quality is often poor. Most Chinese shop owners in Sao Vicente go to China at least once a year to import goods to sell in their shops. ... Typically, goods have to be sold in Cape Verde at more than three times their original price to cover the costs of transportation, import duties and operating costs.

...

The Chinese shops have managed to capture a large proportion of both ends of the Cape Verdean market by providing fashionable goods cheaply. At the lower end, this has resulted in a transformation of business at the municipal market. Many of the stalls have now closed, and those that are still in business specialize increasingly in goods other than clothes. At the top end, many boutiques have suffered competition as a result of the increasingly fashionable stock of the baihuo shops.... Chinese and Cape Verdeans alike commonly assert that the living standard of poor Cape Verdeans has improved with the entry of the Chinese. One shop owner had 'heard that before the Chinese came, very few people wore shoes. At least now they have shoes.' Locals confirm this, saying that the arrival of the Chinese has meant that children in Cape Verde no longer need to go barefoot to school. The other, equally emotive example frequently referred to by Cape Verdeans is that now all parents can afford to buy their children Christmas presents.

(Haugen and Carling, 2008)

Discussion

The article talks about the migrants coming from mainland China and once this flow is established it seems to be self-propelling as they call on relatives to fulfil various tasks. These migrants are entrepreneurs who have entered business for the first time but who felt that the competition, restrictions and racism of Europe did not make it an attractive destination. Instead they talk about how in Cape Verde they are treated with more respect and in some ways similar to the local African populations. The authors also talk about legislative changes in China allied to the liberalization of the economy that has made migration internally and internationally much easier. The Chinese state has also facilitated this internationalization through its diplomacy – 'soft power' in the words of the Kaplan extract in Chapter 3 – by opening up embassies in Cape Verde.

The Chinese migrants entered a new niche around trading in Chinese manufactured goods and providing 'Chinese' services in the form of food and herbal medicines. The extract discusses at some length the nature of these goods, which are essentially cheaply made and low cost but still three times their original price to take into account operating and transportation costs. These goods serve the needs of poorer consumers and so the traders seem to be welcomed and the Cape Verdean consumers also benefit. This, then, is a positive-sum relationship and the point is made that even a few Chinese traders can have a large impact. However, there is evidence that some Cape Verdean traders have suffered from the competition of the baihou shops.

In terms of development as a process of interactions there is an interesting quote about how the Chinese and Africans are the same. Although the woman who is quoted recognizes the racial differences ('yellow people' and 'black people') she frames this in terms of an international division of labour in which both races do 'dirty work'. Although not explicitly stated there is a question behind this – dirty work for whom? This brings us back to questions of hegemony and racism in the international system.

The study suggests that positive impacts on development can be felt through the cheap commodities these Chinese traders bring. In our framework this is a positive-sum scenario because the Chinese manufacturers, Chinese traders and African consumers all benefit. It shows interactions in which Chinese people and goods travel 'out' of China and have developmental impacts in the places they settle due to the goods they sell, the people they employ or the social relationships they form. But are there flows in the other direction, namely 'back to' China?

6.2.2 The brain gain

One of the major drivers of the economic development of China and India – and with it a whole series of cultural and social changes that we touched upon in the previous section on global cities – is the role of their respective diasporas. Migration from India and China was boosted during the colonial period and continued after independence as migrants left for education or employment. In the case of China this outward migration was more restricted by the state but in both cases these countries had sizeable diasporas across Southeast Asia, North America and Western Europe. With the benefits of education and/or entrepreneurial success these migrants had the potential to contribute to the development of their 'homelands' to which they were either directly or culturally attached. In the case of China, the diaspora was extremely influential in investing in the productive capacities that have fired the economic development in the Special Economic Zones (SEZs) along the southern coastal regions, such as Shenzhen (see Figure 6.8a). In India highly skilled migrants have been behind some of the development in India's IT sector, concentrated in a number of cities like Bangalore (see Figure 6.8b) in the south of the country, earning the region the title of 'Silicon Plateau' in contrast to 'Silicon Valley' in California. Here, then, is where international migration and transfers of knowledge back to the rising power have been crucial for its development.

In much of the migration and development literature, as well as policy making, a distinction is made between 'brain drain' and 'brain gain'. When skilled migrants leave a less developed country they take valuable material and mental assets with them which further undermines development. As one policy document puts it:

> The main concern, from a developmental perspective, on the outward flow of skilled people from the developing world arises from the negative consequences on growth and income levels back home. In addition to the

Figure 6.8   (a) Shenzhen, China

Figure 6.8   (b) Bangalore, India

unaffordable loss of the considerable investment undertaken in generating these skills, already poor source countries lose their potentially most enterprising and ambitious young population, limiting future leadership and stifling the development of a more dynamic private sector.

(UNDP, 2007, p. 1)

This is called the 'brain drain' and is more of a zero-sum effect – the gain for the country receiving the migrant is at the cost of the country from which they originate. But what happens if these skilled migrants, or their well-educated offspring, return to the sending country? This is called the 'brain gain' and according to the same document concerns 'the knowledge and skills contribution of migrants outside of their country as potential resources for the socio-economic development of their home country' (UNDP, 2007, p. 1). This is about 'the knowledge elite' who either return or build networks linking themselves to their homeland without actually living there. The benefits are multiple around remittances, education and entrepreneurship.

Activity 6.3

Read the following extract by Saxenian (2005). Picking up on the idea of 'brain gain' how does Saxenian see the role of Chinese and Indian migrants in the development of China and India respectively? What types of connections do they establish? Who benefits from these and over what scale? What are the knock-on effects of this for social change?

Spend no more than 20 minutes on this activity.

> Much of the movement of skilled individuals from developing to advanced countries during the latter part of the twentieth century has involved migration to the United States, specifically Silicon Valley. The region's technology producers grew very rapidly from the 1970s through the 1990s, absorbing scientists and engineers voraciously and irrespective of national origin. Tens of thousands of immigrants from developing countries, who had initially come to the U.S. for graduate engineering education, accepted jobs in Silicon Valley rather than return to their home countries, where professional opportunities were limited. By 2000, over half (53%) of Silicon Valley's scientists and engineers were foreign-born. Indian and Chinese immigrants alone accounted for over one-quarter of the region's scientists and engineers.
>
> …
>
> the same individuals who left their home countries for better lifestyles abroad are now reversing the brain drain, transforming it into 'brain circulation' as they return home to establish business relationships or to start new companies while maintaining their social and professional ties to the United States. When foreign-educated venture capitalists invest in their home countries, they transfer first-hand knowledge of the financial institutions of the new economy to peripheral regions. These individuals, often among the earliest returnees, also typically serve as advisers to domestic policymakers who are anxious to promote technology growth. As experienced engineers and managers return home, either temporarily or permanently, they bring the worldviews and identities that grow out of their shared professional and educational experiences. These cross-regional technical communities have the potential to jumpstart local entrepreneurship, and they succeed over the long term to the extent that they build alliances with technical professionals, businesses, and policymakers in their home countries.
>
> …
>
> The entrepreneurial ecosystem is still in its formative stages in the technology regions of India and China. These regions have seen important early entrepreneurial successes, and both have large

technically skilled workforces willing to work very hard for relatively low wages ... Returning Chinese entrepreneurs have focused primarily on developing products to serve the domestic market, while their Indian counterparts are oriented toward providing software and other services for export.

...

The dynamism of these technology regions is not reducible to cost advantages. Investors in India and China may have initially been motivated by the availability of low-cost skill, but the concentration of technology production has already generated rapidly rising wages and intensifying congestion in these regional economies. Engineering salaries in both Bangalore and Shanghai, for example, are now among the highest in their nations, yet new and established producers continue to cluster there rather than seeking lower-cost locations. The experience of Silicon Valley demonstrates that decentralized economies can flourish long after their labor cost advantages disappear as long as local investors and entrepreneurs are organized to collectively learn, innovate, and upgrade local capabilities – to create and recreate their regional advantage.

The contributions of an international technical community in transferring the institutions of technology entrepreneurship should not be confused with the broader role of a diaspora in the home country. The aggregate remittances, investments, or demonstration effects of a diaspora can affect an economy in a variety of different but largely limited ways. Transnational networks, however, are created by a small subset of highly educated professionals whose potential contributions to economic development are disproportionately significant. These transnational entrepreneurs are not typically drawn from the traditional economic or political elites of their home countries. Rather they are often the top engineering students from middle-class households whose access to education in the United States has landed them in a very different technological and institutional environment – one that they initially master and later transfer to their home countries.

Returning migrant communities are not replicating Silicon Valley around the world.

Wide variations in national economic and political institutions, themselves the products of enormously varied histories and cultures, ensure distinctive and divergent economic trajectories. It is more appropriate to see the emerging regions as hybrids, combining elements of the Silicon Valley industrial system with inherited local institutions and resources ... Regions like Hsinchu, Bangalore, and Shanghai are not replicas of Silicon Valley – although institutions and professional service providers from that region are fast expanding into these new environments. These new regional economies have co-evolved with the Silicon Valley economy. Firms in these regions do not typically seek to compete directly with Silicon Valley producers. They focus instead on developing capabilities in areas that U.S. producers are not pursuing; and over

time they have transformed activities once regarded as mundane and
low-tech into more efficient and dynamic sectors.

(Saxenian, 2005)

Discussion

Saxenian talks more about 'brain circulation' than brain gain to suggest that
these are not one-off movements but that connections and interactions are
ongoing and dynamic. Her main point is that those highly educated software
and other high-tech engineers who were educated in the USA are now the
motivating forces for setting up firms in their 'home' countries.

She makes an important distinction between 'remittances, investments, or
demonstration effects of a diaspora' and the knowledge exchanges of a highly
skilled transnational network. Much of the contribution made by overseas
migrants to their 'home' country, it must be remembered, is through the
relatively small, intra-household transfers of money and gifts that we call
remittances. In 2010 the global value of these was estimated at over
US$300 billion.

But the types of relationship that Saxenian is talking about do not simply
concern money or labour costs. Rather the advantages that these business
start-ups bring are complex and interconnected. Those engineers who set up in
India and China are highly skilled, have acquired new cultural dispositions to
working, have sources of capital and maintain links with the firms in Silicon
Valley. The point is made that these new firms do not simply take
subcontracts from the big US firms but have distinct advantages; they have
'capabilities' that the US companies lack. The outcome is that both the US
and Chinese/Indian firms benefit – a classic positive-sum outcome.

Saxenian is clear that what we see in these new growth areas of India and
China, such as Bangalore and Shanghai, are not facsimiles of California's
Silicon Valley where the engineers cut their teeth. While some of the
organizational practices are similar – such as a lack of hierarchy in firms –
local institutional and political differences help explain why these growth
poles within the rising powers are not the same as Silicon Valley. But she
does acknowledge that these growth areas are not cheap places to live. We
saw earlier in this chapter how the Indian government has been promoting
New Delhi and surrounding urban developments as worthy of global city
status. The new high-tech growth areas in China and India have become
relatively expensive in terms of housing, transport, education, etc. And we are
seeing concentrations of these highly educated, very wealthy and
transnationally oriented migrants that are transforming the social fabric of
these cities, as discussed in Box 6.1.

The example of Cape Verde and the high-tech movers and shakers from
Silicon Valley show how different migration can be and how it links to rising
power development in very different ways. The traders in Cape Verde are not
particularly wealthy but are risk takers. They spotted opportunities in a niche
of the global economy and built on some of the advantages that a rising China
offered – namely cheap goods and a liberalized emigration policy. Their

migration builds on longer histories of labour migration to other developing countries although the recent moves have been largely independent of the Chinese state, which has not discouraged this mobility. This contrasts with some of the big, aid-backed projects that are directly supported by the state. The IT experts are also independent of the state and are not generally from the elites, but they are well educated and willing to take a risk. Their decision to work back in their 'homeland' speaks of the power of cultural ties as well as the changed opportunity structure now that China and India have started to grow so rapidly. However, the location of their work back in China and India is not random, but linked to areas where institutional structures and social networks are most conducive, which in turn leads to regional growth at a sub-national level in cities that are becoming vital to global innovation. In this way the connections between places and people become re-embedded in new geographical configurations, which set in train their own problems of wage and house price inflation and growing inequalities.

6.3 Flows of nature: the case of the environment

Chapter 5 looked at a conceptual framework for understanding the interaction and impacts of the rising powers. Any framework is a simplification of reality in order to help us organize our thinking. The complex nature of international economic relations means there are likely to be a multitude of direct and indirect, positive-sum and zero-sum impacts of a country's growth. An important example of this is how the various interactions bound up in the economic growth of a rising power – commodity trade, production, overseas investment – can impact upon the environment. It is not our intention to detail the multiple relationships between the environment and development in such a short subsection (see Butcher and Papaionnou 2013, for a more detailed discussion on this). Rather we want to show how one channel of interaction can overlap with one or more others and that this has complex (and sometimes contradictory) impacts on development at different scales. As a result it is hard to say definitively how far a bundle of interactions has a positive-sum or zero-sum impact on development. It even throws into question what we actually mean by development since if we take a purely growth-oriented perspective then any growth is good, but if we take a more ecologically sensitive view of development then growth that negatively affects the environment may not be so beneficial.

Taking China as an example, we have seen that the economic reforms of the past 30 years transformed it from an agrarian economy into an industrial and service economy. However, the high economic growth, rapid urbanization and industrialization have taken their toll on the Chinese environment. Today, China faces huge environmental challenges, such as climate change, resource scarcity and pollution of water, soil and air (Watts, 2010). Since 2007, China has been the world's largest CO_2 emitter measured in absolute terms and total CO_2 emissions increased fourfold between 1980 and 2007 (IEA, 2010). While China's economic growth is rapid, its per capita natural resources are relatively small. According to China Economic Net (2004):

> the per capita area of arable land in [China] is only one fifth of the world average, the level of per capita water resources is one fourth of the world

average, and that of forest is one seventh of the world average. The per capita reserves of key mineral resources that support the growth of the national economy like petroleum, natural gas and coal in China are only 11 percent, 45 percent and 79 percent of the **world average**.

(Source: cited in Pamlin and Baijin, 2007, p. 25)

Clearly then the rapid industrialization of China depleted its own environment and implicates other regions through indirect effects of climate change.

Activity 6.4

Look at the cartoon in Figure 6.9. What does it tell us about the sources of China's pollution? What other sources of Chinese pollution might there be?

Spend no more than 5 minutes on this activity.

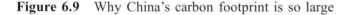

WHY CHINA'S CARBON FOOTPRINT IS SO LARGE

Figure 6.9 Why China's carbon footprint is so large

Discussion

The cartoon clearly blames the export orientation of China's economy, which was discussed in Chapter 5, for the pollution. This is interesting as it implicates western consumption in what is seen to be an 'over there' problem that China has created and which China must clear up. Watson and Wang (2007) found that 23% of Chinese emissions are due to its strong export market and fuelled mainly by exports to the USA and the EU. But is this the only driver or producer of pollution? Clearly, China's rapid economic growth has seen manufacturing increase rapidly in an environment of quite low technology and lax regulation. But China is also building many houses that require land, building materials and energy. Chinese diets for the better off are changing, which means more food production (or import), which can take up land. So there are many ways that China's development impacts upon the environment.

China's domestic environmental record is thus already implicated in international development due to the value chains and commodity flows linking demand in the West with production in China (see Chapter 7 for further discussion on these production networks). But China also gets many of its raw materials from abroad. Chapter 5 mentioned how China's demand for soybeans has implications for producers in Latin America, notably Brazil and

Argentina. But what about the environmental impacts? The following extract gives us some sense of what these impacts might be.

Activity 6.5

Read the following extract by Watts (2005). What are the major environmental impacts of the increased soybean production?

Spend no more than 15 minutes on this activity.

> China's insatiable demand for proteins as well as oil is turning Brazil into the takeaway for the workforce of the world. In the second part of our series, we reveal how the soya trade is creating a gold rush which is deforesting the Amazon.
>
> …
>
> You cannot see the wood for the beans in an ever-widening expanse of the Amazon, and it is increasingly thanks to China. Brazil's boom crop and China's growing appetite are clearing more forest than logging, cattle farming and mining. It is one of the more remarkable developments of a globalized world in which Brazil is rapidly becoming the takeaway for the workforce of the world.
>
> Travelling from Beijing to a farm in the heart of the Amazon showed how far China's reach has extended. It took five flights and nearly three days to reach Santarem, followed by a two-hour drive.
>
> The farmers had also come a long way and at great risk to be here. The Bonettis are from Italian stock. Just as their forebears gave up everything to move from Europe to the new world, they too quit their jobs two years ago and sold their land in the south of Brazil so that they could join the soya gold rush thousands of miles north.
>
> …
>
> But for the pioneers it is a risk worth taking. Amazonian land is cheap. An area the size of a football pitch costs £200. But how could they be sure the soya boom would continue? 'Because of China,' said Mr Bonetti, whose name has been changed to protect him. 'All over Asia, and especially in China, the market is expanding.'
>
> The confidence of the families who are moving to newly cleared land near Santarem reflects a giant shift that is taking place in the global food trade as Brazil becomes a leading supplier of protein for China.
>
> …
>
> Self-sufficient in most food and energy commodities 15 years ago, China must now import millions of kilocalories to fuel its workers just as it needs lakes of international oil to keep its production lines running. Most of the protein comes in the form of soya beans from Brazil, which are used to fatten pigs, poultry and fish that end up on the dinner tables of the world's most populous country.
>
> …

Along with rising demand for the beans in Europe and a poor crop in the US, this contributed last year to the second biggest deforestation of the Amazon in history. Loggers and farmers have already cleared 600,000 hectares and tens of thousands more are added every month.

...

As in China, the losers of modernization are local farmers, who are priced or pushed off their land. Maria dos Santos, of the smallholders union in Santarem, said 500 families had been relocated, a fifth of them by force. Benoir Jean of a French NGO, Groupe de Recherche et d'Echanges Technologiques, said people were being shot and homes burned in the drive to secure land for soya. 'It has created a climate of fear in which people are afraid to talk.'

...

All over Amazonia, China's footprint is getting bigger. Near the northern port of Belemon, an alumina plant is being built to process raw materials for China's producers. Inland, Chinese merchants are negotiating timber deals in Manaus. To the east, forests are being chopped down to provide the charcoal needed for pig-iron exports. The world's biggest iron ore producer, Companhia Vale do Rio Doce, has signed a $1.5bn deal with Baosteel of Shanghai to build a mill with a capacity of 8m tonnes of steel sheet a year. Brazil's state oil firm Petrobras is building a pipeline with a $1bn investment from China's Sinopec.

...

Largely thanks to soya, South American exports to China have grown 570% since 1999. In the process China has overtaken Argentina, Japan and Britain to become the second most important destination, after the US, for Brazilian goods.

With economic clout has come political influence. Brazil's left-leaning president, Luiz Inacio Lula da Silva, has courted Beijing to offset US influence. Last year he headed a 450-member trade mission to China, where he said the two countries could form a relationship unhindered by colonial animosities. 'We are two giants without historical, political or economic divergences, free to think only about the future.'

(Watts, 2005)

Discussion

There's a great deal in this extract regarding the channels of interactions as discussed in Chapter 5. The driver is China's demand and the author talks about how far China's 'reach has extended'. It also implies that this demand extends beyond soybeans to commodities like 'lakes of international oil', which has already been discussed. Local business people – in the case of the Bonetti family, an earlier wave of Italian migrants – are keen to exploit these relatively cheap options of buying up parts of the Amazon to convert to soy production. The impacts on the environment are clear. Forest land is lost and sometimes obtained by violent or illegal means. Subsistence farmers lose out to the big commercial farmers and may be forced to exploit even more marginal land. And the article does not even mention how the loss of trees might affect the carbon balance and with it climate change.

But this one commodity flow is part of a wider engagement between China and Brazil. The article talks of all the other investments the Chinese are making, particularly around natural resources such as iron ore, timber and oil. And with this renewed economic engagement we are seeing shifting international politics, with the former Brazilian President – Lula – hailing a new era of cooperation, and with it a shifting balance of world power as discussed in Chapters 3 and 4.

So, one set of interactions is bound up in other forms of interaction. And while one interaction *in isolation* might be seen to have positive development impacts for the parties concerned, when we factor in other forms of interaction and the impacts associated with them, the picture becomes less clear. In this case China's rise has lifted millions out of poverty and enabled consumers across the world to secure cheap goods and maintain a decent standard of living, and some suppliers of raw materials have benefited from greater demand and higher prices, which are then ploughed back into jobs and further demand.

So far, so good. But once we include the environmental consequences then the picture becomes less rosy. Forests are removed, pollution increases, and climates are changed. Moreover, the extract on soybeans also points to the social impacts. Past migrants to Brazil are part of the recent economic drive into the Amazon and indigenous farmers are displaced and marginalized. This highlights the very complex geography that has been the focus of this chapter.

Historical connections – the Italian migrants to Brazil – are also part of more recent stories, such as China's demand for Brazil's commodities. At one level, while these are all about interactions between countries, it would be tempting to see them as lying outside of the spatial logic of nation states since they are about firms, individuals and regions that cross boundaries. But equally, state policy and diplomacy between states are central to this story. In practice, then, these connections are about both the state and non-state actors operating at and across different scales of development.

Summary and looking forward

This chapter has shed light on the relationships between development, space and scale and added some complexity to the idea that development occurs only at one scale or is 'contained' by a particular territory. Rather it is part of multiple and overlapping connections between many different places and people, often simultaneously. Using case studies of particular locations and flows we examined a number of key ideas.

- First, that development can lead to the concentration of some key activities in particular sites. Here we looked at global cities as nodes in an interconnected world.

- Second, the pursuit of economic opportunities or national goals leads some people to migrate to different places or countries. This can be planned or unplanned but is intimately connected with uneven development.

- Third, all these activities generate environmenal impacts and the 'cause' of these impacts in terms of, say, the markets for the goods that a factory produces, may be far away and not directly affected by the damaged environment. But equally, environmental impacts are felt locally or they can spill over into other scales and have an indirect effect on future development, as in the case of climate change.

The case studies we have looked at involve what we can call 'non-state' actors – cities, migrants or ecological spaces – even though they are intimately and necessarily bound up with a world of states. We have, throughout these chapters on the rising powers, touched on another important non-state actor that is crucial for international development: the transnational corporation. It is to these that we now turn.

References

Alden, C. (2007) *China in Africa*, London, Zed Books.

Berry, J. (2007) *Windrush Songs*, Northumberland, Bloodaxe Books.

Brosius, C. (2008) 'The enclaved gaze: exploring the visual culture of "world class-living" in urban India' in Jain, J. (ed.) *India's Popular Culture: Iconic Spaces and Fluid Images*, Mumbai, MARG.

Butcher, M. and Papaioannou, T. (2013) *New Perspectives in International Development*, London, Bloomsbury Academic/Milton Keynes, The Open University.

ECOWAS-SWAC/OECD (2006) *Atlas on Regional Integration in West Africa* [online], http://www.atlas-westafrica.org (Accessed 21 June 2011).

Globalization and World Cities (GaWC) (2008) *The World According to the GaWC 2008* [online], http://www.lboro.ac.uk/gawc/world2008t.html (Accessed 21 June 2011).

Haugen, H. and Carling, J. (2005) 'On the edge of the Chinese diaspora: the surge of baihuo business in an African city', *Ethnic and Racial Studies*, vol. 28, no. 4, pp. 639–662.

International Energy Agency (IEA) (2010) *IEA Statistics* [online] http://wds.iea.org/ (Accessed 21 June 2011).

Knox, P. (2002) 'World cities and the organisation of global space' in Johnston, R.J., Taylor, P.J. and Watts, M.J. (eds), *Geographies of Global Change: Remapping the World* (2nd edition), Oxford, Blackwell Publishing.

Ministry of Urban Development (2007) *Master Plan for Delhi 2021*, Delhi, JBA Publishers.

Mung, M.E. (2008) 'Chinese migration and China's foreign policy in Africa', *Journal of Overseas Chinese*, vol. 4, pp. 91–109.

Pamlin, D. and Baijin, L. (2007) *Re-Think – Chinese Outward Investment Flows*, World Wildlife Fund, Geneva [online] http://wwf.panda.org/index.cfm?uGlobalSearch=China%E2%80%99s+Outward+Investment+Flows (Accessed 21 June 2011).

Sassen, S. (2001) *The Global City: New York, London, Tokyo* (2nd edition), Princeton, Princeton University Press.

Saxenian, A. (2005) *From Brain Drain to Brain Circulation: Transnational Communities and Regional Upgrading in India and China* [online], http://people.ischool.berkeley.edu/~anno/Papers/scid-2005.pdf (Accessed 21 June 2011).

Stewart, D. (n.d.) 'Windrush', [online] http://www.movinghere.org.uk/schools/Britain/windrush.htm (Accessed 21 June 2011).

United Nations Development Programme (UNDP) (2007) *Case evidence of 'Brain Gain'*, *A UNDP Capacity Development Resource*, UNDP, New York [online], http://lencd.com/data/docs/228-AB-brain%20gain.pdf (Accessed 21 June 2011).

Watson, J. and Wang, T. (2007) 'Who owns China's carbon emissions?', *Tyndall Centre Briefing Note*, No. 23, Norwich, Tyndall Centre.

Watts, J. (2005) 'A hunger eating up the world', *The Guardian*, 10 November 2005 [online] http://www.guardian.co.uk/business/2005/nov/10/environment.china (Accessed 21 June 2011).

Watts, J. (2010) *When a Billion Chinese Jump: How China Will Save Mankind – Or Destroy It*, London, Faber and Faber.

Wilson, D. (2007) 'City transformation and the global trope: Indianapolis and Cleveland', *Globalizations*, vol. 4, no. 1, pp. 29–44.

Further reading

Bridge, G. and Watson, S. (eds) (2010) *The Blackwell City Reader* (2nd edition, Oxford, Blackwell Publishing.

Davis, M. (2006) *Planet of Slums*, London/NY, Verso.

Knott, K. and McLoughlin, S. (eds) (2010) *Diasporas*, London, Zed Books.

Mohan G. and Tan-Mullins, M. (2009) 'Chinese migrants in Africa as new agents of development? An analytical framework', *European Journal of Development Research*, vol. 21, no. 4, pp. 588–605.

Watts, J. (2010) *When a Billion Chinese Jump: How China Will Save Mankind – Or Destroy It*, London, Faber and Faber.

Transnational corporations: significance and impact

Dinar Kale

Introduction

On 31 January 2007, Tata Steel Limited, one of the leading steel producers in India, acquired the Anglo-Dutch steel producer Corus Group plc for US$12.11 billion. The process of acquisition concluded after nine rounds of bidding against a rival interest, the Brazil-based Companhia Siderurgica Nacional (CSN).

The Guardian, a leading English newspaper, covered the story with the title 'Empire strikes back: India forges new steel alliance' and argued:

> It is a dramatic illustration of the shift in the balance of power from West to East: a £5bn bid for Corus, formerly British Steel, by Tata, an Indian industrial conglomerate that has aspirations to turn itself into an Asian version of America's General Electric.
>
> *(Watchman, 2006)*

An editorial in the *Financial Times*, with the very similar title of 'Empire strikes back as Tata bids for Corus', concluded as follows:

> The new trend for foreign purchases [by transnational corporations from emerging markets] has only just begun: the Tata-Corus deal is a dramatic demonstration of the new, self confident mood of Indian business. Over the next 30 years, China and India will grow to dominate the world economy. They will give birth to great industrial companies that own plants all around the world.
>
> *(Financial Times, 2006)*

These quotes reflect the rise of emerging-market transnational corporations (TNCs) and the re-emergence of China, India and Brazil as important players in the world economy. Chapters 3 and 5 discussed how, historically, as major powers change so too does world trade. This change is reflected in the growth of TNCs. Broadly speaking, since the 16th century European regions dominated the world economy with important roles played by The Dutch East India Company (chartered in 1602) and The British East India Company (chartered in 1600), leading to nearly 400 years of involvement by the British in Asia. Over the years, Unilever (1872), Philips (1891), Nestlé (1868) and Imperial Chemicals (0000) continued overseas expansion by opening foreign subsidiaries across the world. The rise of the USA at the beginning of the 20th century was also marked by the growth of American TNCs (see Figure 7.1). In 1901, US companies maintained around 50 overseas manufacturing operations but by 1913 this number had risen to 116 (Dicken, 1986, p. 58). Similarly, the rise of Japan as a global power in the 1970s was reflected in the emergence of TNCs, such as Toyota and Sony, leading TNCs in the automobile and electronics industries respectively.

Figure 7.1   A McDonalds restaurant in Shanghai, China

With these shifts in the global balance of economic power this chapter's main aims are to:

- demonstrate the scale and importance of TNCs in shaping the world economy
- discuss the role of TNCs in facilitating or hindering development
- provide an overview of different models of growth associated with the emergence of TNCs from developing countries.

Section 7.1 discusses key characteristics of TNCs and their significance to international development while Section 7.2 focuses on the changing nature of working practices adopted by TNCs over time. Section 7.3 raises questions regarding the ability of TNCs to help or hurt development efforts, and Section 7.4 documents the emergence of TNCs from developing countries, evaluating the role of national policy in the process.

7.1 What are transnational corporations and why do they matter to international development?

Today there is no sphere of life untouched by products from TNCs, whether in developed or developing countries. According to the United Nations Conference on Trade and Development (UNCTAD, see Box 7.1), in 2007 there were 82 000 TNCs worldwide compared to 7000 in 1970 (WIR, 2009), although in some industries such as petroleum, automobiles, steel and electronics, a significant proportion of world production is accounted for by only a few of these companies.

Activity 7.1

Look quickly around your house and note down the brand names of products you have. How many do you think originate from TNCs?

Spend no more than 10 minutes on this activity.

7.1.1 What makes a company a transnational corporation?

One of the difficulties in discussing the role of TNCs in development is defining the term 'transnational'. Jenkins (1991) points out that there is no universally accepted definition; however, UNCTAD refers to TNCs as enterprises comprising entities in more than one country, which operate under a system of decision making that permits coherent policies and a common strategy (see Box 7.1).

Box 7.1 UNCTAD definition of transnational corporations

UNCTAD defines TNCs as incorporated or unincorporated enterprises comprising parent enterprises and their foreign affiliates (subsidiaries, associates and branches).

A parent enterprise is defined as an enterprise that controls assets of other entities in countries other than its home country, usually by owning a certain equity capital stake. An equity capital stake of 10% or more of the ordinary shares or voting power for an incorporated enterprise, or its equivalent for an unincorporated enterprise, is normally considered as the threshold for the control of assets.

Thus a TNC is a flagship company that holds decision-making powers over entities such as subsidiaries and joint ventures operating in other countries than its home country. They exercise power by holding shares or assets in those subsidiaries or joint ventures and, in particular, facilitate sharing of knowledge, resources and responsibilities with the others.

Note: Incorporation is the forming of a new corporation, a corporation being a legal entity that is effectively recognised as a person under the law.

(Source: WIR, 2009)

7.1.2 Why are transnational corporations important?

TNCs play a major role in the world economy by providing employment, internationalization of financial capital and technology development. For example, UNCTAD estimates that TNCs account for a third of total world exports of goods and services, and the number of people employed by them worldwide totalled about 77 million in 2008 – more than double the total labour force of Germany (WIR, 2005).

TNCs are also major investors in research and development (R&D) and are at the frontiers of innovation in their respective sectors. In 2002, almost 700 of the largest R&D spending firms in the world invested US$310 billion – out of these at least 98% were TNCs. That year TNCs accounted for almost half (46%) of the world's total R&D expenditure (WIR, 2005), most of which is in the information and communication technologies (ICT), automotive and pharmaceutical industries.

R&D spending of some TNCs is higher than that of many countries. For example, in four TNCs (Ford Motor, Pfizer, DaimlerChrysler and Siemens), R&D investments exceeded US$6 billion in 2003 while in Toyota and General Motors it surpassed US$5 billion (see Figure 7.2). By comparison, in developing economies, south-east Europe and the Commonwealth of Independent States (CIS), as a group, total expenditure on R&D only came to US$5 billion in 2002 (WIR, 2005). This shows that TNCs are equally (or more) important players in driving and commercializing innovation in different sectors.

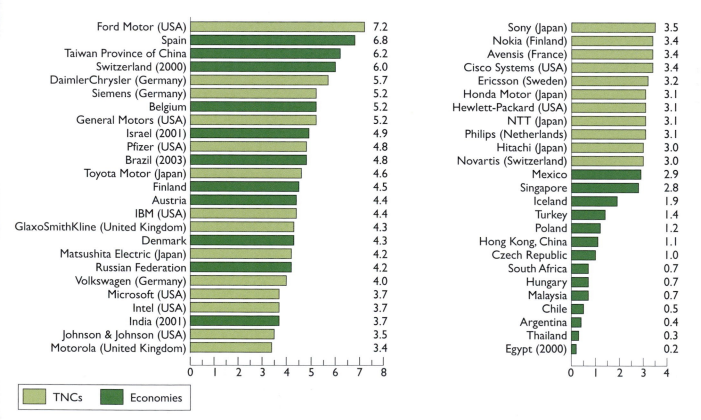

Figure 7.2 R&D expenditure (US$billions) by selected TNCs and economies, 2002 (Source: WIR, 2005)

7.1.3 Which are the top transnational corporations in the world?

Some major TNCs have already been mentioned that you will probably have heard of. This section discusses the major companies with large foreign assets and looks at the sectors in which they operate. Given that we are interested in what difference the rising powers are making we will also look at the changes in composition of the top 100 TNCs from 1990 to 2008.

Activity 7.2

Before proceeding, make a note of which companies and sectors you think are likely to dominate the list of top ten TNCs?

Spend no more than 10 minutes on this activity.

The 100 largest TNCs worldwide represent a major proportion of total international production. Table 7.1 shows the top ten non-financial TNCs by virtue of their **foreign assets** in 1990 and 2008 based on UNCTAD reports. The top ten lists from 1990 and 2008 show the domination of companies operating in primary sectors such as oil, energy, water and food. For example, in 1990 and 2008 the same four companies from the petroleum sector (Royal Dutch Shell, BP, Exxon + Mobil, and Total) appear in the top 10 lists of TNCs. In 2010, the top 10 lists are led by General Electric representing the manufacturing sector, with Vodaphone third, a telecommunications company representing a new economy sector. (Vodafone was not even present in the 1990 top 100 list.)

Previous chapters noted the rise of India, Brazil and China as new growth centres and suggested this may be a sign of the relative waning of established economies. This can be gauged by the rise and fall of TNCs. Indeed, some of the largest US-based TNCs are showing signs of decline. For example, in 1990 General Motors (GM) was the third largest TNC while Toyota was 33rd, but by 2008 Toyota emerged as the fifth largest TNC while GM slipped to 11th place. By contrast, we see the improving presence of TNCs from developing countries. In 1990, there was no company from the global South, but by 1995 two had emerged in the top 100 TNCs list: Daewoo from South Korea at number 52 and Venezuelan state-owned petroleum company, Petroleos De Venezuela, at number 88. Each subsequent year there has been a gradual increase in the number of emerging economy companies. By 2008 there were seven in the top 100: AcerlorMittal, India (no. 10), Hutchison Whampoa Limited, China (no. 25), Cemex S.A., Mexico (no. 55), Samsung Electronics, South Korea (no. 76), Petronas, Malaysia (no. 78), Hyundai Motor Company, South Korea (no. 79) and China Ocean Shipping (Group) Company, China (no. 80).

Let's look at two leading lights of rising power TNCs. In 1990, IBM was ranked at number five, but by 2008 it had slipped to 30th place. Behind these statistics is an important story concerning the acquisition of IBM's Personal Computer Division in 2005 for US$1.75 billion by Chinese manufacturer

Table 7.1 Top ten non-financial TNCs in the world by foreign assets in 1990 and 2008

Rank	1990				2008			
	Name	Country	Sector	Foreign assets (US$bn)	Name	Country	Sector	Foreign assets (US$bn)
1	Royal Dutch	UK/Netherlands	Petroleum	69.2	General Electric	USA	Electrical equipment	401.2
2	Ford	USA	Automobile	55.2	Royal Dutch/Shell Group	UK	Petroleum	222.3
3	General Motors	USA	Automobile	52.6	Vodafone Group plc	UK	Telecommunications	201.5
4	Exxon	USA	Petroleum	51.6	BP plc	UK	Petroleum	188.9
5	IBM	USA	Computers	45.7	Toyota Motor Corporation	Japan	Automobile	169.5
6	BP	UK	Petroleum	31.6	ExxonMobil Corporation	USA	Petroleum	161.2
7	ABB	Switzerland	Industrial and farm equipment	26.9	Total SA	France	Petroleum	141.4
8	Nestlé	Switzerland	Food	00.0	E.On	Germany	Electricity, gas, water	133.6
9	Phillips	Netherlands	Electronics	23.3	Electricité de France	France	Electricity, gas, water	127.1
10	Mobil	USA	Petroleum	22.3	ArcelorMittal	Luxembourg	Metals and metal products	123.6

Sources: WIR, 1991 and WIR, 2010

Lenovo (Wright, 2004). Lenovo is partially owned by the Chinese government and acted as a distributor of equipment made by IBM and other companies. By 1990 it started selling PCs under its own brand name in the Chinese domestic market, which marked the exit of IBM from a market it created with the first IBM PC in 1981. Lenovo is now the third largest manufacturer of personal computers in the world (*Financial Times*, 2004).

Another interesting case is ArcerlorMittal. In 2008, ArcelorMittal, a steel company headquartered in Luxembourg owned by Indian industrialist Lakshmi Mittal, joined the top ten list at number ten. Mittal grew his steel empire by turning around sick steel plants in markets from Trinidad to Kazakhstan, and acquired Arcerlor in 2006. The acquisition was a tense affair and Arcelor's management, who once dismissed Mittal Steel as a 'company of Indians' was forced to backtrack and support the bid under shareholders' threat of revolt. After this acquisition ArcelorMittal emerged as the largest steel company in the world.

7.2 How do transnational corporations operate?

So far we have identified what constitutes a typical TNC in quite abstract terms and looked at the changing distribution of leading firms. But how do they actually operate? This section examines the production practices that revolutionized the working of current TNCs and enabled them to achieve significant **economies of scale** and **economies of scope**. Adoption of practices such as assembly lines, functional specialization and a detailed division of labour laid the foundation for the future growth of manufacturing TNCs. The origin of many of these production practices lies in Henry Ford's innovative techniques to manufacture cars in Detroit. Ford's success resulted in the application of these practices in manufacturing industries all over the world, and the next section will look at Ford's techniques in more detail.

7.2.1 The rise of 'Fordism'

Henry Ford, an automobile magnate and founder of the Ford Motor Company, affected one of the greatest and most rapid changes in manufacturing through transforming working practices involved in the mass production of automobiles (Harvey, 1989). Using innovative practices such as assembly line 'mass' production rather than hand-crafted methods, Ford manufactured the first mass market automobile, known as the 'Model T', in 1908 (see Figure 7.3).

From Ford's system the idea of 'Fordism' emerged. It signifies mass production labour involving assembly-line production, managerial hierarchy and a technical division of labour. It simplified necessary operations that were radically routinized, and so deskilled and intensified the labour process. Advances in machine tools and gauging systems allowed for moving assembly lines, where each worker performed a single, repetitive task. Fordist production systems were also based on 'standardization' – from components to final product. In terms of managerial control it involved top-down decision making where managers and technicians did all the 'thought' work and operatives were required to follow those directives diligently.

Figure 7.3 Model T production line

These practices resulted in assembly line work becoming physically demanding, requiring high levels of concentration, but also excruciatingly boring in a limited, confined environment. These 'Fordist' practices created severe dissatisfaction amongst workers, high personnel turnover and disputes between workers and managers. Faced with these problems Ford started paying higher wages in 1913 – US$5 a day to unskilled labour – and soon other companies followed his lead. This increase in wages – and extension of credit – also ensured workers could afford automobiles, thereby creating a mass market.

While Fordism yielded some benefits, such as improved wages and fringe benefits, and more stable employment, it had its critics, most notably the Italian Marxist, Antonio Gramsci, whom you read about briefly in Chapter 3. Gramsci (1971) argued that Fordist elites were responsible for developing cultural mechanisms to exert control in the wider society. This was an extension of the factory-based logic and created 'standardized individuals' as Fordist managers took interest in the moral and psychological condition of their workers. He stresses that this surveillance of workers' personal lives and other activities outside the workplace was aimed at encouraging the voluntary submission of workers to the labour discipline required by this new order.

7.2.2 From Fordism to post-Fordism

We saw in Chapter 3 that the 1970s was a period of global restructuring. In turn this witnessed significant changes in the organization of industrial enterprises. From the late 1960s social unrest and labour rebellions started dominating the industrial landscape, leading to recession in the USA. This was the environment that gave rise to an era of experimentation in industrial organizations and witnessed the emergence of what has been termed 'post-Fordism' (Kiely, 1998). The shift to post-Fordism involved patterns of 'flexible production', greater responsiveness towards labour and working conditions amongst producers and new capabilities allowing for 'just in time' production. The 'just in time' system is based on production according to actual demand, thereby reducing the requirement of a components inventory and wasteful production time (Schoenberger, 1988). This needed flexibility in the relationship between the core firm and suppliers, and required a far more flexible workforce. For example, Toyota developed core multi-skilled workers able to undertake a number of tasks and provided management flexibility to use their knowledge to promote improvements in the production process. Adaptable technologies also aided diverse production tasks with the use of computer-driven manufacturing. These elements produced an ability to adjust from one process and/or product configuration to another, and subsequently an ability to manage required output rapidly without affecting any efficiency. This flexibility offered opportunities for TNCs to dynamically respond to changes in customized consumer markets.

Managerially, post-Fordism involved decentralized yet highly effective production. These enterprises worked with reduced managerial hierarchies, highly skilled workforces and opportunities for workers to become leaders. For some analysts flexible specialization and its wider regime was a superior model to the crisis-ridden Fordism and thus had potential to be applied on a much wider scale. It was argued that post-Fordist systems avoided workplace tensions by providing better work conditions and wages and with that mitigated costs and inefficiencies of managerial and union bureaucracy (Piore and Sabel, 1984).

However, critics of the post-Fordist paradigm, such as Kiely (1998), argue that this analysis is often not clear enough and tends to be normative. For example, much analysis of Japanese management techniques does not indicate whether these techniques can be easily transferred to different social contexts. According to Kiely, post-Fordism has been unevenly applied across different sectors as well as within them. For example, the automobile industry still operates with Fordist (Model T) as well as post-Fordist (Toyota) strategies. However, labour-intensive industries, such as the clothing sector, are still dominated by Fordist practices. Therefore, rather than seeing the wholesale move to post-Fordism we should see it as coexisting in many cases across sectors. We will return to this point in Section 7.3 on the emergence of sweatshops.

7.2.3 The emergence of global production networks

So far, the ways in which firms might move from standardized to flexible forms of organization have been discussed. But TNCs are, by definition, split between territories that require integration and coordination of their multiple activities. In the 1980s global restructuring of industrial enterprises gave rise to global production networks where the production process for a single product occurred in a number of different firms based in developing and advanced countries. We now examine this in more detail and the implications of these changes to companies operating in developing countries.

As a result of organizational and technological changes, TNCs' linear production models have been replaced by global production chains where interdisciplinary teams work in different locations delivering various components into the production process. TNCs divide the production chain into a variety of discreet tasks, and outsource them to locations that provide cheap and efficient production opportunities, facilitate access to local resources and capabilities, and allow entry into key markets.

Ernst (2000) argued that one of the key developments since the 1970s has been the 'de-coupling' of product development from manufacturing. It has affected the organization of work, accelerated fragmentation of production chains and enhanced competition between low-cost engineering locations around the world. This de-coupling is the result of the increasing separation of product design and development (performed by TNCs) from physical production (organized by contract manufacturing firms). This separation of design and manufacturing fostered a new international division of labour between product design (usually in developed countries) and manufacturing locations (in developing countries). Since then international production has increasingly taken place in the framework of global production networks (GPNs) with TNCs at the centre as a 'lead firm'. TNCs, their affiliates and joint ventures form a strategic alliance in GPNs with contractors, suppliers and service providers, as well as partners. This alliance provides TNCs with quick and cheaper access to resources and capabilities that are complementary to their core competence. While some production moves are due to unique local conditions such as availability of raw materials or markets, most of this reorganization has been to exploit low-cost, less-organized labour forces; laxer labour, safety and environment laws; and lower infrastructural costs in developing countries. The subcontracting of production to low-cost countries has certainly delivered enormous benefits, such as cheaper products and services to consumers in Western countries, albeit with some negative effects on employment. However, the question remains whether the emergence of GPNs will contribute to economic and technological convergence between centre and periphery countries as well as reduce their significant income disparities.

7.3 Do transnational corporations help or hurt the development process?

There is disagreement about whether or not TNCs are engines of growth capable of reducing inequalities and other obstacles to development. Figure 7.4 captures the essence of this debate.

Activity 7.3

In 2000 *The Economist* published an article with the cartoon, shown in Figure 7.4, demonstrating the shifting attitudes to the role of TNCs in world trade and development. Looking at the cartoon, what have been the changing attitudes to TNCs? What might be the reasons for different reactions to TNCs?

Spend no more than 10 minutes on this activity.

Discussion

The four pictures suggest society's attitudes towards TNCs have moved from fear of them in the 1970s as big, irresponsible, monopolistic monsters to nonchalance and indifference in the 1980s, to agents of growth and bearers of foreign capital, technology and knowledge in the 1990s, and now as all powerful and 'evil'.

These trends were reflected in developing country policies towards TNCs, which changed from distrust and control of their activities to liberalization of economies and incentives to attract their technology and capital (Jenkins, 1991). In the 1970s TNCs were denounced as large, monopolistic organizations whose only aim was profit maximization, disregarding any responsibility for the social and economic fabric of society. These opinions led countries to adopt policies that strongly regulated TNCs' activities and in some cases forced them out of their countries. For example, the Indian government enforced the nation's 1973 Foreign Exchange Regulation Act that mandated partial Indian ownership of TNCs operating in the country. Many leading TNCs, including IBM and Coca Cola, closed down their Indian operations rather than accept this (*Time*, 1977).

During the 1990s, perceptions towards TNCs changed, especially in developing economies, modelling the export-oriented growth of South Korea, Singapore and Taiwan, who showed TNCs could drive local development. For

Figure 7.4 Society's attitudes towards TNCs (Source: *The Economist*, 2000)

example, in the 1990s the Indian government opened the economy to TNCs and established special committees and departments to attract investment. Taking advantage of the deregulated open market, TNCs expanded and in the process bought local firms while others lost businesses due to competition (*The Economist*, 2000). The activities, expansion and size of TNCs seemed threatening and as a consequence, by the 2000s, TNCs are again often viewed as monolithic, more powerful than nation states, and bent on destroying livelihoods and the environment.

Box 7.2 summarizes the criticisms of TNCs, and we then look at them in more detail.

> **Box 7.2 Key criticisms of transnational corporations**
>
> **Sweatshops**
>
> TNCs subcontract or outsource production to contractors in developing countries which keeps employees in working environments considered to be unacceptably difficult or dangerous and abusive.
>
> **Race to the bottom**
>
> The increased mobility of international capital and reduction in trade barriers has allowed these companies to exploit differences between countries by (re)locating (or threatening to relocate) their activities to countries with more pliable regimes, providing flexible labour laws or cheaper land (Jenkins, 2005). This is a phenomenon termed as the 'race to the bottom'.
>
> **Social and environment problems**
>
> TNCs align with authoritarian regimes, interfere in national laws for profit and disregard the environment.

7.3.1 Sweatshops

You might have come across the word 'sweatshop', which originated in criticisms of the clothing industry. Profits are said to be 'sweated' out of labourers who work longer and faster under poor working conditions for low wages with no respect to local labour laws mandating overtime pay or a minimum wage (Dreier and Appelbaum, 1999). Due to these working conditions, costs of production remain low and TNCs can reap excessive profits. An example of a company that has come in for a great deal of criticism for its association with sweatshops is Nike.

The Nike global production network

Nike, a leading sport apparel and equipment company, was notorious for its use of contractors operating sweatshops in developing countries (Dreier and Appelbaum, 1999). It was one of the first companies to take advantage of global production opportunities by moving production to cheaper locations around the world. Starting as an importer of Japanese running shoes the company is now a world leader in the design, distribution and marketing of athletic footwear in particular.

In the 1980s, Nike realized the company could achieve better gains from outsourcing than investing in internal resources in the USA (Crain and Abraham, 2008). Identifying its core competences in product development and marketing, the company then built a strategy around designing innovative products that could match ever-changing consumer demands, but outsourcing production to cheaper locations. In 2001, Nike subcontracted the production process of its footwear to 750 contract factories employing thousands of workers primarily in Asia, including China, Vietnam, Pakistan and Bangladesh, while employing only 22 000 in the USA (Locke, 2003).

Figure 7.5 shows a simplified view of Nike's production network. The blueprint of a Nike shoe originates from the Nike Research Lab located in its world headquarters in Oregon, USA. In some cases, where Nike has developed long-term relationships with subcontractors, Nike designers send their designs and styles to these contractors, who in turn develop prototypes. On approval of these prototypes, lead contractors send designs to various plants around the world for production.

Production of raw materials such as rubber, leather and plastic are also outsourced, extracted from places located in close proximity to the factories for manufacturing.

This subcontracting of its production process instead of direct capital investment in a particular place has offered Nike the flexibility of relocating to places that have the lowest production costs. For example, in the 1960s, Nike used to subcontract production to factories in Korea and Taiwan. When wages of these countries rose in the 1980s, Nike switched to the rapidly developing nations of Indonesia, Vietnam and China, which offered low-wage labour.

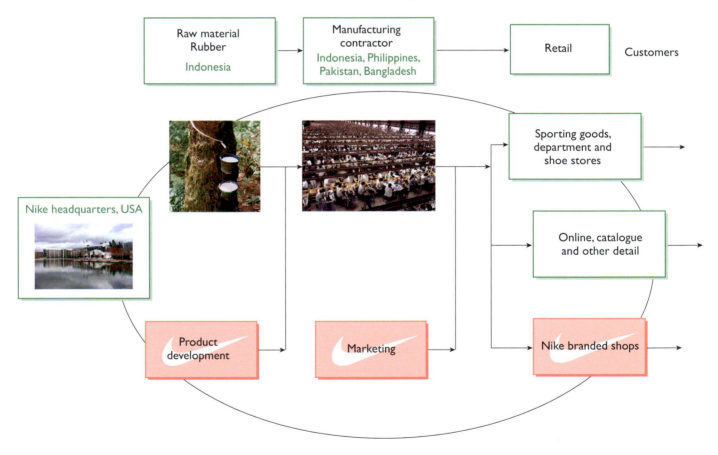

Figure 7.5 Nike's production network (Source: Crain and Abraham, 2008)

By the early 1990s, a key production location was Indonesia. Here six factories employed more than 25 000 workers and supplied over six million pairs of shoes per year. Many of these Indonesian shoe factories only paid 21 000 rupiah (about US$1 per day), less than the minimum wage at the time.

According to official Indonesian government calculations, this minimum daily wage could support only 70% of the living costs of one individual – let alone a family (HBS, 1994). Working conditions were often very poor with intense pressure to meet daily targets, and workers lacked protection from management abuse. The Harvard Business School (HBS) case study on Nike and Reebok depicts the harsh conditions of these factories:

> One worker at Nagasakti Para Shoes, a Nike contractor, said that she and other workers were terrified of managers, 'They yell at us when we don't make production quotas, and if we talk back they cut our wages.'
>
> *(HBS, 1994, p. 5)*

In some instances child labour laws were violated and labourers were found to be handling hazardous material without proper protection (Boje and Khan, 2008). The use of child labour in Pakistan in 1995 created a new wave of protests against Nike and resulted in the Atlanta Agreement: an agreement between the Sialkot Chamber of Commerce and Industry, the International Labour Organisation (ILO), UNICEF and several leading sports goods associations to eliminate child labour from the soccer ball sector.

Nike responded to these accusations by noting that these factories are owned and managed by independent operators, claiming it does not have any control over labour practices. According to the Nike Vice President for Asia:

> 'We don't know the first thing about manufacturing. We are marketers and designers.'
>
> *(HBS, 1994, p. 6)*

In this case, subcontracting the production component of its supply chain to various low-cost regions had enabled Nike to maintain high profits with no responsibility for sweatshop conditions. By 1992 Nike realized this indifferent attitude was damaging the company's reputation and formulated a code of conduct for its suppliers that mandated basic labour and health standards. In 2000 Nike created Corporate Responsibility and Compliance departments and stationed company managers in all manufacturing locations to strengthen labour and environment compliance.

In the mid-1990s, coming on the heels of the Nike child labour controversy, other leading US brands such as Gap, Disney and Levis came under the spotlight concerning the use of sweatshops and child labour (Klein, 2000). In 2005, more major TNCs, such as Walmart and Apple, were added to the list due to the severe treatment of workers by their subcontractors in China. Non-governmental organizations (NGOs), such as Oxfam, continue to campaign on these issues, highlighting the practices of leading brands, but there has also been an argument that consumers must also take some responsibility for demanding cheap products.

7.3.2 Race to the bottom

As we've seen in the Nike example, the reduction of barriers on international trade and the movement of cross-border capital allows TNCs to move their activities from one region to another to exploit differences in wages, regulatory environments and incentives by host governments. As a result, TNCs are accused of relocating their manufacturing plants, outsourcing centres and even R&D set-ups as a way of reaping maximum returns. This has been termed the 'race to the bottom'. Another classic example is the apparel industry. Manufacturers usually focus on the design aspect of product development and outsource fabrication to subcontractors around the world. Look at the labels of the clothes you are wearing now to see where they come from. Apparel is labour intensive but capital investment in machines is quite low therefore it is relatively easy to set up a manufacturing unit. This means that 'there is always some place, somewhere, where clothing can be made still more cheaply' (Dreier and Appelbaum, 1999). As a result subcontractors are severely limited in negotiating terms and conditions of business with 'footloose' TNCs, and low wages reflect workers' lack of power to negotiate better working conditions rather than their low productivity. Dreier and Appelbaum provide a striking description of the production process in the clothing industry:

> Although significant advances have been made in aspects of production technologies, the apparel industry remains low-tech since it involves the sewing of garments. The basic unit of production continues to be a worker sitting or standing at a sewing machine and sewing together pieces of cloth. The contracting system also allows retailers and manufacturers to eliminate much uncertainty and risk. When business is slow, the contract is simply not renewed; manufacturers need not worry about paying unemployment benefits or dealing with idle workers who might go on strike or otherwise make trouble. If a particular contractor becomes a problem, there are countless others to be found who will be only too happy to get their business. Workers, however, experience the flip side of the enormous flexibility enjoyed by retailers and manufacturers. They become contingent labour, employed and paid only when their work is needed.
>
> *(Dreier and Appelbaum, 1999, p. 1)*

There is some disagreement, however, that TNCs engage in a 'race to the bottom'. Drezner (2000) claims that if the core of the argument is that profit-maximising TNCs will move to places with relatively low production costs then TNCs should flock to countries with the weakest regulatory standards since any regulatory standard will increase operating costs. But there is no evidence to support this argument. In fact, Drezner claims that during the 1990s, the majority of TNC investments were directed towards advanced economies, not to poor nations. However, even in wealthier economies, the phenomenon of sweatshops has been uncovered. In Leicester in the UK, for example, sweatshops using low-paid labour supplied mass-market fashion labels such as New Look and BHS (Chamberlain, 2010). However, while the implementation of laws has had some effect on limiting these incidents, more important has been the fear of reputational damage and a consumer backlash.

7.3.3 Social and environmental problems

Another criticism of TNCs, particularly those operating in the commodities sector, is that they have formed alliances with undemocratic or repressive regimes and that they have disregarded local environmental issues to protect their investments. In some cases TNCs have reportedly attempted to amend labour laws or influence local industrial and environmental policies to benefit themselves (*The Economist*, 2000). For commodity businesses, discussed in Chapter 5, fixed investments in the early stages of exploitation are very high compared to start-up costs of consumer business. For example, an oil company setting up a petroleum plant requires a much higher investment than consumer businesses such as McDonalds or Nike. And while return on investments can be huge, it occurs over a longer period of time, therefore the TNC requires stability. As a result commodity businesses try to find a way to secure their investments and profits, including working with governments.

There have been numerous examples of TNCs causing severe social and environmental problems in developing countries and weak governments may fail to take strong action due to the political and financial strength of these companies and the rents they bring to the state. For example, activists have argued that Shell Oil's activities in the Niger Delta have fed conflict, corruption and environmental damage giving rise to civil unrest in this region of Nigeria. Shell is accused of supporting military operations in the 1990s and is too slow in cleaning up oil spills which cause social and environmental problems (Obi, 2009).

However, with the BP oil spill in the Gulf of Mexico, there was a contrasting response from a TNC due to strong US government pressure. In April 2010, an explosion aboard the Deepwater Horizon drilling rig in the Gulf of Mexico killed 11 workers and caused an oil spill (206 million gallons) which leaked until September. The spill caused huge damage to the environment and local industry. Unlike in other regions, such as the EU, the petroleum industry had been able to lobby the US government to relax regulations for deepwater drilling, indicating the power of TNCs at times to influence policy. Deepwater Horizon was drilling in about 1525 m of water, stretching the boundaries of technology in the field, which was also found wanting when they attempted to block the spill after the explosion. The US government held BP responsible for the oil spill and forced it to clean and repair the damage. As a result BP pledged US$20 billion to compensate affected Gulf residents and promote tourism in the area. It has also agreed to support financially a study of the environmental impact. In the end BP spent $32 billion to cover costs of the oil spill (BBC, 2010). These examples clearly show a double standard in some TNCs' behaviour towards social and environmental impacts depending on government structures and the ability of the public to place pressure on them. With increased public awareness TNCs are coming under intense pressure to improve their processes and adopt an attitude of corporate social responsibility.

Probably all of us use products created through a GPN orchestrated by a lead TNC like Nike. Yet we can see that in some cases production of these goods come at a price to people and the environment. However, would you be willing to give up cheap goods and products from TNCs to protect wages and support better working conditions in developing countries?

TNCs and corporate social responsibility

Strengthened by new communication technologies that enable international campaigning, NGOs and public pressure has led to calls for TNCs to address poor working conditions and environmental damage (see Jenkins, 2005, p. 527). Many have responded by developing corporate social responsibility (CSR) practices to counter negative publicity surrounding their activities. Firms outsourcing their production to developing countries have adopted supplier codes of conduct. For example, Levi Strauss developed its Business Partner Terms of Engagement in 1992 after its overseas contractors were accused of bad treatment of workers. In the case of Gap, after several protests in 1995, the company signed an agreement with the National Labour Committee opening its overseas manufacturers to third-party inspections (Spar, 1998).

While some, such as Christian Aid (2004), argue that CSR is simply creating an illusion of the demise of corporate hegemony because it is based on TNCs' concern for their own reputations, and therefore aimed at securing greater profits, there is another side to the debate. There are strong arguments that TNCs also have several beneficial impacts on the development of countries.

Activity 7.4

Make a list of all the potential benefits of TNCs as well as the possible downsides of their activities. Are the beneficiaries different from those who are hurt by their activities or can some scenarios occur where costs and benefits occur together? In terms of the framework introduced in Chapter 5, would you say TNCs are zero-sum or positive-sum for development?

Spent no more than 20 minutes on this activity

Discussion

Zero-sum and positive-sum terms are used to indicate the outcome of negotiations in conflict or dispute situations. A zero-sum outcome will signify that it is difficult for one party to gain advantage without affecting the other party while a positive-sum outcome will indicate a possibility of getting an outcome that will satisfy requirements of all parties involved. Applying this in the case of TNCs' impact on development it is observed that some potential benefits also have a possible downside attached to it. For example, TNCs can help poor people in the developing countries through employment generation although in some industries this can led to exploitation as seen by the sweatshop model. This raises the question of whether it is possible to gain positive-sum development where developing countries and TNCs can achieve their objectives while minimizing harm to people and the environment.

7.4 Transnational corporations: technology transfer and internationalization of financial capital in developing countries

With Drezner's rebuttal of the 'race to the bottom' arguments noted above, there was an acknowledgement that TNCs can do some good for developing countries (see Box 7.3 for a summary). The significant increase of Foreign Direct Investment (FDI) since the 1980s has played an important role in strengthening international economic integration and facilitating technology transfer. TNCs can contribute to technological development in developing countries through different channels, for example local firms use imitation or trial and error strategies to adopt technologies developed by TNCs (Pack and Saggi, 2001). Another route can be via the migration of workers trained or previously employed by the TNCs bringing key knowledge to local firms. In this sense, FDI by TNCs has a long-term effect in building technological capabilities in developing countries.

Box 7.3 Benefits of transnational corporations in development

Technology transfer to different parts of the world

TNCs promote technological development by acting as a mechanism for the transfer of technology and skills from advanced to developing countries.

Employment generation and economic development

TNCs with their production outsourcing generate employment, raise productivity, enhance exports and assist in the economic development of developing countries.

7.4.1 Transnational corporations and technology transfer

The GPNs that you studied in Section 7.2 also have a role in the transfer and diffusion of technology and knowledge. Ernst and Kim (2002) suggest that GPNs create opportunities for local capability formation in low-cost regions such as developing countries and thereby act as a catalyst in global knowledge diffusion. In some cases, TNCs upgrade technological capabilities in local firms by providing them with technical and managerial knowledge. Once a local firm assimilates basic level capabilities, TNCs can transfer more sophisticated knowledge including product and process development, that is, moving local companies higher up the value chain. In many high-tech industries, the difference between knowledge needed for design and manufacturing has been significantly narrowed (Schuler at al., 2006). In this phenomenon, the knowledge gained in manufacturing provides important inputs not only for improving the manufacturing process but also in designing new products. Gradually this enables local suppliers to acquire new capabilities. For example, the research of Murtha et al. (2001) on the flat

screen television industry, one with a highly complex and capital-intensive manufacturing process, shows that engineers working on manufacturing plants in Taiwan provided valuable insights into the designing of new products. Schuler et al. (2006, p. 306) track the shift in flat screen television production from 'Japan (the first high-volume producer), and then to South Korea, next to Taiwan, and now to China and Singapore (the locations that currently have the highest levels of production)'. With this deepening of production capabilities, developing country firms can garner enough expertise to compete on a global scale.

7.4.2 The role of transnational corporations in employment generation and local capability development

In diverse countries and sectors TNCs have helped in creating mass employment, better working conditions and spill-over effects of improving domestic firm capabilities. As noted above, TNCs can work with local suppliers to improve their technical knowledge, usually in the form of machinery, blueprints, production and quality control manuals, product and service specifications and training (Ernst and Kim, 2002). The Mexican automobile and auto component industries are examples of how local capability development can be facilitated by TNCs working with local firms, gaining from the transfer of sophisticated production techniques from associated TNCs (Pack and Saggi, 2001). The entry of US car manufacturers into Mexico was followed by car manufacturers from Japan and Europe but also by international automobile component suppliers. In a short period from this investment there were 300 local auto component suppliers with strong links to these TNC car manufacturers. In some cases, TNCs also introduced management techniques such as best practices in total quality management, continuous improvement processes (the Japanese **kaizan** philosophy) and inventory audits.

FDI also contributed to improving the auto sector's productivity in upstream activities, such as design and R&D. For example, working with local and overseas suppliers and designers Indian firms such as Tata Motors and Mahindra & Mahindra have now designed and developed, respectively, the Tata Nano, the world's cheapest car, and Scorpio, a sports utility vehicle (Kale, 2010). Overall, then, it could be argued that the impact of FDI on increased productivity and competitiveness has ensured that benefits accrue to consumers and labour in the auto industry at least in developing countries. Workers who have lost their jobs in the US car manufacturing industry, in Detroit, for example, as a result of this competition, may see things differently.

There are some who argue that the subcontracting model and incentives to TNCs that have epitomized the 'race to the bottom' can also act as a precursor for better conditions in developing countries. The Nobel Prize winning economist Paul Krugman argues that 'bad jobs at bad wages are better than no jobs at all' (Krugman, 1997). *The Economist* (2000) claims that, specifically in poorer countries, TNCs pay better than domestic companies and create more new jobs faster. For example, in Turkey, salaries offered by foreign firms are 124% above average and their workforces are growing by 11.5% a year compared with 0.6% in local firms. Krugman argues further that in developing countries the export of raw materials generates limited revenues and inefficient domestic manufacturing sectors generate fewer jobs. He goes on to suggest that there has been distinctive improvement in the lives of poor people and this is partly because a TNC provides higher salaries than workers could get elsewhere and has created a ripple effect throughout the economy. As more people become employed, fewer people are dependent on agriculture, so rural wages improve; gradually the pool of unemployed urban people reduces, so companies start to compete with each other for workers, and salaries also begin to rise. Improvement starts taking place as is evident in the cases of South Korea and Malaysia. This is the indirect and unintended result of the actions of TNCs and local entrepreneurs.

In the end he suggests:

> It is not an edifying spectacle; but no matter how base the motives of those involved, the result has been to move hundreds of millions of people from abject poverty to something still awful but nonetheless significantly better.

> *(Krugman, 1997)*

Following on from Krugman's argument it is evident that some countries such as South Korea, Malaysia, China and India have moved from being just a source of cheap labour to a home of TNCs. Operating in diverse sectors, such as automobile, petroleum, pharmaceuticals and IT, and competing globally with European and North American companies, these TNCs are indicative of the emergence of rising powers.

7.5 Transnational corporations from developing countries

The rise of East Asia's Newly Industrializing Countries (NIC), followed by the growth in the rising powers, has led to a new breed of TNCs. The increase in overseas FDI and the new TNCs that embody it from economies as diverse as China, India, Brazil, Korea, Singapore, Malaysia and Taiwan is a remarkable phenomenon. These firms are key players in local economies and, as our opening discussion of Tata showed, are globalizing their business to access markets in developed countries.

7.5.1 From import substitution industrialization to export-led manufacturing

One of the drivers of this change has been the policy environment in the rising powers, which was briefly overviewed in Chapter 3. In the 1960s it was clear that the objective of economic development in general and technological development in particular was not progressing well for many countries. Suspicion of free markets and protection of local industry and technology became the dominant means to achieve desirable development goals, which led to import substitution being the dominant development paradigm. Import substitution industrialization (ISI) in the context of Brazil and India was discussed in Chapter 3. ISI was seen as appropriate for economies which were dominated by agricultural or natural resource sectors that faced declining terms of trade with larger and more industrialized countries (Forbes and Wield, 2002).

Let's look at the main tenets of the import substitution model to see how the change of policy in the rising powers enabled a new type of TNC to evolve. From the beginning of the 1950s Asian and Latin American countries, such as India, Brazil and Mexico, embraced import substitution as a national policy for economic development. Regulated markets and industry protection to achieve development goals formed the basis of this model. Policy was designed to encourage companies to develop everything indigenously and avoid imports of goods from overseas. The Indian government, through strict investment licensing, effectively stamped out domestic competition and through strict import licensing it eliminated foreign competition. For example, in the case of Indian auto industries the government restricted manufacturing of automobiles to only two companies and controlled the number of vehicles each company could manufacture each year.

In some developing countries such as India and Brazil these policies helped in building industrial bases without the use of FDI in the early stages. However, by the 1980s it was clear that countries that had followed ISI were witnessing low economic growth rates in general and low industrial growth rates in particular.

Therefore the dominant policy of ISI changed between 1980 and 1990 towards export orientation policies, following the NIC model. Most countries started abandoning ISI in favour of export-oriented economic policies, involving opening up domestic markets for competition and allowing the free import of goods and technology. Policy focused on development of local firm capabilities through competition and encouraged export of products from domestic firms. It was argued that exporting helped firms to compete with international best practice and operate at an international scale, and this would push them up the product value chain. As a result, the first wave of TNCs that emerged from developing countries were dominated by Latin American and Asian countries, such as Brazil, Argentina, Columbia, Malaysia and India (Dunning et al., 1997). For example, in 1980, Brazil invested over US$1 billion overseas, much of which was accounted for by the giant state-owned enterprise Petrobras. These first-wave TNCs mainly focused on investments in neighbouring and other countries, which were at a similar or earlier stage of their development. Lall (1983) suggested that more than 95 per cent of Brazil's outward investment was in primary sectors such as oil exploration, construction and agriculture while about five per cent of Indian foreign investments were in hotels, banks, insurance and trading ventures. Elaborating on Indian overseas investment, Lall observes that Indian first-wave overseas investments were spread over a much broader spectrum of activity; the largest sector was clothing, accounting for a quarter of total capital held abroad. This was followed by paper and pulp, engineering, food processing and chemicals.

In both Korea and Taiwan the state assisted the growth of enterprises by protecting some sectors for domestic firms and by providing subsidies to firms that met export obligations. For example, Korea restricted entry of foreign firms in the electronics sector and the automobile industry. The policy of import substitution followed by an export-oriented period for particular industries is credited with enhancing Korea's technological learning and deepening industrialization. East Asian TNCs have emerged partly as a result of this process that included state intervention. They are represented in a wider range of industries, in many cases because of deliberate policy choices by government to diversify business. For example, in the early 1960s, Hyundai along with Daewoo were encouraged by the government to enter the car market and develop capabilities to compete in world markets. In 1962, the Korean government allowed imports of parts and provided local market protection from foreign cars, and preferential allocation of foreign exchange was tied to the degree of local content. Hyundai built Korea's first locally designed car, the Pony, in 1975, within a protected home market, and by 1980, Hyundai had achieved 92% local content. Having directed and supported the industry through the risky 'infant stages' of learning, Hyundai went on to develop and produce more new products.

From the late 1980s, Latin American countries, such as Brazil, also opened up their economies and switched to export-oriented policies, but in the face of severe international competition many firms went bankrupt or were forced to downsize. Some Latin American TNCs, such as CEMEX from Mexico, have been able to gain competitive advantage by specializing or intensifying their activities in manufactured goods based on natural resources, such as pulp and paper, petrochemicals and cement.

7.5.2 The rise of transnational corporations from China and India

From the turn of the millennium we witnessed the second wave of developing-country TNCs from China, India and Brazil. This represents quite a different phenomenon, since it is driven more by a search for markets and technological knowledge to compete successfully in the global economy, aimed at industrialized regions such as Europe and the USA (Kale, 2009). Many TNCs from developing countries are no longer competing in markets occupied by incumbents but are creating new markets and technologies by their organizational and strategic innovation (Mathews, 2006), for example the call centre and business process outsourcing sector developed by Indian IT firms and Tata Motors production of the world's cheapest car that targeted a market neglected by other auto TNCs.

The success of these firms results from changing economic conditions in their home countries. For example, a major impetus for Indian firms came from the liberalization of the economy and removal of restrictions on foreign exchange. It was also linked with diasporic networks: the return of skilled, entrepreneurial migrants who had lived and worked in the USA or Europe (see Chapter 6).

Within this broad trend, the emergence of TNCs from China, India and Brazil is particularly notable. By the end of 2004 China had emerged as the fifth largest overseas investor with a total of US$37 billion (Child and Rodrigues, 2005). Similarly, since 2000 there has been a significant increase in overseas investment by Indian industry (Kale, 2009). Firms from rising power countries are making inroads in sectors such as manufacturing (steel) and services (IT) as well as knowledge-intensive sectors like pharmaceuticals. Companies such as Infosys, Lenovo, Tata Steel and ArcelorMittal are now competing at a global level. Tata, the largest business conglomerate from India, has made high profile investments in the UK, while China's Lenovo and Haier have made substantial inroads in the USA.

From both countries, TNCs are investing overseas to access advanced technologies and research capabilities in other countries, as well as to adapt products to new markets and tap specialized knowledge in other developing countries (WIR, 2005). Athreye and Kapoor (2009) argue that this has significant implications for host countries' economic development, as seen in Chapter 3. Industrial policies traditionally encouraged FDI to boost local employment and economic growth,

China and India's economies have been, and still are, particularly in the case of China, characterized by significant government involvement in business and regulation-controlled markets. However, it is important to note that in China the state played a much bigger role than in India and Brazil. The main driving factor for Chinese TNCs is therefore support of the state while Indian TNCs are mainly privately owned firms that the state has encouraged within a framework of neoliberal economic development in order to drive growth. The Chinese government singled out some of the firms as 'national champions', giving them financial support and protection to acquire assets that enable them to compete in the world market. As a result Chinese overseas investments are mainly observed in primary sectors, such as minerals and energy, while Indian investments are in more diverse sectors, such as high technology (IT, pharmaceutical) and manufacturing (auto and steel).

Summary and looking forward

This chapter has given you an overview of the world of TNCs and their role in development. This was important for a number of reasons. In terms of the rising powers the important point is that as these countries move up the international ladder of development their firms tend to internationalize and become key players in their ongoing economic success. This was true of the periods of European and US hegemony as well as when the East Asian states grew to prominence. For the latest group of rising powers that we have been focusing on over the past five chapters, especially China, the state has been an important actor in promoting these firms so that there is nothing that is purely 'economic' in their rise. Once successful, many of these TNCs have a reach and power that exceeds that of many nation states, which makes them important development actors with the ability to exert both positive and negative outcomes on those societies where they operate.

To explore these issues in more detail we:

- reviewed the development and composition of TNCs from a historical perspective to the present day
- examined the debate around Fordism/post-Fordism and the de-coupling of production chains

- contrasted different arguments surrounding TNC activity in developing economies and whether it helps or harms

- looked at the transformation of developing countries' economic models from import substitution to export orientation, and the link to the rise of TNCs from the rising powers of China and India in particular.

It seems likely that over the coming years TNCs from China, India and Brazil will become ever more commonplace in all our lives, just as the Ford Motor Company of Detroit did so many years ago.

References

Athreye, S. and Kapur, S. (2009), 'Introduction: the internationalization of Chinese and Indian firms – trends, motivations and strategy', *Industrial and Corporate Change*, vol. 18, no. 2, pp. 209–221.

BBC (2010) 'Oil rig blaze off Louisiana leaves at least 11 missing', *BBC*, 21 April 2010 [online], http://news.bbc.co.uk/1/hi/world/americas/8634874.stm (Accessed 16 July 2011).

Boje, D.M. and Khan, F.R. (2008) 'Story-branding by empire entrepreneurs: Nike, child labour, and Pakistan's soccer ball industry', *Journal of Small Business Entrepreneurship*, vol. 22, no. 1, pp. 9–24.

Chamberlain, G. (2010) 'British high street chains are named by sweatshop probe', *The Guardian*, 12 December 2010 [online], http://www.guardian.co.uk/business/2010/dec/12/british-high-street-sweatshop-probe, (Accessed 1 January 2011).

Chandler, A.D. (1977) *The Visible Hand: The Managerial Revolution in American Business*, Cambridge, MA, Belknap.

Child, J. and Rodrigues, S. (2005) 'The internationalization of Chinese firms: a case for theoretical extension?', *Management and Organization Review*, vol. 1, no. 3, pp. 381–410.

Christian Aid (2004) *Behind the Mask: The Real Face of Corporate Social Responsibility*, London, Christian Aid, [online], http://www.st-andrews.ac.uk/~csearweb/aptopractice/Behind-the-mask.pdf (Accessed 24 June 2011).

Crain, D.W. and Abraham, S. (2008) 'Using value-chain analysis to discover customers' strategic needs', *Strategy and Leadership,* vol. 36, no. 4, pp. 29–39.

Dicken, P. (1986) *Global Shift: Industrial Change in a Turbulent World*, London, Harper and Row.

Dreier, P. and Appelbaum, R. (1999) 'The campus anti-sweatshop movement', *The American Prospect*, 1 September 1999 [online], http://www.prospect.org/cs/articles?article=the_campus_antisweatshop_movement (Accessed 28 June 2011).

Drezner, D. (2000) 'Bottom feeders', *Foreign Policy*, vol. 121, pp. 64–70.

Dunning, J.H., Van Hoesel, R. and Narula, R. (1997) 'Third World multinationals revisited: new developments and theoretical implications' in Dunning, J.H. (ed.), *Globalization, Trade and Foreign Direct Investment*, Oxford, Pergamon Press.

Economist, The (2000) 'The world's view of multinationals', *The Economist*, 27 January 2000 [online], http://www.economist.com/node/276872 (Accessed 1 January 2011).

Ernst, D. (2000) 'Global production networks and the changing geography of innovation systems: implications for developing countries', *Economics Study Area Working Papers*, no. 9, East-West Center, Economics Study Area.

Ernst, D. and Kim, L. (2002) 'Global production networks, knowledge diffusion, and local capability formation', *Research Policy*, vol. 31, pp. 1417–1429.

Financial Times (2004) 'Lenovo shares slide on $1.75bn IBM acquisition', *Financial Times*, 9 December 2004 [online], http://www.ft.com/cms/s/0/8f21d9aa-4992-11d9-8ce9-00000e2511c8.html#axzz1AUj0s5VG (Accessed 28 June 2011).

Financial Times (2006) 'Empire strikes back as Tata bids for Corus', *Financial Times*, 21 October 2006 [online], http://www.ft.com/cms/s/0/b43abc30-60a0-11db-a716-0000779e2340.html#axzz1SFKlBlze (Accessed 28 June 2011).

Forbes, N. and Wield, D. (2002) *From Followers to Leaders: Managing Technology and Innovation*, London, Routledge.

Gramsci, A. (1971) *Selections From the Prison Notebooks*, ed. and trans. by Hoare, Q. and Nowell Smith, G., New York, International Publishers.

Harvey, D. (1989) *The Condition of Postmodernity*, Blackwell, Oxford.

Harvard Business School (HBS) (1994) 'International sourcing in athletic footwear: Nike and Reebok', *HBS Case Study*, no. 9-394-189, pp. 2–5.

Jenkins, R. (1991) '*Transnational Corporations and Uneven Development: Internationalization of Capital and the Third World*' (2nd edition), London, Routledge.

Jenkins, R. (2005) 'Globalisation, corporate social responsibility and poverty', *International Affairs,* vol. 81, no. 3, pp. 525–540.

Kale, D. (2009) 'International strategies of pharmaceutical firms', published and presented at *'Emerging multinationals': Outward Foreign Direct Investment from Emerging and Developing Economies*, Copenhagen Business School, Denmark.

Kale, D. (2010) 'Sources of innovation and technological capability development in the Indian automobile industry', *The 8th GLOBELICS International Conference Making Innovation Work for Society: Linking, Leveraging and Learning,* 1–3 November 2010, University of Malaya, Kuala Lumpur, Malaysia.

Kiely, R. (1998) 'Globalization, post-Fordism, and the contemporary context of development', *International Sociology*, vol. 13, no. 1, pp. 95–113.

Klein, N. (2000) *No Logo: Taking Aim at the Brand Bullies*, Knopf Canada, Picador.

Krugman, P. (1997) 'In praise of cheap labour', *Slate,* 21 March 1997 [online], http://www.slate.com/id/1918/ (Accessed 18 June 2011).

Lall, S. (1983) *The New Multinationals: The Spread of Third World Enterprises*, Chichester, Wiley.

Locke, R.M. (2003) 'The promise and perils of globalization: the case of Nike', in Kochan, T. and Schmalensee, R. (eds) *Management Inventing and Delivering Its Future*, Cambridge, MA, MIT Press, pp. 39–71.

Mathews, J.A. (2006) 'Dragon multinationals: new players in 21st century globalization', *Asia Pacific Journal of Management*, vol. 23, no. 1, pp. 5–27.

Murtha, T.P., Lenway, S.A. and Hart, J.A. (2001) 'Managing new industry creation: global knowledge formation and entrepreneurship' in *High Technology*, Stanford, CA, Stanford University Press.

Obi, C. (2009) 'Nigeria's Niger Delta: understanding the complex drivers of violent oil-related conflict', *African Development*, vol. 34, no. 2, pp. 103–128.

Pack, H. and Saggi, K. (2001) 'Vertical technology transfer via international outsourcing', *Journal of Development Economics*, vol. 65, pp. 389–415.

Piore, M.J. and Sabel, C.F. (1984) *The Second Industrial Divide: Possibilities for Prosperity*, New York, Basic Books.

Schoenberger, E. (1988) 'From Fordism to flexible accumulation: technology, competitive strategies and international location', *Environment and Planning: Society and Space*, vol. 6, pp. 245–262.

Schuler, D.A., Eden, L. and Lenway, S. (2006) 'Multinational corporations through the uneven development lens' in Jain, S. and Vachani, S. (eds) *Multinational Corporations and Global Poverty Reduction*, Cheltenham, Edward Elgar.

Spar, D.L. (1998) 'The spotlight and the bottom line: how multinationals export human rights', *Foreign Affairs*, vol. 77, no. 2, pp. 7–12.

Time (1977) 'Business: IBM withdraws from India', *Time*, 28 November 1977 [online], http://www.time.com/time/magazine/article/0,9171,919167,00.html (Accessed 1 January, 2011).

Watchman, R. (2006) 'Empire strikes back: India forges new steel alliance', *The Guardian*, 22 October 2001 [online], http://www.guardian.co.uk/business/2006/oct/22/india.theobserver (Accessed 1 January 2011).

WIR (1991) 'The Triad in foreign direct investment', *World Investment Report 1991*, New York, United Nations Centre on Transnational Corporations [online], http://www.unctad.org/en/docs/wir1991overview_en.pdf (Accessed 10 July 2011).

WIR (2005) 'Transnational corporations and the internationalization of R&D', *World Investment Report 2005*, New York, United Nations [online], http://www.unctad.org/en/docs/wir2005_en.pdf (Accessed ??).

WIR (2009) 'Transnational corporations, agricultural development and production', *World Investment Report 2009*, New York, United Nations Centre on Transnational Corporations [online], http://www.unctad.org/en/docs/wir2009pt1_en.pdf (Accessed 28 June 2011).

WIR (2010) 'Investing in a low-carbon economy', *World Investment Report 2010*, New York, United Nations Centre on Transnational Corporations [online], http://www.unctad.org/en/docs/wir2010_en.pdf (Accessed 28 June 2011).

Wright, G. (2004) 'Lenovo buys IBM PC business', *The Guardian*, 8 December 2004 [online], http://www.guardian.co.uk/technology/2004/dec/08/business.china (Accessed 28 June 2011).

Further reading

Forbes, N. and Wield, D. (2002) From Followers to Leaders: Managing Technology and Innovation, London: Routledge.

Jenkins, R. (1991) Transnational Corporations and Uneven Development: Internationalization of Capital and the Third World, 2nd edition, London: Routledge.

Thinking about poverty

Hazel Johnson and Masuma Farooki

Introduction

In spite of the dramatic changes in the world economy that you read about in earlier chapters, and in spite of international efforts such as the Millennium Development Goals (MDGs), world poverty still exists on a grand scale. In 2010, the World Bank reported:

- Estimates … show about 1.4 billion people living below the international poverty line of US$1.25 a day in 2005, equivalent to more than one fourth of the developing world's population.

- … the triple punch of the food, fuel and financial crises [2008] has slowed the pace of poverty reduction and created new risks for the hunger target under MDG Goal 1 and has impaired progress toward other MDGs.

- Compared with what was expected before the financial crisis, by the end of 2010 an estimated 64 million more people [than originally anticipated] are expected to be living on under US$1.25 a day.

(World Bank, 2010)

Nevertheless, the bank also noted:

- Poverty incidence declined from 52 per cent of the global population in 1981 to 42 per cent in 1990 and 25 per cent in 2005. That proportion is expected to be 15 per cent by 2015 [the deadline for the period of action on the Millennium Development Goals].

- Given the above trends, the first Millennium Development Goal (MDG) target of halving the 1990 poverty rate by 2015 remains within reach at the global level.

(World Bank, 2010)

Are these statements by the World Bank compatible or contradictory? As you will see in this chapter, the conceptualization and measurement of poverty is not straightforward. Poverty and development expert, David Hulme, pointed out in 2010 that in addition to around 1.5 billion people who lived in extreme income poverty of under US$1.25 a day (the internationally agreed poverty line of 2005), there were another billion or more who were above this line but under a second established poverty line of US$2 a day. Overall, Hulme estimated that 25% of the world's population were living in extreme poverty (less than US$1.25 a day) with 47% of the world's population living in poverty of less than US$2 a day (Hulme, 2010, p.45).

This chapter examines some of the discussions behind these global trends in poverty and poverty reduction. Specifically, we aim to:

- outline the influential debates about world poverty since the mid-20th century

- discuss contested causes, concepts and measures of poverty

- interpret and reflect on quantitative data about poverty.

We do not necessarily have answers to conflictive data and statements about poverty (and nor do many analysts who have debated them for a long time). But we do provide some background on how poverty is conceptualized, as well as some of the ways in which it is measured. We also link back to earlier chapters that have explored how development can be understood, and the changes that are taking place in the world that influence how we see development, its potential and its contradictions.

8.1 Poverty as a global issue

Activity 8.1

Why should we be concerned about global poverty and about reducing or eradicating it?

First think about your own responses to this question and note down your answers.

Spend about 10 minutes on this activity.

Discussion

David Hulme, mentioned above, published an impressive synthesis of data and arguments about global poverty in 2010. He listed the following reasons for why we should be concerned about global poverty:

- There is a moral case to reduce poverty – there is no reason for allowing, or tolerating, poverty in a world of affluence (Hulme's own position).

- There is a case of self-interest – reducing poverty will reduce the likelihood of conflict and will reinforce social stability. For example, conflicts that emerged in 2010 and 2011 in some of the Arab states, while not simply about poverty, are closely related to the opportunities people have for making a living, particularly young people.

- There is the historical responsibility held by developed countries that have exploited, or otherwise taken advantage of, other parts of the world from colonial times to current trade regimes (which you have read about in earlier chapters, see particularly Chapter 3).

- Hulme also notes the issue of climate change, which has been largely brought about by northern industrialization and northern agricultural practices, but which is likely to bring adverse effects to poor people using basic technologies in vulnerable landscapes in the global South.

To these points we could add another, which links poverty and economic growth. It is possible to have overall growth of an economy while poverty remains. There are two aspects to this phenomenon. The first is that economic growth can be accompanied by increasing income inequality. We return to this point in Chapter 9, which discusses different types and effects of inequality within and between countries, including income inequality. The second is that sustained economic growth relies on internal demand for goods and services, which in turn requires that people have enough income. This kind of challenge has faced the largely export-driven economic growth in China in the early 21st century, for example. As in any other economy, if people do not have enough income to buy goods and services, economic growth will face problems in the longer term.

As it happens, in 2010, the reduction in poverty in China counted for most of the world's poverty reduction. By contrast, while poor people as a proportion of the population in India had declined in 2010, the absolute numbers of people in poverty had grown, creating a serious long-term challenge in spite of being a rising power. On the other hand, the demographics of China and India are different, posing different issues for economic growth and poverty reduction in the medium to longer term. In China, because of the one child policy, the population will become skewed to the ageing end of the spectrum, which will affect the availability of labour for production as well as having cost implications for retirement and healthcare. India, on the other hand, has a relatively youthful population, which implies available labour for production and income creation, but also a huge demand for employment.

China and India are important in thinking about global poverty because of the size of their populations and impact of the size of their populations on the data on world poverty. They should not, though, detract from thinking about the spread and existence of poverty more broadly

Concerns about poverty as a global issue are relatively recent in the history of human poverty as a whole. Although one can trace concern for the poor back to the writings of early philosophers and other thinkers, and to the place of charity in many world religions, the need to act on it in a more global sense has grown with more recent changes in national economies and related population increase, increased understandings of the connectedness of world events and the world economy, and enhanced awareness of the implications of uneven development.

World poverty as a phenomenon began to be addressed seriously after World War II and its aftermath. Hulme (2010, p. 23) cites US President Roosevelt's 1941 Four Freedoms speech: 'The third freedom is freedom from want ... economic understandings which will secure to every nation a healthy peacetime life for its inhabitants – everywhere in the world.' The broad history of this post World War II period saw key changes in the international economy, including the formation and progress of the Bretton Woods Institutions (see Figure 8.1) as economic regulators, and the concomitant process of decolonization during the 1950s. In particular, there is the founding of the United Nations (UN) in 1945, leading over time to a vast UN 'system' of multilateral agencies that reports to the UN General Assembly. The overall panorama is summarized in Chapter 3, and Chapter 12 provides a political analysis of the history of aid.

Some institutions that are part of the UN system, such as the World Bank, have at times pursued policies that have increased rather than reduced poverty, as in the Structural Adjustment Programmes (SAPs) of the 1980s and 1990s (discussed in Chapter 3; there is further explanation in Chapter 12). The problems caused by SAPs, including the generation of further poverty through the liberalization of markets and reduction of state intervention, was reflected

Figure 8.1 July 1944: US delegation to the Bretton Woods Monetary Conference in New Hampshire, USA

in the World Bank's *World Development Report* on poverty in 1990. However, prior to this, as economist Paul Mosley explains, the World Bank went through a series of debates reflecting on changes in the world economy and the persistence of global poverty (Mosley, 2002) – also outlined in Chapter 1. Mosley's account about the influences on the changing perspectives in the World Bank before and after 1990 can be summarized as follows.

Early UN documents on poverty from the 1950s see it primarily as a problem of **unemployment** and **underemployment**. Mosley observes that this was a 'modern insight'. It was based on the idea that the only asset that poor people have is their own labour. Poor people lack other assets, such as physical, social and human capital (concepts we will come back to in Chapter 10). Therefore, in the early 1950s, the focus was on promoting economic growth through investment and technologies that could also (or were thought to) increase employment, and therefore raise incomes of the poor.

Mosley argues that the 1950s and 1960s were seen as positive periods in terms of world development and it was assumed that the policies pursued at that time were indeed having an effect on poverty reduction. However, this view was dispelled by country level poverty studies in the 1970s, which showed that growth was not necessarily leading to a reduction in poverty and that inequality was increasing. In addition, famines in Ethiopia and Bangladesh spurred new interest in poverty.

Famines and new data led to the proposal for *Redistribution with Growth* – a study carried out by the World Bank and the UK Institute of Development Studies (Chenery et al., 1975). This proposal promoted a poverty focus based on:

- a shift of expenditure from industry to agriculture

- within these sectors, a shift from capital-intensive industry to a focus on the informal sector (see Box 8.1)
- a shift from large-scale agriculture and cash crops to food crops.

Box 8.1 Informal and formal sector/economy

The term *informal economy or sector* refers to all economic activities by workers and economic units that are, in law or in practice, not covered or insufficiently covered by formal arrangements. Their activities are not included in the law, which means that they are operating outside the formal reach of the law; or they are not covered in practice, which means that, although they are operating within the formal reach of the law, the law is not applied or not enforced; or the law discourages compliance because it is inappropriate, burdensome, or imposes excessive costs.

(ILO, 2010)

In practice, the term 'informal sector' is used to include activities such as petty trading, self-employment, casual and irregular wage work, personal services and small enterprises. It is characterized by its relative ease of entry, low capital requirements and labour-intensiveness.

It is often thought that the informal sector lacks organization; however, recent studies have shown that there is a high level of organization in the informal sector as well as innovation in technology and markets.

The formal economy or sector encompasses all jobs with normal hours and regular wages that are recognized as income sources on which income taxes must be paid. A formal-sector worker is registered with the relevant authorities (social security, for example) and is, therefore, entitled to the government-provided benefits offered to formal-sector workers.

In practice it refers to larger-scale commercial enterprises and the public sector. It is characterized by relatively stable employment and higher wages than the informal sector; and workers are more often organized.

One particular manifestation of the proposal was **integrated rural development programmes (IRDPs)**. However these programmes often did not succeed because of a lack of internal capacity within countries to integrate rural development, and a lack of adequate aid to support the process.

This initial poverty focus was derailed not only because of project failure but also because of the oil price rises of the late 1970s and the recession of the 1980s. Economic liberalization came to the fore and reinforced views about how economic growth (and poverty reduction) could be achieved in the longer term. This perspective came to dominate policies in spite of the publication of the *Brandt Report* in 1980, and a movement amongst developing countries demanding (in vain) a New International Economic Order. The *Brandt Report* was a seminal document written by the Independent

Commission on International Development Issues, chaired by the former German Chancellor, Willy Brandt, and was based on a line demarcating 'North' and 'South'. The report presented an argument that the North was wealthy because of unequal terms of trade with the South, and aimed to promote redistribution from North to South (Brandt, 1980). Nonetheless, the World Bank turned to 'structural adjustment' (see Chapter 3) as the mechanism for promoting growth, with the idea that growth would indeed trickle down and reduce poverty. Aid became highly conditional on progress made in developing countries (see Chapter 12).

As Mosley notes, the recession and structural adjustment affected different parts of the world differently. The structure of global poverty shifted towards Africa in particular, although living standards were found to have deteriorated in some South American countries too (Cornia et al., 1987). Poverty in South Asia remained static while declining in East Asia. The deterioration also included Eastern Europe.

A debate emerged about 'old' and 'new' poverty. Old poverty was that resulting from low productivity and low wages and income for most people in agriculture and the informal sector; and new poverty arose from SAPs. Mosley argues that there are different responses to these types of poverty. The first requires structural change (for example, land reform or investment in new technologies) while the second requires stimulating global demand and reflation of the economy.

Given the failure of SAPs and the increase in poverty in the 1980s, in particular in Africa, the World Bank (and other institutions in the UN system) was forced to refocus on poverty. This led to some influential publications that have laid markers for the focus on poverty ever since.

In 1990, two documents were published. First, there was the *World Development Report (WDR)* of the World Bank, which proposed an anti-poverty framework of policies and measures based on increasing labour intensity (or productivity), investing in human capital (health and education) and social safety nets. This was a strategy based on different dimensions of poverty, not simply on the income that people earn. The UNDP also initiated an annual report for the first time in 1990, called the *Human Development Report (HDR)*. This report aimed to address the multiple dimensions of poverty but with an even broader perspective (see Box 8.2).

Box 8.2 Extracts from the first *Human Development Report 1990*

Human development is a process of enlarging people's choices. The most critical ones are to lead a long and healthy life, to be educated and to enjoy a decent standard of living. Additional choices include political freedom, guaranteed human rights and self-respect – what Adam Smith called the ability to mix with others without being 'ashamed to appear in public'.

Human development … brings together the production and distribution of commodities and the expansion and use of human capabilities. It also focuses on choices – on what people should have, be and do to be able to ensure their own livelihood. Human development is, moreover, concerned not only with basic needs satisfaction but also with human development as a participatory and dynamic process. It applies equally to less developed and highly developed countries.

(Cited in UNDP, 2010, p. 12)

Ten years later, in 2000, there was the creation of the UN MDGs (introduced in Chapter 1), with the aim of reducing extreme poverty and hunger by 50 per cent between 1990 and 2015. (This was MDG 1, see Chapter 1.) At the same time, a new WDR from the World Bank focused again on poverty (World Bank, 2000) but with a somewhat different emphasis from the 1990 report and strongly influenced by an understanding of the multiple dimensions of poverty. Opportunity, security and empowerment were the new mantras. As noted by Mosley:

> … opportunity and security are the lineal descendants of 'investment in the human capital of the poor' and social safety nets, respectively, but empowerment is quite a new theme. And labour intensity has disappeared off the map – though not because it has become any less true in the twenty-first century that the extremely poor derive most of their income from casual labour only. It remains the case … *that the chronically very poor are those with no assets at all* – and therefore forced by definition to depend either on labour or on connections of some kind for their livelihood.

(Mosley, 2002, p. 60)

With this report, Mosley's point remains that the only resource or asset that all poor people have (except those that are too young, old or sick) is their labour. However, as you will see in Chapters 9 and 10, there may be constraints on gaining employment because of a deficit of skills or discrimination because of gender, ethnicity and age. But what about empowerment? This new emphasis in the WDR of 2000 resulted from a parallel set of studies carried out under World Bank auspices on *Voices of the Poor*. These were first-hand accounts of the different ways that people experienced poverty and their frequent powerlessness to change things. The accounts were collected in three volumes and given worldwide publicity.

However, in 2010, Hulme maintained that the world was still not paying enough attention to global poverty, asking 'Why don't we care ...?' Moreover, in a more recent text, Mosley notes that, while the main focus of anti-poverty policy globally has been in pursuit of the MDGs in the first years of the 21st century, 'a fundamental element missing from the anti-poverty literature, and hence from the global poverty effort, is ... the political motivation to deploy [policies] in support of the poor' (Mosley, 2012).

Understanding the process of changing perspectives on poverty as we have done in this section is an analytical approach. Hulme's question and Mosley's critique of the global anti-poverty effort are normative statements which argue that we should do something (more) about world poverty. This is a typical tension in the study of international development – relating what is (and how it came about) to what might or could be and what is needed to get there.

Activity 8.2

Before continuing, make sure you have understood the main elements of the history of ideas about poverty during the last part of the 20th and early part of the 21st centuries. In particular, you might like to make notes under the following headings:

- Why we should be concerned about global poverty?
- Why may economic growth not always lead to a reduction in poverty?
- Why can poverty be seen as primarily a problem of unemployment and underemployment?
- What is meant by the informal and formal sectors of the economy?
- Why have some economists focused on the role of redistribution: within economies and from the global North to the global South?
- What are the key foci of the *World Development Reports* of 1990 and 2000?
- Why is poverty reduction a political issue?

Spend about 15 minutes on this activity.

8.2 The causes of poverty

How can poverty be explained and what are the reasons for its persistence? This section begins to examine these questions.

Activity 8.3

Imagine you are doing a walkabout in the area where you live. You are probably aware of some streets or houses that seem poorer (or conversely, richer) than others, and you may be aware of parts of the area where you live as being commonly perceived as poor, or depressed, or experiencing some form of deprivation.

In thinking about it, what would you say were the causes of that poverty? Would you say that it was:

- unemployment
- low wages
- low levels of education or skills
- chronic or acute illness or ill-health
- abandonment, e.g. by a breadwinner
- lack of attention by social services
- discrimination on grounds such as ethnicity or age
- other?

Spend about five minutes on this activity.

Discussion

You might say that it was some or all of these ('multiple deprivations' – an idea that we return to in Section 8.3). However, is the list above a list of possible causes or of manifestations of poverty? So, for example, what causes unemployment, low wages, low levels of education and skills, chronic illness, etc.? Is it individual human agency? Is it something about the society in which we live? Is it something about the relationship between the society – or country – in which we live and other countries and economies in the world?

While individuals and households experience poverty and deprivation, and may act on it in positive and less positive ways, we need to look beyond individual people and households to understand causes. To reflect on explanations of poverty, we will go back to Chapter 2, Table 2.2. We are going to take just three of the rows in that table and slightly reorder them. Those we are taking are: the ones on 'main claims/concerns', 'international implications', and 'examples of development practice' (see Table 8.1).

Activity 8.4

Look at the columns on the different approaches to (or theories of) development (Table 8.1) and examine critically the statements below.

Make notes on what you think these statements say or imply are the causes of poverty. (You can also look back at the explanations of the approaches in Boxes 2.1–2.3 and 2.5 in Chapter 2.)

Add notes of your own to reflect on how adequate an account the statements provide in your view. What is missing from the statements? Do elements of the statements need to be combined?

Neoliberalism suggests that the main cause of poverty is distortion in markets and limits on competition, which may result from state interference or the development of **monopolies** or **oligopolies**. These could result in further inefficiencies, limiting employment and hampering access to goods and services, in effect stifling the 'trickle down' of the benefits of economic development. Thus neoliberals were against any form of market distortion, whether it came from the state or from monopolies or oligopolies.

Table 8.1 Elements of key approaches to development

	Neoliberalism	Structuralism	Interventionism	People-centred
Main claims/ concerns	Emphasis on free market solutions and limitations on state/ government action. For a strong but limited state, allowing markets to emerge and work.	Emphasis on the structural bias in world economy against growth and industrialization in developing countries. Need for strong public action in the form of national controls on economic flows (investment, trade) and international regulation to change international commodity markets, technology transfer, etc. More radical versions emphasized 'de-linking' from world economy and national or autarchic development.	Something of a mid-point between neoliberalism and structuralism. Has neoliberal emphasis on market solutions and on capitalism as the motor for development but recognizes market limitations and failures and need for state intervention to address social problems (poverty, education).	Emphasis on meeting human needs (poverty, unemployment, education, housing, etc.) and for policies directed to these ends rather than macro-level aims (economic growth, industrialization, etc.). Emphasizes the negative effects of industrialization strategies.
International implications	Implies that development occurs through liberalized integration between national and world economy, with free flow of trade, investment and finance. Politically for stringent conditions on granting public money through international aid efforts and the like.	Implies a highly regulated and managed relationship between national and international economies; nationalist in political orientation and an anti-colonial/ -imperialist political rhetoric.	Entails liberalization of international economic flows, but also for international public action to achieve social goals. Political rhetoric of international consensus around markets, governance reform and social improvements.	Can contain anti-corporate discourses against multinational corporations as well as radical critiques of impact of World Bank aid projects. Presents a picture of communities struggling against outside (national and international) impositions and exploitation.
Examples of development practice	Structural adjustment policies of the IMF and World Bank Trade liberalization, e.g. through World Trade Organization (WTO)	Import Substitution Industrialization (ISI) policies of 1960s and 1970s campaigns for New International Economic Order of 1970s	Poverty Reduction Strategy Papers (PRSPs) from late 1990s on social sector spending combined with market liberalization and governance reforms in the 2000s	Community-level aid (and empowerment) projects funded by governments and NGOs

Structuralism says that poverty results from the unequal distribution of resources, wealth and power, and the institutions which support this inequality. A typical historical example would be the unequal distribution of land in many countries of South America, which meant that large estate owners (*latifundistas*) were able to dominate economics and politics, while the majority of rural dwellers had very small holdings and/or worked as labourers.

Interventionism posits that unfettered (and 'unplanned' development of) markets creates poverty because it is difficult to guarantee that there will be no distortions; the proposed widespread benefits of capitalist development do not therefore reach everyone. Hence particular kinds of intervention, by the state and by other agencies, are needed.

People-centred development explains the existence of poverty as a result of the focus of intentional development on the need for economic growth (generally of a neoliberal kind) rather than directing intentional development to basic needs and wider dimensions of human life. Taking this perspective further, it also suggests that poverty results from a lack of recognition of the rights of individuals, groups and communities by those in political and economic power.

Spend up to 40 minutes on this activity (up to 10 minutes on each approach).

Discussion

This is not a particularly easy exercise because you have to work backwards from the approach or model of development. However, it is a useful exercise in broader terms as most of what we read does not generally state explicitly what theory or approach is informing it. 'Unpicking the discourse' is an important part of understanding where views come from (just as it is important to understand the nature of data that people use to support their arguments – something we will come to in Section 8.3). Standing back and reflecting critically in this way is also important with respect to our own views and preconceptions, and knowing where our ideas and views come from.

There is another way in which this exercise is useful. It concerns the different ways that the causes of poverty are framed and interpreted. Although not holding equal sway in current debates, there are two broad ways that we identify here:

- Those that attribute poverty to inefficient workings of, and distortions in, the market (or a residual view), which may be related, for example, to global processes of change and their contradictions (such as the financial crisis of 2008 and the role of banks and financial policies; or the unevenness of growth and trade between economies), as well as to ineffective or wrong policies.

- Those that attribute poverty to structural (or relational) causes (for example, the history of colonialism; the nature and progress of capitalism; the dominance and practices of transnational corporations (see Chapter 7); histories and processes of dominance; and the creation and perpetuation of inequality).

The *residual view* considers poverty to be a *residue* of a process of historical change and development that has not reached a certain sector of the population. So, for example, distortion in markets leads to inefficiencies, which means that the benefits of market-based development are not actually trickling down to everyone. In this case, the poor are seen as a residual category and need to be integrated better into markets (which in turn need to work better, etc.).

The second way that the causes of poverty are framed and interpreted sees poverty as an outcome of *social relations*. Social relations are the relationships between people, property and the use of labour in the production of goods and services. A relational approach to understanding poverty (Bernstein, 1992) asks questions such as:

- Who owns or has access to what?
- Who does what?
- Who gets what?
- What do they do with it?

A *relational view*, therefore, examines whether wealth generation by some creates the poverty of others.

Activity 8.5

Taking the two views of how causes of poverty can be explained, how would you map them on to the approaches to development in Table 8.1?

Would you say that a *residual view* of poverty characterizes the neoliberal approach and, to some extent, the interventionist approach? Does a *relational view* of poverty characterize a structuralist approach and, to some extent, a people-centred approach?

Or is it not so straightforward? (Think of arguments for and against in answer to these questions.)

Spend about 20 minutes on this activity.

Discussion

In general, we can say that a residual view of poverty maps on to a neoliberal approach of poverty, in that, as neoliberals might argue, if markets worked better and were more efficient, everyone would be included in them in productive ways and would be able to make a living. Equally, we can say that a relational view of the causes of poverty maps on to a structuralist view of development, given the structuralist focus on inequalities in social and economic processes and on what structures need changing for economic development and poverty reduction to occur. So, for example, structuralists have been concerned historically with unequal access to land for farming as well as the structure of production and employment in farming, or with who controls industry and its profits. The other two approaches in Table 8.1 (interventionist and people-centred) lie somewhere between residual and relational understandings of the causes of poverty. Interventionists would say that poverty reduction cannot be left to the better working of the market but at the same time would not focus so strongly on the structural causes of poverty, while people-centred approaches are more redistributionist in focus.

Before moving on to Section 8.3, we contrast very briefly the positions of three well-known writers. All three support the role of the market and economic growth in development but to different extents because of its perceived relationship to poverty creation and reduction. They are Jeffrey Sachs, William Easterly and Paul Collier.

Sachs wrote *The End of Poverty: How We Can Make it Happen in our Lifetime* (Sachs, 2005). When he wrote the book, he was the director of the Earth Institute at Columbia University and an advisor on the MDGs to the UN. His book is a polemic about 'ending poverty in our time' (Sachs, 2005, p. 1). His main argument about the growth of inequality in the world, and hence relative wealth and relative poverty, is based on the favourable conditions for technological advancement and industrial growth in some parts of the world, particularly Europe and the USA. His argument eschews the idea that growth in one part of the world took place through the exploitation of the poor in another part of the world (although he doesn't deny the negative effects of colonialism). He contrasts the relative rates of growth over the 19th and 20th centuries as explanations of why the USA (for example) was able to develop its economy to such an extent compared with, for example, many African countries. This growth was not at the levels of the rising powers today, which you have read about in earlier chapters, but was consistent over time. Sachs puts particular emphasis on the role of technology in achieving economic growth. His key metaphor is the 'ladder of economic development', which he says can be achieved by all countries through a grand plan for aid and action.

Easterly, a professor of economics at New York University, wrote *The White Man's Burden, Why the West's Efforts to Aid the Rest Have Done So Much Ill and So Little Good* (Easterly, 2006). He is a strong critic of Sachs, of the role of the state and of aid. Like Sachs, his analysis is also growth-centred. But, unlike Sachs, he places much more importance on the role of colonialism and 'chaotic decolonization' in creating world poverty, although he also includes other reasons such as bad governance, often supported by the geopolitics of the West. However, part of Easterly's thesis is that economies have not been allowed to work as they need to. They have been taken over by 'Planners' – internally and through aid programmes – rather than enabling what he calls 'Searchers' to seek for immediate and feasible solutions to problems:

> A Planner … thinks of poverty as a technical engineering problem that his answers will solve. A Searcher admits he doesn't know the answers in advance; he believes that poverty is a complicated tangle of political, social, historical, institutional and technological factors. A Searcher hopes to find answers to individual problems only by trial and error experimentation … . A Searcher believes only insiders have enough knowledge to find solutions, and that most solutions must be home-grown.
>
> *(Easterly, 2006, p. 5)*

While this argument has attractive sides to it, Easterly has been criticized for arguing that the private sector has the answers, for not recognizing the role of the state in society and in development, and also for not recognizing the role of strong players who can influence the geopolitics of world poverty such as the USA (Hulme, 2010, p. 70).

Finally, we turn to Collier, who wrote a book called *The Bottom Billion: Why the Poorest Countries are Failing and What Can Be Done About It* (Collier, 2008). An economist and director of the Centre for the Study of African Economies at Oxford University, Collier asks the question: 'All societies used to be poor. Most are now lifting out of it; why are others stuck?' (ibid, p. 5). Collier argues that there are four traps that individually or together hold such countries back: 'the conflict trap, the natural resources trap, the trap of being landlocked with bad neighbours, and the trap of bad governance in a small country' (ibid). Collier also analyses other dimensions that offer potential yet can also limit the economic growth of poor countries: the challenge of breaking into world trade and diversifying exports; the lack of capital inflows to poor countries and the tendency for private capital to flow out; the migration of skilled labour from those countries to seek employment elsewhere. Collier's own conclusions are that gradualist measures of change (rather than a grand world plan or relying on the private sector) need to be supported by aid programmes and international initiatives, promoting positive forces and approaches at national and regional levels: 'we need to narrow the target [i.e. the bottom billion] but broaden the instruments [i.e. a range of ways of supporting change]' (ibid, p. 192).

These three writers are only some of the contributors to debates about the causes of poverty and 'what is to be done'. We come back to them and other writers in Chapter 12, when we examine the implications of their thinking for aid.

Activity 8.6

To what extent do you think the perspectives of Sachs, Easterly and Collier are informed by a residual or a relational understanding of the causes of poverty, or a mixture of the two?

Spend about 10 minutes on this activity.

Discussion

You only have limited descriptions of the key foci of these writers to go on. However, from these few paragraphs, it could be said that Sachs leans more to the relational view, Easterly to the residual view, and Collier is perhaps somewhere in between. But none of these writers falls straightforwardly into either view, and it is important not to jump to conclusions without reading their texts more deeply. Not leaping to too hasty conclusions is a more general caution for considering the ideas of any writer on poverty and development.

8.3 Conceptualizing and measuring poverty

The above discussion of the causes of poverty is based on assumptions that we know what poverty is and how it can be measured. Note that *conceptualizing* poverty is not quite the same as explaining what *causes* poverty (or having a theory that helps explain what causes poverty).

Conceptualizing poverty is about having a means to capture how poverty is manifested, how we recognize it and how we measure it.

This section discusses two broad ways of conceptualizing and measuring poverty. The first is income, or low income in particular. The second is multiple deprivations or a multidimensional view. There are many variations on the second, but we will try to keep things fairly simple. In addition to these two broad conceptualizations of poverty, we also discuss the notion of 'relative' poverty, the relationship between gender and poverty, and the agency of poor people.

8.3.1 Poverty as low income

Low income is the most commonly used characteristic to conceptualize poverty, and is measured by counting those below an agreed international *poverty line*. The poverty line below which people were considered to be in absolute or extreme poverty in 2010 was US$1.25 per day. In 1990, at the time of the first WDR focusing on poverty, it was US$1.00 per day, revised to US$1.08 per day in the WDR of 2000/2001 and further revised to US$1.25 in 2005.

How is this measure established? The poverty line is based on the minimum consumption needs for an adult. This will obviously vary between countries both in content and in cost. The World Bank has however devised a mechanism for computing **purchasing power parity** (PPP) between countries to enable a global measure to be used. While US$1.25 is the current measure for extreme poverty, and is based on the **mean** for the 15 poorest countries (Hulme, 2010, p. 40), an additional measure of US$2.00 is used to include people who are poor but not in extreme poverty, and is based on the **median** poverty line for all developing countries (ibid).

These measures are subject to re-evaluation (for example, the shift from US$1 per day to US$1.25 per day) and the listings of countries based on the numbers in poverty depend on how national economies change (see Figure 8.2). If you look at the statistical tables of a WDR, you will see that countries are classified according to:

- low income
- lower middle income
- upper middle income
- high income but not a member of the Organisation for Economic Cooperation and Development (OECD) – see Box 8.3
- high income and also a member of the OECD.

So, for example, in 2009, the average gross national income for a low income country was US$503 per annum, whereas that for a high income (OECD) country was US$39 654.

Box 8.3 Organisation of Economic Cooperation and Development (OECD)

The Organisation for European Economic Cooperation (OEEC) was established in 1947 to run the US-financed Marshall Plan for reconstruction of post-war Europe. Canada and the USA joined OEEC members in signing the new OECD Convention on 14 December 1960, and the OECD came into force in 1961.

In 2010, there were 34 OECD member countries worldwide that jointly identified problems and promoted policies to solve them. Through an 'enhanced engagement' programme, there were relations with emerging economies and rising powers (Brazil, China, India, Indonesia, Russia and South Africa). These 40 countries accounted for 80 per cent of world trade and investment.

(Source: Adapted from OECD, 2010)

The poverty line is used to count people below the line (*headcount* – where the *headcount ratio* is the percentage of a population below the line). What a poverty line does not tell you is the distribution of people's incomes below the line. (Who is just below it? Who is a long way below it?) Equally, many people who may be just above the poverty line and therefore considered not to be in extreme poverty, are still exceedingly poor.

The use of low income as the measure of poverty has produced some interesting results in terms of locating global poverty. For example, Collier stated that the 'bottom billion' (based on income poverty) resides mainly in sub-Saharan Africa and South Asia plus a few other countries (e.g. Haiti, Bolivia). The Chronic Poverty Research Centre in the UK mapped the distribution of extreme poverty, where the most chronically deprived appear in sub-Saharan Africa (see Figure 8.2). However, Hulme (2010) made a further calculation which disaggregated data for different states in China and India and suggested that there was a second poor 'continent' (in addition to sub-Saharan Africa) which he called sub-Siberian Asia. When he did these calculations, sub-Siberian Asia included the northern part of South Asia, Burma, Laos, central and western China, Afghanistan and Central Asia.

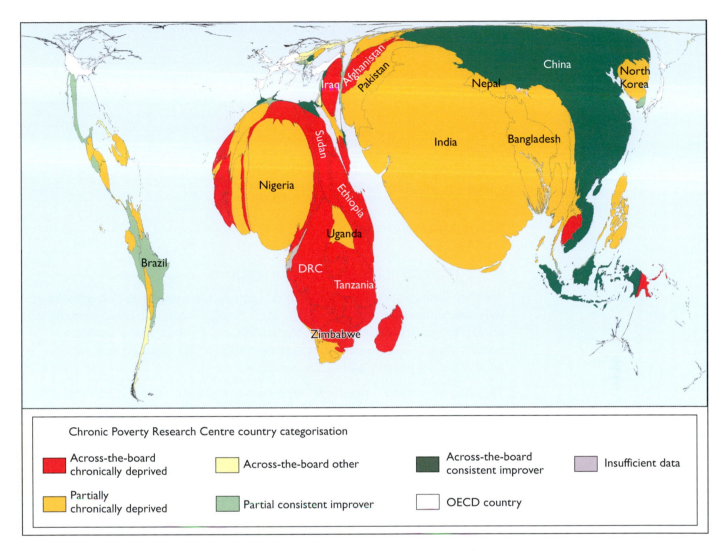

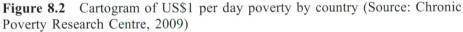

Figure 8.2 Cartogram of US$1 per day poverty by country (Source: Chronic Poverty Research Centre, 2009)

Other analyses of global poverty in 2010 began to contest the idea that the poor were mainly located in low income countries. Sumner, an economist at the UK's Institute of Development Studies, examined global data using different measures of poverty, taking both income and the multidimensional measures of the UNDP. He concluded that most of the world's poor were located in *middle* income countries not in lower income countries (see Table 8.2). Sumner was careful to provide a number of caveats. One was that many states had only recently 'graduated' to middle income status. So, as Sumner noted, his calculations might simply be an effect of this transition. Nevertheless, such analyses raise questions about using income, or only income, as a measure of poverty, and about the limits of our understanding of global poverty trends in relation to changes taking place in the world economy, as well as the distribution of poverty between and within countries.

Table 8.2 Summary estimates – global distribution of the world's poor by country type, 2007/8

	Fragile and conflict-affected countries (%)	Not fragile or conflict-affected countries (%)	Total
Low income	12	16	28
Middle income	11	61	72
Total	23	77	100

Source: Sumner (2010, p. 20)

8.3.2 Poverty as multiple deprivations

Another limitation of seeing poverty simply as low income is that it looks at only one dimension of human life – even though income is fundamentally related to many other aspects of human life. As a result, many analysts of poverty have aimed to construct a more complex and nuanced way of understanding poverty and of measuring it.

The idea of poverty as multiple deprivations has been strongly influenced by the Nobel Prize winning economist, Amartya Sen. Sen (1981) wrote a seminal analysis of famines in which he argued, contrary to many other thinkers, that famine was not so much an issue of supply or shortage of food, as of demand for food. In other words, famines were caused by a failure of demand because people either had no money or not enough other assets to exchange for food. Sen called his analysis an 'entitlement approach' to understanding the causes of famine. A person (or family or household) has an **endowment** of assets that they may own: land, tools or machines, labour power, skills or knowledge, etc. (remembering that many people in the world do not own much more than their labour power). This person (family, household) may be able to produce their own food with this endowment, or produce and sell cash crops, or sell labour for wages. Whatever a person has to exchange for money or goods, Sen called an '**entitlement** bundle'. Someone facing hunger or starvation from famine would not have an adequate entitlement bundle to exchange for food. Such a situation would be exacerbated further if food prices increased.

This early analysis of how a lack of endowments and entitlements could lead to hunger and famine led Sen to think further about the nature of human capabilities. He argued that poverty was effectively the same as capability failure. By capabilities, Sen meant the opportunities and freedoms of a person to do and be what they value. Poverty is capability failure because a poor person does not have the opportunity and freedom to do and be the things she or he values. In later writings, Sen engaged with political philosopher, Martha Nussbaum, about whether there was a set of fundamental capabilities that all human beings ought to be able to enjoy. While Nussbaum drew up such a list (see Box 8.4), Sen resisted it because people may value different things in different contexts, and there is always debate about what is to be valued.

Box 8.4 A brief summary of Nussbaum's list of capabilities

1 Life: living a normal length of human life

2 Bodily health

3 Bodily integrity: bodily freedom

4 Sense, imagination and thought: being able to use the sense, imagine, think and reason

5 Emotions: being able to have attachments

6 Practical reason: having a conception of the good and being able to reflect critically on one's life

7 Affiliation: being able to engage with others; being able to live in dignity and with the respect of others

8 Other species: being able to live with nature

9 Play: being able to enjoy recreation

10 Control over one's environment: being able to participate in political life/civil liberties; being able to have property, equal opportunities in employment/economic rights

(Source: Nussbaum, 2000, pp. 78–80)

Activity 8.7

How far do you agree with Nussbaum's list in Box 8.4? What might you add or delete from the list with respect to the context you live in, and why?

Spend about 15 minutes on this activity.

Sen's work was extremely influential in the UN and particularly the UNDP, which, with the first HDR in 1990, initiated ways of measuring different dimensions of human life that would provide a more complex and more sensitive measure of poverty (or, alternatively, well-being). The UNDP did indeed select some aspects of human life that were seen as fundamental to the quality of people's existence and that could be taken as indicators of development. They cluster around three dimensions: health, education and income. There have been a number of changes over time in how these three dimensions are used to construct an index of human development. Some of the main ones are outlined in Box 8.5: the Human Development Index (HDI), the Gender Inequality Index (GII) and the Multidimensional Poverty Index (MPI).

Box 8.5 Multidimensional measures from the UNDP

Gender Inequality Index (GII) is a measure that captures the loss in achievements due to gender disparities in the dimensions of reproductive health, empowerment and labour force participation. There are five indicators used to construct this index: maternal mortality; adolescent fertility; parliamentary representation; secondary educational attainment and above; and labour force participation. The values of the overall index range from 0 (perfect equality) to 1 (total inequality).

Human Development Index (HDI) is a composite measure of achievements in three basic dimensions of human development – a long and healthy life, access to education and a decent standard of living. These three dimensions are measured respectively by: life expectancy at birth; mean years of schooling and expected years of schooling; **Gross National Income per capita** (GNIpc). For ease of comparability, the average value of achievements in these three dimensions is put on a scale of 0 to 1, where greater is better, and the indicators are aggregated.

Multidimensional Poverty Index (MPI) is a measure of serious deprivations in the dimensions of health, education and living standards that combines the number of deprived and the intensity of their deprivation. There are ten indicators used across these dimensions: for health – nutrition and child mortality; for education – children enrolled and years of schooling; for living standards – assets, floor, electricity, water, toilet and cooking fuel. A household is considered to be multidimensionally poor if is deprived in at least 2–6 indicators.

(Source: Adapted from UNDP, 2010, p. 13; p. 26; p. 91; pp. 95–96)

There is another important aspect to understanding poverty as multiple deprivations. The idea of multiple deprivations is that they tend to act as a vicious circle, one dimension reinforcing another (see Figure 8.3). There are other dimensions, for example, people with low levels of literacy have difficulty participating in organizational and political life and therefore have less influence in terms of social and economic change.

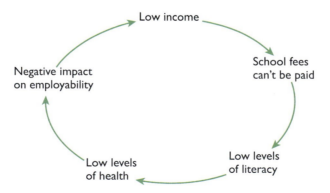

Figure 8.3   Multiple deprivations

Activity 8.8

Table 8.3 shows you two different components of the HDI against the HDI rank in 2010.

Looking at this table by column, check some of your assumptions about GNIpc. Would you have expected incomes to be higher or lower in:

- Germany or Norway?
- Chile or Brazil?
- China or South Africa?
- Kenya or Sudan?

Next check your assumptions on **life expectancy at birth** for the same list of countries. Which would you have expected to have higher or lower life expectancies?

Table 8.3 The HDI rank and the HDI components

HDI rank		Life expectancy at birth (years)	GNIpc (US$)
	Very high human development		
1	Norway	81.0	58 810
4	United States of America	79.6	47 094
10	Germany	80.2	35 308
12	Korea (Republic of)	79.8	29 518
26	United Kingdom	79.8	35 087
	High human development		
45	Chile	78.8	13 561
56	Mexico	76.7	13 971
65	Russian Federation	67.2	15 258
73	Brazil	72.9	10 607
83	Turkey	72.2	13 359
	Medium human development		
89	China	73.5	7 258
95	Bolivia	66.3	4 357
101	Egypt	70.5	5 889
110	South Africa	52.0	9 812
119	India	64.4	3 337
	Low human development		
128	Kenya	55.6	1 628
145	Haiti	61.7	949
154	Sudan	58.9	2 051
155	Afghanistan	44.6	1 419
165	Mozambique	48.4	854

Source: compiled from data given in UNDP (2010)

What do you think explains the low life expectancy of South Africa in particular (and of all the countries with low human development)?

Allow about 15 minutes for this activity.

Discussion

With respect to the final question on life expectancy in South Africa, in spite of its having the highest income in the group of five medium human development countries that we have selected, in 2010 HIV/AIDS had severely affected the health of the population and hence the average years that people could expect to live. This also applied to some other African countries. The case of Sudan was probably more an outcome of civil war.

Table 8.3 demonstrates that the components of the rankings of the HDI are not necessarily uniform or move in the same direction. Overall, the composite nature of the HDI makes it more sensitive to different aspects of a country's development in ways that cannot immediately be grasped simply by looking at income. To illustrate this further, we have taken some countries with similar income but different HDIs, and similar HDIs but different incomes. These are shown in Tables 8.4 and 8.5 and are used in Activity 8.9.

Activity 8.9

First examine Table 8.4, in which there are seven pairs of countries that have similar income but different HDIs. Why do you think this is?

Then examine Table 8.5, which shows six pairs of countries with similar HDIs but different GNIpc. What explanation would you give?

Spend no more than 10 minutes on this part of the activity.

If you want to find out more, or whether this situation has changed, you can search online for the following resources:

- The latest Human Development Report of the UNDP, which will have tables at the back to show the other elements of the HDI.

- Country profiles: you could search for national government websites, or the website of the World Bank.

Just search for data on one pair of countries in each table and spend no more than 30 minutes on the second part of this activity.

Table 8.4 Similar income, different HDI (2010)

Country	GNIpc (constant 2008 PPP US$)	HDI	Rank
Mali	1171	0.31	160
Nepal	1201	0.43	138
Afghanistan	1419	0.35	155
Bangladesh	1587	0.47	129
Pakistan	2678	0.49	125
Vietnam	2995	0.57	113
Turkey	13 359	0.68	83
Chile	13 561	0.78	45
Saudi Arabia	24 726	0.75	55
New Zealand	25 438	0.91	3
Austria	37 056	0.85	25
Australia	38 692	0.94	2
United Arab Emirates	58 006	0.82	32
Norway	58 810	0.94	1

Source: compiled from data given in UNDP (2010)

The data in Table 8.4 reflect pairs of countries that have similar GNIpc but different HDI scores and ranks. This can arise for two different reasons. First, you will remember, the HDI is a composite measure of life expectancy, education and income, while the GNIpc is only a measure of average income. Therefore countries may have similar income levels, but differences in the other two categories will give them different HDI scores. For example, taking Pakistan and Vietnam, Pakistan has a life expectancy of 67.2 years, while Vietnam has a life expectancy of 74.9 years. In Pakistan, mean years of schooling average at 4.9 years while for Vietnam the value is 5.5 years. It is only for GNIpc that their values are similar.

The second reason has to do with the measure of GNIpc itself. The measure is calculated by dividing the total national income of a country by its population; it is therefore an average figure. Countries may have a large national income but a large population as well (for example, Bangladesh has a GNI of US $86.6 billion and a population of 145 million). The average may be similar to a country with low national income but also a smaller population (for example, Afghanistan, which has a population of 32 million and a GNI of US $10.6 billion). Similarly in other cases, the GNIpc average of two countries may be similar even though there may be large income inequalities in some countries (where the number of poor is much larger, but the smaller richer population has a disproportionate share of the national income), while in the other country income is more evenly spread in the population.

These points are important to understand that although we have 'measures' of poverty and development, these are often complex composites or averages, and these numbers may not fully reflect the different faces of poverty.

Table 8.5 Similar HDI, different income (2010)

Country	GNIpc (constant 2008 PPP US$)	HDI	Rank
Congo	3258	0.49	126
Cambodia	1868	0.49	124
South Africa	9812	0.60	110
Indonesia	3957	0.60	108
Russian Federation	15 258	0.72	65
Peru	8424	0.72	63
Mexico	13 971	0.75	56
Saudi Arabia	24 726	0.75	55
Italy	29 619	0.85	23
Hong Kong, China (SAR)	45 090	0.86	21
United States of America	47 094	0.90	4
New Zealand	25 438	0.91	3

Source: compiled from data given in UNDP (2010)

For Table 8.5, the inverse relationship holds. It is possible for the quality of life as represented by the HDI to be relatively high compared with the level of average incomes. There may be a number of reasons. One might be a more equal access in a society to healthcare or to food (and hence longer life expectancy), and also to education even if incomes are relatively low. This reason in turn might be the result of policies to invest in education and health or subsidized food. A well-known example is the state of Kerala in India, which has a very high literacy rate and good healthcare system relative to people's incomes as a result of local state policies as well as the existence of a range of private and non-governmental healthcare providers.

8.3.3 Relative poverty

We turn to the concept of relative poverty because, as it will quickly be deduced from the above discussion, poverty is not the same experience with the same dimensions in every context. Amartya Sen gives the famous comparison of the life expectancy of men in Harlem, New York and Bangladesh in the early 1990s, where Harlem men had less chance of reaching 40 than men in Bangladesh. This relative deprivation is explained by the different 'baskets' of goods and services that men in each context required to survive (or in Sen's terms, realize their capabilities). Sen further notes:

> While the rural Indian may have little problem in appearing in public without shame with relatively modest clothing and can take part in the life of the community without a telephone or television, the commodity requirements of these general functionings are much more demanding in a country where people standardly use a bigger basket of diverse commodities.
>
> *(Sen, 1992, p. 116)*

The concept of relative poverty can also be used to understand the different experiences of poverty within a country as well as between countries. Poverty is relative to the lives of other people within the country. Thus, in Sen's example, men in Harlem in the early 1990s were poor relative to men in other areas of New York.

In 2011 in the UK, for example, households were considered poor if they had less than 60% of the national median income – a threshold that rises or falls as median incomes rise and fall. In 2008/2009 the Rowntree Trust estimated that 13.5 million people (or 22% of the population of the UK) were living in households below this threshold – a very startling figure. While this figure had been stable over a period of years, even more startling was that the number of people living below an income of 40% of the national median had increased. In absolute terms, it was the highest since records began in 1979 (see Figure 8.4). When figures were disaggregated for ethnicity, it was found that twice the proportion of people from ethnic minorities lived in low income households compared with the white population.

Disaggregating such data helps to understand much better the nature of poverty and who experiences it. It also helps to think about possible explanations (or issues to investigate). Other aspects that one could look at are the geography of poverty within a country: is it concentrated in particular regions, for example? This has been an important dimension in the discussion of poverty in India, where particular states (for example, Orissa, Bihar) experience much higher levels of poverty than other states.

Another dimension of relative poverty has also been alluded to earlier: people living in relative poverty tend to be excluded from many aspects of social life, from participation in the local community to engagement in national politics. The concept of 'social exclusion' is one that you might come across in many contexts and is an area of debate amongst those who study poverty in both high-income and low-income countries.

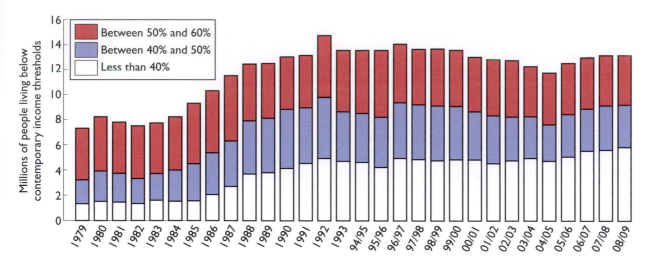

Figure 8.4 Number of people in low-income households (Source: The Poverty Site, 2010)

So you can see that once you start to look more closely at poverty data, and examine the relative deprivation between groups or sectors, you get a much more nuanced picture.

8.3.4 Gender and poverty

An important way in which data need to be nuanced is in the relative experiences of poverty of men and women. This is because, in many countries and in many respects, there is inequality between women and men both within society at large and within households and families. There are different areas of life in which these inequalities are manifested and have poverty impacts. For example, in the public sphere, men and women often receive different wages for similar work, while in the household, men and women may have different access to food. Women may also experience forms of deprivation in the public sphere such as relative exclusion from public life (although these deprivations also affect poor men). Within the household, there may be inequalities between men and women in access to and command over income, but particularly in responsibilities in the 'reproductive' sphere – that is, all the work involved in the care of human beings which is usually carried out by women (Pearson and Sweetman, 2011, p. 4).

We will come back to the gender dimensions of poverty, inequality and livelihoods in the following chapters. However it is important to think about these nuances, as poverty impacts on men and women differently – both in the public sphere and in the household. For example, Elson, Pearson and others analyzed how the recession that began with the sub-prime mortgage crisis in the USA in 2008 was likely to have specific effects on low-income women in the different spheres of their lives, both directly in northern countries as well as indirectly in the South. However crises can also have unexpected effects or offer opportunities for change. Elson (2011, p. 45) noted at the time: 'the crisis may also provide opportunities to challenge and transform gender norms, through collective action by civil society or governments.'

8.3.5 Poverty and agency

The last point brings us to a final debate, namely the agency of poor people. For example, Sen's notion of capabilities and freedoms incorporates a strong sense of agency. That is, people act on their own situations in different ways, in deciding what core things they value. Agency is, of course, constrained by poverty, although poor people can act with agency in small ways in their own lives and may act with greater impact if they are organized (for example, in community groups, peasant associations, unions, etc.). From this point of view, Sen's perspective is not simply about individual choice but also about the social arrangements and forms of organization that people create to improve human existence. This might be by the poor themselves, and it might be by other organizations and governments on behalf of poor people.

Ignoring the agency of poor people in conceptualizing poverty has been a source of critique. One example is the work of Rahnema (1996) who examined the different ways that poverty can be seen: as material deprivation, by poor people themselves, by how others in society view poor people, and by how things are seen differently in different contexts over time. In reflecting on these dimensions and on global responses to poverty, he suggests that the agency of poor people themselves is notably absent. Without such agency, as he argues, many millions would have had even shorter lives. He notes:

> The way planners, development actomaniacs and politicians ... are presenting their case, gives the uninformed public a distorted impression of how the world's impoverished are living their deprivations. Not only are these people presented as incapable of doing anything intelligent by themselves, but also as preventing the modern do-gooders from helping them.
>
> *(Rahnema, 1996, p. 169).*

Rahnema is referring both to individuals' and households' survival strategies and to social movements of poor people working to change their conditions of existence, a dimension we come back to in Chapter 11.

Other writers have picked up on the 'post-development' views of Rahnema and others (see Robbins, 2013). For example, Nederveen Pierterse (2002) argues that it is not simply a question of rejecting growth or particular forms of development as espoused by international organizations. He observes (ibid, p. 101) that 'less market participation does not necessarily imply more social participation'. Nevertheless he also points out that action is needed – but of what kind?

Some writers have examined the 'political spaces' within which poor people take action (such as the social movements mentioned by Rahnema). For example, Engberg-Pedersen and Webster (2002, p. 255) note that 'the poor are constantly seeking to manoeuvre within given conditions'. In the view of Engberg-Pedersen and Webster, this manoeuvring involves political activity, not only in the sense of political parties (although some unions or peasant leagues are affiliated to political parties), but in the sense of contesting the economic and power relations that create and reinforce poverty (see Figure 8.5).

Figure 8.5 Action by and on behalf of the poor: protesting against poverty at a demonstration organized by the Association for the Taxation of Financial Transactions for the Aid of Citizens (ATTAC) and the Moroccan Association for Human Rights (AMDH), 2009

We return to the agency of the poor in Chapter 11.

Summary and looking forward

This chapter has outlined some of the ways that poverty is conceptualized and measured, and some of the issues that arise as a result. You will have realized that poverty is a contested concept in how writers and organizations see its causes, how it is conceptualized and how it is measured. There are differences too in how people play down or highlight the role of aid and intervention, and the agency of the poor. In particular, you will have identified a number of key thinkers and international institutions in shaping the debates. Other key points include:

- the continuing persistence of, and concerns about, world poverty
- the trends in thinking within major institutions such as the World Bank and UNDP about how to address global poverty
- how different theories of development understand the causes of poverty
- the differences between relational and residual views of poverty
- the differences in perspective between some well-known writers about poverty
- the conceptualization of poverty as low incomes and as multiple deprivations
- how income poverty and multiple deprivation poverty are measured
- the meaning of relative and chronic poverty
- the importance of gender in considering how poverty is manifested and what its impacts might be
- the role of poor people as active agents in the daily struggle against poverty.

This chapter has also taken you from the global to the local and has started to indicate how poor people have agency and ways of being that need to be understood if we are to have a more nuanced understanding of poverty, inequality and livelihoods. A well-known economist from Princeton University, Angus Deaton, wryly commented: 'Given all of the problems [of understanding and measuring poverty], it is worth returning to the idea the people themselves have a very good idea of whether or not they are poor' (Deaton, 2010, p. 38). We will come back to some of the more local and individual experiences of poverty, livelihoods and the role of poor people's agency in Chapter 10. You will have noticed too that there is a strong relationship between poverty and inequality. Inequality is the focus of Chapter 9.

References

Bernstein, H. (1992) 'Poverty and the poor' in Bernstein, H., Crow, B. and Johnson, H. (eds) *Rural Livelihoods. Crises and Responses*, Oxford and Milton Keynes: Oxford University Press in association with The Open University.

Brandt, W. (1980) *North-South: A Programme for Survival, Report of the Independent Commission on International Development (The Brandt Report)*, London, Pan Books.

Chenery, H., Bell, C., Duloy, J. and Jolly, R. (1975) *Redistribution with Growth*, Oxford, Oxford University Press.

Chronic Poverty Research Centre (2009) *The Chronic Poverty Report 2008–09: Escaping Poverty Traps*, Manchester, Chronic Poverty Research Centre, also available online at http://www.chronicpoverty.org/uploads/publication_files/CPR2_ReportFull.pdf (Accessed 2 August 2011).

Collier, P. (2008) *The Bottom Billion: Why the Poorest Countries Are Failing and What Can Be Done About It*, Oxford, Oxford University Press.

Cornia, G.A., Jolly, R. and Stewart, F. (1987) *Adjustment with a Human Face*, Oxford, Oxford University Press.

Deaton, A. (2010) 'Price indexes, inequality, and the measurement of world poverty', *Presidential Address*, American Economic Association, Atlanta, January 2010.

Easterly, W. (2006) *The White Man's Burden: Why the West's Efforts to Aid the Rest Have Done So Much Ill and So Little Good*, Oxford, Oxford University Press.

Elson, (2011) – add details!

Engberg-Pedersen, L. and Webster, N. (2002) 'Political agencies and spaces' in Webster, N. and Engberg-Pedersen, L. (eds) *In the Name of the Poor: Contesting Political Space for Poverty Reduction*, London and New York, Zed Books.

Hulme, D. (2010) *Global Poverty: How Global Governance is Failing the Poor*, London, Routledge.

Hulme, D., Moore, K. and Shepherd, A. (2001) 'Chronic poverty: meanings and analytical frameworks', *CPRC Working Paper 2*, Manchester, IDPM, Birmingham, IDD.

International Labour Organization (ILO) (2010) *Resource Guide on the Informal Economy* http://www.ilo.org/public/english/support/lib/resource/subject/informal.htm [online] (Accessed 2 August 2011).

Mosley, P. (2002) 'International institutions and the fight against global poverty' in Johnson, H., Mosley, P., Olsen, W. and Pearson, R., *Poverty and Inequality*, U213 International Development: Challenges for a World in Transition, Milton Keynes: The Open University.

Mosley, P. (with Chiripanhura, B., Grugel, J. and Thirkell-White, B.) (2012) *The Politics of Poverty Reduction*, Oxford, Oxford University Press.

Nederveen Pieterse, J. (2002) *Development Theory: Deconstructions/Reconstructions*, London, Thousand Oaks New Delhi, Sage.

Nussbaum, M.C. (2000) *Women and Human Development: The Capabilities Approach*, Cambridge, Cambridge University Press.

Organization of Economic Cooperation and Development (OECD) (2010) *History* [online], http://www.oecd.org/document/25/0,3746, en_36734052_36761863_36952473_1_1_1_1,00.html (Accessed 20 March 2011).

Rahnema, M. (1996) 'Poverty' in Sachs, W. (ed.) *The Development Dictionary: A Guide to Knowledge as Power*, London, Zed Books.

Robbins, P. (2013) 'Perspectives on development, technology and the environment' in Butcher, M. and Papaioannou, T. (eds) *New Perspectives in International Development*, London, Bloomsbury Academic/Milton Keynes, The Open University.

Sachs, J. (2005) *The End of Poverty: How We Can Make It Happen in Our Lifetime*, London, Penguin.

Sen, A. (1981) *Poverty and Famines: An Essay on Entitlement and Deprivation*, Oxford, Oxford University Press.

Sen, A. (1992) *Inequality Reexamined*, Oxford, Clarendon Press.

Sumner, A. (2010) 'Global poverty and the new bottom billion: what if three-quarters of the world's poor live in middle-income countries?', *IDS Working Paper No. 349*, Sussex, Institute of Development Studies.

The Poverty Site (2010) *Numbers in Low Income* [online], http://www.poverty.org.uk/01/index.shtml (Accessed 2 August 2011)

United Nations Development Programme (UNDP) (2010) *Human Development Report. The Real Wealth of Nations: Pathways to Human Development*, New York, UNDP.

World Bank (2000) *World Development Report 2000/2001: Attacking Poverty,* World Bank; Oxford University Press USA, also available online at http://web.worldbank.org (Accessed 2 August 2011).

World Bank (2010) *Poverty* [online], http://go.worldbank.org/2UJWJC2XG0 (Accessed 30 November 2010).

Further reading

Hulme, D. (2010) *Global Poverty: How Global Governance is Failing the Poor*, London, Routledge.

Mosley, P. (with Chiripanhura, B., Grugel, J. and Thirkell-White, B.) (2012) *The Politics of Poverty Reduction*, Oxford, Oxford University Press.

Useful websites

University of Manchester Chronic Poverty Research Centre: http://www.chronicpoverty.org/

The UK Poverty Site: http://www.poverty.org.uk/

United States Census Bureau on Poverty: http://www.census.gov/hhes/www/poverty/index.html

The World Bank: http://www.worldbank.org/

Inequality – does it matter?

9

Joseph Hanlon

Introduction

Inequality is a matter of life and death as, for example, poor people are more likely to be ill and die younger than their richer neighbours. And inequality is increasing across the world, driven by almost unimaginable increases in wealth for some people, while the majority is largely left behind. This has caused growing concern, even at the International Monetary Fund (IMF) (see Box 9.1).

> ### Box 9.1 IMF warns inequality threatens economic and social stability
>
> In a speech given in 2010, Dominique Strauss-Kahn, Managing Director of the IMF, said this:
>
> > Adam Smith – one of the founders of modern economics – recognized clearly that a poor distribution of wealth could undermine the free market system, noting that: 'The disposition to admire, and almost to worship, the rich and the powerful and … neglect persons of poor and mean condition … is the great and most universal cause of the corruption of our moral sentiments.'
> >
> > This was over 250 years ago. In today's world, these problems are magnified under the lens of globalization. …
> >
> > Lurking behind [globalization] was a large and growing chasm between rich and poor – especially within countries. An inequitable distribution of wealth can wear down the social fabric. More unequal countries have worse social indicators, a poorer human development record, and higher degrees of economic insecurity and anxiety. …
> >
> > Fundamentally, the growth model that co-existed with globalization was unbalanced and unsustainable. …
> >
> > Inequality may have actually stoked this unsustainable model. …
> >
> > Inequality goes against notions of fairness and solidarity, but it also threatens economic and social stability…
> >
> > The mandate of the IMF is economic and financial stability, the sure foundation of human development. We care about inequality not only on grounds of common decency, but because inequality threatens this stability.
> >
> > *(Strauss-Kahn, 2010)*

Poverty and inequality are linked, but they are not the same thing. Poverty, as discussed in Chapter 8, is often measured as 'a lack' of something, such as income, health or education. However, the causes of poverty were linked to the social relations between structures. For example, many people do not have enough food and are malnourished. But is the problem a general lack of food, so that everyone is hungry? Or is it the distribution of the food, so that some are hungry and some are not, which is an 'inequality'? In other words, inequality is a measure of the relative position of groups of people. If poor people are malnourished because they cannot afford food, even if it is available, we might point to this as a link between poverty and inequality. This connection between poverty and inequality, however, is subject to intense debate, so the aims of this chapter are to:

• help you understand and analyze inequality

• explain how inequality can be quantified and some of the issues involved

• demonstrate and examine the links between poverty and inequality, and why inequality matters for development.

Measurement and comparison are central to any discussion of inequality, so the first half of this chapter looks at how we can use tables, graphs, comparisons and simple statistical techniques to quantify inequality. Economic status is a key indicator of inequality, and you will see there are two ways to measure income. You will also see that there can be many different inequalities and that their interaction is complex. We can talk about inequality between countries, or between people within countries, or between groups (e.g. 'racial' groups or regions), and even within families. There are many types of inequalities, such as health, education, housing, power and vulnerability to climate change. These are partly related to money, and income inequality will be a central issue of this chapter.

The second half of the chapter focuses on the issue: to what extent is the problem poverty in general, and to what extent is the issue inequality? If people are dying unnecessarily, should we take action to reduce inequality, or is poverty a spur for people to 'better' themselves? The debate within the development community is sometimes expressed as: does 'development' and a general increase in income make everyone better off – characterized as 'a rising tide raises all boats' – or does growth only benefit the better off and increase inequality, leaving the poor behind – characterized as 'a rising tide sinks leaky boats'?

9.1 Inequalities in maternal health

We start by looking at two linked types of inequality where income is only part of the question, and other factors also come into play: maternal **mortality** and literacy. The Asian Development Bank (Purdue, 2008) has noted that: 'Maternal health is inextricably linked to development, poverty reduction, and social inclusiveness. Maternal **morbidity** is both a cause and a consequence of poverty. It reflects unequal access and outcomes for women based on class, caste, wealth and power.' As such, maternal mortality is seen as an accurate marker of both development and inequality and was chosen as part of Millennium Development Goal 5 (see Chapter 1). (Target 5a aims to reduce the maternal mortality ratio by three quarters between 1990 and 2015.) The global differences are huge: in Malawi, one woman dies out of each 88 women giving birth, while in Italy one woman dies for every 25 000 giving birth. In other words, a Malawian woman is 280 times as likely to die in childbirth as an Italian woman (see Table 9.1). That is serious inequality.

Table 9.1 Maternal mortality

	Number of maternal deaths for each 100 000 live births	One death for this many live births	2009 GDP per capita, US$/year
Malawi	1140	88	3269
Brazil	55	1820	8121
Jamaica	34	2940	4471
Iran	28	3580	4540
United States of America	17	5880	45 989
France	10	10 000	41 051
UK	8	12 500	35 165
Germany	7	14 300	40 670
Italy	4	25 000	35 084
Within the USA			
Black or African American	36	2780	
Washington DC (US capital)	38	2630	
States of Indiana & Vermont	3	33 300	
Historic			
England 1851–60	470	212	2640*
England 1931–40	358	279	6000*

* 1990 'international' or PPP dollars.
Sources: Hogan et al., 2010 (for global maternal deaths); Center for Disease Control, n.d. (for US maternal deaths); Loudon, 1992 (historic data); World Bank, 2009 (global GDP data); Maddison, 2010 (historic GDP data)

Table 9.1 compares rates of maternal mortality in various countries. It shows that wealth in a country is not the only determining factor – Brazil has almost double the per capita income of Iran, yet it also has double the maternal mortality. And looking at five developed countries, the USA has the highest per capita GDP but the poorest maternal mortality. Finally, we look within the USA, and see a huge variation – the best states do as well as the best European countries, while in the nation's capital, Washington DC, and for black women in general, the death rate is higher than in Jamaica or Iran. Factors other than money are coming into play, including access to healthcare and racial discrimination. This is underlined by the way that maternal mortality did not change significantly in England for nearly a century, despite a more than doubling of per capita GDP, as noted in Table 9.1.

Look more closely at the table to see how we have used the statistics. In the text above the table, the likelihood of a woman dying each time she gives birth was used, citing the figure of one woman dying in Malawi out of each 88 giving birth, and that is shown in the second column of figures. But data for maternal mortality is usually presented as in the first column, the number of maternal deaths for each 100 000 live births (1140 maternal deaths for Malawi). As you can see in the first column, this format is easier for making comparisons. But the two numbers are linked: 100 000 / 1140 = 88.

Maternal mortality is just one very harsh inequality. The World Bank's *World Development Report 2006* (World Bank, 2006) focused on 'Equity and Development' and the bank noted that 'differences in life chances across nationality, race, gender, and social groups will strike many readers as fundamentally unfair. They are also likely to lead to wasted human potential and thus to missed development opportunities.' Box 9.2, from the 'overview' of that report, gives an example of the unfair differences. We will come back to fairness later, but we want now to look more at inequalities.

Box 9.2 The real cost of inequality

Consider two South African children born on the same day in 2000. Nthabiseng is black, born to a poor family in a rural area in the Eastern Cape province, about 700 kilometers from Cape Town. Her mother had no formal schooling. Pieter is white, born to a wealthy family in Cape Town. His mother completed a college education at the nearby prestigious Stellenbosch University.

On the day of their birth, Nthabiseng and Pieter could hardly be held responsible for their family circumstances: their race, their parents' income and education, their urban or rural location, or indeed their sex. Yet statistics suggest that those predetermined background variables will make a major difference for the lives they lead. Nthabiseng has a 7.2 per cent chance of dying in the first year of her life, more than twice Pieter's 3 per cent. Pieter can look forward to 68 years of life, Nthabiseng to 50. Pieter can expect to complete 12 years of formal schooling, Nthabiseng less than 1 year. Nthabiseng is likely to be considerably poorer than Pieter throughout her life. Growing up, she is less likely to have access to clean water and sanitation, or to good schools. So the opportunities these two children face to reach their full human potential are vastly different from the outset, through no fault of their own.

Such disparities in opportunity translate into different abilities to contribute to South Africa's development. Nthabiseng's health at birth may have been poorer, owing to the poorer nutrition of her mother during her pregnancy. By virtue of their gender socialization, their geographic location, and their access to schools, Pieter is much more likely to acquire an education that will enable him to put his innate talents to full use. Even if, at age 25, and despite the odds, Nthabiseng manages to come up with a great business idea (such as an innovation to increase agricultural production), she would find it much harder to persuade a bank to lend her money at a reasonable interest rate. Pieter, having a similarly bright idea (say, on how to design an improved version of promising software), would likely find it easier to obtain credit, with both a college diploma and quite possibly some collateral.

With the transition to democracy in South Africa, Nthabiseng is able to vote and thus indirectly shape the policy of her government, something denied to blacks under apartheid. But the legacy of apartheid's unequal opportunities and political power will remain for some time to come. It is a long road from such a (fundamental) political change to changes in economic and social conditions.

As striking as the differences in life chances are between Pieter and Nthabiseng in South Africa, they are dwarfed by the disparities between average South Africans and citizens of more developed countries. Consider the cards dealt to Sven – born on that same day to an average Swedish household. His chances of dying in the first year of life are very small (0.3 per cent) and he can expect to live to the age of 80, 12 years longer than Pieter, and 30 years more than Nthabiseng. He is likely to complete 11.4 years of schooling – 5 years more than the average South African.

(World Bank, 2006, p. 1)

9.2 Literacy, power, and other inequalities

As Box 9.2 shows, there is a whole spectrum of inequalities, including education, which has a marked influence on well-being. In Europe, at the time of writing, adult literacy rates were over 98%, and in Latin America, Indonesia, South Africa and China over 90%. Many poor countries have relatively high literacy rates. But in Benin, Senegal, Afghanistan and Ethiopia, literacy rates were below 45%, meaning that more than half of adults could not read and write (UNDP, 2011). The adult literacy rate in India in 2001 was 65%, but that hid a range of inequalities. In the south Indian state of Kerala, adult literacy was over 90% while in Bihar it was below 50%. For all of India, 76% of men were literate, but only 54% of women. India's constitution (article 46 and part XVI) refers to 'scheduled castes', which are groups that had been subject to 'social injustice' and are about 16% of the population. The designation remains controversial but there is no question that scheduled castes suffer from relative inequality within India. In particular, the scheduled castes have lower adult literacy rates – 67% for men and 42% for women. However, inequalities can be reversed. The Indian state of Punjab had such low literacy rates for scheduled castes that it launched a campaign to change the situation in the 1990s, raising the literacy rate from 41% in 1991 to 56% in 2001 (Kaur and Kumar, 2008). This is still below the national average, but it is evidence that inequalities can be addressed.

This analysis of literacy in India brings to the fore just how many dimensions there are to inequality. First, there are spatial inequalities, between countries and between regions within countries. Within countries, there are inequalities between groups or social categories, such as gender, caste, ethnic or religious differences, which can also become a cause of conflict and violence (see Hanlon, 2013). Second, there is a range of measurable inequalities such as literacy and maternal mortality where a transfer of resources could redress the inequality and reduce the associated poverty (discussed further in this chapter).

Finally, there are other sets of inequalities that are important but less obvious. Inequalities in power tend to perpetuate other inequalities, so that the illiterate, for example, are often less powerful in the community and in the country, making it harder for them to take action to reduce these inequalities. Gender divisions are important in much of the world, with women having less power. This inequality is highlighted within the family, where girls may have less food and be less likely to go to school than boys. We cite just two of many studies. One looked at family expenditure in Ethiopia, and found that more family money was spent on boys than girls (Koohi-Kamali, 2008). Another, in Bangladesh, found girls receive less food than boys; however, more money is spent on girls' clothing than boys' (Cockburn et al., 2006).

Inequality is not special to the global South. Amartya Sen, the Nobel Prize winning economist cited in Chapter 8, noted that inner-city African Americans in the USA often have a lower life expectancy than those born in poorer regions of the world, such as Jamaica or parts of India and China, because of unequal access to factors such as healthcare, education and social cohesion.

Activity 9.1

Reflect on an inequality close to you, that is, within your household, workplace or community. Think about the source of the inequality and its implications. For example, if you choose unequal heights, ask if this is a natural variation, or if some people are shorter because they were poorer and were more poorly fed as children, and ask if those people now face disadvantages because of their smaller stature. Or if you consider power within the household or workplace, ask how some people came to be more powerful and what is the significance of those inequalities.

Spend about 10 minutes on this activity.

9.3 Rising income inequality

The previous section has highlighted that there is a range of inequalities. However, while income is not the only marker of inequality, it is the most important, and has a direct impact on most other inequalities. But how do we measure if a person is richer or poorer than a neighbour, a person in another country or an ancestor. How do we compare countries? How do we measure inequality? This section tackles some of these very difficult (and often controversial) measurement issues, with a stress on tables and graphs. We will do this in four steps:

- comparing incomes with a common currency, the US dollar
- comparing countries over time
- showing inequality

- better measures of inequality.

9.3.1 Comparing incomes with a common currency, the US dollar

Although controversial, the US dollar had become the international currency by the end of the 20th century, so comparisons, for example, between personal income or national GDP, are often made using this currency. To be sure, a US$1 bill (banknote) is the same everywhere, but it does not buy the same amount in every country. The World Bank has established its International Comparison Program, which every five years compares prices across the globe, and calculates what it calls a purchasing power parity (PPP) exchange rate as discussed in Chapter 8. The bank explains:

> PPPs are price relatives. In their simplest form they show the ratio of prices in national currencies of the same precisely defined product in different countries. For example, if the price of a kilo of oranges of a specified quality is 45 rupees in country A and 3 dollars in country B, the PPP for such oranges between the two countries, when B is the base country, is the ratio 45 to 3 or 15 rupees to the dollar. In other words, for every dollar spent on oranges of the specified quality in country B, 15 rupees would have to be spent in country A to obtain the same quantity and quality of oranges.

> *(World Bank, 2011)*

These figures can make a difference in how we see a country. For example, for 2009, the World Bank said India's per capita GDP was US$1134 at official exchange rates, but US$3270 at PPP – nearly three times as much. These calculations are not just technical; there is a significant amount of guesswork in estimating price relatives, and some economists question their validity. Table 9.2 compares three European countries.

Table 9.2 Comparison of three European countries

2009 GDP	GDP per capita, US$, official exchange rate	GDP per capita, US$ PPP
France	41 051	33 655
Germany	40 067	36 267
United Kingdom	35 165	36 496

The order is significantly different depending on whether one looks at the official exchange rate or at PPP. But which gives the true picture?

PPP allows us to compare countries, but to compare GDP or other figures over time, it is sometimes useful to correct for inflation, and, as with PPP, try to estimate the buying power of those dollars in other years. When this is done, all the figures will be based on dollars of a particular year. Again, this can make a difference in how you see things. For example, global aid (Official Development Assistance (ODA)) was roughly constant from 1990 to 1996 in the dollars of each year, but if measured in 1990 dollars, it actually fell by 12%, and thus the 'real' amount of aid was declining in that period.

Economic historian Angus Maddison (1926–2010) developed techniques that allowed him to estimate GDP per capita going back as much as 2000 years; all his data were based on 1990 PPP dollars (which we used in Table 9.1 for historic English comparisons). Figure 9.1 plots some of Maddison's historic data.

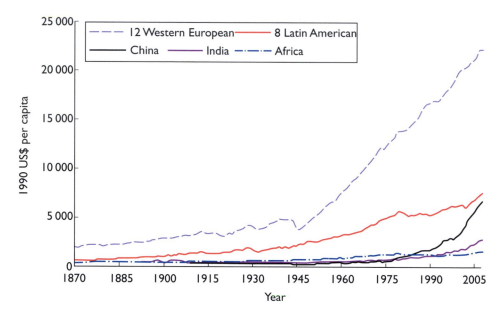

Figure 9.1 GDP per capita since 1870, given in 1990 US$

(Source: Maddison, 2010)

Activity 9.2

Look at Figure 9.1, which shows per capita income (in Maddison's 1990 US dollars) since 1870. What does this graph tell you?

Spend about 10 minutes on this activity.

Discussion

Looking first at Western Europe, you will see it was already richer than the other countries, even in 1870. Second, there was a steady increase in average GDP for the next 70 years. In 1945, we see a sharp drop caused by World War II, and then we see a dramatic increase. Compare this to Latin America, which also grew steadily over 70 years – by the 1920s it had reached European incomes of 50 years earlier. You will also see that income continued to grow steadily, not suffering the drop for World War II, but also not having the post-war spurt. China, India and Africa remain very poor for much of the time, but China suddenly starts to grow in the 1980s and has nearly caught up with Latin America in only 30 years. India, too, has started to grow, leaving Africa behind.

9.3.2 Comparing countries over time

Figure 9.1 allowed us to make comparisons between countries and also to look at those differences over time. Thus, for example, Figure 9.1 appears to show a rapidly widening gap between the incomes of Africa and Western Europe.

Maddison concluded that in the year 1000 Iran, Iraq and Turkey were the richest countries in the world, but their per capita income was only double that of the poorest countries (for which data can be found). By 1500, Italy was the wealthiest, but had only triple the income of the poorest country. By 1820, Western Europe was wealthiest, but had only five times the wealth of the poorest country. Table 9.3 looks at estimates by Maddison and his team at four points in recent history, setting out the richest and poorest countries.

Table 9.3   Richest and poorest countries – GDP per capita in 1990 PPP US dollars

1820*	1900	1975	2008
Richest			
Netherlands 1838	UK 4492	Switzerland 17 224	USA 31 178
UK 1706	New Zealand 4298	USA 16 284	Norway 28 500
Belgium 1319	USA 4091	Sweden 14 575	Ireland 27 898
Poorest			
South Africa 415	Brazil 678	Bangladesh 529	Niger 514
New Zealand 400	India 599	Cape Verde 525	Burundi 479
Nepal 397	China 545	Guinea 517	Democratic Republic of the Congo 249
Ratio richest to poorest			
5	8	33	127

* Fewer countries were available for inclusion in the 1820 data. Small oil states in West Asia have been excluded from this analysis.
Source: Maddison, 2010

Activity 9.3

Table 9.3 gives the three richest and three poorest countries (for which Maddison could make estimates) at four points in time. This table tries to use constant value dollars. First compare the richest country in 2008 with the richest in 1820. What do you see? Next look at the figures for the poorest countries. What do they tell you?

Don't spend more than 5 minutes on this activity.

Discussion

The comparison reveals that the average person in the richest country in 2008 (the USA) was almost 17 times as wealthy as the average person in the richest country in 1820 (The Netherlands). The figures for the poorest countries show that the wealth of the average person in these countries has actually decreased since 1900. You will see from this graph just how dramatically the difference between rich and poor countries has increased in recent years.

Table 9.2 also shows that the increasing wealth in the global North and worsening poverty in Africa has dramatically increased the gap between the poorest and wealthiest over the past century, from 8 to 1 in 1900 to 33 to 1 in 1975 to 127 to 1 in 2008. Numbers like this are hard to conceptualize in text so we often put them into tables, like Table 9.2, and graphs. Figure 9.2 is another way of showing this data. The scale on the left (known as the y axis) is the ratio of average income in the richest country to average income in the poorest country at various dates (shown on the horizontal, or x axis).

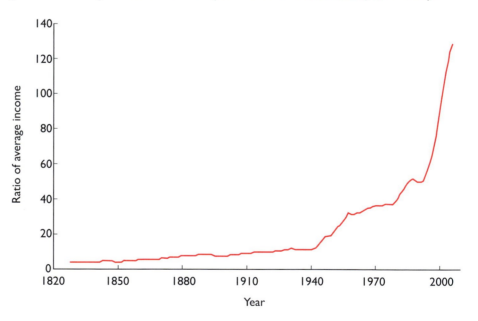

Figure 9.2   Growing global inequality: ratio of richest country per capita income to poorest country per capita income (Source: based on Maddison, 2010)

9.3.3 Showing inequality

So far we have compared countries by comparing average or mean income. But countries are big or small, and can be more or less equal, so we need better ways to look at inequality. Again, graphic representations are useful. Suppose for the moment that we only compare five people, and suppose they all have the same income. We could line up a set of five equal size people, as shown in Figure 9.3.

Figure 9.3   Using five people to show equal income

Let us use these five figures to represent the entire population of the world in 1820. First, we ask the world's population to queue up according to income, the poorest first, and then divide them into five equal groups (known as **quintiles**). We find that the poorest fifth had only 4.7% of the world's income, while the richest fifth in 1820 had 56.3% – more than half of the world's income. One way to use the figures of people to represent the quintiles is to use their size – the area of the figure – to represent their share of income, with the poorest quintile 'small figure' on the left and the richest quintile 'large figure' on the right. Figure 9.4 shows this.

4.7%   8.8%   12.2%   18%   56.3%

Figure 9.4   Using five figures to show global income distribution in 1820. Percentages show the share of global income for each quintile, and the size of the figure shows the relative share of income.

Instead of drawings of people, we can simply use bars, all the same width. In Figure 9.5 data are shown as simple bar charts. Perfect equality (Figure 9.3) in which everyone has the same income is shown in chart (a), the world in 1820 (Figure 9.4) is shown in chart (b), and we now add the world in 2000 as chart (c). Figure 9.5 also shows the Gini and Theil coefficients, which are inequality measures that we define in Section 9.3.4.

In 1820 the richest fifth (20%) of the world's population had 56.3% of the world's income – 12 times the income of the poorest fifth. And we can say that inequality is increasing because by 2000 the richest fifth had 74.1% of the world's income – 49 times the income of the poorest fifth, so we argue that the world has become less equal.

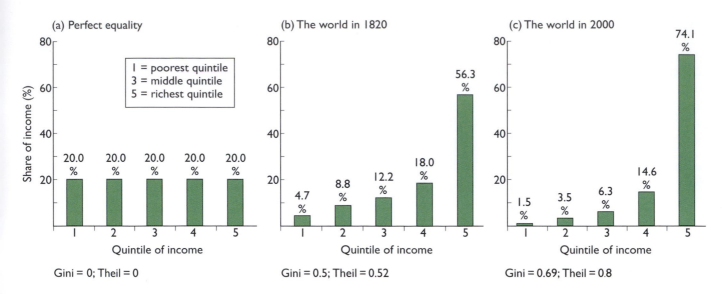

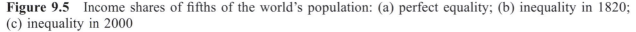

Figure 9.5 Income shares of fifths of the world's population: (a) perfect equality; (b) inequality in 1820; (c) inequality in 2000

Remember that inequality is not the same as poverty. Between 1820 and 2000, the average income of the people in the world increased fourfold. So, although the poorest fifth of the population has a much smaller share of the world's income, they are nevertheless somewhat better off now than poor people were in 1820. But the richest fifth of the world's population is nearly seven times as rich as its equivalent group in 1820. So the rich *are* getting richer, but the poor are not getting poorer, on average. Thus, when looking at charts, it is important to remember that they help you visualize differences, but only tell part of the story.

The next step is that instead of bars, we can just draw lines. Figure 9.6 shows the income distribution of three different countries. The populations of the three countries are divided into groups that are each 1/10th (10%) of the population, known as **deciles**, lined up according to income, with the poorest on the left. Chile has much more unequal income than many other countries, and the chart shows that the poorest people in Chile are as poor as the poorest in Ghana, while the richest in Chile are wealthier than nearly everyone in Portugal. Figure 9.6 also shows the Gini coefficient for the three countries.

9.3.4 Better measures of inequality

Studying Figure 9.6, we said that Chile 'seems' more unequal than the other two countries. But it is not precise to say Chile 'seems' more unequal. Clearer measures are needed. So the next step is to turn these graphic visualizations into numbers that can be used for comparisons. Statisticians and economists have developed various ways to measure income inequality. None of these are simple, but the Lorenz curve and Gini coefficients are widely used and are easier to understand because they are based on graphic and visual representations of inequality.

Economist Max Lorenz was a doctoral student in 1905 when he published his famous method to describe income inequalities. His system is based on

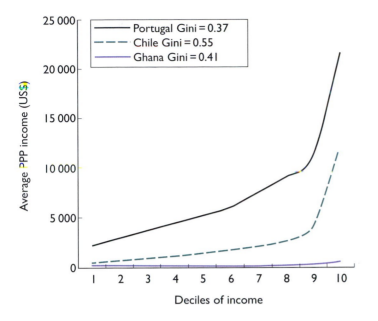

Figure 9.6   Comparison of Portugal, Chile and Ghana using deciles and income data from 1999–2003 (Source: UNU-Wider, 2008)

cumulative share of income. Suppose we again imagine a parade of people, the poorest first, who each go past a window where they collect their income, until the richest person goes by and takes all the money that remains. What Lorenz shows in his graph is the total share of money that has been taken by each person.

In Figure 9.5 we used quintiles, and in Figure 9.6 we used deciles, simply because five bars looked neater in Figure 9.5 while ten points gave a smoother graph in Figure 9.6, and we might have also used hundredths to create an even smoother graph. Our choice of how we divide populations reflects availability of data and presentation, and does not make a fundamental difference. Note that one of the neat things about the Lorenz curve is that it does not matter if we use quintiles, deciles, or even hundredths, because we are always showing the income of the everyone below a point.

Now let us return to our bar chart in Figure 9.5, of incomes by quintiles, and present them as Lorenz curves. The key graph is perfect equality, in which each quintile has the same share. Remember that we are doing cumulative percentages. Tables 9.4 and 9.5 show how we work this out.

Table 9.4 Percentage shares of income if income is distributed equally

Quintile	1	2	3	4	5
Share of income (%)	20	20	20	20	20

Now we do it cumulatively. So 20% of the population is just the first quintile. But 40% of the population is quintiles 1 and 2, and thus has 40% of the income. And 60% of the population is the income of quintiles 1, 2 and 3, and so on.

Table 9.5 Cumulative percentage share of income when income is distributed equally

Proportion of population (%)	0	20	40	60	80	100
Cumulative share of income (%)	0	20	40	60	80	100

That always gives a straight line at a 45 degree angle, as shown in Figure 9.7.

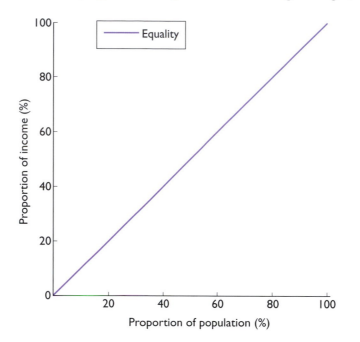

Figure 9.7 Equality of income distribution

In Figure 9.5 we gave the distribution of incomes for global quintiles in 1820 and 2000. Using that to calculate cumulative income shares, we can produce the Lorenz curves for 1820 and 2000. Table 9.6 gives the incomes per quintile and Table 9.7 gives the cumulative incomes, producing the Lorenz curves in Figure 9.8.

Table 9.6 Percentage shares of global income by quintile

Quintile	1	2	3	4	5
1820 share of income (%)	4.7	8.8	12.2	18.0	56.3
2000 share of income (%)	1.5	3.5	6.3	14.6	74.1

Again, when we calculate cumulative shares; the first 40% of the population is the sum of quintiles 1 and 2, and so on.

Table 9.7 Cumulative percentage shares of global income

Cumulative percentage of population (%)	0	20	40	60	80	100
1820 cumulative share of income (%)	0	4.7	13.5	25.7	43.7	100
2000 cumulative share of income (%)	0	1.5	5.0	11.3	25.9	100

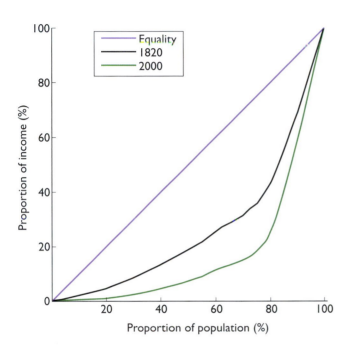

Figure 9.8 Lorenz curves of global income

Note that the line for 2000 is further away from the equality line. We argued that the global income distribution in 2000 had become more unequal than it had been in 1820, and the Lorenz curve demonstrates that conclusion. So, to come back to the earlier statement that Chile 'seems' more unequal, it is possible to create a clear measure and to demonstrate the comparison with other countries using a Lorenz curve.

Activity 9.4

It is sometimes easier to understand graphs such as Figure 9.8 if we think about a specific example of people and money. So let us assume we have five children and we are going to divide an allowance of €100 between them. (To keep everything looking similar, we have consciously chosen five children so we are working in quintiles, and €100 so that the total amount of money €100 = 100%.)

Equality would mean giving each child €20. But suppose we give less money to the younger children, and we distribute the allowance as €5, €10, €15, €30 and €40.

Now, draw the equality and Lorenz curves for the five children.

Your first step is to make a table with the cumulative proportions. Remember the poorest always comes first. Your table will look similar to Table 9.8 and the curves should look similar to Figure 9.9.

Table 9.8 Cumulative allowances of children, in Euros

Proportion of children (%)	0	20	40	60	80	100
Cumulative allowance if all were equal (€)	0	20	40	60	80	100
Cumulative allowance for our 5 children (€)	0	5	15	30	60	100

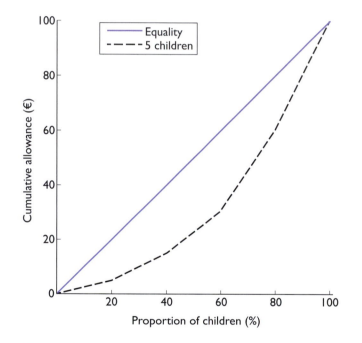

Figure 9.9 Lorenz curve for allowances for five children

Now, suppose the eldest child is at university and needs more money, so we give her a bigger share of the allowance, and take some away from some of the others. Say we change the distribution to €2, €5, €10, €22, and €60.

Next, calculate the cumulative allowances and on the same graph draw the new Lorenz curve.

Although it may be justified, we feel that the second distribution of allowances is less equal than the first. That means that the second Lorenz curve should be below the first one, farther away from the equality line.

Third, think of another distribution of allowances for these five children, and graph that Lorenz curve. (Remember, however you distribute the money, to do a Lorenz curve the child with least always comes first in the parade.)

Is your new allowance distribution more or less equal than the others?

Spend about 15 minutes on this activity.

Now that we have seen how the Lorenz curve works in a simple case, let us apply the technique to two countries, to see which is more equal.

Activity 9.5

Consider Sweden and the USA. This time we will present the data in deciles (a tenth of the population). The basic distribution of income is shown in Table 9.9.

Table 9.9 Share of income, by deciles, for Sweden and the USA, 2000

Decile of income	1	2	3	4	5	6	7	8	9	10
Sweden (%)	4	6	7	7	8	9	11	12	14	22
USA (%)	2	4	5	6	7	8	10	12	16	30

First look at the data. Does one country seem less equal, with less income going to the poor and more income going to the better off?

Now draw the Lorenz curves for Sweden and the USA as in the previous activity.

Which country is more equal? Does this correspond to what you thought before you drew the curves?

Spend about 10 minutes on this activity.

You have now seen how to draw curves which give you a picture of inequality. The next step is to actually give numbers to inequality. The Italian statistician Corrado Gini made that step in 1912. Go back to Figure 9.8 and you will see that the 1820 line is closer to the equality line than the 2000 line. That means the area between the equal line and the 1820 line is smaller than the area between the equal line and the 2000 line, and this area is a possible measure of inequality. Figure 9.10 shows this.

As expected, B is larger than A. To create a number that we can use for comparisons, Gini used the area under the equality line as the starting point. This is shown in Figure 9.11.

The Gini coefficient is defined as being the area between the equality line and the Lorenz curve (A or B in this example, shown in Figure 9.10) divided by the area under the equality line (C in this example). Area A turns out to be exactly half of area C. As the Gini coefficient for 1820 is A/C, that means the Gini coefficient is 0.5. The area of B is obviously larger than the area of A, so we would expect that the Gini coefficient for 2000, which is B/C, is larger also, and it turns out to be 0.69.

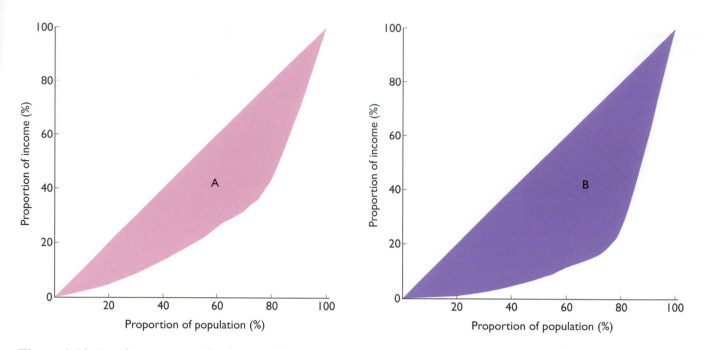

Figure 9.10 Area between equality line and Lorenz curves for 1820 (A) and 2000 (B) global income distribution

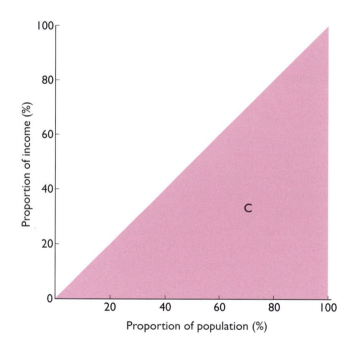

Figure 9.11 Area under the equality line

The Gini coefficient is the most commonly used measure of inequality. It is always between 0 and 1, and the closer to 1 the greater the inequality. This corresponds to what we expect to find – the Gini is larger for 2000 than for 1820.

We can also calculate the Gini for the five children in Activity 9.4. For the more equal distribution the Gini is 0.3, while in the second distribution in which we gave more than half the total allowance to the oldest child, the Gini is 0.45. We selected those distributions intentionally, because in 2003 the Gini coefficient for Sweden was 0.3 and for the USA was 0.45.

Finally, you may sometimes find that a Gini coefficient is presented multiplied by 100, so that the Gini of Sweden would be presented as 30 rather than 0.30.

Activity 9.6

So far we have simply presented measures on inequality. But in Activity 9.4 we reduced the discussion to five children and gave distributions that gave Gini coefficients that corresponded to major countries.

Thinking about a group of five children you know, are such distributions fair or unfair? Can we even ask that question?

Spend no more than 5 minutes on this activity. We will return to this question in the next section.

The Theil index

Statisticians have also developed other, more complex inequality measures, including the Theil index, which we will not even try to explain. Like the Gini it runs from 0 to 1, and it is coming more into use because the Theil index increases more quickly as inequality becomes greater, and because we can use it later to separate the components of inequality. Economists François Bourguignon and Christian Morrison were able to look at global inequality back to 1820, and they used the Theil index to separate two components – inequality within countries (that is, how the rich people compare to the poor people within a country) and inequality between countries (how the income of people in Britain compares to the income of the people in India). Figure 9.12 shows an unexpected result.

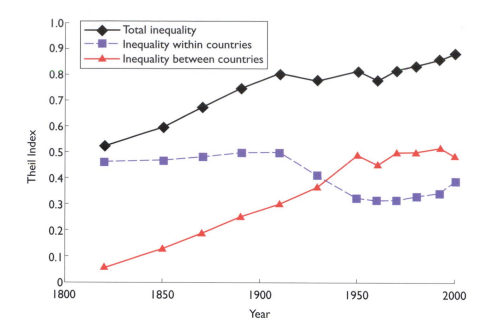

Figure 9.12 Theil index of global inequality, separated by domestic and international inequality (Source: based on Bourguignon and Morrison, 2002, and Dikhanov, 2005)

The line for inequality between countries (the line with the triangles) shows that in 1820, nearly all countries of the world had similar average incomes, and thus were similarly poor. But with colonialism and the industrial revolution, income rose in Europe and the USA much more rapidly than elsewhere (see Figure 9.1), so there was a sharp increase in economic inequality between countries. Through the 19th century, inequality within countries (the second line with squares) changed very little. Then, in the first half of the 20th century, wages rose and there were more social benefits, so inequality within individual countries dropped significantly, while inequalities between countries continued to increase, meaning that total global inequality (the top line, with diamonds) did not change much for half a century. But the second half of the 20th century and especially the beginning of the 21st century shows that inequality between countries stopped increasing and may actually now be declining slightly – largely due to the growth of China – while inequality within countries increased significantly from 1970 to 2000. Indeed, the International Labour Organization found that between 1990 and 2005 there was an increase in income differentials, sometimes quite large; only in Brazil and Mexico was there a decrease in income differences.

9.4 Does income inequality matter?

It is not just the differentials in incomes between countries, but also between people, which are increasing dramatically. The US magazine *Forbes* declared that Mexican businessman Carlos Slim Helú was the world's richest man in 2010. His fortune was US$54 billion, and his income in 2009 was US$18 billion, according to *Forbes*. This one man earned more money in 2009 than many entire countries in that year, including Malawi, Madagascar, Rwanda, Botswana, Laos, Haiti and Albania.

These spectacular income inequalities have occurred largely since 1975, and have triggered an intense debate. As discussed in Subsection 9.3.4, inequality declined within countries through much of the 20th century. Anthony Bebbington argues that it was the power of social movements and trade unions which pushed the reduction of poverty in industrialized countries. In broad terms, governments in the 1945–1975 period (and some would argue in response to the global economic crisis in 2008) followed the strategy advocated by the economist John Maynard Keynes (1883–1946). This argued for a stress on demand from consumers, which would promote growth as businesses invested to increase supply to meet the demand. Keynes put a much greater stress on the role of government to maintain demand, for example through public spending on social welfare and job creation. He wrote: 'To dig holes in the ground, paid for out of savings, will increase, not only employment, but the real national dividend of useful goods and services' (Keynes, 1936, p. 220).

But growth in the late 20th century was linked to neoliberalism (see Chapter 2), which aimed to restrict the role of government and promote the agency of the individual instead. Advocates of this policy (see, for example, Hayek, 1948, 1960) essentially argued that richer people were more likely to save, invest, create jobs and produce more goods at lower prices, thus increasing the well-being of the poor. This was called 'supply-side economics', meaning that the rich should be supported with tax cuts and other benefits to allow them to invest and create an increased supply of goods. It was promoted by the USA and Britain in the early 1980s, and was pushed by the World Bank and the IMF for developing countries.

Even during the ascendency of supply-side economics, many economists and agencies, including the UN Conference on Trade and Development, continued to promote demand-side economics for developing countries. The key difference is that in supply-side economics money goes to the rich in the hope that they will invest (thus creating the income boom of the late 20th century), while in demand-side economics money goes to the middle class and poor in the hope that they will spend. The eminent economist John Kenneth Galbraith (1908–2006) said neoliberalism was nothing more than 'trickle-down economics', hoping that a bit of wealth would eventually trickle down to the poor. He said it was like the late 19th century 'horse and sparrow theory', that 'if you feed the horse enough oats, some will pass through to the road for the sparrows' (Galbraith, 1982).

Jason Myers, in his book *The Politics of Equality*, argues that this dramatic shift in the 1980s reflected a major increase in inequalities of power. Myers (2010, p. 125) points to the 'sweeping counter-attack that Western capitalists and their political allies' successfully launched against trade unions and social movements. Inequalities of power at national and global levels were behind political changes that promoted increases in inequality and a reduction in attempts to reduce poverty in industrialized countries. According to Myers (2010, pp. 91–92), the UNDP warned in 1997 that 'some multinational corporations command more wealth and economic power than most states do'; they bypass local jurisdictions and have no incentives to contribute to poverty reduction. The 'welfare state' was reduced in many industrial countries, just as taxes were cut for corporations and better-off people, and inequality began to increase sharply. Globally, the USA and other industrialized countries used their power in the international financial institutions such as the World Bank and the IMF, to impose neoliberal policies on developing countries (see Chapter 2).

These economic shifts and the increase in inequalities in wealth and power were matched by a change in the underlying political philosophy that contributed to the hegemony of ideas of neoliberalism (see Chapter 3). John Rawls (1921–2002) proclaimed the concept of 'Justice as Fairness', which included individual liberty and accepted some inequality, but also put great stress on creating institutions which would act 'to the greatest benefit of the least advantaged members of society' (Rawls, 1972). The philosophical response to 'Justice as Fairness' came from Robert Nozick (1938–2002), who suggested an 'Entitlement Justice' and argued that absolute priority should be given to inviolable individual rights, and especially to property rights. Nozick (1974) described individual human beings as 'self-owners' who are entitled to their bodies, abilities and labour, and the fruits of the use of their talents, abilities and labour. Those who were more skilled or harder working would earn more, and this would inevitably create justified inequalities.

The intellectual battle between Nozick and Rawls was often seen as between individual liberty and institutions that could benefit the least advantaged. Another aspect of the debate is which 'rights' are important. The Universal Declaration of Human Rights, adopted by the UN in 1948, used the language of justice and rights and guarantees not only political rights, but also economic rights. Article 17 of the Universal Declaration says 'Everyone has the right to own property alone as well as in association with others. No one shall be arbitrarily deprived of his property.' But Articles 23 and 25 guarantee a right to work and the right to an 'adequate' standard of living; does this come into conflict with Article 17? Conservatives argue that Article 17 should be seen as a prohibition on high taxes because it deprives people of the profits from their work, and are thus saying that for the rich, inequality is a right. But satisfying Articles 23 and 25 may require the intervention of the state and transfers from rich to poor, either directly through redistribution, or through taxation paying for heath and education. Does Article 17 take precedence, or does increasing inequality (in wages, power, access to healthcare, etc.) violate the rights of the poor to an adequate standard of living as set out in Articles 23 and 25?

The late 1990s saw various attempts to find a middle path, largely around trying to reduce non-economic inequalities while continuing to accept income differences. The Millennium Development Goals (MDGs) were first proposed in 1995 by the OECD's Development Assistance Committee (DAC), which has members from all the main donor countries except China. They were adopted by the UN in 2000. Of the eight goals, only one relates to income inequality and poverty. All the others relate to education, health, gender and environment. Target 5a, for example, is about reducing maternal mortality – the inequality cited at the beginning of this chapter. There was also an increasing interest in transferring money from rich to poor. With the end of the Cold War, net aid (defined by the DAC as ODA and measured in 2008 US dollars) fell from US$84 billion in 1990 to US$69 billion in 1997, but then rose steadily to US$124 billion by 2009. At the same time, some of the fabulously rich began to give large amounts of money for development. The Bill and Melinda Gates Foundation was created in 1994. In 2010 it had endowments worth US$36 billion, largely from Bill Gates and Warren Buffett, the world's second and third richest men in 2010, according to *Forbes*. The foundation concentrates on health (particularly vaccines), agriculture, micro-finance and disaster relief. In 2009, it gave US$3 billion in grants; this was more than each of 11 members of the DAC, including Switzerland, Belgium and Australia.

Activity 9.7

Does the level of aid from wealthy individuals give them more influence in development policy? What do you think are the implications of this? Should individuals have the right to set development polices, because of their wealth?

Spend no more than 15 minutes on this activity.

Philosophically this middle path was set out by the Nobel Prize winning economist Amartya Sen, who concentrated on the individual rather than on institutions, but who also argued that rights were of no use if they could not be exercised. As explained in Chapter 8, he developed the concept of 'capabilities' which are 'the substantive freedoms he or she enjoys to lead the kind of life he or she has reason to value.' In other words, capabilities are not just rights, but the actual possibilities open to a person. Capabilities are such things as the ability to live to old age, engage in economic transactions and participate in political activities; these reflect what people value, and will be different for different individuals. This can be seen as 'agency', the ability of a person to achieve their aims and goals, and perhaps to influence their community and society. Poverty can then be defined as a lack of capabilities or agency as well as lack of money, and inequality then becomes the relative position, with some people having significantly more power or agency than others. In his 2010 book *The Idea of Justice*, Sen argues strongly against a single definition of justice, noting that individuals and groups can disagree and that the definition changes with time. But he makes two points. First, justice needs to be defined through broad discussion which cannot be 'parochial', that is, only involving the views of a small group. Second, that justice should be seen as a relative rather than absolute. It is not about finding the best solution, but about finding a better position than the present one in a move toward some sort of 'social justice'. He may not agree with Rawls about there being some abstract 'justice', but he does argue that 'the world in which we live has so much deprivation of one kind or another (from being hungry to being tyrannized)', and that this is morally and politically unacceptable (Sen, 2010, p. 415).

Finally, growing concern about the environment is beginning to shift thinking on inequality, because of the large inequalities in energy use and the impact of climate change (Smith, 2013). On average, a person in a rich country adds ten times as much carbon to the atmosphere as a person in a poor country. But key impacts of climate change, including drought and rising sea levels, are disproportionately affecting poor countries. Boyce (2007, p. 1) argues that:

> Those who are relatively powerful and wealthy typically gain disproportionate benefits from the economic activities that degrade the environment, while those who are relatively powerless and poor typically bear disproportionate costs. All else being equal, wider political and economic inequalities tend to result in higher levels of environmental harm.
>
> *(Boyce, 2007, p. 1)*

Thus, 'more equitable distributions of power and wealth in human societies' (ibid) are important for safeguarding the environment.

9.5 Do more equal societies do better?

The international financial institutions are becoming more concerned about inequality, as noted in Box 9.1. Martin Ravallion, Senior Research Manager in the World Bank, wrote a 2007 article entitled simply 'Inequality is bad for the poor'. In it, he concentrated on economic growth, and said: 'inequality is bad for growth', 'countries with higher initial inequality experienced lower rates of growth' and 'poor people in high inequality countries face a double handicap: such countries will tend to experience lower growth rates and the growth that does occur will have less impact on poverty (Ravallion, 2007, p. 50).

This has direct implications for development policy. The UN Research Institute for Social Development (UNRISD) points out in 'Combating poverty and inequality' (UNRISD, 2010) that 'in contrast to the experiences of countries that were successful historically in reducing poverty, contemporary poverty reduction strategies have increasingly focused on "targeting the poor"'. But this runs 'counter to the evidence from countries that have successfully reduced poverty over relatively short periods. UNRISD research shows instead that progress has occurred principally through state-directed strategies which combine economic development objectives with active social policies.' Key is the creation of 'jobs that are adequately remunerated and accessible to all' and 'comprehensive social policies that are grounded in universal rights'. Employment creation represents an important channel for reducing inequality. Finally, UNRISD notes that the MDGs 'do not directly address inequality'.

The strongest challenge to rapidly growing inequality was the book *The Spirit Level: Why More Equal Societies Almost Always Do Better*, by two health economists, Richard Wilkinson and Kate Pickett (Wilkinson and Pickett, 2009). They analyse a broad range of data, and come to two conclusions. First, increasing income is important, but only up to a point. Above US$25 000 per capita income (the income in 2009 of the Czech Republic and Portugal), further income does not make people happier or live longer. Second, health and social problems are closely related to inequality within rich countries, and also within US states. A range of things are more serious in less equal countries, such as: the more unequal have relatively more people with mental health problems and obesity, and have higher murder, imprisonment, teenage pregnancy and infant death rates, but lower life expectancy and educational attainment. Precisely why is unclear, but the authors suggest that in more divided societies hierarchies are stronger, trust is lower and people worry more about self-esteem and self-worth. This creates stress and mental and physical health problems. The key point of *The Spirit Level* is the claim that inequality harms both rich and poor, and more equality increases mental and physical health for everyone.

The challenge to these conclusions came from a British centre-right think tank, Policy Exchange, in a provocative booklet *Beware False Prophets* written by Peter Saunders (Saunders, 2010). He argues that data on homicides is biased because of the very high murder rate in the USA (which has one of the highest income inequalities), 'which probably has more to do with its gun control laws than its income distribution'. Similarly (more equal) 'Scandinavian nations routinely appear at one end of many of [*The Spirit Level*] graphs, and the (less equal) Anglo nations often appear at the other. But these differences probably reflect a deeper divergence between Nordic and Anglo cultures.'

But for Saunders, the core difference is political. In Box 9.3, we quote Saunders's characterization of the debate. His comments are subjective and he uses loose terms like 'left-wingers' and 'right-wingers', and you may want to consider whether these are accurate characterizations of the position or simply caricatures. Politics does matter. In the 1980s, the economics of neoliberalism and the libertarian philosophy of Nozick dominated the political era of Ronald Reagan and Margaret Thatcher. The return to structuralist explanations of poverty (Chapter 2) and the growing importance of the egalitarian philosophies of Rawls and Sen in the early 21st century were linked to a political shift which was less conservative and more concerned with inequality on moral grounds. This shift, as noted in this chapter, was reflected in the thinking of the International Financial Institutions (IFIs) – the World Bank, the IMF and regional development banks, such as the African Development Bank – with both the IMF and World Bank increasingly treating inequality as a problem. Whether or not one accepts Saunders' description of the debate, it is a useful reminder of the centrality of politics to all discussions, not simply about inequality, but development in general.

Box 9.3 The view from the right

Is inequality unjust?

More than any other single issue, economic inequality has for generations functioned like a litmus test of political ideology:

- The majority on the left believe in equalising incomes and wealth. Few left-wingers think income differences should be flattened completely, but they do think it is wrong that anybody should receive a lot more than anybody else. They therefore tend to favour tax and welfare policies which aim, not only to improve the living standards of those at the bottom, but also to reduce the prosperity enjoyed by those at the top. Seen in this light, the fact that Britain's income distribution is more unequal than that of most other western European countries, coupled with the evidence that it has increased significantly over the past 30 years, is a serious cause for concern.

- For those on the political right, concern about the way incomes are distributed is more muted. Few right-wingers disapprove in principle of 'progressive' taxation and the provision of state welfare benefits, but they worry that redistributive policies like these can destroy work incentives, and they believe it is right that people who work hard and exploit their talents should enjoy the material rewards that come with success. From this perspective, what really matters is not equality of outcomes, but equality of opportunity. Provided there are no major barriers to people competing for material rewards, it is not 'unfair' if some end up with more than others.

(Saunders, 2010, p. 13)

Summary and looking forward

This chapter has looked at the sharp increase in income inequality, globally and within countries, and has noted that this has not improved the lot of the poorest people in the world. We looked at ways to measure income inequality, and considered issues of inequality within countries and between countries. Income is perhaps the most important component of inequality, but not the only one. There are inequalities in health, education and power that can be a matter of life or death. For example, the poorest women are much more likely to die in childbirth. Inequalities occur between and within countries, between groups, and even within families. Inequality is not the same as poverty, but where large inequalities leave the worst off deprived and in poverty, with fewer opportunities, we often consider this unfair or unreasonable. Finally, we have looked at issues of fairness and justice, and at the ongoing political, economic and philosophical debates about inequality. These issues will be picked up and explored further in the following chapters, giving case studies and examples to which your own judgements can be applied about what is fair, just, and equal.

References

Bourguignon, F. and Morrison, C. (2002) 'Inequality among world citizens: 1820–1992', *American Economic Review*, vol. 92, no. 4, pp. 727–744.

Boyce, J.K. (2007) 'Is inequality bad for the environment?', *University of Massachusetts Political Economy Research Institute Working Paper 135* [online], http://www.peri.umass.edu/fileadmin/pdf/working_papers/working_papers_101-150/WP135.pdf (Accessed 3 August 2011).

Centers for Disease Control and Protection (n.d.) *Wonder Online Databases* [online], http://wonder.cdc.gov/ (Accessed 31 August 2011).

Cockburn, J., Razzaque, A. and Razzaque, M.A. (2006) 'Child poverty and intrahousehold allocation: analysis of a Bangladeshi household survey with individual consumption data', *5th PEP Research Network General Meeting*, 18–22 June 2006, Addis Ababa.

Dikhanov, Y. (2005) 'Trends in global income distribution, 1970–2000, and scenarios for 2015', *Occasional Paper 8 for the UNDP Human Development Report 2005*.

Galbraith, J.K. (1982) 'Recession economics', New York Review of Books, 4 Feb 1982, http://www.nybooks.com/articles/archives/1982/feb/04/recession-economics/ Accessed January 2012).

Hanlon, J. (2013) 'Fear and development', in Butcher, M. and Papaioannou, T. (eds) *New Perspectives in International Development*, London, Bloomsbury Academic/ Milton Keynes, The Open University.

Hayek, F.A. (1948) *Individualism and Economic Order*, South Bend Indiana, Gateway Editions.

Hayek, F.A. (1960) *The Constitution of Liberty*, London, Routledge and Kegan Paul.

Hogan, M.C., Foreman, K.J., Naghavi, M., Ahn, S.Y., Wang, M., Makela, S.M., Lopez, A.D., Lozano, R. and Murray, C.J.L. (2010) 'Maternal mortality for 181 countries, 1980–2008: a systematic analysis of progress towards Millennium Development Goal 5', *Lancet*, vol. 375, pp. 1609–23.

Kaur, N. and Kumar, S. (2008) *Literacy Rate and Gender Gap in Scheduled Castes Among Different Religions* [online], http://www.capabilityapproach.com/pubs/NavjeetKaur.pdf (Accessed 3 August 2011).

Keynes, J.M. (1936) *The General Theory of Employment, Interest, and Money*, New York, Harcourt Brace.

Koohi-Kamali, F. (2008) 'Intrahousehold inequality and child gender bias in Ethiopia', *World Bank Policy Research Working Paper 4755*, The World Bank.
Loudon, I. (1992) *Death in Childbirth: an International Study of Maternal Care and Maternal Mortality*, 1800–1950, Oxford, Oxford University Press.

Loudon, I. (1992) *Death in Childbirth: An International Study of Maternal Care and Maternal Mortality, 1800–1950*, Oxford, Oxford University Press.

Maddison, A. (2010) *Historical Statistics of the World Economy: 1–2008 AD* [online], http://www.ggdc.net/MADDISON/Historical_Statistics/horizontal-file_02-2010.xls (Accessed 31 August 2011).

Myers, J. (2010) *The Politics of Equality*, London, Zed Books.

Nozick, R. (1974) *Anarchy, State, and Utopia*, Oxford, Blackwell.

Purdue, B. (2008), 'Statement submitted to the UK All Party Parliamentary Group on Population Development and Reproductive Health', 9 December 2008, Manila, Asian Development Bank.

Ravallion, M. (2007) 'Inequality is bad for the poor' in Jenkins, S.P. and Micklewright, J. (eds) *Inequality and Poverty Re-Examined*, Oxford, Oxford University Press.

Rawls, J. (1972) *A Theory of Justice*, Oxford, Oxford University Press.

Saunders, P. (2010) *Beware False Prophets*, London, Policy Exchange, also available online at: http://www.policyexchange.org.uk/assets/Beware_False_Prophets_Jul_10.pdf (Accessed 3 August 2011).

Sen, A. (2010) *The Idea of Justice*, London, Penguin.

Smith, M. (2013) 'Vulnerability in a world risk society' in Butcher, M. and Papaioannou, T. (eds) *New Perspectives in International Development*, London, Bloomsbury Academic/Milton Keynes, The Open University.

Strauss-Kahn, D. (2010) 'Human development and wealth distribution', speech given in Agadir, Morocco, 1 November 2010, available online at: http://www.imf.org/external/np/speeches/2010/110110.htm (Accessed 3 August 2011).

United Nations Development Programme (UNDP) (2011) UNDP Database: International Human Development Indicators, [online], http://hdrstats.undp.org/en/indicators/6.html (Accessed 21 July 2011).

United Nations Research Institute for Social Development (UNRISD) (2010) 'Combating poverty and inequality', *UNRISD Research and Policy Brief 10*, May 2010.

UNU-WIDER (2008) World Income Inequality Database V2.0c May 2008 [online], http://www.wider.unu.edu/research/Database/en_GB/database/ (Accessed 1 March 2012).

Wilkinson, R. and Pickett, K. (2009) *The Spirit Level: Why More Equal Societies Almost Always Do Better*, London, Allen Lane.

World Bank (2006) *World Development Report 2006: Equity and Development,* World Bank [online], http://www.worldbank.org (Accessed 3 August 2011).

World Bank (2009) World Bank Data [online], http://data.worldbank.org/indicator (Accessed 1 March 2012).

World Bank (2011) *What are PPPs?* [online], http://go.worldbank.org/A3R6KFYSR0 (Accessed 3 August 2011).

Culture, livelihoods and making a living

Daphne Chang, Masuma Farooki and Hazel Johnson

Introduction

From considering the debates on poverty and inequality, and how they have changed over time, we now turn to how poor or low-income people make a living. For low-income people, making a living is both simple and complex. It is simple at the level of basic needs that have to be met. It is complex in terms of how those needs are, or are not, met in practice. Making a living usually involves an extensive and diverse range of activities, connecting different types of production and trade, the rural to the urban and the local to the national and international. Shifts in demographics, such as increasing urbanisation, have impacted on livelihood strategies. For those who live in rural areas, there has been a decline in the numbers engaged in agriculture, although most of the income for the poorest households still comes from this sector (World Bank, 2008, p. 77). An increasing number of people in both rural areas and towns are working in multiple forms of small business and trade, formal and informal sectors, often with several sources of low-level income.

This chapter focuses on three dimensions of livelihood. The first is the cultural dimension. Although the world seems to be becoming more homogeneous – the international spread of particular industries, brand names, use of mobile phones and so on – how people live their lives, the things they value and the norms they live by take many different shapes and forms and affect people's perceptions of what is considered a 'good life'. The second dimension is vulnerability. For poor and low-income people, making a living and ensuring the livelihood of families and households can easily come under threat. We examine some of the conditions under which this occurs as well as the ways that people exert agency in difficult circumstances. Finally, we examine the national and global linkages in the livelihoods of low-income people, by looking at how workers in the South are connected to international production and trade.

In exploring these three dimensions, we will start with the local and end with the international, using case studies and different approaches. The approaches we use are: (i) a cultural perspective; (ii) focusing on sustainable livelihoods approach; and (iii) using a value chain analysis. Although we wish to locate development in its international setting, it is important to examine the local if we are to understand the everyday challenges of making a living. Poor people's livelihoods are connected in complex ways to the international economy: from the things they produce and sell to the things they buy. To see these interconnections and relationships, we need to look at micro-level processes in households and communities as well as macro-level processes of international production and trade. In summary, the aims of this chapter are to:

- provide frameworks for understanding the livelihoods of low-income people

- identify how poor people are both constrained and exert agency in making a living
- locate the everyday challenges of making a living in an international context.

Note that we use both the terms 'livelihoods' and 'making a living' in this chapter. By livelihoods we tend to mean the range of activities, including social activities, which support or constrain the overall process of making a living. Making a living tends to refer to the production of goods or services for sale or consumption and the earning of wages or other forms of income in cash and kind. However, in practice the terms are often used in a similar way.

10.1 Understanding livelihoods from a cultural perspective

What is meant by 'culture'? If you find defining 'culture' difficult, you are not alone – the concept is an ambiguous one. To *describe* a group of people as sharing the same 'culture' such as 'the Maasai culture', 'Scottish culture' or 'working class culture' can be open to vague and misleading generalisations. However, taking 'culture' for granted leads to misconceptions of poverty, of the livelihoods that people pursue, and of interventions to alleviate poverty.

An *analytical* rather than descriptive way of attributing phenomena associated with 'culture' would be to focus on differences. For example what is it that makes a person 'Maasai', 'Scottish' or 'working class'? In order to do this, we focus on the specifics that mark out a group of people from others in terms of traditions, customs, values, world views, religious practices, perceptions, belief systems, symbols, languages and codes of morality. In short, the word 'culture' can be used to mean some or all of these dimensions of human life.

Box 10.1 outlines dimensions of pastoralists' livelihoods in East Africa. Pastoralists are people who make a living from the herding of livestock, often moving from place to place. The following activity asks you to read Box 10.1 and make links between culture, livelihoods and understandings of poverty.

Activity 10.1

Make a list of the key features of livelihood for pastoralists as outlined in Box 10.1.

Using your list, compare the meanings and significance given to those features by pastoralists with the meanings and significance given to them in the culture you most identify with.

Referring back to the concepts of low income, multiple deprivations and relative poverty in Chapter 8, how useful do you think these concepts are in understanding pastoral life and livelihoods?

Spend no more than 30 minutes on this activity.

Box 10.1 The poor are not us

Pastoral economies in the context of East Africa rest upon livestock – sheep, goats, donkeys and especially cattle. Cattle milk is the dietary staple. The meat of sheep and goats supplement the diet and the meat of cattle is essential during all ceremonies. Milk, meat and sometimes blood have symbolic and social significance. Pastoralists not only rely on the livestock for subsistence, they also use the skins of the cattle, goats and sheep for clothing, hides for sleeping, and sacks for storage and carrying. The horns of cattle are made into snuff boxes and cups. Dung is used for fuel and plaster on walls and on the roofs of huts. Donkeys are mainly used as pack animals to carry water and belongings when migrating during the dry seasons.

Cattle are seen as wealth. They are the most important medium (in the past the only medium) of exchange and accumulation. They are the currency for bridewealth as well as for the payment of fines for social transgressions. Exchange of livestock between friends and relatives is the basis of social relationships. These relationships are a social and financial safety net when natural and human disasters strike. Generous donation of livestock during rituals and ceremonies is an important way to build up one's reputation and authority. Therefore, cattle also symbolise prestige (Spencer, 1988). Waller's description of the economic and social relations amongst the Maa-speakers in the central Rift Valley in the 19th century still holds true today. He says: 'Large holdings of stock create an impression of competence, responsibility, and stability, enabled a man to extend his network through gift exchanges and hospitality …' (Waller, 1985, p. 104).

On the other hand, loss of stock (or access to stock) due to diseases, drought and cattle rustling would effectively exclude the individual from participating in social functions and force such an individual to become a dependant in his own community or, worse, to leave pastoralism altogether.

The Poor Are Not Us is the title of a book edited by Anderson and Broch-Due (1999). By exploring the self-perceptions and community consciousness of pastoralist societies in East Africa, Anderson and Broch-Due (1999, p. 3) begin their volume by arguing that 'the poor' by definition are not the people who practise pastoralism.

Anderson and Broch-Due further discuss how such perceptions and community consciousness contrasts starkly with the interventions put forward for alleviating poverty amongst pastoralists. They say:

> … images of poverty and East African pastoralism have in recent years become inextricably bound up together in apocalyptic scenes of drought, famine and warfare. Media presentations of swollen-bellied children, skeletal figures in drought-stricken landscapes and pitiful refugee camps are so powerful that, rather than stimulating critical examination of the

complex causes of the crisis, they have circumvented it and urged upon planners the simplest of diagnoses and cures – pastoralism is not a strategy for survival, it is a recipe for disaster and impoverishment … while planners see the reduction of livestock and moves towards sedentarization and cultivation as the ways to prosperity, pastoralists tend to see these as the very definition of poverty itself.

(Anderson and Broch-Due, 1999, p. ix)

Not surprisingly, these interventions often fail because they encourage pastoralists to become 'poor' materially and socially.

So how does understanding different cultures help better explain people's experiences or perceptions of poverty and what constitutes a valued livelihood in their context? Let us look at some of the issues raised in Activity 10.1.

Poverty as low income. According to Box 10.1, a poor pastoralist is someone who does not have any livestock. Research by Chang (2002) on Maasai pastoralists in Kenya shows that when a male Maasai has an income but no cattle, he would be considered 'poor' in many ways. Investing money in livestock would be a priority because income per se is meaningless according to this world view. An intervention to alleviate poverty through sedentarization as outlined in Box 10.1 could be at best inappropriate and at worst counterproductive.

Poverty as multiple deprivations. This conceptualization of poverty argues for a more complex and nuanced approach. One of the multi-dimensional measures used by the United Nations Development Programme (UNDP) is the Human Development Index (HDI), composed of life expectancy, education and Gross National Income per capita (GNI pc) (see Chapter 8). Although a lack of access to education can be seen to be the cause of poverty, or its persistence in some contexts, educational provision can deprive households of their labour force, which includes children. Furthermore, educational projects for pastoralists can often fail because the provision of education is sedentary (classrooms are concrete buildings and schools are at fixed locations) whereas pastoralists are often on the move.

Thus what constitutes deprivations in one cultural context might not be applicable in another. For example, large families are often stereotyped as 'poor families'. However, large families can provide labour for production, additional income and support for people in their old age when there is no formal social security. In such circumstances, small families may be viewed as poor families, and population control projects may fail if interventions ignore the cultural (and economic) meanings of family size.

Chapter 8 noted that Amartya Sen, who was influential in developing the conceptualization of poverty as multiple deprivations, refrained from arguing for a set of fundamental capabilities universal to all. The above examples illustrate that deprivation, and capabilities to address them, need to be contextualised culturally.

Relative poverty. In Chapter 8, the concept of relative poverty was also discussed. The concept of relative poverty can be useful in analyzing the cultural dimensions of poverty and livelihoods, and the kinds of interventions that might be appropriate or inappropriate. For example, Box 10.2 contains an extract from the business plan published by the UK government's Department for Work and Pensions (DWP) in November 2010. It aims to cover the period from 2011 to 2015. Someone who is familiar with the cultural context of the UK will not be surprised with the language, wording and issues raised. However, with closer scrutiny, the relationship between poverty and welfare, 'responsible behaviour' and employment, and the role of paid work as a solution, may depend on who you are, your background and where you live in the UK. Would, for example, a single mother who claims social benefits see the plan in Box 10.2 the same way as a middle-aged business man?

Box 10.2 An extract from the plan of the UK's Department for Work and Pensions

The Department for Work and Pensions has an ambitious agenda of reform which aims to create a new welfare system for the 21st century; to transform the opportunity for people without jobs to find work and support themselves and their families; and to ensure that the most vulnerable in society are protected. We will focus on the [government's] values of freedom, fairness and responsibility and put welfare spending on a sustainable footing.

Over the course of the business plan period, our reforms will:

- tackle poverty and welfare dependency through a simplified welfare system that encourages and incentivises people to find work, rewards responsible behaviour and protects the most vulnerable
- promote high levels of employment by helping people who are out of work, including people in disadvantaged groups, to move into work
- help people meet the challenges of an ageing society and maintain standards of living in retirement
- provide opportunity, choice and independence to enable disabled people to take an equal role in society.

(Source: Department for Work and Pensions, 2010, p. 2)

Obtaining a livelihood therefore has a wider meaning than simply making a living. Strategizing for a livelihood that can be sustained in a particular cultural context is an integral part of social life. The example of the livelihood strategies pursued by a Maasai–Kikuyu mixed domestic unit (Box 10.3) illustrates this well.

Box 10.3 is adapted from an ethnography that describes and examines Maasai–Kikuyu intermarriage (Chang, 2002). The Maasai (pastoralists) in the Ngong area of Kenya and the Kikuyu (who tend to be agriculturalists and traders) have intermarried for a number of generations. A typical Maasai–Kikuyu basic domestic unit is comprised of a couple from two different groups of people who have different histories and cultural and linguistic backgrounds. Kikuyu wives in the mixed household/homestead have the direct responsibility for their dependents' subsistence. Although they do not appear to 'accumulate' or 'invest', like their pastoral husbands, many Kikuyu wives have better access to cash than their husbands by selling surplus crops from their plots and milk from the cows. Wives do not, however, have rights to dispose of cows.

The idea of a household (see Figure 10.1) comprising a nuclear family (in this case with a male household head) applies to monogamous Maasai–Kikuyu intermarriage. However, many Maasai men practice **polygyny** later in life. Maasai and Kikuyu women in mixed homestead/households have different access to resources, hence different 'bargaining' powers.

In Ngong, such a domestic unit is often split into individual subunits as a way to negotiate differences between Maasai husbands and Kikuyu wives. For a Maasai husband, a split unit is a way to manage the conflict between him and his Kikuyu wife and other wives. For a Kikuyu wife, a split unit enables her household to be autonomous and avoids daily aggravation with co-wives. But it can also result in lost opportunities to participate in discussions about the allocation of her husband's resources.

Figure 10.1 A Maasai household or compound

A close look at the strategies of male and female actors in their marital context reveals that their livelihood strategies serve domestic purposes and also often have 'public' meanings. For example, for Maasai men, a diversified livelihood leads to prosperity, which in turns grants them social status in the community. For Kikuyu women, joining a social group such as a women's guild provides them with emotional and financial support in the home, and grants them moral authority in the community. Focusing on the actors' strategies for trying to achieve 'the good life' illustrates how they attain endowments and entitlements (Chapter 8) within their domestic unit and how they attain social status and authority in the community.

Activity 10.2

Think about how you define and strategize for a good life in your own situation. What are the factors that influence your strategies?

Now read in Box 10.3 how Maasai men and Kikuyu women strategise for the good life. As you read the box, make notes on the key elements for men and for women in terms of their perceptions of the good life. How and why have they been changing over time?

Spend no more than 20 minutes on this activity.

Box 10.3   Livelihood strategizing for the good life

Maasai men

'I am extremely rich. Look at my cattle – they're mine and no one else's … The sheep – they're mine. You see this village – there are young people in it and there are old people – they're mine. Children, elders, women, old women, little boys – all mine. It's I who control (*a-itore*) them all. This is how I come to be an important person … I do not share with anyone … I am the owner who is in charge (*a-itore*). I control people and I control cattle' (Llewelyn-Davies, 1981, p. 330).

The above quotation epitomized the Maasai men's ideals and perceptions of 'the good life' in the 1980s: control of livestock (cattle in particular), human resources and the authority to dispose of them. Three concepts are pertinent to the economic, social and political ideals for Maasai men, namely pastoralism, polygyny and **patriarchy**. Collectively, they constituted Maasai men's 'good life' as they perceived it. Prosperity derived from the pastoral mode of subsistence and having a polygynous homestead well endowed with wives and children is part and parcel of being a patriarch for the Maasai.

Data from field work by Chang in 1996–7 found that the strategies for subsistence had changed amongst Maasai men in some contexts but the ideals that drove people towards 'the good life' had not.

Amongst the men's strategies for subsistence, pastoralism was still the ideal form of lifestyle. However, keeping a family herd for subsistence was no longer viable in Ngong by the mid-1990s because of the small area of land available and lack of access to dry season grazing land and water supply. Milk was no longer relied on as the main staple.

Many young men engaged in wage employment and cattle trade. They often talked about finding a Kikuyu wife because Kikuyu women were renowned for their hard work. Kikuyu women's agricultural expertise would help to diversify Maasai husbands' means of subsistence; furthermore, the surplus crops could then be sold to bring in extra cash.

Men with small families often talked about the political and social pressure to have their children educated. The demand for school fees and the inability to utilize their children's labour caused considerable stress. Nevertheless, most Maasai men saw the importance of education and would try their best to provide some level of primary education for their children.

More financially established men were often preoccupied with diversifying their means of subsistence further and obtaining social status. They did so by marrying a Maasai wife. Being able to have one wife who would work on land and another wife who would look after livestock was an important livelihood strategy for the Maasai men, while having two wives afforded them the social status of being a polygynist (adapted from Chang, 2002, pp. 138–176).

Kikuyu women

Chang also describes Kikuyu wives' strategies for 'the good life'.

Women on the windward side of the Ngong Hills engaged in agriculture, petty trading, wage employment and work in the service sector to sustain themselves and their households. In contrast, most women living on the leeward side of the Hills appeared to concentrate on only agriculture and petty trading for their subsistence. As their right to dispose of milk (and manure and skins) had greatly diminished, wives in Ngong no longer actively practised pastoralism for subsistence. However, on the leeward side they still provided milking labour on their husbands' herds. Milk in this case was no longer the staple in the household whereas maize was. In contrast to Maasai women who had diminished autonomy due to their husbands' increased control over pastoral by-products, Kikuyu women's right to dispose of their crops was not disputed. Matters related to agriculture and farming were seen by their Maasai husbands to be exclusively a woman's domain.

All women (Kikuyu and Maasai alike) managed to derive staples from their farming. Kikuyu women in particular not only placed great reliance on farming to maintain their dependants but also many of them were seen to be involved in some kind of petty trading to supplement what they could harvest from their plots. Educating their children (girls and boys) was seen to be an active strategy for a good life to Kikuyu women. In contrast to their husbands, who frequently strategized for prosperity, women in Ngong did not view accumulation of wealth as important. For them, 'security' in various forms was perceived as crucial. For example, Kikuyu wives felt strongly about the importance of a legalized marriage because this secures their inheritance in the event of their husbands' death. Kikuyu women in Ngong also articulated a perception of a good life by strategizing for status, influence and autonomy. They perceived that participating in various Christian fellowships and becoming a church elder not only provided them with an enlarged social network but also lent them moral authority in the community. These associations and networks could further contribute to 'security' in a time of crisis (adapted from Chang, 2002, pp. 253–254).

You will have noticed that we have been using the term household, and that Maasai–Kikuyu households have their own particular characteristics. Kabeer (1994, p. 92) states that 'the household (or domestic unit) generally refers to a group of co-resident persons who share most aspects of consumption and draw upon a common pool of resources for their livelihood.' The term 'household' does not necessarily mean the same as the term 'nuclear family', as it may include non-family members (such as servants or labourers) as well as more distant family members who may have particular roles or are being cared for.

But, as Kabeer notes, this definition of household can be rather vague for gathering data and challenging for policy makers who want to promote better livelihoods. In Development Studies, the need for a better understanding of different types of household arose originally from failures of interventions to improve livelihoods at the local level. In particular, there was frequent omission of women's roles in the household and in the economy, the household often being represented by a household head, who was often assumed to be a man (although many households are in practice headed by women). In addition, the roles of other household members, such as children, or girls in particular, could be invisible, when they might be contributors to income. Concern grew further with the realization that men and women in households might have different sources of income and control over different resources and outputs (as in the Maasai–Kikuyu example). It was noticed that women might have access to land or might work on land, but might not have control over what was produced or the income from it.

All these issues meant that those seeking to understand rural livelihoods needed to consider what went on *inside* households and, in particular, needed to investigate inequalities within the household and their implications (as noted in Chapter 9). Distribution of food within the household, for example, could be very unequal and might mean that women, girls or older people may not have had the same access to food as men and boys. So it was not enough to think about poor households or household livelihoods on their own. The activities of household members, what they had control over, who took decisions about use of resources and outputs was also essential.

Activity 10.3

Box 10.3 described how Maasai men and Kikuyu women go about strategizing for 'the good life'. By doing so, it also outlined the activities undertaken by men and women in Maasai-Kikuyu households.

Think about your own and other people's experiences of households and families.

- Have households and families been synonymous?
- Have men and women had the same or different roles and responsibilities within them?

- Has the income coming into the household or family been shared between men and women or have there been different controls over different income streams?

- Has some of the income for the household or family come from other family members or other people who don't live there?

- In turn, have there been financial flows to others outside the household or family unit?

How do your answers for the above compare with what you have learned about Maasai-Kikuyu households?

Spend about 10 minutes on this activity.

As you will have realized, understanding the relationship between households and livelihoods involves understanding **gender relations** and **gender divisions of labour**. In addition, understanding how people in households make a living and what the implications are for the household overall has to take into account the composition of the household, the resources that household members have access to, what relationship they have with the household head (whether male or female), whether they are able to have control over what they produce or earn, and what they are able to do with it. Therefore, the questions asked by Bernstein (Chapter 8, p. 188) are as pertinent to the social relations within households as they are to the wider context of making a living:

- Who owns or has access to what?

- Who does what?

- Who gets what?

- What do they do with it?

To these questions we can add:

- Do the household members have equal access to resources?

- If not, how is inequality created?

- How do understandings of different cultural values help interpret the answers to these questions?

10.2 Livelihood vulnerability and the sustainable livelihoods approach

We now move to the second of our dimensions – vulnerability. Making a living for low-income people is often focused on basic conditions of existence – food, clothes and housing. Healthcare and education are usually the first things that people will spend money on if they have enough income. As observed in Section 10.1, these basic dimensions of livelihood and the meanings attached to them may be expressed and valued differently.

We are going to consider some examples from Krishna (2010), who gathered low-income people's views about what constitutes basic necessities and when they consider themselves no longer to be poor across several countries in the global South and the USA. He also collected first-hand accounts about how people's livelihoods could change – both downwards into poverty and upwards into **social mobility**. We are now going to look at two such contrasting stories from the rural areas of Rajasthan, India (see Figure 10.2).

Figure 10.2   Farming in Rajasthan

To analyze these stories, we are going to use a 'Sustainable Livelihoods Approach' (SLA). The SLA is a framework that emerged from discussions between academics and policy makers in the UK and elsewhere towards the end of the 1990s as a means to understand better the ways that poor people make a living. The SLA suggests that examining poor people's capital assets enables researchers and policy makers to understand what keeps people poor, as well as identifying how poor people make a living. The approach has been used, debated and adapted in different ways by researchers over the years, and discussions on its use and value continue. It has also been used and elaborated by development organizations and institutions to inform policies that have the potential to reduce vulnerability and make livelihoods more sustainable.

So what is meant by capital assets and what do they include? The SLA identifies five types of capital:

- *Natural capital:* natural resources, such as land, water, biodiversity.
- *Social capital:* the social networks and access to local groups and associations that people have; also the relations of trust that have been built up.
- *Human capital:* the knowledge, skills and abilities that people bring to bear on making a living; as well as education, training and knowledge from experience, health is important for being able to use these capabilities.

- *Physical capital:* physical infrastructure such as roads, transport and other communications, energy, etc. This might also include tools, machines, etc.
- *Financial capital:* savings, credit, remittances and social funds, such as state aid or pensions.

Activity 10.4 explores stories from Krishna's research.

Activity 10.4

Read the two stories in Box 10.4, making notes on what access the people in each case have to:

- natural capital
- social capital
- human capital
- physical capital
- financial capital.

You might find it useful to draw a matrix such as the one in Table 10.1 to make your notes. We have put in a few points in the table to get you started.

Table 10.1   Matrix for the analysis of access to capital assets

Types of capital	Heera's household	Shantilal's household
Natural	Originally owned land and cattle.	
Social		An older relative who helped Shantilal's father get a job.
Human	No real information although presumably considerable knowledge about looking after cattle.	
Physical		No real information, but it's obviously possible to get to Ahmedabad.
Financial	Initially had financial resources from livestock farming; once cattle and land were sold, financial resources were only from borrowing, and subsequently from waged work.	

Spend no more than 30 minutes on this activity.

Box 10.4 Two livelihood stories

Heera's story, Rajasthan, India

Twenty years ago, Heera and his family were among the more prosperous households within this village.

'We owned land. We also owned many heads of cattle. But things changed for the worse, and today we are among the poorest people in our village, the recipients of community handouts on religious holidays. My father fell ill about 18 years ago. We must have spent close to 25 000 rupees on his treatment, but to no avail. When my father died, we performed the customary death feast, spending another 10 000 rupees. We sold our cattle, and we also had to take out some loans. We worked harder in order to repay these debts. Then, about ten years ago, my wife fell seriously ill, and she has still not recovered. We borrowed more money to pay for her medical treatments. More than 20 000 rupees were spent for this purpose. It became hard to keep up with our debts. Somehow we could make do for another two or three years. Then the rains failed for three years in a row, and that was the end of the road for us. We sold our land. Now, my sons and I work as casual labour, earning whatever we can from one day to the next.'

Shantilal's story Rajasthan, India

Shantilal's household is one among many that has escaped poverty. When he was a young boy, they faced very difficult circumstances. They possessed no land of their own. His mother and father worked on other people's farms and in their homes. They had no other sources of income. On days when no offer of paid work was made to the parents, the family survived by borrowing grains from the local merchant. A high rate of interest was levied from the borrowing family, which was also required to pledge a portion of its future earnings to the lender.

An older relative visited them one day and persuaded Shantilal's father to go with him to Ahmedabad, an industrial city, located about 250 kilometers away from their village. This relative worked for a cotton textile mill, and he helped Shantilal's father find a position in the same processing unit. Unloading raw cotton from famers' carts was seasonal work, gruelling and poorly paid, but it provided the family with additional income for four months of every year. Shantilal's parents used part of this amount to pay for their children's education. They also bought a small herd of goats and built some additions to the family home.

In time, Shantilal also travelled to Ahmedabad in search of a job. Because he was educated, more than his father and others, he was made responsible for overseeing their work and keeping the daily accounts. Shantilal also has a seasonal job. He is hired by the cotton mill for a few months following the harvest, and he spends the rest of his time in his village. This family has overcome poverty but they have not yet become prosperous. There is still no refrigerator or television in their home, but there is no need any more to make do with less food. Shantilal's three children, two sons and a daughter, attend the village school. He has plans to pay for their college education.

(Source: Krishna, 2010, pp.12–13)

As you undertook this activity, how well did you think the idea of types of capital amongst poor and low-income households and individuals stood up?

The idea of capital – particularly financial and physical capital – is usually linked to the idea of **accumulation**. Yet any accumulation that comes about through sustainable livelihoods is often so small that it is difficult to compare it to the process of accumulation in a firm or large business. In fact, the type of production in subsistence-oriented farming has often been characterized as 'simple reproduction'. Simple reproduction means that producers, such as farmers or small businesses, are only able to maintain their access to resources (land, inputs, tools) and to reproduce labour (food, clothing, housing) at current levels of existence. A household that only achieves such a level of production is not necessarily able to expand what they do ('expanded reproduction'). Whether small farms operate like small firms has been an ongoing debate in Development Studies.

What about the other types of 'capital'? The term human capital is routinely used in discussions of education. Coleman (1997, p. 83) states that 'human capital is created by changes in persons that bring about skills and capabilities that make them able to act in new ways.' This change could, of course, happen through education and training, but equally it could occur through 'learning from life'.

The SLA also refers to social capital, a concept that Coleman helped to elaborate and contributed to in terms of its current usage and popularity in development debates. He notes (ibid):

> Social capital … comes about through changes in the relations among persons that facilitate action. If physical capital is wholly tangible, being embodied in observable material form, and human capital is less tangible, being embodied in the skills and knowledge acquired by an individual, *social capital is less tangible yet, for it exists in the relations among persons.* Just as physical capital and human capital facilitate productive activity, social capital does as well. For example, a group within which there is extensive trustworthiness and extensive trust is able to accomplish much more than a comparable group without that trustworthiness and trust.

(Coleman, 1997, p. 83)

Forms of association, organization and collective action among poor people are able to achieve much more in terms of improving livelihoods than individuals alone, and they are also important in terms of being part of social life. However, there has, as ever, been considerable debate about the concept of social capital, in particular given that relations between people are often unequal, involving different kinds of power. Groups and associations can exclude as well as include people and reinforce divisions, so social capital will not necessarily or always have positive consequences.

10.2.1   Livelihood assets and livelihood vulnerability

What is Krishna's own view of the two livelihoods described in Box 10.4? Instead of SLA, Krishna uses an approach called 'Stages of Progress', which helped him answer two questions:

- Why do some poor people escape from poverty?
- Why do some non-poor people fall into poverty?

Krishna reconstructed household histories to try and find some explanation. He observed that analyzing what assets people have does not in itself provide an explanation. The important aspect is why people's assets change over time.

Krishna's own conclusion about the stories above and many others he collected, was that it was 'ordinary events, such as frequent ill-health episodes, crop diseases, expensive marriages and funeral ceremonies, lack of affordable credit, and the like' (2010, p. 14) that threw people into poverty. He also posited that, in policy terms, ordinary events are easier to control and to do something about. And, indeed, there has been a very strong focus on social protection by researchers and in international aid policies of the early 21st century.

But why are some people vulnerable to ordinary events? It may be, as in Heera's household, that it was simply a series of events over time that reduced their ability to make a living. However, it is well known in the UK, and is also the case in other parts of the world, that indebtedness amongst people who are already impoverished can push them further into debt, for example because of high interest rates imposed by unscrupulous lenders. Such exploitation of misery was illustrated in the early stages of Shantilal's story.

Why such exploitation of misery occurs is based on the ability of certain people, groups or organizations to exert power over others. In the story of Shantilal, the local merchant was able to exert power over Shantilal's family ('A high rate of interest was levied from the borrowing family, which was also required to pledge a portion of its future earnings to the lender'). This kind of indebtedness can also take more extreme forms, called debt bondage or forced labour, where an individual or household is held in ongoing obligation to a creditor or landlord (or is trapped in even more pernicious forms such as the sex trade, see Aradau, 2013). So while there may be many 'ordinary events' to which individuals and households fall prey, understanding the institutional context and the social relations in which people live helps to explain why it may be difficult to move out of poverty.

On a more positive note, Shantilal's story also demonstrates the role of agency and self-determination in being able to take advantage of opportunities for making a living. Shantilal himself is even better placed because he has some schooling, enhancing his capabilities for earning an income. Note too that education was a priority in this household once basic necessities were met.

10.2.2 SLA and historical processes: linking the local to the international

As we pointed out, SLA has been debated, discussed, criticized and elaborated by many researchers and policy makers. One elaboration that aims to understand asset change over time is the 'asset accumulation' approach developed by anthropologist Caroline Moser (2009). Moser studied how poverty and livelihoods changed over a 30-year period (1974–2008) in a suburb of the city of Guayaquil on the coast of Ecuador. In constructing what she calls an 'asset accumulation index', Moser aimed to understand the dynamics of urban livelihoods by examining how poor people strategize their 'asset portfolios' and how they change over time. So at an early stage of the urban settlement, setting up a community committee (social capital) was important for all the families to gain access to services and to build their livelihoods. At another stage, education (human capital) became crucial if families wanted to improve their standard of living. In addition, based on their greater human capital, some of the younger generation migrated to Spain to seek better employment and a better life (although in practice this proved harder than they imagined).

Tracing inter-generational histories is important for understanding how livelihoods change over time and why (you will also have noticed that conditions were changing for Maasai pastoralists). Understanding the changes in how people make a living also requires understanding the larger context.

One example can be seen from Shantilal's story in Box 10.4. The village-based livelihood of his family depended on migration to Ahmedabad to work in a cotton mill (see Figure 10.3). Ahmedabad is a site of substantial manufacture and export of textiles, and many major retailers in the global North rely on imports from India, including from mills in Ahmedabad. So you can immediately see how the livelihood of Shantilal and his family in a Rajasthan village depended on a cotton textile mill 250 kilometres away, which was probably exporting textiles around the world.

These linkages are a growing dimension of making a living for many low-income people in the countryside as well as towns, and may both increase and reduce vulnerability. For example, the 2008 *World Development Report* (World Bank, 2008) notes that, globally, agriculture alone cannot provide enough employment for rural populations. It observes (ibid, p. 202):

> because of the low elasticity of demand for food, the agricultural labour force will in the long run decline, not only relatively but absolutely, as is already happening in Latin America and the Caribbean, and in Europe and Central Asia. Agricultural advance alone will not meet the rural employment challenge. The rural non-farm economy will also have to be a key source of new jobs [particularly for landless people].

In rural areas, the production of high-value crops (particularly in horticulture) may lead to an increase in demand for agricultural labour. However, changes in rural employment may also have other effects: for example the 'feminization' of rural wage labour, that is, the substitution of male workers by women because of cost cutting or male migration. Although such changes

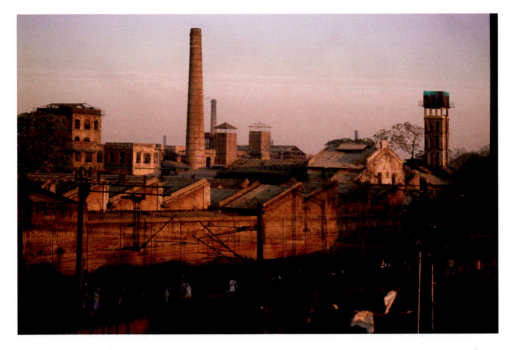

Figure 10.3   Picture of an Ahmedabad cotton mill

may provide job opportunities for women, there is also frequent wage inequality between women and men working in agriculture.

Links to the world economy thus offer new opportunities for employment, but the effects may not be straightforward nor the same for men and women, or for people from different cultural backgrounds or nationalities. We turn to such issues as part of our third dimension to livelihoods, the connection between the local and the international, in Section 10.3. As you read this section, aim to note the specific effects for different groups of people (including women's roles in production and processing) and other actors involved in the global production and marketing outlined.

10.3 Global value chains

In our daily lives we consume products that are often made outside the country we live in. Much of our food is grown in other countries, and our clothes come from as far away as China and Madagascar. The international trade in manufactured products increased by 72 per cent between 2000 and 2009, with nearly 40 per cent coming from developing countries (UNCTAD, 2010). The processes and actors involved in delivering these products to our shelves can often be complex and multi-layered. For example, the flowers we find in our local supermarkets may be grown on smallholder farms in Kenya, packaged to the specifications of a large transnational corporation (TNC), and then flown by specialist logistic firms so they arrive fresh and ready for sale.

This section examines the processes that affect employment and wage conditions of low-income workers and producers at the end of the production chain. Concern over those conditions has influenced Fair Trade agreements, and involved the International Labour Organization (ILO) and non-governmental organizations (NGOs) in the campaign for 'decent work'. We will come back to such interventions in Chapter 11. Here we look at what affects the conditions of those working in globally connected production and distribution, and how to understand them.

First some background, following on from the discussion on TNCs in Chapter 7. Initially TNCs relocated production facilities in developing countries to benefit from lower wage costs, access local markets and side step import tariffs. Production was either owned by the TNC itself, or the use of subsidiaries and licences ensured the parent company kept hold of production facilities. In more recent years, this production process has become fragmented, with more and more firms choosing to 'source' from local companies in developing countries, rather than owning production facilities. Advances in information technology and transport since the 1980s have seen an expansion of developing countries participating in international trade in this way.

Now a single consumer product may have passed through various stages of processing in a number of different countries before making it to our stores. As discussed in Chapter 7, the network and environment in which such production takes place are referred to as Global Production Networks (GPNs). In order to understand production systems that employ people in one country, use raw material from another and result in final consumption in yet another, we can use value chain analysis. The 'mapping' of a value chain shows the processes and actors involved in production, from its initial stages, to reaching the market and beyond. These maps cover the physical transformation of raw materials into products, and highlight the relationships between the actors involved. A value chain can be drawn for manufactured or agricultural products as well as for services such as banking or tourism. The principles of mapping a value chain are outlined in Box 10.5.

Figure 10.4 shows a simple value chain for a consumer product, indicating the major actors and processes involved in the production. The right-hand side of the figure shows the physical process of transformation, from the inputs to producers, to the provision of finished goods to traders, who then sell them in wholesale markets to local retailers or export them to global retailers. The left-hand side of the figure shows the services that support this physical activity, such as the provision of finance to input suppliers and producers, or cross-cutting support services, such as telecommunications and logistics. Other services may be more specific to the sector itself, for example furniture production may require certification that the wood was sourced from sustainable forests. All of these relationships are embedded within a domestic and international environment.

In reality, of course, the process is much more complicated. However, value chain analysis can be useful in studying and understanding how people make a living and the constraints on their jobs and sources of income. This is because the approach maps the power relations between major actors and stakeholders and the environment within which these processes take place. Thus changes can be focused on particular actors and impacts can be understood in a 'complete picture', both of which lead to better policy design and interventions to tackle livelihoods, as we will see in Chapter 11.

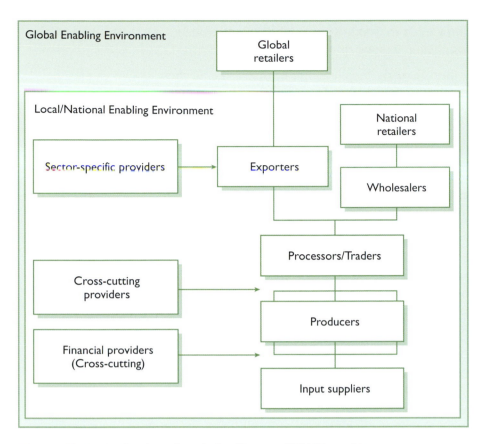

Figure 10.4 A simple value chain (Source: USAID, n.d.)

Box 10.5 The structural components of a value chain analysis

Final (demand) markets

In drawing a value chain you must identify the final market where the product or service is eventually sold. The nature of this market, such as the quality and price required, time and flexibility of delivery, etc., can have an important impact on the production process. For example, in Europe there are legal standards for consumer products that must be fulfilled before goods can be exported, such as food hygiene standards or lead content in toys, consumer preferences for Fair Trade or organic products.

Vertical and horizontal linkages

The production process is generally broken down into smaller segments, where each segment is carried out by the most efficient firm in the category. For example, Japan is more efficient at designing new electronic consumer goods, while South Korea is more efficient at producing the components for these goods. China's low wage relative to the other two countries means that it is the cheapest at assembling these goods. Therefore a product designed in Japan has its components manufactured in South Korea and the final product is assembled in China before being shipped to consumers in the USA.

One firm is rarely large enough to undertake all these activities and the production process depends on linkages between firms. Vertical linkages refer to the firms above or below in the production process. Therefore the design firm is linked vertically to the manufacturing firm, which is then vertically linked to the assembling firm. Horizontal linkages refer to interaction between firms that share a similar function. For example, Silicon Valley in the USA has a number of information technology firms working, collaborating and competing in the same area. These are horizontal linkages.

Input (supply) markets

The raw materials for the product may be produced locally, such as cotton for a textile factory, or imported, such as chip boards from abroad to assemble computers locally. The input providers for the producers and their ownership need to be identified (local or foreign, part of a franchise or subsidiary).

Enabling environment

This refers to the networks, rules and standards within which the production chain operates: the left side of Figure 10.4. Finance and insurance, logistics and transportation, the tax and investment schemes, training and apprentice programmes, all affect the production process. Such factors can affect the cost of production and ability to follow standards set by final markets, etc.

Production is never a static process, and there are dynamic components within value chain analysis that focus on the relationships between actors. There are three major elements:

- *Governance.* This refers to the power exercised by a firm in relation to other actors in a value chain; the setting of prices, volume, standards, quality and occasionally the production process itself. For example, IKEA, the Swedish furniture retailer, sets the designs and price at which it will obtain furniture from its suppliers. It also specifies standards, such as fire safety and wood sourced from sustainable forests. Other companies, such as Nike, set standards to ensure child labour is not used by any of their suppliers. Such firms therefore are the 'dominant' firm in the chain and govern the production process of those who supply it.

- *Competition versus cooperation.* Firms within a chain, in both vertical and horizontal linkages, may compete and cooperate with each other to gain market shares. For example, a number of smallholder farmers in Kenya will cooperate to fulfil a large order from a European supermarket, while clothing firms in China will compete on price to supply foreign retailers. Depending on the nature of the final market, firms may well compete and cooperate within the same chain.

- *Upgrading for development.* This refers to an increase in the skill set of a firm, in the product or in the production process, to allow the firm to reap greater returns on its investment. Innovation and adaptation of new knowledge and skills is essential for this process. For example, firms that compete on low wages to win contracts for assembling goods can increase their returns by branching out into the production of inputs in the assembly process. Upgrading is essential if a firm wishes to develop, but the opportunities for upgrading may be limited or vast depending on its location within the value chain.

GPNs enable developing countries to participate in international trade and generate local employment. However, the opening up of economies has also brought risks. Workers are often from poor backgrounds, with little social or legal protection in their working environment. As production systems have become global, there is an increasing need to ensure that the livelihoods of people in low-income countries are not adversely affected by such exposure.

To illustrate these issues, we are going to examine the value chain of the cashew nut industry in Mozambique. This next subsection draws on the work of Hanlon and Smart (2010).

10.3.1 Cashew nuts anyone?

Cashew nuts go well with salads or on their own and are readily available in supermarkets all year around. But where do they come from? India may spring to mind, and, if so, that would be correct. Some 40 per cent of international exports of cashew nuts are accounted for by India. India also imports unprocessed nuts from a number of countries, processes them and then re-exports them to the European Union and other countries.

One of the countries that provide India with raw cashew nuts is Mozambique and its story illustrates the multi-layered, trans-dimensional process that impacts the livelihoods of people in low-income countries.

In 1977, Mozambique was the largest global producer of cashew nuts but it saw declining production and employment over the following three decades. Investment in the industry had been declining since 1972 and the civil war in 1977 nearly wiped out production. In the mid-1990s the sector was privatized, revival began and some of the highest employment and production figures were recorded for the sector in 1998. However, during the 1995–2001 period conditions set by the World Bank and the IMF in a Structural Adjustment Programme (SAP) led to the imposition of free market reforms in the agricultural sector. Mozambique, like a number of other African countries, required new loans from the World Bank and the International Monetary Fund (IMF) to repay previous loans taken from commercial banks and other institutions in the past decade. SAPs were imposed as a condition for receiving these new loans. This led to the second decline for the sector, wiping out nearly all the gains made post-1990 and leaving only four functioning factories. In 2001, the government of Mozambique took more aggressive steps towards supporting the sector, and with contributions from international NGOs and local institutions, the industry had sprung back to 18 factories and 6000 workers by 2006.

The cashew is an unusual nut as it grows outside the cashew fruit and hangs below it (see Figure 10.5a). The fruit itself is edible and can also be used to make beer, while the kernel is contained in a hard shell. Cashew trees in Mozambique grow along the coastal region and are able to survive on poor land. Peasants and smallholder farmers (mostly women) grow cashew trees and collect the kernels to sell to factories that process them.

Figure 10.5   (a) Cashew fruit; (b) cashew nuts being shelled; (c) processing of cashew nuts

The processing of cashew kernels involves the boiling or steaming of the nut to make the shell more brittle, the cracking of the shell and removal of the nut by hand, the sorting of kernels (broken versus whole), oven drying, peeling the skin, sorting the kernel into different grades and vacuum packing in plastic bags. They are then ready for export. Shells are broken with either pedal-operated machines or high-tech machinery (see Figure 10.5b); the peeling of the skin and sorting into grades is done by hand. The processing of cashews therefore can be labour-intensive and women tend to be a large part of the labour force (Figure 10.5c). Since remuneration is near or just above minimum wage, most workers will have other sources of income such as animal husbandry and farming.

Within the Mozambique value chain there are three major sets of actors: the peasants who grow and harvest the nut; middle men who buy from the farmers and sell to the factories; and the factories themselves. The portion of raw kernel not used by the local processing factories can be exported to other countries, such as India. Figure 10.6 shows a simplified version of the Mozambique cashew nut value chain, with the production process on the right and the actors that influence this process on the left.

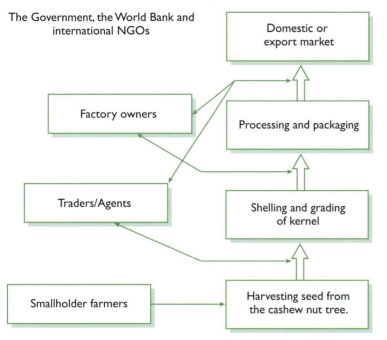

Figure 10.6 The Mozambique cashew nut chain (post-2001) (adapted from Hanlon and Smart, 2010)

Activity 10.5

Consider Figure 10.6, which shows the value chain of the Mozambican cashew nut industry post-2001.

With the information above, put yourself in the shoes of the following actors and make a note of what you would want to see happen to improve the returns to your part of the production process:

- smallholder farmer of cashew trees
- female factory worker processing cashew nuts
- factory owner
- Indian importer.

Spend no more than 10–15 minutes on this activity.

Discussion

Smallholders and farmers of cashew nuts bear the risk of climate variations, disease and other factors that could affect their output, therefore insurance against natural disasters could be considered helpful. These farmers earn low incomes and may not have the capital to use insecticides and fertilizers that would assist in improving their harvests. Apart from assistance in lowering the costs of farming inputs, higher prices for their output would also benefit the farmers.

Female factory workers involved in the processing of cashew nuts would benefit from higher wages, job security and other benefits such as health coverage. A clean and safe space at the factory floor, and security of their labour rights would ensure a decent work environment. They would be helped by the right to organise so that they can collectively bargain for better working conditions with their employers. Since women are the primary caretakers of their families, flexible working hours would also be beneficial.

The factory owner benefits from minimizing costs and maximising the price for his output. That means buying raw cashew nuts at the lowest possible rates and keeping wages low will help increase his profits. If he can receive subsidies from the government for his exports, he could further increase his profits. As the 'seller' of cashew nuts, he also needs to be able to compete in the international markets and be able to find buyers for his produce. This often means finding the best price possible in highly competitive international markets. Any tax or tariff placed on his exports would harm his business.

The Indian importer buys semi-processed cashew nuts from a number of countries and his profits are determined by the difference between the price he pays for these and the price he can receive for his processed cashew nuts. Since India supplies a large share of the global markets, the Indian importer is looking to acquire a large volume at the lowest price possible. However, the quality of the raw material is also important and the 'cleaner' the product, the less effort (and cost) he endures in the processing. Thus for the Indian importer the ideal situation is to be able to buy cheap, high-quality semi-processed cashew nuts. Being one of the largest customers for these, he carries substantial power in being able to negotiate price from his suppliers.

Before 2001, Mozambique was exporting most of its raw kernel and so was unable to benefit from the higher prices of processed cashew nut sales. With the government's aim to rehabilitate the entire industry in 2001, the value chain approach helps to explain where and how intervention at various levels was made and its impact on the livelihoods of people.

First, the cashew trees needed attention. Insecticide spraying programmes were introduced to increase the yield from existing trees, most of which had been affected by powdery mildew since the 1980s. New varieties of more productive and disease-resistant trees were also introduced. Since peasant farmers were often too poor to afford these services, they were made available by the government and international NGOs. When international NGOs and local institutions began to focus on peasant farmers for spraying programmes post-2001, they focused on men. Research, however, suggested that most tree owners were women, so the number of farmers to actually benefit from the scheme was limited (an example of poor understanding of household dynamics, which we discussed in Section 10.1).

Second, the kernel is removed from the shells. Some efforts had been made by NGOs to encourage small-scale firms, organized within peasant communities, to shell the cashew and then offer it for sale to factories for sorting and packaging. However, these projects tended to collapse when the NGOs withdrew. This is related to two issues: managerial capability within the community and the nature of cashew processing (the larger the scale, the more profitable the operations).

Third, the cashew nuts must be packaged and marketed. When the World Bank and the IMF imposed neoliberal policies on the country in the 1990s, the government was forced to reduce the export tax on raw cashews. The tax on exports of raw cashews was aimed at promoting domestic processing; reducing the tax meant that domestic processing declined. Factories were closed down and workers, mostly basic wage earners, lost their jobs. Since 2001, this policy has been reversed allowing the sector to thrive again. Larger factories have also banded together – assisted by international NGOs, the government and financial and business services – to market their output under one brand name, and meet international food production standards. The large factories have been able to expand production and employment, benefiting from the managerial skills of expatriate managers and owners from other developing countries who have experience of working in challenging business environments.

In conclusion, the value chain of the Mozambique cashew nut helps illustrate three points. First, the success of the chain depends on all nodes of the chain: success in Mozambique has been the result of substantial support from the government and donors along the entire value chain. Second, decisions made at one level, for example by the World Bank to impose the neoliberal policies of the 1990s, have effects down the entire chain, for example and impact on the producers and workers at the bottom of the chain. Third, a domestic production chain is not an isolated unit: it operates within a larger context, such as the state of the economy, the state of the competition and international standards.

So the next time you casually pick up a pack of cashew nuts in your local grocery store, check the label to see where they come from; you may be the final consumer of a chain starting in the coastal regions of Mozambique!

Summary and looking forward

In this chapter, we have examined three perspectives on livelihoods and how low-income people make a living. In doing so, we have noted dimensions of power and agency, and have considered different scales of analysis, from very local stories to international linkages, as well as how the dynamics of making a living change over time.

The first perspective focused on the cultural settings in which people build their livelihoods and the values they attribute to different activities and to creating a 'good life'. Looking at some aspects of the Maasai–Kikuyu households in Kenya revealed that Maasai men and Kikuyu women had different but complementary strategies. Such strategies could potentially be conflictive once an additional spouse entered the household, but the relative independence of the family units within the household also enabled a degree of complementarity to be maintained. From this it could be seen that the concept of household and family is a variable one, and that gender relations in households and in making a living affect processes and outcomes. Men and women within households can also exert different types of agency in accordance with cultural values and external pressures that might be on them (such as shortage of land or drought).

The second perspective examined vulnerability by using the Sustainable Livelihoods Approach, an approach that has been adapted in different ways by researchers and international organizations working in development. SLA was used to identify the capital assets of two rural households in India. Analyzing the assets of the households in the stories revealed that the concept of capital – and its different types – is not necessarily straightforward in understanding the behaviour of people trying to make a living from small farms and enterprises. Reflecting on two livelihood stories also provided an understanding of how people with low incomes may fall into or move out of poverty, and how asset change over time can reduce or increase vulnerability. Again, power and agency were crucial dimensions in explaining how vulnerability is increased or mitigated. In addition, in the case of one household we identified how livelihoods were linked to urban-based and globalized agro-industry. This observation led us to discuss the nature of rural–urban linkages as well as the changing nature of agriculture and rural employment, including, in some parts of the world, the 'feminization' of labour.

Finally, the third perspective was to use the global value chain approach to analyze how livelihoods of rural producers and workers in agro-industry are connected to the foods we buy in our local supermarket. This section demonstrated how making a living at one end of the chain was affected by a whole set of processes and actors through the chain to the consumer. Using a global value chain approach, it is possible to analyze the power and agency of actors along the chain to influence processes and outcomes. How global value chains are governed is therefore crucial with respect to the outcomes for those at the bottom end of the chain. In such chains, collective agency on the part of those at the bottom of the chain may be crucial. This aspect will be picked up again in Chapter 11, which examines interventions to promote livelihoods.

References

Anderson, D. and Broch-Due, V. (eds) (1999) *The Poor Are Not Us: Poverty and Pastoralism in Eastern Africa*, Oxford, James Currey.

Aradau, C. (2013) 'Human security or human development in a world of states' in Butcher, M. and Papaioannou, T. (eds) *New Perspectives in International Development*, London, Bloomsbury Academic/Milton Keynes, The Open University.

Chang, D. (2002) 'Pursuing the good life in hard times: a comparison of men's and women's strategies in Maasai/Kikuyu marriages in Kenya', Unpublished PhD thesis, University of London.

Coleman, J. (1997) 'Social capital in the creation of human capital' in Halsey, A.H., Lauder, H., Brown, P. and Stuart Wells, A. (eds) *Education, Culture, Economy, and Society*, Oxford and New York, Oxford University Press.

Department for Work and Pensions (2010) *Business Plan 2010–2015*, November [online], http://www.dwp.gov.uk/docs/dwp-business-plan-2011-2015.pdf (Accessed 24 March 2010).

Hanlon, J. and Smart, T. (2010) *Do Bicycles Equal Development in Mozambique?* London, Boydell and Brewer.

Kabeer, N. (1994) *Reversed Realities: Gender Hierarchies in Development Thought*, London, Verso.

Krishna, A. (2010) *One Illness Away: Why People Become Poor and How They Escape Poverty*, Oxford, Oxford University Press.

Llewelyn-Davies, M. (1981) 'Women, warriors, and patriarchs' in Ortner, S. and Whitehead, H. (eds) *Sexual Meanings: The Cultural Construction of Gender and Sexuality*, Cambridge, Cambridge University Press.

Moser, C.O.N. (2009) *Ordinary Families, Extraordinary Lives: Assets and Poverty Reduction in Guayaquil, 1978–2004*, Washington, Brookings Institution Press.

Spencer, P. (1988) *The Maasai of Matapato*, Manchester, Manchester University Press.

United Nations Conference on Trade and Development (UNCTAD) (2010) UNCTAD Statistics Overview [online], http://www.unctad.org/Templates/Page.asp?intItemID=1584&lang=1 (Accessed December 2010).

USAID (n.d.) 'The value chain framework', *Briefing Paper* [online], http://Pdf.Usaid.Gov/Pdf_Docs/PNADP302.Pdf (Accessed 27 March 2011).

Waller, R. (1985) 'Economic and social relations in the central Rift Valley: the Maa-speakers and their neighbours in the nineteenth century' in Ogot, B.A. (ed.) *Kenya in the Nineteenth Century*, Nairobi, Bookwise.

World Bank (2008) *Agriculture for Development: World Development Report*, Washington, The World Bank.

Further reading

Kaplinsky, R. and Morris, M. (2001) *A Handbook for Value Chain Research*, Ottawa, IDRC.

Krishna, A. (2010) *One Illness Away: Why People Become Poor and How They Escape Poverty*, Oxford, Oxford University Press.

Moser, C.O.N. (2009) *Ordinary Families, Extraordinary Lives: Assets and Poverty Reduction in Guayaquil, 1978–2004*, Washington, Brookings Institution Press.

Interventions to promote livelihoods

Jane Cullen, Masuma Farooki, Hazel Johnson, Julius Mugwagwa and Claudio Velasco

Introduction

Chapters 8 and 10 introduced the ways that poverty, livelihoods and making a living can be analyzed and understood. You saw it was important to ask questions such as: Who owns or has access to what? Who does what? Who gets what and what do they do with it? In other words, understanding the relations between different actors holding different resources and power, and their cultural and historical contexts, is an essential part of explaining different types of livelihood, vulnerability and opportunities for making a living. Asking such questions can be used at different scales, from understanding livelihoods in households and communities to analyzing the international or global dynamics of why people remain in poverty. They can also be used to evaluate livelihood strategies and the possibilities of making a (better) living. These 'bottom line' questions add to the cultural frameworks and tools such as the Sustainable Livelihoods Approach (SLA) and its variants, which you considered in Chapter 10. And they are a fundamental part of analyzing global value chains. This chapter will elaborate further on these questions by aiming to:

- locate interventions for promoting livelihoods within debates on actions for and by the poor

- enable you to study different types of intervention (innovation, finance, organization, health, education)

- provide a framework for evaluating social relations, power and agency in interventions to promote livelihoods.

As we have seen, livelihoods also change over time: in response to wider social, economic and political changes, because of changes in policy, or because of individual and collective actions. This chapter therefore examines different kinds of intervention aiming at enhancing livelihoods, in other words, intentional development (Chapter 1). We provide a series of case studies of intervention, which you will have the opportunity to evaluate. The case studies are at different scales: from international initiatives on health to local income generation. They also involve different actors: from international organizations to local farmers and community groups, involving different kinds of power and power relations.

11.1 Changing ideas and approaches: what sort of interventions and by whom?

First, let us review some of the thinking about poverty reduction and livelihood creation in the international development arena. Views about intervention in the early 21st century are not quite where Development Studies started out (Bernstein, 2005). The early days of development studies were as much concerned with international relations as International Studies, and with understanding how changes in the world economy, world politics and power relations affected and brought about the uneven development of nations as well as different sectors and populations within them. Much has changed over time, including a growth of concern with development as a practice as well as a historical process. The ideas of people-centred development and participation have formed part of these more recent currents, although they are both informed by a vision of development that is not simply (or even necessarily) growth-centred, but puts people's concerns and needs first.

There is not necessarily a contradiction between growth and putting people first. Indeed, many economists argue that growth is needed for poverty reduction, as we have seen. There may, however, be a contradiction between kinds and speed of growth and putting people first. For this reason, the role of the state and other actors in development, and the kinds of development vision being promoted, are also important in terms of outcomes. The 2010 *Human Development Report (HDR)* notes in its summary:

> Our results … confirm, with new data and analysis, two central contentions of the *HDR* …: that human development is different from economic growth and that substantial achievements are possible even without fast growth. Early *HDRs* pointed to the Indian state of Kerala and countries such as Costa Rica, Cuba and Sri Lanka that attained much higher human development than other countries at their incomes. These achievements were possible because growth had decoupled from the processes determining progress in the non-income dimensions of human development.
>
> *(UNDP, 2010, p. 7)*

The *HDR*'s recommendations include:

> *Think of principles first*. Asking whether a particular policy is a general prescription for human development is not the best approach, because many policies work in some settings and not in others …
>
> *Take context seriously.* State capacity and political constraints are examples of why and how context matters …
>
> *Shift global policies.* Numerous challenges such as international migration, effective and equitable trade and investment rules, and global threats such as climate change, are beyond the capacity of individual states …
>
> *(UNDP, 2010, pp. 11–12)*

As well as the Human Development Index (HDI) that was first mentioned in Chapter 8, the United Nations Development Programme (UNDP) perspective focuses on other dimensions of human life such as empowerment (civil and political rights), inequality (income inequality, gender inequality), vulnerability (to shocks, for example the financial crisis of 2008) and sustainability (threatened, for example, by climate change). Some of the case studies of intervention below address these dimensions of livelihood – for example, how low-income people exert agency and become more empowered; and how livelihoods can be made more sustainable – as well as some of the contradictions and challenges.

A further issue is raised by the *HDR* principles and foci: whose responsibility is it to intervene to promote the livelihoods of low-income people? In Chapter 1, we considered the idea that intervention is to 'ameliorate the disordered faults of progress' (Cowen and Shenton, 1996, p. 00). Cowen and Shenton also discuss the idea of 'trusteeship' (ibid, p. 00): 'the intent which is expressed, by one sort of agency, to develop the capacities of another. It is what binds the process of development to the intent of development.' In other words, trusteeship is what binds the purposes of development practice (intentional development) to the history of unplanned change. The challenge then is who is entitled to develop the capacity of others and what legitimacy do they have to do so?

While the state is one agent that can legitimately be tasked with such trusteeship in the context of democracy (this is more complicated when the form of state is imposed), there are many other organizations that assume such trusteeship; from the international organizations of the UN system to small community-based non-governmental organizations (NGOs). The basis of their legitimacy may be questionable in some cases. However, there are organizations of the poor, from social movements to community groups, that can also claim legitimacy, perhaps even more than that of many NGOs. In addition, these different forms of trusteeship and agency are very likely to involve differences of vision and interest, which makes working together quite challenging.

The place of poor people in intervention has also been subject to some debate. On one hand, policy makers and development professionals have been keen to advocate the participation of the poor in interventions. On the other, this espoused promotion of poor people's participation has been criticized for being rather instrumental, and for not taking into account the differences and power relations within poor communities (Hickey and Mohan, 2004). For example, the different positions of men and women, or other forms of social difference such as age or ethnicity can be neglected or misunderstood.

There are other issues of an institutional kind. The poverty agenda set by the World Bank in the 1990s, and its extension into the 21st century, recognized the multidimensional nature of poverty (although income and consumption measures are still used). However, in spite or because of this, Moser (2009, p. 23) argues that poverty reduction has become more a methodology of how to pursue development, that is, a technical exercise, rather than a political challenge to address the causes of poverty. In addition, Moser argues (ibid, p. 24), 'Poverty is seen not only as a problem of the poor but also as their responsibility.' She suggests that, in paying close attention to the characteristics of poverty and the poor, researchers and policy makers have diverted attention from wider structural changes. As Webster and Engberg-Pedersen (2002, p. 4) have argued: 'to place emphasis upon the agency of the deprived does not have to imply that, given the opportunity, they can pull themselves up by their own bootstraps and overcome impoverishment.'

It is, however, important not to ignore the place of the poor in planned interventions, in particular social movements, community and other types of organization. Webster and Engberg-Pedersen (also mentioned in Chapter 8) have published studies of poor people's organizations and discuss the 'political spaces' in which organizations and associations of the poor can emerge and act. By 'political space' they mean 'the types and range of possibilities present for pursuing poverty reduction by the poor or on behalf of the poor by local organizations' (Webster and Engberg-Pedersen (2002), p. 8). They suggest that certain conditions are necessary: there is a need for institutional channels through which policies can be discussed and influenced; poverty has to be acknowledged as a significant issue; and there have to be activities ('social and political practices') of poor people that can act as a basis for influencing change. Such conditions are not automatic, but Webster and Engberg-Pedersen are making the point that action by the poor is a complex process and does not simply depend either on an enabling environment or on calls for their direct participation.

Moser's own work on the settlement of Indio Guayas in Guayaquil, Ecuador (mentioned in Chapter 10, p. 252) provides an illustration. Her study showed how poor people can organize themselves in the face of very challenging conditions. When the group of people she studied came to settle in Indio Guayas, originally in 1978, they set up a committee: the Indio Guayas Committee (IGC). Moser relates how the IGC had to deal with all the basic infrastructure that the community needed for everyday life, going outside the area to try and bring services in, and working within the area to enable services to be accessed by those living in the community. From her field notes on those early days, she drew the diagram in Figure 11.1, which shows the flow of needs and services to meet them within and from outside the community. However, although the IGC was able to mobilize the community and provide cohesion, there were also sources of conflict – a common phenomenon in any process of change where there are serious resource issues. As Moser states (2009, p. 75): 'The scarcity of resources within the community, as well as politically motivated allocations made in an intentionally partial manner, meant that conflict management and negotiation skills were always needed.'

These issues and debates are challenges for many types of intervention. For example, can engagement in different markets provide an avenue out of poverty for low-income people by promoting enterprise and employment? Or should the focus be on provision of low-cost products and services that low-income people can afford to buy or obtain? The potentially enormous market for low-cost products that could at the same time improve the wellbeing of poor people is something that has caught the attention of researchers as well as transnational corporations (TNCs) (Kaplinsky et al., 2009).

While such market development by large or formal sector companies may take place, low-income people may also produce new products and services through their own enterprise. However, they are often challenged by the settings in which they live and work, which may not have potential for product development and marketing. There are instances, however, when such innovation can be promoted through the interventions of research and development organizations working with low-income producers.

The term 'innovation' is used in multiple ways, from common sense means of making a change to quite specific meanings around technological changes that are brought to market. Claudio Velasco and colleagues, whose case study on

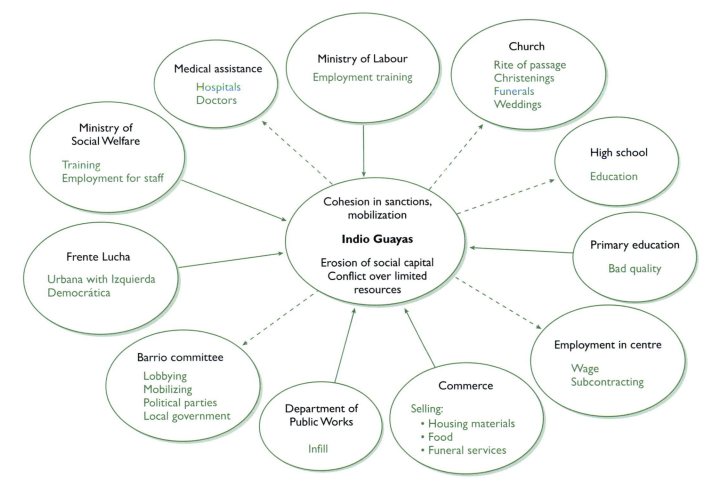

Figure 11.1 Flow chart of institutions and individuals into and out of Indio Guayas (Source: Moser, 2009)

innovation for poor farmers in the Bolivian highlands is presented in Section 11.2, states:

> innovation is the presence of diverse agents playing different roles and interacting between them in the process of generation, accumulation, diffusion and use of knowledge in response to market opportunities or other social needs, and the formal and informal institutions in which such a process is embedded.
>
> *(Velasco et al., 2009, p. 66)*

This seemingly complex statement means that an innovation is not just an invention. It is something that multiple actors with different knowledge may be involved in generating and that can be marketed or have a wide outlet and use. Innovation also needs an appropriate institutional framework or setting to be successful and to be sustained. Velasco's case study (Case study 6) is about how innovation can benefit poor farmers and involves both technological change and an organizational setting to make it work.

Innovation is therefore not only technological, albeit embedded in social processes. It is also social, for example when new ways of doing or organizing things are adopted on a large scale. For example, the 2010 *HDR*

(UNDP, 2010) discusses ideas and innovations that have changed approaches to healthcare and education in recent times. UNDP's use of the term innovation is more in the sense of the diffusion of new ideas and practices throughout these sectors that have changed many things for the better. Health and education are fundamental dimensions of well-being and livelihood and we consider new initiatives in the case studies below.

11.2 Using analytical frameworks to evaluate cases of intervention

As you know from Chapter 2, this book has three central themes running through the chapters: history, power and agency, and scale. If you are not sure about how these themes were introduced, you can turn back and refresh your memory now.

This chapter is primarily concerned with the issues of power and agency, and to some extent with scale. Power and agency are closely connected with social relations – who owns or controls what, who does what, who gets what, what they do with what they gain?

Power may be of different kinds, for example:

- power over what others have or do, that is, a form of control over others
- power to enact or to do something
- power with others to enact or to do something – a collective form of power.

Some types of power may be quite subtle – for example, power may be reflected in everyday norms and language or practices that we all tend to accept, or things that we all believe to be true. The philosopher Michel Foucault argued that truth and power are intimately related because what societies hold to be true is often upheld and reinforced by governments or other powerful institutions, and represented in many small ways through speech, the media and political rhetoric (Rabinow, 1984). This is part of cultural hegemony, discussed in Chapter 3. On the other hand, power can be contested in many ways, from individual actions to social movements.

Contestation is a manifestation of agency: that is, action to try and bring about change. Agency can be tactical in nature – improving but not changing the status quo, such as initiatives to increase wages or gain status in the community. Agency can also be strategic, bringing about more fundamental changes in social, economic and/or political processes. Another type of distinction is whether agency is individual or collective. That is, is it of the type that was seen in the case of Heera and Shantilal in Chapter 10: individual efforts or efforts by the household to grapple with their slide into poverty, or is it of the type seen in the improvements to the conditions of cashew nut workers where several organizations were involved in a collective effort (even if there were different interests at stake)? Another distinction has been made by Mackintosh (1992) between action that is for private benefit (that is, the interests of those taking the action) or for public benefit (that is, beyond the interests of those taking the action). We will see examples of both in the case studies below.

There is an important relationship between power and agency, for example in who is able to exert agency in a particular context and what kinds of power limit people's agency. Appreciating this relationship provides better understanding of how interventions to improve livelihoods may be supported or undermined.

In the rest of this chapter your active reading is crucial. We provide you with a framework for thinking critically about the case studies and you will need to make notes on the case studies to complete your understanding. We include some brief reflections on the nature of power and agency in these case studies in Section 11.3.

Activity 11.1

The purpose of this extended activity is to enable you to think critically about the nature of the social relations, power and agency in particular interventions to promote livelihoods and making a living. In the light of the discussion above, you will have realized that intervention is not free of contention or conflict, and that different voices, interests, roles and responsibilities may prevail.

The six case studies below involve interventions at different scales – from worldwide interventions to national or very local. Sometimes more than one scale is involved. Some of the case studies involve public action and some private action. Some involve public ends and some private ends. Some involve a mixture of types of action. Try to recognize and note these differences.

Read through all the case studies first. (Note that Case study 5 on education for livelihoods in Bangladesh has two different examples within it.)

Then select two that are of particular interest to you. Try to choose two that are quite different from each other so that you can see how different types of power and agency are exerted.

Make notes on:

- the key social relations between the different actors involved
- who has power
- who has agency.

You can use Table 11.1 for this purpose. Note that you may not be able to answer all the questions in the matrix. Evaluating real world phenomena is often carried out with imperfect information. In such situations, it is useful to identify what is missing or what else you would want or need to know.

As an extension to this activity, you might find it useful to make additional notes making links where relevant to the three dimensions of analysing livelihoods discussed in Chapter 10: cultural dimensions; sustainable livelihoods approach; global value chains.

Table 11.1 Matrix for analysing the social relations of interventions on livelihoods

List the main actors	Who owns or controls what?	Who is doing what?	Who is getting what?	What are they doing with it?	Who in your view has power in this situation and why?	Who in your view is exerting agency and how?	Who in your view is benefiting?

Case study 1: Who made your T-shirt?

We start with a case of intervention in a global value chain, as it uses an approach to understanding livelihoods that is already familiar to you from Chapter 10.

The garments industry was established in the 1970s in Bangladesh, as a response to trade opportunities opened up by the **Multi Fibre Agreement** (MFA). In 2009, garment exports accounted for nearly 80 per cent of Bangladesh's exports and were valued at US$15 billion. Europe and the USA remain the major destinations for these exports, with large apparel brands and retailers such as JCPenney, Wal-Mart, H&M, Marks & Spencer, Zara and Carrefour sourcing directly from Bangladesh since the mid-1980s. The emergence of the garment sector has generated employment opportunities for women, who were largely confined to traditional roles in the private sphere of the home rather than the public sphere of employment (Barrientos, 2007). Around 3 million people, most of them women, are employed by the garment sector.

Global buyers place orders, specified by design, quality and price, with domestic firms. Local firms (first-tier suppliers) primarily use their own production facilities but will also source from other local producers to complete the order. These latter firms are often referred to as second- and third-tier suppliers.

The international garments industry is very competitive, based on price as well as brand reputation. A number of developing countries, such as China and Vietnam, compete with Bangladesh on low costs, related mainly to the low wages given to garment workers. While ensuring the costs of production are kept low, these firms also have to 'protect' the repute of their retail customers. Brands such as Zara and Marks & Spencer are 'highly visible' brands, targeted by labour activists and consumer groups and more prone to losing business if stories of 'sweatshop labour' surface.

Thus international buyers govern parts of the value chain in Bangladesh as they set specific product requirements and enforce specific process codes, such as following international labour regulations, a ban on the use of child labour and a good working environment. The Bangladesh garment sector offers an interesting mix of actors that has an impact on the workers. First is the local firm itself, the second is the government, the third is international firms that source clothes from the country and, finally, there are international organizations such as the International Labour Organization (ILO) and NGOs.

Wages in the garment sector tend to be higher than other sectors (such as domestic workers), and are more likely to be paid on time and with provision of employment benefits. In 2010, garment workers in Bangladesh were involved in a number of protests, demanding fairer wages (see Figure 11.2). The minimum wage, as determined by the government, was raised from 1662 taka (US$43) to 3000 taka (US$75) a month. The new wage included an allowance for medical expenses and housing. The workers had demanded 5000 taka, and NGOs (such as the UK-based Action Aid) had calculated US$150 to be the living wage, that is the wage level that would allow the workers to afford nutritious food, health and education for their families. The workers received support from as far away as garment workers in Mexico!

Figure 11.2   Garment workers in Bangladesh protesting for better wages

There were other concerns. Most workers reported having a lack of information of their rights, occupation segregation, discrimination in wage and gender pay gaps, long working hours, little employment security, lack of childcare facilities or maternity leave, and poor working conditions. Formation of trade unions and associations has been problematic.

The government had argued against raising wages further as it would affect the ability of the sector to compete with other low-cost exporters, such as China. NGOs on the other hand argued that western companies could afford to pay the higher wage without raising prices for consumers in the North. Whereas, in a domestic production chain, an increase in wages would be the domain of trade unions and government, within global production networks, international organizations may actively campaign on behalf of workers. Therefore, the livelihoods of workers in Bangladesh can be affected by campaigns run in Europe and North America.

In 2010, to address working conditions, international buying houses and clothing store retailers were setting and enforcing labour standards within first-tier suppliers. Local factories not adhering to these standards were being removed from the parent companies list of suppliers and not awarded further contracts unless changes were made. GAP and other leading brands have been subjecting factories they use to regular inspections by independent auditors. These audits focus on checking that no child labour is used on the factory floor and require implementation of local fire regulations, having emergency exits marked and regular evacuation drills. Ethical trading standards for those firms receiving direct orders from overseas have seen improved working conditions and code compliance in factories. Even though local firms are audited, those that they outsource to (second- and third-tier companies, that is, those firms that supply inputs to local firm such as buttons, zips, embroidered pieces, etc.) are not as yet within the audit sphere, but efforts are underway to monitor the working conditions of all actors in the value chain.

Other organizations, such as the ILO, have been actively involved in improving working conditions for garment workers, under the 'Decent Work' program. Decent work was defined by the ILO as 'under conditions of freedom, equity, security and dignity, in which rights are protected and adequate remuneration and social coverage is provided' (ILO, 2000). The objective has been to ensure that globalized production provides social protection, rights and social dialogue as well as employment. In collaboration with UNICEF and the Bangladesh Garment Exports Manufactures Association, the ILO has also helped implement a ban on child labour within the garment industry. Brands and retailers joined together in the MFA Forum, where trade unions and NGOs get together with producers to increase productivity as well as build sustainability in the garments sector in Bangladesh. Although much needs to be done in ensuring decent work for all, international organizations and firms can play a constructive role in the livelihoods of those in low-income countries.

Case study 2: Innovative approaches for delivering health solutions

Developing countries, particularly those in Africa, suffer from a significant disease burden. The World Health Organization (WHO) estimates that malaria, which particularly impacts children and those living in Africa, affects nearly 3.2 billion people a year and kills 1.2 million. Nearly 40 million people globally are infected with HIV/AIDS and 65 per cent of all new infections occur in Africa (Kalua et al., 2009). Ensuring effective and sustainable health delivery to needy populations is an onerous challenge in both developed and developing countries, but more so in the latter because of many contextual challenges that result in systemic weaknesses to the health delivery programmes.

The logical starting point, therefore, is the strengthening of health systems, so that technological solutions to the health challenge can be delivered efficiently. However, the task of strengthening health systems is a daunting one, starting from the fact that everywhere in the world, health is but one issue in a bigger context of development challenges. These challenges vary among countries, spawning great diversity in what constitutes a health system in one setting versus a health system in another.

Developing universal solutions to such challenges, therefore, becomes a challenging task, while at the same time tailoring solutions to specific contexts (health technologies included) becomes an expensive and time-consuming process. Ultimately, however, if health systems addressing the needs of all people are to emerge and be sustainable, they have to be integrated with the local social setting (Chataway et al., 2010).

Improving public health is a hugely complex process. It relies, in part, on products that work reaching people who need them. In addition to significant scientific challenges involved in tackling disease, there needs to be market demand to fund the product development. Once a product is developed, effective health systems, good infrastructure and skilled staff are required to distribute it to those in need. Crucially, these products must be affordable to some of the world's poorest people.

Scientific and technological innovation in the area of health has gone some way towards reducing the disease burden in resource-poor communities. For example, while they do not cure the disease, treatment of HIV/AIDS with drugs does increase life expectancy and is seen as being partly responsible for the reduction in the international AIDS death rate.

The International AIDS Vaccine Initiative (IAVI) is one of the organizations that has played a prominent role in spearheading technological innovation in the quest for HIV/AIDS vaccines and drugs. IAVI was initiated in 1996 as a not-for-profit organization based out of New York. Following initial activities as an advocacy organization (promoting the need for funding for AIDS vaccine research), its attention became focused on becoming actively involved in AIDS vaccine research (ibid). This started as a brokering role, in which IAVI provided an entity around which others within the AIDS vaccine community could coalesce. Gradually, IAVI has become much more of a knowledge integrator, moving from promoting science done by others to building its own laboratories within which to conduct applied science.

While IAVI is taking on the characteristics of a knowledge integrator in the area of the science of AIDS vaccine research, in terms of its work in developing countries and advocacy in the global health arena, it is more of a knowledge broker (Chataway and Hanlin, 2008). It shapes the agenda through providing voice and capabilities for new or previously unheard actors. This role is based on IAVI's understanding of the need to work in collaboration with others, particularly in terms of its work in developing countries. IAVI learnt early on through problems with its initial clinical trials in Kenya and India that it needed to be seen as inclusive and a real partner and not as an external US-based company imposing a 'technological fix'. It therefore places an emphasis on letting others lead, while being the central node in a network of government and non-governmental agencies, including research organizations, local communities and industry. This is how IAVI conducts much of its advocacy work in developing countries, in preparation for clinical trials, and at an international level in discussions around the AIDS vaccine and neglected disease policy agendas (Orsenigo et al., 2007).

Case study 3: The case of genetically modified cotton in India and South Africa

There is much debate about the potential benefits (and costs) of genetically modified (GM) crop technology for developing countries. GM technology is an arm of biotechnology: techniques that use living organisms (plants, animals or micro-organisms) or their parts to make or modify a product or improve these organisms for specific uses. The number of countries growing 'biotech crops' rose from zero in 1996 to 25 in 2009. The International Service for the Acquisition of Agribiotech Applications (ISAAA) reported that, in 2009, 14 million farmers planted 134 million hectares of 'biotech crops', and of these, 13 million (90 per cent) were small and resource-poor farmers from developing countries (James, 2009).

The case of GM cotton and smallholder farmers in India and South Africa is one that has been extensively studied by both proponents and opponents of this new form of biotechnology. The cases below illustrate some of the realities around developing and delivering this technology to farmers.

Bt and the Beast

'Bt and the beast' is how cotton scientist Keshav Raj Kranthi refers to the controversial GM cotton so widely planted in India (Padma, 2006). The 'beast' is the American bollworm (see Figure 11.3) – a moth larva that devours cotton bolls — while Bt is its nemesis, a protein crystal from the bacterium *Bacillus thuringiensis* (see Figure 11.4).

In 2006, four years after the Indian government allowed farmers to grow Bt cotton, which is genetically modified to contain the Bt toxin, the government's department of biotechnology and the biotechnology industry said it had led to decreasing use of insecticides and improved yields.

But meanwhile, another picture of India's Bt saga was emerging – one that pointed to a pressing need for an enquiry into just how successful GM technology has been in India.

Figure 11.3   The American bollworm

There were warning signs, for instance, of the bollworm's resistance to the Bt toxin. The media and NGOs pointed to a worrying rate of suicide among cotton farmers in parts of India, though a direct link between the deaths and Bt cotton remained to be established. Further, the monitoring of where and how the cotton was being grown was also poor, and a market for legal and illegal, fake and real, Bt cotton has sprung up.

Given GM's chequered history in the country, and the polarized opinions of the pro-GM government and industry, and anti-GM activists, the need for a serious, inclusive scientific debate was said to be desirable but often impossible to achieve.

Meanwhile, the story of Bt-cotton production by smallholder farmers was being said to be 'the success story that never was'. Genetic Resources Action International (GRAIN) argued that despite claims that Bt cotton will catapult African farmers out of poverty, a report in 2005 revealed that the majority of Bt small-scale cotton farmers on the Makhathini

Flats in South Africa had stopped planting Bt cotton because they could not repay their debts.

It cited a five-year study by Biowatch South Africa, which showed that small-scale cotton farmers in Northern KwaZulu Natal Province had not benefited from Bt cotton and that the hype surrounding this case was just that – a media hype created by biotechnology companies to try and convince the rest of Africa to approve GM crops. The study was said to show that Bt cotton has failed on a number of fronts: farmers were in debt and credit institutions had withdrawn from the area because farmers could not repay their loans, and the number of farmers planting cotton had dropped by 80 per cent since 2000. One farmer had commented: 'Four years ago we were told we would make lots of money but we work harder and make nothing' (Pschorn-Strauss, 2005).

Figure 11.4 Bt cotton

In Makhathini, Bt cotton was said to have compounded the problems that African cotton farmers typically face. After the introduction of Bt cotton, the Makhathini farmers were hit with droughts and low cotton prices. Since Bt cottonseeds were double the price of non-GM cotton, farmers increased their debt to be able to plant it, thereby increasing their risk.

Only four farmers of the total sample of 36 Bt cotton farmers said to have been followed in the study made a profit. The net loss for these 36 farmers was US$83 348. Such debt and income problems were rampant for Makhathini farmers. According to a local Land Bank official, farmers in Makhathini owe an average of US$1322 per farmer and around 80 per cent of them have defaulted on their loans.

'With the Makhathini miracle now in tatters, the GM industry is bound to dig up another 'success story,' said Elfrieda Pschorn-Strauss, one of the researchers. In South Africa, the GM industry was said to have already shifted its attention to the promotion of GM maize, citing yields of up to 400 per cent for small farmers in some areas. She added that: 'It would be wise to keep in mind the rise and fall of the Makhathini farmers whenever the industry talks about the benefits of GM crops for the poor' (Pschorn-Strauss, 2005).

(Sources: Adapted from Padma, 2006; Pschorn-Strauss, 2005)

Case study 4: Micro-credit – a world initiative to promote livelihoods?

The Nobel Prize winning economist, Joseph Stiglitz, has stated that micro-credit is one measure that works in terms of promoting livelihoods and reducing poverty (Stiglitz, 2010). The Grameen Bank – the most famous micro-credit scheme in the world – was launched in the 1970s by Mohamed Yunus. There are now micro-credit schemes in many countries around the world (including the USA), particularly targeting women borrowers to promote their income-generating capacities. A fundamental aspect of the Grameen idea is the formation of groups of borrowers. The relationship between people in the group is key both to organizing the loans and for repayment, because peer pressure and solidarity underpins the process. In small or tightly knit communities, this process can be very powerful. Others have also argued that the formation of groups and group solidarity, particularly for women, is just as important to members as the income derived from loans and investments.

The 'social capital' (see Chapter 10) dimension of micro-credit schemes is, however, being challenged by some forms that micro-credit has been taking (*Financial Times*, 2010). Some initiatives aim to make micro-credit operate more like a bank, so that group formation and the building of relationships is given very little time as the schemes aim to make the process more efficient. This, it has been suggested, has led to an increase in non-repayment of loans. On the other hand, after the world economic crisis which started in 2008, it has also been argued that women have become further indebted because the crisis has had an impact, whether directly or indirectly, on jobs, incomes and access to services affecting health, education and care of children (Pearson and Sweetman, 2011, p.5). Even so, micro-credit is still seen as having great potential promoting incomes and group organization. Below is a report on the start-up of a micro-credit scheme among low-income people in New York, USA. Note that this report is from 2008, the year the sub-prime mortgage crisis hit the United States.

Small loans, significant impact after success in poor nations, Grameen Bank tries New York

Robert Shulman, Washington Post Staff Writer

Monday, 10 March, 2008; Page A03

NEW YORK – 'Señoras!' calls the banker, summoning her borrowers to attention at their first loan-repayment meeting.

The small-business borrowers – day-care providers, clothing sellers, jewellery makers – crowd into the living room where their children are napping, eating cereal and watching TV.

They are part of a nascent lending program created by Muhammad Yunus, a Bangladeshi economist who won the 2006 Nobel Peace Prize for developing the Grameen Bank, which uses micro-loans to help eradicate poverty in developing nations.

But these women are not in Bangladesh, they are in Queens [New York]. They are among the first 100 borrowers of Grameen America, which began disbursing loans in January. This is the first time Grameen has run its program in a developed country. 'I just want to live a little better, and one day own a little house or something,' said Socorro Diaz, 54, a borrower who sells women's lingerie and jewellery. 'I'm trying to change my life. Bit by bit.'

Grameen America, which offers loans from US$500 to US$3000, hopes to reach people like her, part of the large segment of poor Americans without access to credit, said Ritu Chattree, the vice president for finance and development.

They are bakers who can only buy enough eggs and milk for a day's work because they cannot afford a restaurant refrigerator to store ingredients. They are vendors who borrow money daily to rent a cart. They are hair salon owners who take out loans every time they need to buy shampoo.

They often use pawn shops, or fall prey to check-cashing stores, loan sharks, and payday lenders, which can charge interest rates of 200 or 300 per cent, Chattree said. 'You think this is normal, because you grew up with it,' said Yunus of such high-interest lending in a recent interview with the *Financial Times*. 'This is an abnormal situation, because of the problem with the financial system, so we have to adjust the financial system.'

His adjustment begins with this experiment in the immigrant neighborhood of Jackson Heights, Queens.

Three groups of five borrowers attend the meeting in the apartment of Jenny Guante, 40, who makes silver and gold jewellery and runs a home day care. Some are making weekly loan payments; the largest payment is US$66 on a US$3000 loan. Guante, the group's chairwoman, counts the money carefully before passing it to Alethia Mendez, the Grameen staff member who serves as community banker and center director.

'I've known these people forever,' said one borrower in the roomful of immigrants from the Dominican Republic. 'We grew up together. We went to school together around the corner.'

That bond helps people make payments, said Chattree. If one woman is having trouble repaying a loan because, say, her husband is sick and she has to care for him and the children, another of her group might pitch in to help with child care. Loan disbursements for the whole group are slowed if one person defaults, she said.

After the meeting, as several women drift off into the kitchen with a calculator to discuss their plans, 10 new prospective borrowers stop by the apartment.

The program began in 1974, when Yunus lent US$27 to a group of poor villagers and realized that even small amounts could make transformative differences. He set up the Grameen Bank, which has since disbursed about US$6 billion in tiny loans to about 7.4 million Bangladeshi micro-entrepreneurs, mostly women in businesses such as street vending and farming.

In Bangladesh, Grameen also functions as a savings bank, makes college and housing loans, and operates projects in areas such as telecommunications, yogurt production and solar energy.

The problem with capitalism, Yunus says, is its distinction between companies pursuing profit and charities pursuing good. His bank model operates with corporate efficiency, but pumps profits back into social objectives.

The borrowers in Queens are following Grameen's self-sufficient model in the developing world.

But Yunus acknowledges that the United States is different from the seven countries where Grameen operates its loan programs, or the dozens of others where Grameen has offered technical advice.

Here, there is more regulation, so a person cannot just set up a cart and sell cakes without a permit.

The welfare system discourages income-generating activities, Yunus says. 'If you earn a dollar, that dollar is to be deducted from your welfare check. If you want to quit welfare, then you lose your health benefits,' he told the *Financial Times*.

Rules for setting up a bank are cumbersome for a micro-operation, and Yunus has met with the head of the Federal Reserve and members of Congress to discuss creating more flexible legal frameworks.

Grameen America will break even when it has 20 000 borrowers, Chattree said, a scale she expects to achieve in three to five years.

That is something that no American micro-lender has achieved, said Michael Chu, a specialist in micro-finance at Harvard. 'In general, the feeling is that micro-finance doesn't work in the States,' said Chattree, even though many groups, including some aided by the Grameen Trust, have followed the Grameen model.

Other micro-lenders and academics say that if anyone can spark discussion on the issue, Grameen can.

(Source: Shulman, 2008)

Case study 5: Education for livelihoods in Bangladesh

In 2010, Bangladesh was the seventh most populated country in the world, with somewhere between 142 and 159 million inhabitants. While the majority of the population is rural-based, there is significant migration to cities, especially Dhaka, the capital. Bangladesh is seen as an emerging economy, having moved into the medium development country category (UNDP, 2003), and is a key global centre for the garment industry (see Case study 1), which accounts for about 75 per cent of its total export earnings (Haider, 2007). In 2010, its low-cost skilled labour force was significantly cheaper than that of other emerging economies such as China.

Can education help children to move out of poverty as they move into adulthood? In 2010, Bangladesh had an estimated 35–40 million children aged between 5 and 14. Of these, an estimated 8 million were working children (USDOL, 2010), employed in agricultural work, such as labouring in rice fields, or in small workshops in the cities. Much employment is hazardous, such as brick-chipping or working with toxic materials. Girls are frequently employed as live-in domestic labour, working up to 58 hours a week. But, as noted in Chapter 10, working children contribute to family income (the World Bank estimated up to one third of household income in the poorest families in 2007), a reality that cannot be ignored.

In 2010, compulsory education in Bangladesh lasted five years with an official finishing age of 10 years old. Although there have been many programmes to promote school education amongst poor families, millions of children had never enrolled in school or dropped out. Data from 2009 estimated that 69 per cent of those who do complete the five years of compulsory schooling were unable to read news headlines in newspapers properly, and 87 per cent could not do simple mathematical calculations (IRIN, 2009). There was a strong correlation between the proportions of children who dropped out and families continually in 'food deficit', that is, the poorest families (Ahmed et al., 2007).

While this evidence might seem to suggest that children's education is not transformative for the poor, the work of two Bangladeshi NGOs presents a compelling counterargument. BRAC (originally the Bangladesh Rural Advancement Committee) and UCEP (Underprivileged Children's Educational Programs) both began their work in the 1970s, soon after independence. Arguably, both demonstrate through their work that education for children helps to improve both their employability and their life chances. Each NGO, however, takes quite a different approach.

The work of UCEP

UCEP started in 1972, aiming to provide a high-quality intensive catch-up primary and lower secondary education for those who had already dropped out from primary school (see Figure 11.5). Funded by a consortium of international donor partners, such as the UK Department for International Development (DFID) and the Swiss Agency for Development and Cooperation (SADC), a UCEP education is relatively expensive, at more than twice the cost per student of government-run vocational programmes, but UCEP argues that this higher investment is worthwhile in the long run.

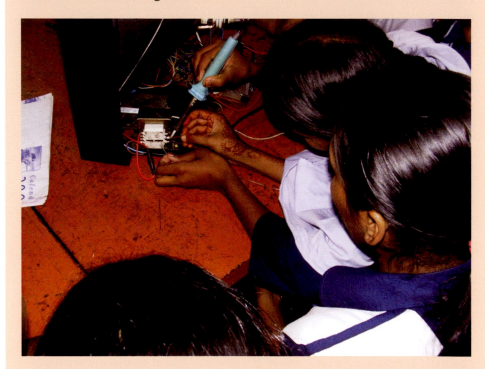

Figure 11.5   Working with youngsters from poor backgrounds

The main objective of UCEP is 'to improve the socio-economic status of the urban poor and support industrial growth by generating skilled manpower' (UCEP, 2008). Children living in the cities can combine their participation in UCEP with part-time or full-time work. This is an 'earning and learning' model for children who have dropped out of state education: children whose parents typically work as domestic servants, hawkers, factory workers, shop assistants, rag pickers, porters and day labourers. UCEP schools are close to poor neighbourhoods so that UCEP staff maintain close links with the communities, including home visits to parents to encourage support and inhibit dropout. Entry to UCEP programmes is competitive, with entrance tests for a place on the Integrated General and Vocational Education (IGVE) programme, and competition among the highest achieving graduates from IGVE for places at the UCEP Technical Schools.

The UCEP IGVE combines an abridged Bangladesh National Primary and Lower Secondary Curriculum with vocational education designed to help with employment on graduation. Every aspect possible of the learning is linked to employment: when learning the alphabet in English, for example, 'T' is for 'tape-measure' and 'S' is for 'screwdriver'. Children have an intensive school day at the IGVE schools, with even greater use of a shift system than the state primary schools.

According to UCEP, IGVE graduates have the chance of better-paid employment on finishing because they have the chance to move on to a UCEP Technical School. These are well-resourced centres with highly qualified staff, where students complete an apprenticeship in a trade such as auto mechanics, tailoring, weaving or plumbing. Graduates from these schools are reportedly in high demand. The gender balance in the schools is 50:50, although girls are clustered in trades traditionally accepted as suitable for females, such as textiles, and there is a preponderance of boys in trades such as auto mechanics.

UCEP has competitive entry and a modest scale: its programmes covered 32 000 children in 2010, although it aimed to scale up to 50 000. Would a large increase in scale lead to compromises in quality? UCEP's years of success in transforming hard-to-reach children into young people who can move into skilled national and international employment suggest that its programmes ought to benefit many more than are currently able to enjoy them.

The work of BRAC

In 2010, BRAC was the world's largest NGO, working in all districts of Bangladesh and having spread to other countries in Asia, including Afghanistan, Sri Lanka and Pakistan as well as sub-Saharan Africa. BRAC began in the aftermath of the civil war in Bangladesh in the early 1970s, first working to provide post-conflict rehabilitation, and then moving into long-term rural community development. The success of BRAC's **social enterprises** has allowed it to develop its non-income activities such as education at a large scale.

Figure 11.6   The education programme of BRAC

BRAC began education for children in the mid-1980s with 22 one-room schools, increasing to more than 30 000 primary schools across Bangladesh, and teaching about one million children, mainly in rural areas (see Figure 11.6). The education is free. The model is a one-teacher one-room school, only set up when there are 30 or so children, a local person – usually female – prepared to act as an unqualified teacher, and the backing of the local community to construct the schoolhouse. The schoolroom is basic with no heating, lighting or electricity and with an earth floor covered with a cloth, and there are no desks or chairs. But each child is provided with a pile of reading and writing materials and the classroom is always bright and highly decorated. The school day lasts only 3 hours and is arranged to suit the other responsibilities of families and children, such as work. There is no homework.

The children cover the five years of primary school in four years and the one teacher stays with this same group of children the whole time. The BRAC Primary School programme has developed its own curriculum and its own certification. It places a strong emphasis on child-centred pedagogy and inclusiveness: 65 per cent of primary students are girls. Every class includes children with special needs and there are first language programmes for children from ethnic minorities. The dropout rate from BRAC schools is very low, with a completion rate in its primary schools from start to finish of 93 per cent.

BRAC primary education is non-formal but BRAC has the capacity to negotiate easy transitions from its primary schools into government-funded lower secondary education and has high transition rates of more than 90 per cent. BRAC children often outperform children from government schools.

That BRAC schooling stops at the end of primary can be seen as a serious disadvantage and the organization is now working to provide support for state-funded secondary level education. In practice, students may find it difficult to make the necessary adjustments and parents may see little point in their continuing their education. Over-age when they began primary school, BRAC primary graduates will be adolescents capable of working in the fields, or helping with domestic work and family-caring responsibilities. For rural girls, early marriage is a common expectation.

Conversely, it could be argued that BRAC offers an education that enables children to make better lives for themselves while continuing as members of a rural community, helping meet some of the challenges of rural employment, raised in Chapter 10. And as adults, these children will be in a position to improve their communities by strengthening community organizations, increasing the accountability of local government in rural areas, developing human rights awareness and the role of women and improving awareness of health issues and the environment, as well as improving their chances of a better livelihood than their parents.

BRAC and UCEP

These are two very different approaches to the question of whether education can improve the lot of poor youth moving into adulthood. UCEP's work was predicated on helping relatively few children make a relatively big transformation in their lives. The work of BRAC, on the other hand, implied smaller changes in the livelihood of a much larger group of children. The two programmes are informed by different views of what education is for, with the tight focus of the UCEP approach linked directly to employability, and the child-centred approach of BRAC linked to wider forms of empowerment of people and communities. But both are based on the idea that innovation in education can improve the livelihood prospects of children when they are adults.

Case study 6: New markets and food processing technologies for potato farmers in Bolivia

Changes in urban consumption and new actors in food markets (supermarkets, food industries and retailers) are exercising increasing pressure over production practices and resources of small farmers and other small- and medium-scale enterprises (SMEs) in the market chain in Bolivia. They have limited access to information, services, technology and capital, and inferior bargaining power to compete in a changing context. Although market opportunities are a trigger for innovation, the question of how and to what extent development interventions can help poor farmers benefit is a challenging question.

To meet this challenge, the Bolivian Andean multi-stakeholder platform (ANDIBOL) was set up. ANDIBOL brings farmers' associations together with traders, processors, researchers, extension agents, service providers and others, to foster pro-poor innovation. Amongst other activities, ANDIBOL has established links with market agents to develop better quality *chuño*-based products (products using freeze-dried potatoes) which have a higher price and export potential. The platform is facilitated by PROINPA (a private research and development, R&D, organization) and represents 13 core (organizational) members including four farmers' associations with around 200 (individual) members, processing firms, development projects, NGOs and other service providers (Devaux et al., 2009).

Market opportunities as source of technical innovation

Based on the initial results from commercializing Chuñosa (clean, selected and bagged *chuño*) in supermarkets of La Paz and Santa Cruz (the two main cities in Bolivia), the manager of a medium-scale firm dedicated to processing and commercializing natural Andean products, called Ricafrut, explained that it was necessary to improve *chuño* quality to respond to urban consumers' requirements, especially in terms of standard size and shape, cleanliness and absence of peel and pest damage.

Researchers in ANDIBOL started the hunt for technical alternatives to solve quality problems at field level. They found a local retailer who had invented a manual machine to remove *chuño* peel. They also found that another R&D organization (CIFEMA) had already developed a prototype of a manual machine to classify fresh potatoes. The performance of this machine, however, was never tested with the kind of potatoes that farmers use to obtain *chuño*.

Adapting and improving the peel remover machine

The researchers, working with a local mechanic, introduced the first changes in the manual machine used by the retailer (see Figure 11.7). The new version was assembled. *Chuño* producers from four communities tested the improved machine during two months. The manager of Ricafrut visited the production area to see how the machine performed and verify if the *chuño* fulfilled market quality standards.

Two months later, in a meeting with farmers, researchers and local authorities, the results were presented and further suggestions to improve the process were made. The CIFEMA experts were contacted and they introduced modifications to improve durability, facilitate the reparation and replacement of parts, and even investigated how to diminish noise from the machine.

Interviewed by the researchers, *chuño* producers highlighted the following results from the new, improved machines:

- 'Now we have more time available for other activities; the time required to peel 12 kg has been reduced from 4 hours to 20 minutes.'

- 'Normally *chuño* was peeled by women; now with the machine, men and women share this work.'
- 'We obtain clean *chuño* and without peel and we are able to satisfy the quantity of *chuño* required by the Ricafrut manager.'
- 'Ricafrut no longer refuses our *chuño*.'
- 'In the local market our clean *chuño* also receives a higher price.'
- 'We need peeler machines in each community; however, the price is high (US$400 each) and we are not able to buy them.'
- 'We will try to get funds from the local government to buy more machines.'

Adapting and improving the classifier machine

Researchers then bought a classifier and demonstrated it to farmers. To make the machine usable to classify *chuño*, the first idea was to change the sieves used to classify potatoes in the original model for sieves specially designed to select *chuño*. However, the farmers turned down this idea, arguing that the process of selection starts with the classification of fresh potatoes, and therefore the only thing … to do was to adapt the shape and size of the sieves according to the kind of potatoes that they use to *obtain chuño*.

As with the peeler machine, the new classifier was distributed to be tested in four communities and after two months further suggestions for improvements were made. With 24 improved potato classifiers in use in 16 different communities, initial information about performance was gathered from the farmers:

- 'The time required to classify potatoes has been reduced from 12 hours to 5.'
- 'Normally we women were in charge of this extremely hard work; our hands suffered injuries. Now we join this work with men and our hands no longer suffer.'
- 'We have *chuño* of better quality because working with selected potatoes [of a standard size] the freezing process acts uniformly.'
- 'We also obtain benefit from selling our fresh potatoes, because we obtain better prices in the local market by classifying potatoes [according to their] size.'
- 'As well as with the peeler we are not able to buy this machine due the price (US$350 each), but we want it. We are going to look for support from the local government.'

Figure 11.7 Three different potato peelers. (a) Peeler machine first model; (b) peeler machine second model; (c) peeler machine final model

(Source: Adapted and abbreviated from Velasco et al., 2009)

11.3 Thinking about power and agency

The social relations in these case studies reveal different types of power and agency. We take just two of them here and briefly reflect on them.

First, we turn to Case study 1 on garment workers in Bangladesh. Here we have a chain of actors (or agents) from consumers to retailers (who are also global buyers) to the national firms and the women workers. We also have organizations that represent or work with those actors: consumer groups; the government of Bangladesh and the Bangladesh Garment Export Manufactures Association, which wish to safeguard the national industry; and national unions, international campaigning organizations, the ILO and UNICEF, all supporting the workers' interests. Some of these entities wield considerable power; however, the case study shows that there have been complex negotiations to improve working conditions. This involves, on one hand, protecting different powerful interests (whose brands and names would be undermined by stories of child labour or other 'indecent work'). On the other hand, these powerful interests have been put under considerable pressure by the garment workers supported by the international organizations. While the process was, as described in the case study, 'constructive', one couldn't help feeling that the garment workers faced considerable challenges in organizing and in gaining better working conditions. As noted in Chapter 10, a global value chain analysis helps to identify key links in the manufacturing stages, as well as the stakeholders and actors that affect the production process. Thus the global value chain framework assists in identifying points where interventions can be made to improve the conditions of workers at the bottom of the chain. Value chain analysis does not necessarily enable an investigation into other aspects of women's lives that their working conditions may have an impact on, such as their reproductive roles in the household. However, the changes that need to be made involve active agency and challenges to power relations in the value chain.

By contrast, Case study 6 on pro-poor innovation for potato farmers in Bolivia appears to be a much less hierarchical context, partly because a platform was established to bring together actors in the market chain, including researchers and others with particular areas of expertise. The intention of the platform was both to enable small-scale potato farmers to take advantage of new markets, and to promote technological changes to ensure the quality of the product desired by consumers (upgrading). At a much smaller scale, Case study 6 resonates to some extent with Case study 1 in that some similar types of actors were involved (low-income producers and companies having a key stake in the market). However in this instance, the mediating organizations were local R&D bodies that worked with farmers and companies to make the technological changes needed for product upgrading. In addition, an essential part of the process of realizing technological change was to involve, listen to and make changes required by the potato farmers as well as the manager of the company, Ricafrut. Finally, although we do not have very much information about gender divisions of labour in potato farming and potato processing, we saw that the eventual innovations proposed could have positive effects on reducing the negative impacts for women doing the processing work.

In spite of the relatively flat hierarchies of this situation, what kinds of power do you think were exerted and how? From the case study (a much abbreviated version of the original article), you do not have enough information to be able to answer this question fully. However, one might imagine that the company manager could exert his voice as he was the outlet for the processed potatoes. In addition, there is often power embedded in knowledge and expertise, even though in this case there seemed to be a working engagement between the knowledge and expertise of the potato farmers and that of the researchers.

Finally, notice the different scales of these two examples of intervention, the different complexity of actors, and their different dynamics. They are also different in that the garment workers are wage workers in a large industry while the potato farmers are individual smallholders in the Andean highlands. Although the latter were producing for a local buyer, in this case niche potato products from South America now reach international markets too. Both sectors are thus dynamic and constantly changing, with different challenges (for example, scale; individual versus collectively organized production; the range of interests and different types of capital) and similar issues (control over markets; know-how; prices for what's produced or wages received – and who benefits).

11.4 Summary and looking forward

This chapter has presented an opportunity for critical reflection on the nature of intervention and agency at different scales, involving different forms of power and agency, and also raising questions about who should intervene and on behalf of whom. The case studies have mainly focused on the agency of the poor and what place their agency has in intervention. But they have also focused on the agency of other organizations and the role they can play in either promoting or impeding change. It is always important to reflect on whose responsibility it is to intervene, on whose behalf, with what end in mind, whether intervenors have legitimacy and on what it might be based. These are challenging and much debated issues.

The chapter has highlighted that appreciating the roles of power and agency in interventions to promote better livelihoods is necessary to understand how and why different interventions may succeed or fail. Some of the cases you studied in this chapter involved aid, which has its own power dynamic. It is one of the most well-known forms of intervention but also one of the most contentious. Its role and usefulness is much debated and Chapter 12 will explain why.

References

Ahmed, M., Ahmed, K.S., Khan, N.I. and Ahmed, R. (2007) *Access to Education in Bangladesh: Country Analytic Review of Primary and Secondary Education*, University of Sussex, CREATE/Dhaka, BRAC University, IED.

Barrientos, S. (2007) 'Global production systems and decent work', *Working Paper No. 77*, Geneva, ILO.

Bernstein, H., 'Development studies and the Marxists' in Kothari, U. (ed.) *A Radical History of Development Studies: Individuals, Institutions and Ideologies*, Cape Town, London and New York, David Philip and Zed Books.

Chataway, J. and Hanlin, R. (2008) 'Sustainable (vaccine) development: the International AIDS Vaccine Initiative (IAVI) and capacity building', *Health Partnerships Review*, pp. 43–5.

Chataway, J., Hanlin, R., Mugwagwa, J. and Muraguri, L. (2010) 'Global health social technologies: reflections on evolving theories and landscapes', *Research Policy*, vol. 39, pp. 1277–88.

Cowen, M. and Shenton, R.W. (1996) *Doctrines of Development*, London, Routledge.

Devaux, A., Horton, D., Velasco, C., Thiele, G., López, G., Bernet, T., Reinoso, I., Ordinola, M. and Pico, H. (2009) 'Collective action for market chain innovation in The Andes', *Food Policy*, vol. 34, pp. 31–8.

Financial Times (2010) 'Micro-credit crisis. India's small lenders face scrutiny', 2 December 2010, p. 15.

Haider, M.Z. (2007) 'Competitiveness of the Bangladesh ready-made garment industry in major international markets', *Asia-Pacific Trade and Investment Review*, vol. 3, no. 1, pp. 3–27.

Hickey, S. and Mohan, G. (eds) (2004) *Participation: From Tyranny to Transformation?*, London and New York, Zed Books.

International Labour Organization (ILO). (2000) 'Investing in human capital: focus on training ', *Modular Package on Gender, Poverty and Employment,* Geneva, ILO.

Integrated Regional Information Networks (IRIN) (2009) *Bangladesh: Report Blasts Primary School Education*, Bangladesh, http://www.unhcr.org/refworld/docid/4993ea3b14.html (Accessed 20 December 2010).

James, C. (2009) 'Global status of commercialized biotech/GM crops: 2009', *ISAAA Brief No. 41*, Ithaca, New York, ISAAA.

Kalua, F.A., Awotedu, A., Kamwanja, L.A. and Saka, J.D.K. (eds) (2009) *Science, Technology and Innovation for Public Health in Africa*, Monograph, Pretoria, Republic of South Africa, NEPAD Office of Science and Technology.

Kaplinsky, R., Chataway, J., Hanlin, R., Clark, N., Kale, D., Muraguri, L., Papaioannou, T., Robbins, P. and Wamae, W. (2009) 'Below the radar: what does innovation in emerging economies have to offer other low-income economies?', *International Journal of Technology Management and Sustainable Development*, vol. 8, no. 3, pp. 177–97.

Mackintosh, M. (1992) 'Introduction' in Wuyts, M., Mackintosh, M. and Hewitt, T. (eds), *Development Policy and Public Action*, Oxford, Oxford University Press in association with The Open University.

Moser, C.O.N. (2009) *Ordinary Families, Extraordinary Lives: Assets and Poverty Reduction in Guayaquil, 1978–2004*, Washington, Brookings Institution Press.

Orsenigo, L., Chataway, J., Brusoni, S., Cacciatori, E. and Hanlin, R. (2007) 'The International AIDS Vaccine Initiative (IAVI) in a changing landscape of vaccine development: a public private partnership as knowledge broker and integrator', *European Journal of Development Research*, vol. 19, no. 1, pp. 100–17.

Padma, T.V. (2006) 'GM in India: the battle over Bt cotton', *Science and Development Network*, 20 December 2006 [online], http://www.scidev.net/en/features/gm-in-india-the-battle-over-bt-cotton.html (Accessed 14 August 2011).

Pearson and Sweetman (2011).

Pschorn-Strauss, E. (2005) 'Bt cotton in South Africa: the case of the Makhathini farmers', *Seedling*, 26 April 2005, Spain, GRAIN, also available online at http://www.grain.org/article/entries/492-bt-cotton-in-south-africa-the-case-of-the-makhathini-farmers (Accessed 15 August 2011).

Rabinow, P. (ed.) (1984) *The Foucault Reader: An Introduction to Foucault's Thought*, London, Penguin Books.

Shulman, R. (2008) 'Small loans, significant impact after success in poor nations, Grameen Bank tries New York', *The Washington Post*, 10 March 2008 [online], http://www.washingtonpost.com/wp-dyn/content/article/2008/03/09/AR2008030901617.html?hpid%3Dtopnews&sub=AR (Accessed 15 August 2011)

Stiglitz, J. (2010) 'Reducing poverty: some lessons from the last quarter century', Presentation to the Chronic Poverty Research Centre Conference 'Ten Years of War Against Poverty', Manchester, 8 September 2010.

Underprivileged Children's Education Programmes (UCEP) (2008) 'About UCEP' [online], http://www.ucepbd.org/ (Accessed 15 August 2011).

United Nations Development Programme (UNDP) (2003) 'Millennium Development Goals: a compact among nations to end human poverty', *Human Development Report 2003*, New York, Oxford University Press.

United Nations Development Programme (UNDP) (2003) 'The real wealth of nations: pathways to human development', *Human Development Report 2010*, New York, UNDP.

UNICEF (2008) 'Basic education for urban working children', *UNICEF Fact sheet* [online], http://www.unicef.org/bangladesh/Education_for_Working_Children_(BEHTRUWC).pdf (Accessed 15 August 2011).

United States Department of Labor (USDOL (2010) *2009 Findings on the Worst Forms of Child Labor – Bangladesh*, USA, online at: http://www.unhcr.org/refworld/docid/4d4a67f71a.html (Accessed 25 March 2011).

Velasco, C., Esprella, R., Flores, P. and Foronda, E. (2009) 'Dealing with innovation in response to market opportunities and poor farmers' needs: the case of the Bolivian Andean Platform promoting technical and commercial innovation in the native potato market chain in the Andean highlands in Bolivia', *15th Triennial Symposium of the International Society for Tropical Crops*, Lima, Peru, 2–6 November 2009, International Potato Center (CIP), Lima, Peru, pp. 65–72.

Webster, N. and Engberg-Pedersen, L. (eds) (2002) *In the Name of the Poor: Contesting Political Space for Poverty Reduction*, London and New York, Zed Books.

Further reading

Lawson, D., Hulme, D., Matin, I. and Moore, K. (2010) *What Works for the Poorest? Poverty Reduction Programmes for the World's Extreme Poor*, Rugby, Practical Action Publishing.

Prahalad, K.C. (2010) *The Fortune at the Bottom of the Pyramid: Eradicating Poverty through Profits*, New Jersey, Pearson Education.

Webster, N. and Engberg-Pedersen, L. (eds) (2002) *In the Name of the Poor: Contesting Political Space for Poverty Reduction*, London and New York, Zed Books.

International action to reduce poverty

William Brown and Joseph Hanlon

Introduction

Sugar sales fell by a third as the consumer boycott took hold, and 1.5 million people signed petitions. This may sound like many present-day campaigns, but it took place in Britain in 1792. The campaign was to end slavery, and the consumer boycott was of sugar produced on plantations in the West Indies. Shops began to advertize non-slave sugar and imports of sugar grown in India by 'freemen' jumped tenfold. The campaign was successful and contributed to Britain banning the slave trade in 1807.

This was probably the first time that ordinary citizens in an industrialized country carried out a major campaign to improve the status of people in what we now call the global South. Over the subsequent two centuries there have been many similar campaigns including those against atrocities in the Belgian Congo, the anti-colonial movements of the 1940s and 1950s, and the global campaign in the 1960s, 1970s and 1980s against apartheid in South Africa. In the 1990s and the first decade of the 21st century, this tradition continued, with mass movements aimed at reducing poverty in the South, first in the Jubilee Debt campaign of the 1990s then in the Make Poverty History campaign in 2004–05. You can no doubt think of many other examples. Despite the varied aims of the campaigns, what they share is a collective effort to improve the conditions of people in the global South and to change the policies of governments in the industrialized North.

These citizen campaigns were based on two assumptions: that people in richer countries have a responsibility toward people in poorer countries; and that the policies of governments in the North could affect people in poorer countries for good or for ill. For example, in the second half of the 20th century, governments of the North were increasingly active, providing aid to poorer countries and formulating international plans of action and declarations aimed at poverty reduction. Both non-governmental organization (NGO) and government action on poverty, across national boundaries, has been a very important example of *intentional* international development (see Chapter 1).

Therefore, the aim of this chapter is to look at international action on poverty:

- outline key elements and histories of international NGO and government action on poverty reduction
- analyze the relationships of power involved in international aid
- introduce the debate about the effectiveness of aid as a means of reducing poverty.

We examine two histories: that of citizen action in formal NGOs and that of governments' and international organizations' action on poverty via aid. We then detail the main features of aid, first by looking at its history, through which we trace how political actors in the North pursue aims relating to poverty in the South, addressing questions of power and agency. Second, we look at the contested areas of aid policy and the bargaining between governments of North and South around aid. Finally, we question whether aid is effective as a means of reducing poverty, and outline some of the positions in a debate that has run for many years.

12.1 NGOs and poverty in historical perspective

Early successful civil society campaigns targeted their own governments and others in the industrialized countries as well as conditions overseas. The anti-slavery movement, noted above, was aimed at forcing the British and other governments to outlaw slavery in their countries and colonies, and then to ban the trade in slaves. These were long campaigns. Twenty years passed before Britain banned the slave trade in 1807, and slavery continued in British colonies until 1928, when it was outlawed under pressure from the League of Nations, a forerunner of the United Nations (UN). The campaign against the actions of Belgian colonialists in the Congo at the end of the 19th century had over a million supporters across the industrialized world (Hochschild, 1999). All this was before most people had telegraphic communication, let alone high-speed broadband, and shows transnational civil society campaigns are not a product of the internet age.

The anti-apartheid campaign in the 1960s, 1970s and 1980s was aimed at isolating South Africa's white minority government. South Africa was expelled from many international organizations, and increasingly strong sanctions and embargoes were imposed. Again, global campaigning seemed to be successful. Nelson Mandela of the African National Congress was released after 27 years in prison and elected President in 1994 in the first non-racial election.

These were campaigns organized around notions of human rights and directed at changing the policies of governments. However, they form only one part of a wider category of development action centred on NGOs, and part of a broader trend of an increase in numbers, scale and activity of civil society groups. Some of this rise in civil society campaigning has been explicitly political in its focus, while some has had more charitable aims and purpose, including taking direct action to try to reduce poverty.

This trend goes back to Christian missionary activity from the 19th century and earlier, linking 'aiding the poor' to spreading the gospel and 'saving souls'.

Save the Children is regarded as one of the first modern NGOs. It was founded in 1919, just after World War I, to campaign against the blockade imposed on the defeated Germany. The new organization claimed that children were dying on the streets due to lack of food, and it mixed campaigning with direct assistance. Similarly, the Oxford Committee for Famine Relief, now Oxfam, was set up in 1942 during World War II, to campaign against the allied blockade of Nazi-occupied Greece, which was blocking food shipments.

Since then civil society movements have grown massively and some of them are referred to as NGOs. The term NGO is used very loosely, but refers to not-for-profit organizations that are legally independent of governments. They can include trade unions, business associations and faith groups, as well as those established specifically to respond to wars, natural disasters and other emergencies, and increasingly dealing with poverty in the global South. Those that act in more than one country are often called international NGOs (INGOs). It is difficult to even estimate a number but the Union for International Associations (UIA) estimated that while in the late 19th century there were under 200 INGOs, by 1990 there were around 6000, and by 2010 over 50 000 (UIA cited in World Bank, 2010). More than 13 000 NGOs and civil society organizations (CSOs) were registered with the UN by 2010 and there are 70 000 development NGOs listed in the 2011 Directory of Development Organizations (available online at: http://www.devdir.org/index. html).

The international development NGO industry has grown into a big 'business', with an annual income of at least US$40 billion per year in the early 21st century (Ridell, 2007, p. 259). NGOs like Oxfam, World Vision and Care had been country-based, but their national centres were pulled together in order to become major international organizations. In 2009, the biggest was probably World Vision International, with an income of US$2.6 billion, larger than the aid budget of small countries such as Belgium and Switzerland. Two other well-known development NGOs are Care USA (2009 budget of US $700 million, of which US$441 million came from governments) and Oxfam Great Britain (2010 income US$368 million, of which US$148 million came from governments and US$86 million from Oxfam shops and other trading (Oxfam, 2011)).

As these figures show, although development NGOs raise some money from the general public, they are increasingly dependent on government funds, and carry out contracts for governments, UN agencies and development banks. Such size and funding raises two questions. First, as many have become large international organizations, have they become more concerned about ensuring income and protecting tens of thousands of jobs, and thus less fleet of foot? Second, does financial backing reduce independence from government and hence limit the critical tone of campaign messages?

Campaigns on poverty in the 1990s and 2000s highlighted these divides. The Jubilee 2000 campaign, established in the late 1990s, called for the 'cancellation of the unpayable debt of the world's poorest countries by the year 2000' (Jubilee 2000 Coalition, 1999). In probably the first global petition, 24 million signatures were collected in 166 countries. For the first time, southern campaigns played a central role, as southern civil society began to challenge the view that the global South was responsible for its own poverty. The campaign was highly successful in three ways. First, it took what had been considered an obscure technical issue, which supposedly could only be understood by economists, and turned it into an easy-to-understand campaign. Second, it joined together local campaigns in the North and the global South. Third, it was big enough to put pressure on world leaders, who had to deal with the issue at several international meetings. By 2009, US $106 billion of poor country debt had been cancelled (Yanacopulos, 2009). But its success had put pressure on governments, and also created tension in the INGO movement, which felt that Jubilee 2000 took attention (and perhaps donations) away from established INGOs.

Figure 12.1   A Make Poverty History demonstration, Edinburgh, July 2005

The Make Poverty History campaign in 2004–5 (see Figure 12.1) picked up where Jubilee 2000 left off, and became one of the most notable development campaigns of the early 21st century. However, it was structured in a very different way. It targeted the 31st summit of the G8 (Canada, France, Germany, Italy, Japan, Russia, UK and the USA, with the EU as an observer) in Gleneagles, Scotland on 6 July 2005, arguing for further debt cancellation, increased aid, and fair trade. There were similar campaigns in most G8 countries, and they were successful in keeping aid, debt and developing country poverty on the global agenda. However, instead of being a free-standing campaign putting pressure on governments, this was largely organized by a coalition of British NGOs and enjoyed support from the UK government, with both Prime Minister Tony Blair and Chancellor of the Exchequer Gordon Brown giving tacit and at times explicit backing (Harrison, 2009).

This was controversial. NGOs normally hope to influence key decision makers, and have a critical edge. Some observers argued that the message from the Make Poverty History campaign shifted from an argument about justice, that is, that changes to aid, debt and trade policies were needed because the South had a *right* to such remedial action, to an argument based on humanitarianism, charity and simply increasing aid. These changes amounted to the North 'doing good' *for* the poor. Political support from government, the ostensible target of campaigns, is double-edged, providing evidence of impact but also the danger of co-option, that is, support for the campaign becomes useful 'political capital' for those in power (Harrison, 2009).

Activity 12.1

As NGOs become larger and more dependent on government funding, have they become more part of the establishment and lost their edge and critical tone? Note down some of the benefits and dangers for NGOs campaigning on poverty if they get financial and political backing from governments.

Spend no more than 5 minutes on this activity.

Discussion

You might identify several different benefits and dangers, for example one clear benefit for NGOs is increased political influence, while a clear danger is loss of autonomy.

12.2 Governments, aid and poverty

The idea of the North 'doing good' for the poor can be traced back to arguments in support of Empire and its 'civilizing' mission (see Chapter 3). The European powers and Japan established colonial empires in the 18th and 19th centuries to provide raw materials and markets for their economic development. Nevertheless, imperial powers also argued that they were improving the lives of their colonial subjects. Edmund Burke in his speech on the India Bill in 1785 said that Britain had become directly responsible for the welfare of the Indian peoples 'as a sacred trust'. This led to the concept of 'trusteeship' and the argument that the political, social and economic policies of the imperial powers would prepare indigenous peoples for self-government. Britain and France undertook sporadic efforts to 'intentionally' develop their colonies, for example through Britain's Colonial Development Act of 1929 (Havinden and Meredith, 1993; Chafer, 2002). In 1932 the British government sent Lord Moyne to Kenya, and he proposed the establishment of a 'Native Betterment Fund' that would receive half the hut and poll taxes paid by Kenyan 'natives', but it was not implemented because of settler resistance (Berman, 1990, p. 194). Attention on developing the colonies increased in response to the impact of the 1930s Great Depression in Europe, riots and strikes in the West Indies and a number of British African colonies in the late 1930s, and political pressures from both within colonies and international criticism arising through the League of Nations Mandates Commission.

After World War II there was also rising nationalist pressure within the colonies, and pressure from anti-colonialist powers like the USA and anti-colonial movements in Europe. In 1960, the UN General Assembly passed Resolution 1514 proclaiming:

> All peoples have the right to self-determination; by virtue of that right they freely determine their political status and freely pursue their economic, social and cultural development. Inadequacy of political, economic, social or educational preparedness should never serve as a pretext for delaying independence.
>
> *(UN General Assembly, 1960)*

As well as an insistence on independence, developing countries also made a forceful claim to a right to development and a continuing obligation on the part of the industrialized world to assist the new states in their development efforts (see Adams, 1997; Jackson, 1990). With the start of the Cold War, both capitalist and communist states began to vie for the allegiance of the colonies coming to independence (see Hanlon, 2011). This provided part of the context for a 1949 speech by US President Truman, seen by some as the foundation of contemporary development aid. In it he set out a new task for the industrialized world:

> We must embark on a bold new program for making the benefits of our scientific advances and industrial progress available for the improvement and growth of underdeveloped areas. More than half the people of the world are living in conditions approaching misery. Their food is inadequate. They are victims of disease. Their economic life is primitive and stagnant. Their poverty is a handicap and a threat both to them and to more prosperous areas. ... I believe that we should make available to peace-loving peoples the benefits of our store of technical knowledge in order to help them realize their aspirations for a better life. ... This should be a cooperative enterprise in which all nations work together through the United Nations and its

specialized agencies whenever practicable. It must be a worldwide effort for the achievement of peace, plenty, and freedom.

(Truman, 1949)

By the 1950s, development aid had become increasingly institutionalized as a part of 'the architecture of international relations' (Riddell, 2007), and the clamour to increase aid in order to reduce poverty was reiterated in numerous reports, commissions and UN resolutions.

Activity 12.2

Review the background on the history of aid given in Sections 12.1 and 12.2. Note down any factors that might detract from aid being used as a means to reduce poverty.

Spend no more than 5 minutes on this activity.

Discussion

Aid policy has been directed at generating growth and broad economic development, as well as at the more specific concern of alleviating poverty. Altruism, charity and obligation have also played a part in why industrialized countries give aid. But it has always been clear that other motives also exist – for example, to fend off nationalist anti-colonial pressures during the era of empire and particularly to support allies during the Cold War. Developing countries were able to exercise leverage on the industrialized world in the context of the Cold War by playing one superpower off against another. With the end of the Cold War, other motives have included political stability, ensuring access to mineral resources and other raw materials, and creating opportunities for foreign investment.

12.3 What is aid?

Aid has evolved a complex language and structure of its own, not least due to the numerous uses and forms of aid and the multiple actors involved in it. In one of the most comprehensive books on aid, *Does Foreign Aid Really Work?*, which we draw on extensively in this chapter, UK-based academic Roger Riddell distinguished various kinds of aid (2007, pp. 17–19). The generic term **'foreign aid'** includes all transfers, that is, money, goods and skills, military and civilian aid, and both grants and loans. Within this mix is Official Development Assistance (ODA). This is defined by the Development Assistance Committee (DAC) of the Organisation for Economic Co-operation and Development (OECD) as aid coming from states and other official agencies that is used with the objective of promoting the welfare of developing countries, and which is concessional (that is, contains a grant element of at least 25 per cent, even if the rest is a loan). Riddell also points to NGO-delivered aid and humanitarian and emergency aid. Of these three types of aid, ODA is the largest category followed by NGO-delivered aid (about 30 per cent of ODA in total size) and humanitarian and emergency aid (about 20 per cent of ODA). There is also some overlap between the types of aid, and the boundaries are blurred in that much NGO-aid comes from governments, as does much humanitarian aid.

Furthermore, much of the aid delivered by INGOs, or used for humanitarian and emergency work, comes from states' ODA budgets, although some is raised by INGOs from campaigns. INGOs both deliver aid for emergencies and engage in more long-term aid projects.

ODA forms a part of the overall range of foreign policy instruments that donor states possess. It is inherently political in this sense of being a part of the public policy of those states and an instrument that might be used for purposes other than development and poverty reduction. Figure 12.2 locates ODA within the broader spectrum of donor states' foreign policy instruments.

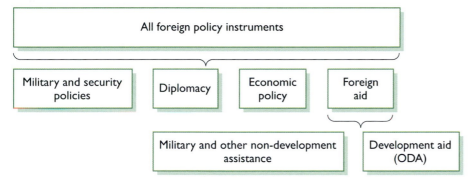

Figure 12.2   ODA and foreign policy instruments

Activity 12.3

To check your understanding of ODA, try to answer these questions:

1   What are the three criteria that define ODA and what problems might arise in trying to measure the amount of it?

2   Can you foresee any problems if ODA is seen *both* as a foreign policy instrument *and* a mechanism through which to reduce poverty?

Spend no more than 5 minutes on this activity.

Discussion

For question 1, problems of measurement may include the difficulty of dividing government from business investment. Aid for building state capacity, particularly in law enforcement and military fields, might be seen as developmental, or might be seen as military or political aid to a friendly state.

For question 2, governments often make development aid dependent on the recipient country taking certain political or economic actions. This was truer in the Cold War era, but 'aid' still sometimes goes to dictators or those who will vote the 'right way' in the UN.

The final complication is that there is a multiplicity of aid channels. Aid can go directly from one government to another (**bilateral aid**). It can be channelled through international institutions like the World Bank, other development banks or UN agencies (**multilateral aid**), or it can go through INGOs. Next is the issue of just where the aid goes. Donors can carry out projects themselves (often done by INGOs and faith groups) or directly support projects carried out by others. World Bank loans, for example, are sometimes to build specific infrastructure such as dams. Aid can also go to support programmes helping in economic policy reform, or sometimes directly to governments to support a ministry budget such as health or education (known as a sector-wide approach), or to particular areas within a ministry budget such as primary education or road building. When aid goes through a central government or ministry budget, donors normally negotiate the budget details and uses of the aid with recipients, a process that is dependent on the relative power held by each (discussed further in Section 12.5).

12.4 Aid and poverty reduction: historical overview

You had a brief introduction to the changing thinking on poverty within the UN system in Chapter 8 (Section 8.1). In this section, we develop the specific historical trajectory of aid and its architecture.

The first step toward aid as we now know it was the creation of the World Bank at the Bretton Woods conference in 1944, which also created its sister organization the International Monetary Fund (IMF). The bank's formal name, the International Bank for Reconstruction and Development, points to its initial focus: rebuilding war-torn Europe. However, it increasingly targeted economic development in the South and became the pre-eminent development institution both in terms of dispersal of funds and, together with the IMF, in its domination of policy agendas. Its constitution and funding mean that industrialized countries have had overwhelming influence on the bank's policy for much of its existence.

12.4.1 The early years

From the 1950s through to the 1970s, development finance was a combination of loans from commercial banks, governments and the World Bank, and slowly increasing amounts of ODA. Much of it was directed to infrastructure projects – roads, dams and some industrial development. Economic growth was the priority and the obstacles were seen as lack of capital for investment and imports combined with a lack of skills and technology. The rise of ODA reflected both bilateral aid stimulated in part by the USA and the Cold War (see Truman's speech) and the increasing attention being given to developing countries by the World Bank during the 1950s.

But questions began to be raised about the role of aid, and World Bank President Robert McNamara set up the Pearson Commission in 1969 – one, if not the first, of many international commissions set up to review the results of aid efforts (Riddell, 2007). Even then, the focus of the Commission was firmly on the need for developing countries to 'move forward into industrialisation and the technological age' (cited in Riddell, 2007, p. 31). This was an era of economic growth in the world economy. World GDP increased by 4.9 per cent (average per year) between 1950 and 1973, compared to 3.1 per cent between 1980 and 2000 (Maddison, 2001, p. 262). It was also the era of the rapidly growing 'Asian Tiger' economies such as Japan and South Korea, and there was a broad feeling that more money would lift poor countries out of poverty.

Under McNamara's leadership, the World Bank began to shift the focus of aid towards poorer people. World Bank programmes, and other donors such as the European Union (European Economic Community as it then was called), began funding what was called 'integrated rural development' (see also Chapter 8), with a mix of economic and agricultural development, as well as new attention on the social sectors of health and education.

Activity 12.4

Pause here and try to note any connections between these early debates over aid and wider debates over development that you encountered in Chapters 1 and 2.

Spend no more than 15 minutes on this activity.

Discussion

The move between trying to use external finance to stimulate general economic growth, and targeting such finance on lifting poor people out of poverty is one example of the wider tension within development between intentional efforts aimed at the development goal of economic growth and structural transformation of societies, and the sometimes competing goal of achieving specific targets relating to human welfare and well-being (see Chapter 1). This reflects the conflict between structuralist approaches to development (emphasizing large-scale investment, industrialization and economic growth) and people-centred development emphasizing targeted, and sometimes more small-scale, action on specific human welfare needs, including poverty reduction (see Chapter 2).

12.4.2 1975 and beyond: a political mood change

By the early-1970s, post World War II economic growth in the industrialized countries was slowing down. Industrialized countries were pushed into recession by the 1973 oil price rise, and this was exacerbated in the USA by the high cost of the Vietnam War. Banks had been accustomed to high profits in the boom era, but suddenly there was less in the North to invest in and lower potential profits, so banks increased risky lending to the global South. Much of the lending was reckless, as banks pushed countries to borrow money they did not need. Developing country debt jumped from US$161 million in 1975 to US$537 million in 1980 (Hanlon, 2009).

Then, as you have seen in Chapters 3 and 8, the end of the 1970s saw a political 'mood change', as three global transformations occurred. The first was an economic crisis in the industrialized countries, caused in part by the second, much more serious, oil price rise of 1979. This caused industrialized countries to suddenly cut lending to the South and dramatically push up interest rates to try to extract money from the South. This triggered a debt crisis because Southern governments could not repay the loans; later they borrowed simply to repay old debts, and by 1990 total debt had jumped to US $1330 million. Figure 12.3 shows how from 1984 to 1991, poor countries actually gave the North more in loan repayments than they received in new loans. The cash shortfall was made up with aid, and the desperate need for aid to repay loans meant that donors were able to impose harsher conditions. In the 1970s, poor countries were still able to borrow from banks if they rejected donor conditions; now this was no longer possible.

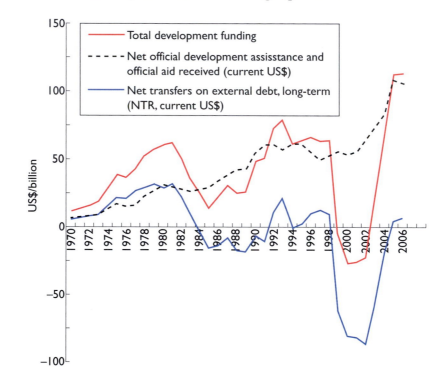

Figure 12.3   Development finance flows

The second transformation was directly linked to the first, and was a shift in economic thinking in the North. Elections in the UK and USA saw Margaret Thatcher become prime minister of Britain in 1979 and Ronald Reagan president of the USA in 1981. Both radically changed economic policies, taking a very hard line on reducing the role of the state and reducing restrictions on capital and free enterprise, an approach that later became known as 'neoliberalism' (see Chapter 1).

Third, Reagan intensified the Cold War, and developing countries were increasingly forced to choose sides, and take assistance from either East or West, but not both.

As Figure 12.3 shows, in the 1980s developing countries were suddenly receiving only half as much in external finance as they had received in the late 1970s. This change was so sudden that many developing countries found themselves in economic crises, and could not pay for basic imports. Through the 1970s, international aid policy had supported state-led development and a focus on economic growth based on inflows of development funding. In the 1980s, the Washington-based international financial institutions (IFIs), the IMF and the World Bank shifted to an emphasis on the market, reflecting both the new neoliberal ideology and the sharp fall in development finance. The IFIs said the developing countries had to go through a profound 'structural adjustment' to respond to the new reality. The IFIs promoted what came to be labelled the 'Washington Consensus' (Williamson, 1993), which included cut backs in state expenditure (including cuts to social sectors such as health and education), reducing the role of the state sector in the economy (for example, through privatization) and liberalization of trade, currency and finance. Structural Adjustment Programmes (SAPs) were built on existing IMF approaches (for instance, a very similar IMF package was adopted in the UK in 1976).

The Washington Consensus insisted that establishing the conditions for economic growth by restoring 'market fundamentals' was a prerequisite to reducing poverty, and that wealth generated by economic growth would 'trickle down' to the poorest. Structural adjustment was, and remains, extremely controversial. Its proponents argue that it was an inevitable and necessary response to the failure of state-led development, while its opponents pointed to the centrality of state involvement in the economic development in Europe in the late 19th century and the newly industrialized countries of Asia in the late 20th century, and also argued that a strong state role was needed to redress the malign heritage of colonialism. In any case, the effects of structural adjustment were severe: raising food prices, reducing public services, introducing charges for education and health and creating short-term economic contraction.

12.4.3 1990s–2000s: controversy and change

By demanding economic liberalization in return for aid, SAPs connected aid to political struggles over wider economic policies in a very direct way and prompted a series of debates that continue today. Here we will cover two of these: an 'internal versus external' debate, and a debate about the impact of programmes of economic liberalization on poor people.

In the first of these, disagreements raged between those who argued that the continuation of poverty and low economic growth was caused by features of the world economy that disadvantaged the South, such as unfair trade or the economic policies imposed from outside, and those who argued that the primary problems were the policies and governance structures within countries of the South. The former 'external' position has been a mainstay of structuralist critiques of development for some time (see Chapter 2) but was taken further by the UN Development Programme UNDP) in its 1999 *Human Development Report*. That report claimed 60 countries had become poorer since 1980 – the period of the Washington Consensus. The report argued that:

> Today's globalization is being driven by market expansion – opening national borders to trade ... [but] when the market goes too far in dominating social and political outcomes, the opportunities and rewards of globalization spread unequally and inequitably – concentrating power and

wealth in a select group of people, nations and corporations, marginalizing the others.

(UNDP, 1999, p. 2)

The latter, 'internal' position was taken by the World Bank, the IMF and many donor countries in the 1980s and 1990s; it saw the cause of poverty as lying within poor countries, in poor governance, greedy elites and poorly run economies. Change therefore needed to be imposed from the outside and donors insisted on policy changes as well as far-reaching changes to how the governments of recipient countries were run in return for aid. As one World Bank researcher put it in 1990: 'the governance of African states has to be *systematically rebuilt* from the bottom up' (Landell-Mills cited in Williams and Young, 1994). The external or structuralist approach, which saw poverty as rooted in colonialism and historic exploitation, saw the Washington Consensus policies as a new colonialism, opening up developing countries to northern-controlled transnational companies.

The second area of debate was closely linked and focused on the impact on poverty of the economic and political reforms promoted by donors. Even by the end of the 1980s, a rising chorus of aid analysts and NGOs were denouncing the effect of cut backs in state expenditure on the poor (for example, Cornia et al., 1987). Indeed, under pressure from NGOs and recipient governments, and with only limited success in restoring growth to countries adopting adjustment measures, the Washington institutions and other donors began to create additional funding programmes to accompany SAPs in order to alleviate the 'social dimensions of adjustment'. As noted in Chapter 8, the World Bank had begun to give greater emphasis to poverty reduction, albeit focused on market-based solutions (World Bank, 1990). Nevertheless, a shift had begun and increasingly donors and their critics began to realize that even 'making markets work' might also entail 'making the state work'. With the fall of the Berlin Wall, many western donor states began to insist on political reforms, including the holding of elections, a commitment to 'good government' and programmes to tackle developing country corruption. In a landmark World Development Report in 1997 *The State in a Changing World*, the World Bank (1997) also appeared to step back from some of the more strident anti-state rhetoric of the 1980s.

12.4.4 New consensus? The Millennium Development Goals

The mid-1990s were a period of substantial flux in aid policy. Aid levels were falling (see Figure 12.3) which caused concern in the aid industry; during a seven-year period poor countries actually gave more money to rich countries in debt repayments than they received in new loans and aid. Meanwhile critiques of structural adjustment's failure to reduce poverty were gaining wider acceptance. With a new World Bank President (James Wolfensohn) and with centre-left governments in power in the USA and UK, the insistence on market-based reforms was supplemented with a shift to refocusing on poverty reduction as the main purpose of aid policy.

The ten-year period 1995–2005 involved both conflict and compromise within the aid industry, as donors and the IFIs tried to keep a market-led, neoliberal approach with the new focus on poverty that required reversing at least some of the cuts of the state and social spending. Within the World Bank, divisions began to appear between those who held to the argument that liberalization was working and those who claimed the bank's policies were failing to reduce poverty. Among the latter was Joseph Stiglitz, Senior Vice President and Chief Economist of the World Bank, who was forced to resign because he continually pointed out that the huge falls in poverty were only taking place in China and not in those countries which followed World Bank policies.

The World Bank re-emphasized targeted aid to the poorest as its over-riding mission for the first time since McNamara's Presidency of the Bank, and its 2000 World Development Report was called *Attacking Poverty* (World Bank, 2000). Even the IMF, until the late 1990s reluctant to depart from its bedrock of economic orthodoxy, renamed its structural adjustment fund as the Poverty Reduction and Growth Facility (PRGF) in 1999, arguing poverty reduction was now the 'linchpin of its lending to low income countries' (IMF, 2009).

Acting in concert, the World Bank and the IMF then made Poverty Reduction Strategy Papers (PRSPs) the focus of both debt relief programmes (writing off debt owed to donors, including the Washington institutions themselves) and concessional lending. In principle, PRSPs were to be formulated by recipient governments in consultation with a range of domestic social interest groups and 'stakeholders' and with external donors. In place of the often antagonistic bargaining over adjustment conditionality, the image donors – and many recipients – now presented was of a new partnership for development. The World Bank, and donors such as the UK, went as far as to declare that 'conditionality doesn't work' (DFID, 2005). Such rethinking lay behind the 2005 *Paris Declaration on Aid Effectiveness*, signed by over 100 donor agencies and recipient governments, and which committed donors to helping recipient countries to 'exercise effective leadership over their development policies' (OECD, 2005).

In parallel with this, and partly pushing it forward, were the Millennium Development Goals (MDGs). The DAC wanted to promote an increase in aid, and in 1996 took six UN summit targets as the International Development Goals (IDGs). Their statement says 'those of us in the industrialised countries have a strong moral imperative to respond to the extreme poverty and human suffering that still affects more than one billion people' (OECD, 1996). This was taken up by the new Secretary General of the UN, Kofi Annan. The UN adopted a Millennium Declaration in 2000 and the IDGs were transformed into the MDGs in 2002. Sakiko Fukuda-Parr, who was Director of the UNDP Human Development Report Office, and later became Professor of International Affairs at the New School, New York, has written extensively about how the MDGs were turned into an international norm, which reversed the decline in aid. She stressed that the MDGs focused 'on people and the ends of development – something around which a common vision could be established – rather than the means to get there, which was fiercely contested' (Fukuda-Parr, 2012). However, the MDGs were written not at a UN conference, but by a small team from the UNDP, the World Bank and the OECD, with relatively little input from developing countries (see also Hulme and Scott, 2010, p. 66). Fukuda-Parr stresses that in order to reach consensus, the MDGs ignored human rights, empowerment, the centrality of growth and the need for redistribution and the reduction of inequality.

The MDGs were intended to influence the content of PRSPs; however, the World Bank and IMF were lukewarm in their support and sought to control national development and poverty reduction plans (Dijkstra, 2005; Stewart and Wang, 2004, cited in Hulme and Scott, 2010). Although MDG 1 was about poverty reduction and job creation, the stress by donors was on MDGs 2 to 6, about children, gender, education and health. Fukuda-Parr, in a study of 22 developing country PRSPs, found that almost all 'focus on economic liberalization and social investments. ... Of the 60 MDG indicators, those that received virtually no mentions were those most important for ensuring that growth is inclusive and pro-poor' (Fukuda-Parr, 2008). She also looked at donor documents, and found they emphasized poverty, but not empowerment, social integration, jobs, equality or pro-poor growth. Thus 'the post 2000 architecture of international development has changed in terms of instruments and narratives, but not in content' (Fukuda-Parr and Hulme, 2009).

For their part, by the start of the 21st century many African governments had begun to make much more forthright rhetorical commitments to both political and economic liberalization. A key signal of this change was the launch in 2001 of the New Economic Partnership for African Development (NEPAD), led by Thabo Mbeki of South Africa and Olusegun Obasanjo of Nigeria. This committed African governments, among other things, to democracy and good political, economic and corporate governance, and to forging a new, more equal relationship with donors, in return for which they hoped to attract increased aid and foreign investment.

This new 'deal' won its seal of approval at the 2005 Gleneagles meeting of the G8 group of largest economies where, led by Britain, donors pledged to double ODA, write off debt and liberalize trade in return for commitments from the poorest countries to stay true to the PRSP process. Nevertheless, serious doubts continued about either side living up to its promises.

At the level of relations between donors and recipient governments, the first decade of the 21st century seemed to present a picture of greater consensus around poverty reduction, while the theoretical debates in development policy were converging on what Brett calls a 'new synthesis in the mainstream development community' (Brett, 2009, p. xix). The MDGs received a level of continued and sustained attention, unusual for UN development declarations (Hulme and Scott, 2010, p. 6), and they provided a useful reference point for NGOs who used MDG targets to 'grab media attention' in their campaigns. In the words of one review, 'The MDGs, though flawed, can potentially be seen as a significant step towards the emergence of an international social norm that sees extreme poverty as morally unacceptable in an affluent world' (ibid, p. 3).

Activity 12.5

To check your understanding, try to answer the following questions:

1   Based on this description, how would you characterize aid policies at the end of the 2000s, using the categories of neoliberalism, structuralism and interventionism (see Chapter 8, Activity 8.4).

2   How might the rise of China, discussed in Chapter 3, have affected aid policies?

Spend no more than 15 minutes on this activity.

Discussion

In answer to question 1, the dominant approach reflected interventionist ideas in so far as aid agencies recognized a key role for the state and governance in reducing poverty. However, a strong neoliberal current remained in the emphasis on market solutions and on economic liberalization.

In answer to question 2, the key new dimension was the rise of donors outside of the OECD DAC group. As you have seen in Chapters 3 and 6, China provides an alternative source of finance for some poor countries, representing a challenge to the ability of western donors to enforce their views of how poverty reduction might be achieved.

12.5 Aid power and agency

In this section we ask whether the practice of aid supports or undermines the image of consensus presented at international summits. We confine our discussion to bilateral and multilateral ODA rather than aid delivered through NGOs.

As you have seen, taken at face value, by the end of the 2000s, there was general agreement and a concerted international effort around aid consisting of:

- a focus on poverty reduction (codified in the MDGs and PRSP process)

- a relationship based on partnership (in which donors supplied finance to support 'recipient-owned' poverty reduction strategies)

- an agreement about the broad institutional parameters within which poverty reduction and economic growth would take place, involving a limited but effective state and the expansion of markets.

However, ODA most often is delivered by one government or a multilateral institution like the World Bank or the EU to a recipient government. Therefore, there still has to be a formal process of stipulating what will be paid, when, in what form and for what purposes. Even if there is broad agreement between donor and recipient, there will be negotiation over which roads are built, which economic policies are followed, if priority is to be given to primary or secondary education, etc.

We're going to begin assessing this process of negotiation by using some simple diagrams, then adding some more complexity as we go on. We proceed in three steps: first, a very simple view of consensus around aid; second, a slightly more complicated view of negotiations over aid; and, finally, a more expanded discussion of the factors that influence these negotiations. The first two steps are illustrated by the use of Figures 12.4 and 12.5. This kind of approach, using fairly abstract representations, is found in a number of disciplines including economics and in international relations. As you will see, the rather sanguine image of an aid partnership begins to look increasingly problematic as we move through these three steps.

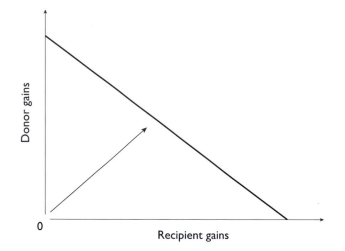

Figure 12.4   Aid negotiations as consensus

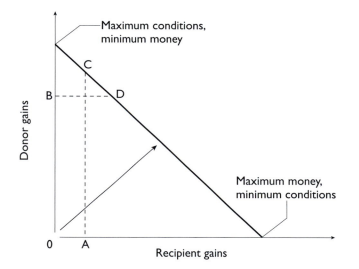

Figure 12.5   Aid negotiations as bargaining

For our first step, in Figure 12.4, we start with the idea that by providing aid, both parties – a donor and a recipient country – gain something and broadly agree on these gains. Both see a need for external finance to be provided to the recipient country and both believe that this, coupled with changes internal to the recipient country (reforms to governance and management of national budgets for health and education systems, say), will help to reduce poverty.

They may also agree on changes to macroeconomic policy to increase growth through, say, liberalization.

In Figure 12.4, the horizontal axis represents the recipient's gains – what the recipient wants to get from the aid negotiation. The vertical axis represents the donor's gains – what *it* wants to get from the aid negotiation. The diagonal line represents the maximum gains that both parties, added together, can get. The letter O represents the Origin, the point at which negotiation begins. Where both parties are essentially in agreement about the disbursal of aid and the reforms the recipient will take, the aid agreement is a straightforward matter of coordination, moving the parties from the origin (represented by the arrow) out towards the diagonal line delivering mutual gains to both sides. As you know from Chapter 3, situations of cooperation where there are net gains like these are known as positive-sum interactions. Here aid is a form of development cooperation delivering things that both sides want to see – finance, reform and poverty reduction. Although very simplified, the image we are given from the rhetoric about aid is not so far from this picture.

In step 2 we take off the rose-tinted spectacles. As you've seen already, despite contemporary rhetoric around 'partnership', the relationship between donors and recipients has often been more conflictual than Figure 12.4 suggests. Aid agreements have always contained a mix of commitments from recipients (poverty reduction targets, governance changes, macroeconomic reforms, and so on) and from donors (specified amounts of money delivered according to an agreed timetable). Very often donors have sought to get recipients to do more reform in exchange for an amount of aid, and recipients seek to get more aid in return for fewer conditions. Rather than complete consensus around an aid deal, there is a process of bargaining where each side is exchanging something for something else it wants. These processes of bargaining may still result in agreements, and when they do they are still genuine examples of international cooperation because it is voluntary, either party could walk away, and both get, or believe they will get, some benefit. However, it is a form of cooperation within which there is a struggle over the balance of gains. In this, each party tries to exert its power to achieve the ends it wants. If you look at Figure 12.4 again, the gains (represented by the mid-point on the diagonal line) are more or less equally shared. However, more often things aren't so balanced. Although both parties get something from the aid deal – otherwise they would not agree to it – the balance of gains may be much less equal.

In Figure 12.5 we have made two main changes: we've introduced a recognition that the gains each party seeks to get from an aid deal are different, and we've added a recognition that each party has a minimum acceptable level of gains from a deal – the point at which it would not agree to a deal.

Let's work through that diagram. First, in contrast to Figure 12.4, we recognise that donors and recipients are pulling in somewhat different directions. 'Recipient gains' – what the recipient wants to achieve, or what are sometimes called **state preferences** – are for increasing amounts of inward finance in the form of aid. The recipient seeks to minimize the policy changes it has to make in return for aid. The donor on the other hand wants to see a range of policy changes in return for a minimum amount of aid. The straight diagonal line represents, as with Figure 12.4, the sum total of gains of both parties added together. Different points along that line signal different divisions of the gains. At the extreme right of the line, where it touches the horizontal axis, the recipient is getting a maximum amount of money for minimum conditions. At the extreme left, where it touches the vertical axis, the donor is imposing the maximum conditions for minimum aid.

How do we know where agreement will be reached? A key to understanding a bargaining situation like this is to ask 'what is the minimum each party would find acceptable?' This is defined as its **fallback position** – the gains that a party can get without an agreement and the point where it would walk away from the deal. For our recipient country it might be a minimum level of aid; for a donor it might be key policy changes it wants to see.

In Figure 12.5 the fallback position of the recipient is given by the letter A – it will not agree to any deal that gives it less aid than that (that is, anywhere to the left of that point on the horizontal axis). For the donor, its fallback position is given by the letter B – it will not agree to any deal that gives it fewer conditions, policy changes and reforms, etc., than that (that is, anywhere below that point on the vertical axis). If we extend these points via the dotted lines, onto the diagonal line it gives us points C, corresponding to the recipient's fallback position, and D, corresponding to the donor's fallback position. We know the recipient isn't going to agree to anything above and to the left of C, and the donor to anything below and to the right of D. An agreement will therefore have to lie somewhere on the line between C and D for it to be acceptable to both parties.

Activity 12.6

To check your understanding of Figure 12.5, study the diagram and try to explain in your own words what it is showing.

If you need to, compare your discussion of the figure with the one given above.

Spend no more than 5 minutes on this activity.

Discussion

As is suggested by the diagram, such a deal (that is, between points C and D on Figure 12.5) would be closer to the donor's interests than the recipient's – it is getting a lot of reform for not much money. The recipient's fallback position in this scenario is rather weak – it would accept even a fairly small amount of aid therefore it cannot credibly threaten to walk away and has to accept much of the donor's terms.

Many instances, particularly in the structural adjustment era, were akin to a situation like this. Recipients were in a weak position: they were in situations of economic crisis, were desperate for aid and had no one to turn to other than the World Bank and the IMF. Donors came to hold a very strong position; they grouped together and coordinated their actions among themselves.

Bilateral donors sometimes cut off aid to countries that didn't agree to IMF and World Bank deals, weakening developing countries' fallback positions.

To begin step three, and expand the background to this kind of negotiating position, look at Activity 12.7.

Activity 12.7

To think about how power in aid relationships changes, try to identify the factors that might strengthen a recipient country's bargaining position. If it helps, take the role of a government representative and consider the options open to you when facing a donor like the World Bank. Then, consider what factors might affect the donor's power.

Spend no more than 5 minutes on this activity.

Discussion

Once you start unpacking the factors that lie behind these simple diagrammatic representations you'll see that a complex of political factors influence the bargains around aid. An indicative, but far from exhaustive list, would include for recipients:

- the overall extent of aid dependency, which includes how much of a country's GDP, or the government's budget, is reliant on aid
- the existence or not of economic crisis, which in turn will affect the urgency with which recipients will seek donor funding
- the availability of other funding streams (other official donors, remittances, philanthropic donations, inward investment)
- the capacity of the government to negotiate effectively and articulate a strong idea of the national interest
- the strength of the government vis-à-vis domestic opposition and support.

For donors, the reverse of these apply, but in addition:

- the extent to which the donors coordinate action among themselves and use their advantages in terms of technical, research and policy resources, person-power and an ability to claim 'we know best'
- the wider strategic context – whether donors have to provide funding to support allies regardless of the content of the aid deal
- the overall amount of ODA on offer and whether there is pressure within donor organizations to increase aid spending.

One result of this analysis is to recognize that given these multiple influences on the power of states in aid negotiations, the particular circumstances of different countries and donors matters a great deal. A thorough study of aid negotiations (Whitfield, 2009) showed just how varied these relationships were, even among African countries that on some measures were quite similar. While donors were able to exert, for a time at least, coercive power over states such as Zambia and Tanzania, others were more able to resist. In Whitfield's study both Rwanda and Ethiopia were shown to be less susceptible to donor pressure as both had political and strategic importance to Western states outside of the aid relationship. The rise of inward financing from China and India also suggested, for the limited number of countries who were affected, a major shift in their bargaining position (as discussed in Chapter 6).

Despite the pressure that donors undoubtedly have been able to apply by threatening to withdraw aid, their power to achieve their desired outcomes, far-reaching economic and political reform, was often less than it appeared on first glance. Indeed, donors increasingly became aware that aid deals were not the end of the story. *Implementation* of agreements often left political actors in recipient states considerable scope to evade and backslide on promises. As the UK's DFID 2005 review of conditionality concluded: 'Put simply, conditionality which attempts to "buy" reform from an unwilling partner has rarely worked' (DFID, 2005, p. 10). The shift in aid policies from the late 1990s, towards an emphasis on fulfilment of PRSPs *before* aid was released, and on country ownership of reform packages, was in part recognition of these limits. However, throughout the period since, there remained considerable divergence between donors and recipients over the appropriate policies that needed to be implemented.

By the end of the first decade of the 21st century, the aid for poverty reduction picture was therefore mixed. The much-vaunted post-Gleneagles increases in aid were being delivered in a patchy way. Some, such as the UK, the USA and Japan were thought to be on the way to meeting their commitments while others such as France and Italy were far behind (Africa Progress Panel, 2009). The financial crisis and ensuing recession of 2007–09 put even more pressure on aid budgets. Progress on meeting the MDGs was also slow with many arguing that some key targets would be missed (Hulme and Scott, 2010). This redoubled debates about the use of aid as a tool for poverty reduction, the issue we discuss in Section 12.6.

12.6 Can aid end poverty?

We noted in Section 12.2 how aid had become a central feature of international relations in the wake of independence of many Southern countries. Indeed, in 1970 the UN General Assembly declared that:

> While a part of the world lives in great comfort and even affluence, much of the larger part suffers from abject poverty, and in fact the disparity is continuing to widen … each economically advanced country will progressively increase its official development assistance to the developing countries and will exert its best efforts to reach a minimum net amount of 0.7 per cent of its gross national product at market prices by the middle of the [1970s].

(UN General Assembly, 1970)

The 0.7 per cent figure remains a widely accepted, but very rarely met, global target. In the 40 years after that pledge, donors gave US$2 trillion to developing countries. Did it work? As you have seen in Chapter 8, the global record on reducing poverty is mixed. Further, as Table 12.1 shows, the reduction since the 1980s has been very uneven. Only in China has the absolute number of people in poverty fallen significantly, from 835 million to 208 million. Of particular note, because it was the focus of so much aid effort after 1980, is sub-Saharan Africa where the proportion of the population in poverty remained stubbornly around 50 per cent. We know from Chapter 8 that there are many issues around the measurement of poverty. Nevertheless, in Africa at least, there is a case to answer that aid had not delivered the poverty reduction gains that were hoped for. In the period of the table (1981–2005) sub-Saharan Africa received US$244 billion in aid, while China received US$33 billion, and India US$22 billion. So aid does not seem to be correlated with poverty reduction. Why not?

Table 12.1 How many people are poor?
World Bank estimate of people earning less than US$1.25 per day

	Total number (millions)			Percentage of population in poverty (%)		
	1981	2005	Change	1981	2005	Change
China	835	208	↓↓	84	16	↓↓
India	421	456	↗	60	42	↘
Other Asia and Pacific	371	266	↘			
Sub-Saharan Africa	214	391	↑	54	51	→
Latin America and Caribbean	42	46	→	12	8	↘
Total	1896	1377	↓	52	25	↓
Total, excluding China	1061	1165	↗			

(Source: adapted from Chen and Ravallion, 2008)

Much of the controversy over changing aid policy, surveyed in Section 12.4, was animated by questions of whether aid 'works', though over the years the focus of debate has shifted to whether aid helps economic growth, whether it improves governance, whether it can promote trade or industrialization, and so on. However, in the 21st century the rising prominence of poverty reduction as the overarching goal for aid policy, and the commitments of some industrialized countries to redouble their aid efforts, gave the debate a new focus.

Activity 12.8

You encountered three significant contributions to the aid and poverty debate in Chapter 8 in the ideas of Sachs (2005), Easterly (2006) and Collier (2007). Pause here and look again at the ideas of these three writers (see Chapter 8, Section 8.2). Try to identify where each of them stand on the following questions:

* Will poverty be reduced through unintentional processes of development or intentional development actions? (see Chapter 1 for a description of these terms)
* Can aid help to reduce poverty?

Spend no more than 15 minutes on this activity.

Discussion

In Sachs' view, poverty in many countries was reduced through processes of 'unintentional development', in the sense that broad processes of technological change helped to increase growth and raise living standards. However, in terms of the aid debate he is a strong advocate of its role as a mode of intentional development, reducing poverty, particularly through funding technological change.

Easterly sits on the other side of the debate, emphasizing unintentional development processes, particularly through the actions of markets as the chief mechanism through which to stimulate growth, and deeply sceptical of the 'top-down' plans of donors. Easterly and Sachs disagree fundamentally on the relationship between aid and poor governance, with Sachs arguing that poor governance is a result of poverty while Easterly (in accord with many donors) sees poor governance as a major cause of continued poverty. Nevertheless, even Easterly recognized that aid has contributed to improvements in some of the specific indicators of development, such as life expectancy and infant mortality.

Finally, Collier sits somewhere between these two viewpoints. Collier sees unintentional processes of development in the form of trade, capital flows and migration as being key to growth and to poverty reduction. He shares the view that markets are key to poverty reduction. Nevertheless, in line with interventionist views of development, he argues that intentional development actions, by both donors and recipients, are needed for this potential to be realised. Aid plays a role, for Collier, in helping to stimulate necessary changes (for instance, to governance) and supporting efforts of poor countries to escape 'poverty traps'. However, significant questions were also raised about Collier's work, with one World Bank study questioning the reliability of the data upon which his work, and the bank's own policy recommendations, rested (Banerjee et al., 2006, pp. 52–53).

Between 2006 and 2010 others joined the debate. Supporting some of Easterly's arguments, the Zambian-born Dambisa Moyo, who worked at Goldman Sachs and the World Bank, argued that aid fosters dependency, encourages corruption and perpetuates poor governance and poverty (Moyo, 2009). She argued that African governments should be forced to borrow from banks, which would impose discipline on borrowing countries.

Riddell's 2007 study tried to make some overall sense of the debate over the efficacy of aid. He claimed there is plenty of evidence of ODA 'contributing positively' to growth and poverty reduction; the problem is that 'aid works, but not nearly as well as it could' (Riddell, 2007, p. 381). He identified a number of problems, not least those caused by the sheer number of competing donors who remain in almost total control of their aid, and that because of political, strategic and commercial interests they are not prepared to give up that control. Thus 'the aid which is provided is not allocated in any systematic, rational or efficient way to those who need it most' (ibid, p. 386).

Riddell also pointed out that funding linked to the MDGs and to recurrent costs of health and education ministries actually increases aid dependence, because it reduces funds going to long-term development. Instead, development should be accelerated by using more aid money to develop the productive capacities of poor countries. In contrast to the opponents of aid, Riddell found that aid saves lives and promotes development, but he called for fundamental change in an aid industry. 'Many poor countries,' he argued, 'have been ill-served by the rigidity and narrowness of much of the macro-level policy advice [from the IFIs] which prove inadequate to address their complex, structural and long-term problems' (ibid, p. 254). In contrast to Collier, he claimed that 'the lack of effectiveness of aid at the national level has been due, in part, to the deficiencies of the policy advice given by donors' (ibid, p. 364).

12.6.1 Aid through direct cash transfers

One option suggested by Riddell is to give more aid through direct cash transfers (see Figure 12.6) – that is, giving money directly to poor people through child benefit, non-contributory pensions and family grants. We conclude by considering this idea.

Figure 12.6 Cash transfer scheme – Maria Nilza, 36, and mother of four, shows her 'Bolsa Familia' social plan card in Serra Azul, north of the state of Minas Gerais in Brazil (Source: http://www.guardian.co.uk/global-development/poverty-matters/2010/nov/19/brazil-cash-transfer-scheme)

The book *Just Give Money to the Poor: the Development Revolution from the Global South*, by Hanlon et al. (2010), found that 45 countries in the global South were giving cash transfers to 110 million families, and largely funding these through tax or other domestic revenues, such as mineral sales. The lead was taken in the late 1990s by three middle-income countries: South Africa (with a pension and child benefit), Brazil (with a pension and family grant) and Mexico (with a family grant). Several aspects seem key to cash transfers. First, they are rights-based: anyone who meets the criteria has the right to the grant. Second, they do not target the poorest of the poor, but are broad-based; sometimes there is a condition, particularly school attendance, but it is a condition that poor parents usually want to fulfil. Third, cash transfers are long term; even where grants are means tested, qualifications are usually only checked again after two or three years. This means that poor people are assured of grants and can plan on them. This, in turn, encourages investment, for example taking the risk of buying better seed instead of saving the money, knowing that if the crop fails there will at least be a grant next year. Cash transfers thus provide immediate extra income to the poor, but they also start a positive economic spiral, both because the money is spent locally, generating new jobs and increasing agricultural production, and because many poor people invest some of the money in an attempt to increase their income.

Summary and looking forward

International action to defend people in the global South and promote development is not new. Citizen actions included anti-slavery campaigns of the late 18th century, while NGOs, government and multilateral development aid began in the first half of the 20th century. But aid is not simply altruistic. It is linked to donor foreign policy and also to internal or external explanations of poverty, for example the question of whether the poor are to be blamed for their poverty because of their 'poor' governance, or are the rich to be blamed because of past colonialism, present imperialism and an unfair global economic system? Questions over the balance between leaving space for a free market to function, and directly intervening to promote development, as well as the power balance between the rich and poor, donors and recipients, continue to be debated.

References

Adams, N. (1997) *Worlds Apart: The North-South Divide and the International System*, London, Zed Books.

Africa Progress Panel (2009) 'An agenda for progress at a time of global crisis: a call for African leadership', *Annual Report of the African Progress Panel*, Geneva, Africa Progress Panel, [online], http://www.africaprogresspanel.org/EN/publications/AnnualReport2009/20090610-APP2009_Annual_Report_EN.pdf (Accessed 28 January 2010).

Banerjee, A., Deaton, A., Lustig, N. and Rogoff, K. (2006) *An Evaluation of World Bank Research, 1998–2005*. Washington, World Bank [online], http://siteresources.worldbank.org/DEC/Resources/84797-1109362238001/726454-1164121166494/RESEARCH-EVALUATION-2006-Main-Report.pdf (Accessed 24 August 2011).

Berman, B. (1990) *Control and Crisis in Colonial Kenya: The Dialectic of Domination*, London, James Currey.

Brett, E.A. (2009) *Reconstructing Development Theory: International Inequality, Institutional Reform and Social Emancipation*, Basingstoke, Palgrave Macmillan.

Chafer, T. (2002) *The End of Empire in French West Africa: France's successful decolonisation?*, Oxford, Berg.

Chen, S. and Ravallion, M. (2008) 'The developing world is poorer than we thought, but no less successful in the fight against poverty', *World Bank Policy Research Working Paper 4703*, Tables 6 and 7, pp. 42, 44 [online], http://www-wds.worldbank.org/external/default/WDSContentServer/IW3P/IB/2010/01/21/000158349_20100121133109/Rendered/PDF/WPS4703.pdf (Accessed 25 August 2010).

Collier, P. (2007) *The Bottom Billion: Why the Poorest Countries are Failing and What Can Be Done About It*, Oxford, Oxford University Press.

Cornia, G.A., Jolly, R. and Stewart, F. (1987) *Adjustment with a Human Face: Protecting the Vulnerable and Promoting Growth*, Vol. I, Oxford, Oxford University Press.

Department for International Development (DFID) (2005) 'Partnerships for poverty reduction: rethinking conditionality', *UK Policy Paper*, March, London, [online], http://collections.europarchive.org/tna/20100423085705/http://dfid.gov.uk/Documents/publications/conditionality.pdf (Accessed 18 March 2011).

Dijkstra, G. (2005), 'The PRSP approach and the illusion of improved aid effectiveness: lessons from Bolivia, Honduras and Nicaragua', *Development Policy Review*, vol. 23, no. 4, pp. 443–464.

Easterly, W. (2006) *The White Man's Burden: Why the West's Efforts to Aid the Rest Have Done So Much Ill and So Little Good,* Oxford, Oxford University Press.

Fukuda-Parr, S. (2008) 'Are the MDGs priority in development strategies and aid programmes? Only few are!', *Working Paper 48*, Brasilia, International Poverty Centre, United Nations Development Programme.

Fukuda-Parr, S. (2012) *Millennium Development Goals (MDGs): For a People Centered Development Agenda?*, London, Routledge (in press April 2012).

Fukuda-Parr, S. and Hulme, D. (2009) 'International norm dynamics and "the end of poverty": understanding the Millennium Development Goals (MDGs)', *BWPI Working Paper 96*, June 2009, Manchester, Manchester University Brooks World Poverty Institute.

Hanlon, J. (2009) 'Debt and development' in Haslam, P., Schafer, J. and Beaudet, P. (eds) *Introduction to International Development*, Don Mills, Ontario, Oxford University Press.

Hanlon, J. (2011) [book 2 chapter 1]

Hanlon, J., Barrientos, A. and Hulme, D. (2010) *Just Give Money to the Poor: The Development Revolution from the Global South*, Sterling, VA, Kumarian Press.

Harrison, G. (2009) 'The Africanization of poverty: a retrospective on "Make poverty history"', *African Affairs*, vol. 109, no. 436, pp. 391–408.

Havendin, M. and Meredith, D. (1993) *Colonialism and Development: Britain and its Tropical Colonies, 1850–1960*. London, Routledge.

Hochschild, A. (1999) *King Leopold's Ghost: A Story of Greed, Terror and Heroism in Colonial Africa*, Basingstoke, Macmillan.

Hulme, D. and Scott, J. (2010) 'The political economy of the MDGs: retrospect and prospect for the world's biggest promise', *Brooks World Policy Institute Working Paper*, no.110, Manchester.

International Monetary Fund (IMF) (2009) 'The Poverty Reduction and Growth Facility', *Factsheet* [online], www.imf.org/external/np/exr/facts/pdf/prgf.pdf (Accessed 18 March 2011).

Jackson, R.H. (1990) *Quasi-States: Sovereignty, International Relations and the Third World*, Cambridge, Cambridge University Press.

Jubilee 2000 Coalition (1999) *Breaking the Chains: All You Need for the Final Push*, London, Jubilee 2000 Coalition.

Kiely, R. (2007) *The New Political Economy of Development*, Basingstoke and New York, Palgrave Macmillan.

Maddison, A. (2001) *The World Economy: A Millennial Perspective*, Paris, OECD.

Moyo, D. (2009) *Dead Aid: Why Aid is Not Working and How There is a Better Way For Africa*, New York, Farrar Straus Giroux.

Organization of Economic Cooperation and Development (OECD) (1996) *Shaping the 21st Century: The Contribution of Development Co-operation*, Paris: OECD [online], http://www.oecd.org/dataoecd/23/35/2508761.pdf (Accessed 20 September 2011).

Organization of Economic Cooperation and Development (OECD) (2005) *Paris Declaration on Aid Effectiveness*, Paris, OECD.

Oxfam (2011) *Oxfam Annual Report and Accounts 2010–11*, Oxford, Oxfam.

Riddell, R. (2007) *Does Foreign Aid Really Work?*, Oxford, Oxford University Press.

Sachs, J. (2005) *The End of Poverty: How We Can Make It Happen in Our Lifetime*, London, Penguin.

Stewart, F. and Wang, M. (2004), *Report on the Evaluation of Poverty Reduction Strategy Papers (PRSPs) and the Poverty Reduction and Growth Facility (PRGF)* Washington DC, IMF.

Truman, H.S. (1949) *Inaugural Presidential Address*, 20 January 1949 [online], http://www.trumanlibrary.org/whistlestop/50yr_archive/inagural20jan1949.htm (Accessed 18 March 2011).

United Nations Development Programme (UNDP) (1999) 'Globalization with a human face', *Human Development Report* New York, United Nations, [online], http://hdr.undp.org/en/reports/global/hdr1999/ (Accessed 18 March 2011).

UN General Assembly (1960) *Resolution 1514: Declaration on the Granting of Independence to Colonial Countries and Peoples* [online], http://www.un.org/documents/ga/res/15/ares15.htm (Accessed 18 March 2011).

UN General Assembly (1970) *Resolution 2626: International Development Strategy for the Second United Nations Development Decade* [online], http://www.un.org/documents/ga/res/25/ares25.htm (accessed 18 March 2011).

Whitfield, L. (ed) (2009) *The Politics of Aid: African Strategies for Dealing with Donors*, Oxford, Oxford University Press.

Williams, D. and Young, T. (1994) 'Governance, the World Bank and liberal theory', *Political Studies*, vol. 42, no. 1, pp. 84–100.

Williamson, J. (1993) 'Democracy and the "Washington Consensus"', *World Development*, vol. 21, no. 8, pp. 1329–1336.

World Bank (1990) *Poverty: World Development Report 1990*, Washington, World Bank.

World Bank (1997) *The State in a Changing World: World Development Report 1987*, Washington, World Bank.

World Bank (2000) *Attacking Poverty: World Development Report 2000*, Washington, World Bank.

World Bank (2010) *Defining Civil Society*, Washington, World Bank [online], http://go.worldbank.org/4CE7W046K0 (Accessed 28 January 2011).

Yanacopulos, H. (2009) 'Cutting the Diamond: Networking economic justice' in Kahler, M. (ed.) *Networked Politics: Agency, Power and Governance*, New York, Cornell University Press.

Further Reading

Collier, P. (2007) *The Bottom Billion: Why the Poorest Countries are Failing and What Can Be Done About It*, Oxford, Oxford University Press.

Moyo, D. (2009) *Dead Aid: Why Aid is Not Working and How There is a Better Way For Africa*, New York, Farrar Straus Giroux.

Riddell, R. (2007) *Does Foreign Aid Really Work?*, Oxford, Oxford University Press.

Epilogue

Theo Papaioannou and Melissa Butcher

In this book we have sought to provide you with a good theoretical and practical grounding of international development in today's fast-changing world. To achieve our aim, we have first explored specific meanings and theories of development. Some of them emphasize unplanned processes of social change while some others focus on individual and collective actions. Despite their differences, all key ideas and debates about development are concerned with historical transformations of human lives at local, national, international and global levels. The fact that all human societies interact at different scales implies that development as such takes place within the wider international and global system. Therefore, we have highlighted that different agents of development, including individuals, businesses, non-governmental organizations, social movements and governments, exercise different powers in terms of promoting and/or imposing ideas of social transformation. A crucial theme of this book is that ideas and theories of international development, whether neoliberal, structuralist or interventionist, are contested. In this sense we can conclude that there is not just one correct approach to social change, but rather many different and competing approaches, some of them more plausible and less problematic than others.

To illustrate the contested nature of international development and its complex processes that invoke history, agency, power and scale, we have focused on the most important phenomenon of today's changing world: the rising powers of China, India and Brazil. As you have seen, this phenomenon has not only political and economic implications but also social and spatial ones. China, India and Brazil have increased their hegemonic role in the international political system (for example, demanding a greater voice in the United Nations) and within economic structures (for example, the impact of their increasing consumption on trade). However, with rising powers there is also an implied fall of others if we regard development as a zero-sum interaction (see Chapter 3). As you have read, the dominance of current hegemonic powers such as the USA appears to be increasingly challenged. The consequence is the emergence of countries such as China and India as new drivers of international development that inevitably alters the character of the international order. However, if we regard development at times as a positive-sum process, these changes could also have benefits for other regions in the world. For example, China's growth has contributed to the lifting out of poverty of millions of people in Asia and Africa.

The competing theories of international relations, including realism, liberalism and Marxism, have each taken a different perspective on China's rise as a hegemonic power (see Chapter 4). Realists insist on the possibility of conflict between China and existing hegemonic powers, for example the USA. By contrast, liberals emphasize the interdependence between the two powers and Marxists stress their uneven development and geopolitical competition. Despite their differences, these three perspectives on the rising powers need to be backed by historical and empirical evidence that can be found, for example, in their economic indicators, especially their exceptional growth since the late 1990s (see Chapter 5). This growth is due not only to their industrialization but also to their size.

The impacts of rising powers are multiple, overlapping and even contradictory. For example, you have seen that various interactions in terms of trade, production and overseas investment can impact not only upon the economy and society of developing countries such as those in Africa but also on their environment. Such impacts are often directly linked with the role of Chinese, Indian and Brazilian transnational corporations (TNCs; see Chapter 7). Again we can see where TNCs can be involved in both zero-sum and positive-sum development, increasing both opportunities and economic growth in developing countries, but also criticized for their role in labour exploitation or environmental problems.

The shift in the global distribution of economic growth that these emerging powers highlight also impacts on the location and intensity of poverty and inequality, as well as the possibilities and problems of sustaining livelihoods in both the global North and the global South. The first conclusion of our examination is that poverty remains a global issue that needs to be politically, as well as socially and economically, addressed. Although there are different views about the causes of poverty, almost all of them concentrate on structural problems (interventionist theories of development) and/or market inefficiencies (neoliberal theories; see Chapter 8). This is not surprising since, as you have read, it is only very recently that poverty began to be conceptualized and measured as multiple deprivations. Similarly, there are many types of inequalities, including income and health inequalities, with differing impacts on levels of poverty. The vulnerabilities created by poverty and inequality can be addressed through the creation of secure, productive livelihoods but, as you have read in Chapter 8, making a living and ensuring the livelihood of families and households can come under threat from shifts in power and centres of economic production. For example, if the (re)distribution of resources and/or capabilities are only left to competitive institutions of the free market, or if the state intervenes to reorient the economy away from 'traditional' forms of production.

Debates over inequality and livelihoods have become embedded in our understanding of social justice. Contemporary theorists of justice, including liberal egalitarians such as Rawls and libertarians such as Nozick, have proposed different political solutions to these persistent problems of poverty and inequality (see Chapter 9). Such solutions may be institutional but have implications for public policies targeting particular livelihoods, for example low-income people or people without jobs who try to find work and support themselves and their families. In addition, there are important cultural dimensions to poverty and inequality that need to be taken on board in any sustainable livelihood approach (see Chapter 10). As can be seen from the examples in Chapter 11, livelihoods are not isolated phenomena of development but rather part of global value chains and production systems that express multiple types of power and agency. The improvement of lives of poor people is not a foregone conclusion of this multiplicity, so historically we have seen civil society campaigns and social movements at both local and international levels attempting to intervene in social and economic change (see Chapter 12). International agency in the form of government aid also remains an important factor in poverty reduction and development.

This critical analysis of historical processes, power relations and agency at different scales highlights new perspectives on international development in the 21st century that are taken up in the second volume of this book series, *New Perspectives in International Development*.

Glossary

accountable governance

Where those in positions of power are held to account by members of the public.

accumulation

A debated concept, depending on different approaches to economic theory. At its simplest, it is the transformation of a certain amount of capital or money into a greater amount of capital or money. This process may happen by any number of means: investment, trade, speculation, exploitation, etc.

analytical

Views based on understanding of how development actually occurs in practice.

anarchy

Not to be confused with the everyday meaning of the word as chaos or disorder, anarchy in International Studies refers to the absence of a single, recognized 'world' government with the ability to make and uphold laws.

autocracy

A system of government based on the power of a single person, or autocrat.

bilateral aid

Aid that goes directly from one country to another.

capitalism

A system of social relations in which owners of capital hire labour in return for wages; production is for sale in the market rather than direct consumption by producers; and profits are realized by owners of capital after payment of costs of production.

Cold War

A period after the end of World War II when the world was polarized between a communist 'East' and a capitalist 'West'. It ended with the fall of Communism in the 1980s and 1990s.

decile

One-tenth of a population.

diaspora

A migrant community originating from a single place but spread around the world, yet still connected to that original place in terms of their identity if not their physical connections.

diplomacy

The practice of conducting negotiations between representatives of groups or states.

East Asian Tigers

Refers to the highly developed economies of Hong Kong, Singapore, South Korea and Taiwan, which exhibited high economic growth rates in the 1980s and are considered high-income countries now.

economies of scale

Produced by spreading fixed expenses, especially investments in plant and equipment and the organization of production lines, over larger volumes of output. As production increases, the cost of producing each further unit falls.

economies of scope

Produced by exploiting the division of labour – sequentially combining specialized functional units, especially overheads such as reporting, accounting, personnel, purchasing, or quality assurance, in multifarious ways so that it is less costly to produce several products than a single specialized one.

empowerment

Enabling an individual, community or organization to have control and authority over their own lives and actions.

endowments

The owned assets and personal capacities that an individual or household can use to establish entitlement to food.

entitlements

The relationships, established by trade, direct production or sale of labour power, through which an individual gains access to food.

European Enlightenment

A period of philosophical thought within Europe in the 17th and 18th centuries associated with scientific reasoning, logic and rationality (as opposed to customs and beliefs). It is often seen as the philosophical starting point of 'modernity' or the change in social and economic relations towards capitalism.

fair trade

The supply and purchase of goods that meet certain welfare criteria, for example in relation to wages or working conditions for workers involved in the production and distribution of the goods.

fallback position

In a bargaining model the position determined by how each party would fare if no agreement was reached (sometimes called a 'threat point').

foreign aid

All transfers by one government to aid another including money, goods and skills, and includes military and civilian aid, and both grants and loans.

foreign assets

The total fixed and current assets outside the home country.

Foreign Direct Investment

(FDI) The net inflows of investment that acquire a 'lasting management interest', which means ten per cent or more of voting stock in an enterprise operating in an economy other than that of the investor. It is the net flow of money invested in the acquisition by a foreigner of physical assets, such as plant and equipment, with operational control either residing with the parent company or control over production governed by part-ownership of production through shares and stocks.

gender divisions of labour

How labour is divided between men and women in society. There are many dimensions: reproductive activities and domestic work in the household; the kinds of work done, or occupations and positions held, by men and women, and whether these differences correlate to differences in remuneration. While the gender division of labour may seem to have some biological dimensions (most obviously in child-bearing), differences are largely socially constructed through particular assumptions and values about the place and roles of men and women in the household and in society.

gender relations

Gender relations are part of social relations. They refer to the ways that men and women relate over the whole range of social organization, access to resources, remuneration, distribution consumption, exercise of authority and power, and participation in social, political and religious life.

globalization

At its most general, the increasing inter-connectedness of the world, through various avenues including increased flows of economic, political and religious ideas across regions.

global South

Interchangeable with the South. See South.

Gross Domestic Product

(GDP) The value of all the goods and services produced within a country in a given period.

Gross National Income per capita

(GNIpc) Sum of value added by all resident producers in the economy plus any product taxes (less subsidies) not included in the valuation of output plus net receipts of primary income (compensation of employees and property income) from abroad, divided by mid-year population.

hegemony

In its general meaning, a situation where a political actor (such as a state or a social class) or a set of ideas (such as an ideology or theory) exercises *de facto* influence over, and leadership of, others, despite the absence of any formal standing as a 'leader'.

imperialism

A form of authority whereby an empire or nation holds power over foreign countries, either through indirect means or by formally holding colonies and dependencies.

Import Substitution Industrialization

(ISI) A national development strategy that uses import tariffs and quotas to limit imports and promote higher domestic production of goods that would have been imported otherwise.

industrialization

A process of change, both social and economic, involving the mechanization of social productive activity with the use of inanimate sources of power (fossil fuels and electricity rather than horses and oxen); the invention and diffusion of new technical knowledge; and changes to how work is organized, especially the use of wage labour and large scale factory production.

integrated rural development programmes

(IRDPs) attempt to lift rural people out of poverty through the promotion of rural enterprise and associated services. This approach requires backward and forward linkages (inputs to production and markets for output) and supporting institutions (for example, mechanisms to obtain credit). Perhaps the best known is the IRDP of India which was conceptualized in 1978. Although having some success, it was challenged by the structural causes of poverty and limits to enterprise.

international law

Law that governs the conduct of independent nations in their relationships with one another. It differs from other forms of law since it is concerned with provinces rather than private citizens.

international organization

Organization with an international membership and/or presence. There are two main types – international non-governmental organizations (such as Greenpeace) and those made up of sovereign states (such as the World Bank).

international system

Regularized and substantial interaction between states or across state borders which can include political, military, economic, cultural and social activity.

kaizan

Japanese for improvement or change for better. Kaizan philosophy is focused on a continuous improvement process driving incremental changes in products and processes.

life expectancy at birth

Number of years a newborn infant could expect to live if prevailing patterns of age-specific mortality rates at the time of birth were to stay the same throughout the infant's life.

market

Any system that brings buyers and sellers of goods and services together in conditions of exchange and/or competition, whatever the nature of the goods and services.

Marshall Aid

US aid in the immediate post World War II period designed to boost capitalist production in Europe.

Marxism

Approaches that are rooted in the ideas of Karl Marx. They centre on the analysis of capitalism as a specific and inherently conflict-laden way of organizing society.

mean

The sum of the numbers divided by however many numbers there are in the group.

median

The middle value in a group of numbers ranked in order of size.

monopoly

When the production of a good or service with no close substitutes is carried out by a single firm with the market power to decide the price of its output. This is different from 'perfect competition', in which no single firm can affect the price of what it produces. Typically, a monopoly will produce less, at a higher price, than would be the case for the entire market under perfect competition.

morbidity

The probability or likelihood of suffering an illness or disease.

mortality

The probability or likelihood of dying.

Multi Fibre Agreement

(MFA) An agreement governing the trade in textiles and garments from 1974 to 2004, creating export opportunities for developing countries by establishing quotas for each country.

multilateral aid

Aid that is channelled through international institutions such as the World Bank or UN agencies.

nation state

A state that claims sovereignty over and on behalf of a territory and people. The term implies a congruence of cultural groupings (a nation or people) and territory and hence distinguishes nation state from other types of state, though in fact there is almost never an exact match of nations and territories.

New International Economic Order

A programme of action developed in the 1970s to reduce the gap between developed and developing countries. The actions put forward related to more favourable terms of trade and development assistance.

normative

Views based on our values as to how development should occur.

North

The most economically developed countries of the world, most of which are in the Northern hemisphere, although some, such as Japan, Australia and New Zealand are not. Can also be referred to as 'global North'. See also South.

Official Development Assistance

(ODA) Grants (or loans containing at least a 25% grant element) given to developing countries by governments and other official agencies.

oligarchy

A form of rule where the power is held by a small number of people.

oligopoly

When a few firms dominate a market. Often they can together behave as if they were a single monopoly, perhaps by forming a cartel, or they may collude informally, by preferring non-price competition to a price war.

Opium Wars

Two wars during 1839–1842 and 1856–1860 between Britain and China. They were the culmination of diplomatic and trade tensions in which opium grown in British India was sold to China in an effort to redress a trade imbalance, but the growing drug problems in China forced a response from the Qing Dynasty.

participation

The active and equitable involvement of all stakeholders.

patriarchy

Originally an anthropological term to describe a social system where authority is vested in the male head of household and/or other male elders. The term has also been used to describe the dominance of men over women in society.

However, the latter take very different forms in different social contexts and is under constant negotiation and change.

polygyny

The practice of having more than one wife.

power

Has more than one meaning and is used with reference to individuals, organizations and states. Often it refers to the degree of control or influence over others. But it also refers to the control someone or something has over their own activity, for example the degree of freedom someone has to live their own life as they wish to.

price boom

A period experiencing steadily rising prices rather than a momentary price hike in one period.

price index

A means of comparing prices by using a base year (for example 2005) as being equal to 100. All other price changes are then recalculated as relative to the base year.

protectionism

A policy of limiting trade from other countries in order to nurture domestic industry which faces a competitive threat from foreign exports.

purchasing power parity

(PPP) The exchange rate that equates the price of a basket of identical traded goods and services in two countries.

quintile

One-fifth of a population.

realism

A major school of thought within the discipline of International Relations. It refers to an approach that prioritizes national interests over other questions of ideology or morality.

remittance

Transfer of money from a migrant worker to their home country.

social enterprise

A business that has social objectives, rather than simply maximizing profits. Profits are often directed towards social purposes either in the business or in the wider community.

social mobility

People's ability to move upwards or downwards in social status because of changes in income, type of work or other culturally defined characteristics.

soft power

The ability to secure goals through co-option and attraction rather than force or coercion. It is associated with the work of Joseph Nye.

South

Encapsulates the common experience of a group of countries and their similar position relative to global capitalism. The term 'the South' was initially used to denote the group of countries previously referred to as the 'Third World' or those countries that were seeking an alternative path to development (neither capitalism nor socialism). More recently, 'the South', or 'global South', is used to refer to what are sometimes called 'developing' countries as it denotes countries at different – usually lower – stages of economic development than those in 'the North'. As geographic terms the 'South' and the 'North' are not completely correct, as there are some southern nations (New Zealand, Australia) which would not be included in the 'South'.

sovereignty

A claim by states to a right to rule. More fully it is a form of authority, the power of command associated with a socially recognized right to rule.

state

As a political institution, a compulsory political organization, operating in a given territory, which successfully upholds a claim to a monopoly of the legitimate use of physical force in the enforcement of its order. The term 'state' is also sometimes used as synonymous with 'nation state' or 'country'.

state preference

What a state seeks to do or achieve in the international system.

Structural Adjustment Programmes

(SAPs) Policy packages secured by the Bretton Woods Institutions as conditions on loans. They are based on neoliberal economic policies and typically include the following elements: (i) liberalization of markets – letting markets determine prices, involving removing price controls, liberalizing financial markets and having less intervention in labour markets; (ii) liberalizing trade by removing import quotas, reducing tariffs and having realistic exchange rates; and (iii) reducing the role of the state in the economy by privatizing state enterprises and cutting government expenditure.

surplus

The term has different economic meanings. The Marxist use of the term means the new value created by workers in excess of their own labour-cost, and this new value is taken by a capitalist as gross profit. This 'appropriation of surplus' is at the heart of the capitalist system.

technological innovation

The process of combining or using existing 'technological' resources for introducing a new product to the market and/or the world. A technological innovation can either be a physical entity, such as a car, saucepan or pill, or a process, such as a new way of marketing or financing a product.

terms of trade

A ratio between an exported commodity bundle and the imported manufactures bundle for a country. It is a relative term, and therefore changes in either commodity or manufacturers' prices will have an impact on the ratio.

underemployment

Work that does not allow the full use of someone's skills or capacities. There are several manifestations: working for shorter periods than normal working hours; working less intensively than one is able or willing to work; working at a lower level of productivity than able to do; earning less than able or willing; working in a production unit that has lower than normal productivity.

unemployment

Usually restricted to the wage economy; not in paid employment or self-employment but available for employment and actively seeking it.

West

The countries of Europe, North and South America (the East being Russia, China, the Middle East and Asia more generally). The terms became dominant in relation to the Cold War, see Cold War.

world average

Calculated by dividing the total amount of resources available globally by the total global population.

world systems theory

An approach emphasizing a unit of analysis larger than nation states, 'world systems', and specifies these as divided into groups of countries in a dominant core, a subordinate periphery and an intermediate semi-periphery.

Acknowledgements

Grateful acknowledgement is made to the following sources for permission to reproduce material in this book.

Figures

Figure 1.1 © Thomas Mukoya/Reuters; **Figure 1.2** © Car Culture/Corbis; **Figure 1.5** Anne S.K. Brown Military Collection, Brown University Library; **Figure 2.1** © Lebrecht Music and Arts Photo Library/Alamy; **Figure 2.2** Justin Cormack, used under a Creative Commons Attribution-Share Alike 2.0 Licence; **Figure 2.3** Baby Milk Action; **Figure 3.1** Strange, S. (1988) 'States and Markets', Pinter Publishers; **Figure 3.3** NASA; **Figure 3.3** Adapted from Ellis, E. and Esler, A. (2001) 'World History:Connections to Today', Prentice Hall International (UK) Limited; **Figure 3.6** © National Maritime Museum, Greenwich; **Figure 3.7** © Gamma-Keystone/Getty Images; **Figure 3.9** Watts, J. (2005) 'A hunger eating up the world', The Guardian, November 10 2005. Guardian News and Media Limited; **Figure 3.9** Taken from: http://ageofempires.wikia.com/wiki/Portuguese; **Figure 4.1** Library of Congress, Prints & Photographs Division, photograph by Harris & Ewing, LC-DIG-hec-16835; **Figure 4.3** © liu jiansheng/Xinhua Press/Corbis; **Figure 4.4** © Scott Barber/Getty Images; **Figure 5.2** © Carol Lee/Alamy; **Figure 5.2** Curt Reynolds/United States Department of Agriculture; **Figure 5.3** © HOANG DINH NAM /AFP/Getty Images; **Figure 5.7** United Nations Conference on Trade and Development; **Figure 5.8** World Integrated Trade Solution; **Figure 6.1** © Illustrated London News Ltd/Mary Evans; All Rights Reserved; **Figure 6.10** © www.CartoonStock.com; **Figure 6.2** © Illustrated London News Ltd/Mary Evans; **Figures 6.4** and **6.5** Dr Melissa Butcher; **Figure 6.6** Found SF: Shaping San Francisco and the San Francisco Museum and Historical Society; **Figure 6.7** © Blend Images/Alamy; **Figure 6.8a** © Panorama Media (Beijing) Ltd./Alamy; **Figure 6.8b** © Richard Ianson/Getty Images; **Figure 7.1** © Karen Cowled/Alamy; **Figure 7.2** UNTAD (2005), World Investment Report 2005, UNCTAD (UN conference on trade and development); **Figure 7.3** © Getty Images; **Figures 7.4a**, **b**, **c** and **d** © Kevin Kallaugher/www.kalcartoons.com; **Figure 7.5** Nike; **Figure 8.1** Library of Congress, Prints & Photographs Division, photograph by Harris & Ewing, LC-DIG-hec-16835; **Figure 8.2** 'Cartogram © 2006 SASI Group (University of Sheffield), design © 2008 CPRC (University of Manchester)'; **Figure 8.3** Hulme, D. (2010) Global poverty:how global governance is failing the poor. 2010 Routledge; **Figure 8.5** © ABDELHAK SENNA/AFP/Getty Images; **Figure 9.2** Angus Maddison; **Figure 9.3** Sourced; **Figure 10.1** © Angelo Cavalli/Getty Images; **Figure 10.2** © iStock.com/Nancy Nehring; Figure 10.3 © Robert Harding Picture Library Ltd/Alamy; **Figure 10.4** SAID The Value Chain Framwework Briefing Paper, USAID. The United States Government; **Figures 10.5b** and **c** Joseph Hanlon; **Figure 11.1** Moser, C.O.N. (2009) Ordinary families, Extraordinary lives: assets and poverty reduction in Guaquil, The Brookings Institution Press; **Figure 11.2** © AFP/Getty Images; **Figure 11.3** Scott Bauer/United States Department of Agriculture, Agricultural Research Service; **Figure 11.4** © inga spence/Alamy; **Figures 11.5** and **11.6**

Jane Cullen; **Figures 11.7a**, **b** and **c** Taken from: 'The Triennial Symppsium of the International Society for Tropical Crops', International Society for Tropical Crops; **Figure 12.1** Make Poverty History; **Figure 12.6** © AFP/Getty Images.

Text

Box 1.1 page 13 United Nations; **Activity 5.2 page 117** Jopson B., Wallis W., (2009), 'Congo Cuts Back Aid Deal with China', Financial Times Syndication; **Box 6.1 page 131** GaWC, Loughborogh University; **Activity 6.2 page 136** Haugen, H.O. and Carling, J. (2005) 'On the edge of the Chinese diaspora: The surge of baihuo business in an African city', Ethnic and Racial Studies, Vol 28, No 4 July 2005, Routledge, Taylor & Francis; **Activity 6.3 page 141** Saxenian A.L., (2005) 'From Brain Drain to Brain Circulation: Trasnational Communities and Regional Upgrading in India and China', Watson Institute for International Studies, Brown University; **Activity 6.5 page 146** Watts J., (2005) 'A Hunger Eating up the World', The Guardian News & Media Limited; **Box 9.2 page 210** World Bank, (2005) Equity and Development, World Development Report 2006, World Bank and Oxford University Press; **Box 10.3 page 241** Chang, D. (2002) Livelihoods in Kenya, Pursuing the good life in hard times: a comparison of men's and women's strategies in Maasai/Kikuyu marriages in Kenya. Unpublished PhD thesis University of London; **Box 10.4 page 247** Krishna, A. (2010) Refilling the the pool of poverty, One illness away, Oxford University Press; **Case study 1 page 271** Barrientos S., (2007), 'Global Systems and Decent Work', ILO Publications; **Case Study 3 page 275** BT and the beast, Science and Development Network www.scidev.net, December 20 2006, The content of SciDev.Net is made available under a Creative Commons Attribution 2.0 licence.; **Case Study 4 page 279** (2011) 'Small Loans, Significant Impact After Success in Poor Countries Grameen Bank Tries New York', The Washington Post; **Case Study 6 page 285** Taken from: 'The Triennial Symposium of the International Society for Tropical Crops', International Society for Tropical Crops.

Index

value chains 254
concentration of capital 83, 84
conditionality 311–12
conditions of development 43
condominiums 132
conflict 80, 93
    Marxist theory of imperialism 83, 84–5
    realism 78–9, 80, 81, 88–9
    and the rise of China 88–9, 90, 93–6
    see also warfare
Congo 117-18, 293, 294
Congress Party 73
consensus 307–9
consumer boycotts 38–9, 293
consumption 52, 111
contingency 82
coolie trade 135
cooperation 85
    between China and the USA 89–90, 93–6
    liberalism 79, 81–2, 89–90
    value chains 254
    see also international organizations
corporate social responsibility (CSR) 167
Corus Group 151
cotton, genetically modified 275–8
Cowen, M. 265
Cox, R. 55–6
crises 202
    debt crisis 66–7, 71, 301–2
    global financial crisis 90, 278, 312
    oil crises 65–6, 301
critical reflection 41
Cultural Revolution 68, 107
culture 52
    cultural perspective and livelihoods 235, 236–44, 260
cumulative share of income 218–23

D

Daewoo 155, 172
dams 7
Das, G. 49
Deaton, A. 205

debt
    individual
      GM cotton 277
      livelihood vulnerability 247, 249
    national
      Democratic Republic of Congo and aid from China 117–18
      Jubilee 2000 campaign 293, 295
      Make Poverty History 293, 296
debt bondage 249
debt crisis 66–7, 71, 301–2
'Decent Work' programme 273
deciles 218, 219, 325
de-coupling of product development and manufacturing 159
Deepwater Horizon oil spill 166
defensive realism 89
deforestation 147
demand-side economics 227
Democratic Republic of Congo (DRC) 117–18
Deng Xiaoping 68, 94
Department for Work and Pensions (DWP) 239
'dependency' syndrome 65
dependency theory 44
Detroit 11, 12
developing country status 111–12
development 2, 5–29, 321
    goals see goals of development
    international process 19–27
    meanings of 6–8
    multiple aspects 51
    routes to see routes to development
Development Assistance Committee (DAC) 228, 298, 305
development debates 2, 31–48
    agency and power 32, 37–41
    history of development thinking 32, 32–7
    key approaches to development 45–7
    questions of scale 32, 41–5
diasporas 127, 172, 325
    brain gain 139–44

diplomacy 21, 54, 326
    see also soft power
direct cash transfers 315–16
direct impacts 112–15
Directory of Development Organizations 295
diseases, major 14
Disney 164
disruption, in the international system 53–7
dollar, comparison of incomes with 213–15
dominant social strata 55, 56
domination 85
Dreier, P. 165
Drezner, D. 165
Dutch East India Company 60, 72, 151

E

East Asian Tigers 110, 326
Easterly, W. 189–90, 313–14
economic crisis (from 2007) 90, 278, 312
economic growth/development 10, 13, 44, 99–123, 300–1
    analytic perspectives 100–1
    inequality and 230–2
    pattern in Brazil, India and China 105–10
    patterns of industrialization 101–5
    and people-centred development 264
    and poverty 178–9
    rising powers 52
      as drivers of international development 112–22
    TNCs and 168, 169–70
    why rising powers affect other countries 110–12
economic interactions 22
economic nationalism 72
economic policy
    changes and the development of TNCs 170–2
    development trajectories of rising powers 67–73